M000107203

A terrific, refreshing memoir – a compelling story well told. The story of Jorma Ollila is the story of Nokia, among the most improbable and astonishing technology success stories at the turn of the 21st century. Nokia and Ollila also had their share of failures, which are candidly acknowledged, including the most recent past. But Ollila reminds us not to count Nokia out, echoing Muhammed Ali's assertion that "impossible is just an opinion."

— John Thornton, Chairman of the Board, Brookings Institution, Professor and Director of Global Leadership, Tsinghua University in Beijing, and former President of Goldman Sachs

Nokia: Where it all went wrong, by the man who made it the world's biggest mobile company. The biography of Jorma Ollila, CEO of Nokia during its stratospheric rise, offers glimpses from inside the company as it underwent massive change. The book, co-written with Harri Saukkomaa, focuses on Ollila's achievements, his ambitions, and overcoming adversity.

— Olli Sulopuisto, *ZDNet*

Interesting inside story from the CEO. Ollila's career as the leader of Nokia was exceptionally long and triumphant. It was interesting to read the background of strategic decisions and changes we've seen during the years. Ollila also said that besides decisions, luck and turbulence of markets made Nokia succesful – and that same turbulence also plummeted Nokia's mobile phone business.

— Jari Pirhonen, Security Director, Samlink, *Goodreads*

[Against All Odds] will undoubtedly become one of Finland's economic history classics. That's why it is worth reading even now.

— Eeva-Leena Vaahtio, Ph.D., author of *Recruiting Success* and *More Out of Life*

Like reading a detective story.

— Seija Telaranta, *Talking About Leadership*

The book is very well written, which makes it very readable. And the work is surprisingly open. It shows the mistakes made by the company, which no one could have avoided. The book is definitely worth reading.

— Paavo Vasala, *Media Week*

Nokia's former CEO, Jorma Ollila's biography offers an excellent overview of how Finland's first international brand was born and how it crashed. The book should be read in parallel with the Jobs biography.

— Seppo Mölsä, Managing Editor, *Rakennuslehti (Building Journal)*

One of the most fascinating stories in Finland's recent history is the rapid rise of Nokia, thanks to the establishment of its mobile phones as a global brand in the 1990s, the decline in the company's success in the 2000s, and its eventual abandonment of mobile phones. The boom was personified by the company's talented CEO Jorma Ollila. His interesting memoirs are readily accessible to a non-specialist readership.

— Juha Honkala, *Books from Finland: A Literary Journal*

The book is actually quite exciting to read.

— Matti Mattila, *Wizzit Magazine*

The book is very good and recommended. It has a lot to offer all those interested in management.

— Pauli Forma, Director of Working Life Services, Keva

AGAINST ALL ODDS

AGAINST ALL ODDS

Leading Nokia from Near
Catastrophe to Global Success

Jorma Ollila
& Harri Saukkomaa

Translated from Finnish by Richard Powell

MAVEN HOUSE

US edition published by Maven House Press, 4 Snead Ct., Palmyra, VA 22963; 610.883.7988; www.mavenhousepress.com.

US edition copyright ©2016 by Jorma Ollila and Harri Saukkomaa. All rights reserved.

US edition published by agreement with Jorma Ollila, Tekir Oy/Harri Saukkomaa and Elina Ahlback Literary Agency, Helsinki, Finland.

Mahdoton menestys: Kasvun paikkana Nokia
Copyright ©2013 Jorma Ollila, Tekir Oy/Harri Saukkomaa ja Kustannusosakeyhtiö Otava
Original edition published by Kustannusosakeyhtiö Otava, 2013

While this publication is designed to provide accurate and authoritative information in regard to the subject matter covered, it is sold with the understanding that the publisher is not engaged in rendering legal, accounting, or other professional service. If legal advice or other expert assistance is required, the services of a competent professional person should be sought. — From the Declaration of Principles jointly adopted by a Committee of the American Bar Association and a Committee of Publishers and Associations

Library of Congress Control Number: 2016932950

Hardcover ISBN: 978-1-938548-70-3
ePUB ISBN: 978-1-938548-71-0
ePDF ISBN: 978-1-938548-72-7
Kindle ISBN: 978-1-938548-73-4

Printed in the United States of America.

10 9 8 7 6 5 4 3 2 1

CONTENTS

PART III: MASTERS OF THE UNIVERSE

FOREWORD

By Jorma Ollila

THE OUTLOOK FOR BOOKS BY CHIEF EXECUTIVES, and especially for the memoirs they write, is poor. Their recollections rarely enthrall readers. The company grows, its revenue and profits rise, it gets into difficulties, and a crisis ensues. Days are full of meetings, discussions, strategy groups, and travelling. Looking back, it's easy to gloss over the mistakes, while success is always the fruit of good planning and brilliant leadership. I don't believe in hindsight, or in rationalizations after the event.

Nevertheless, one can always learn something from history, though the most important lesson is probably that events do not repeat themselves when one is running a company.

All these reservations and doubts churned about in my mind when, at the request of my Finnish publisher Otava, I began, at the beginning of the 2000s, to think about writing a book. I decided that the book would describe my own role in and perspective on the story of Nokia, which is unique in Finland, Europe, and indeed the world. I decided I would also write about other people who had a part in this story. I would describe how things felt as they happened. This is what I have tried to do throughout. Only the end of the book was written in the last year; the rest was written as things happened. The book was written over the course of more than ten years, and I hope that its long period of gestation will only add to the reader's pleasure.

The reader should bear in mind that I am not a historical researcher, and my book is not intended as an objective company history. Martti Häikiö has written an excellent history of Nokia from 1865 to 2000. Its abridged English translation is a worthy background for any reader. My book is intended to portray only my own perspective, observations, and experiences of Nokia at different stages in its development. I have selected the events that left the strongest impression on me, or struck me as interesting and important.

The book goes up to 2010, when Stephen Elop took over as chief executive. This was a conscious choice. It is still far too early to evaluate recent events at Nokia. Also, I stepped down as chairman of the board of directors in spring 2012, so I really don't have much first-hand knowledge of what has happened at Nokia recently. The epilogue, however, goes up to the beginning of September 2013, after the decision to sell Nokia's mobile phone business to Microsoft.

Harder than knowing what to write about Nokia was deciding what to say about myself. My media image has only a distant relation to reality. It's not easy to write about private matters, and I haven't given a full account of them. I particularly wanted to illuminate how I became chief executive. I didn't plan my career at all, but many factors came together to make it what it was. I have also described my childhood and my roots in Ostrobothnia, because I believe they are significant. But above all I believe that in Finland it's possible for people to get on in life irrespective of their background, if the will and the effort are there.

I was a young adult in the 1970s. I wanted to give my own account of that time both in Finland and in the wider world. It's only one viewpoint, but I have tried to be honest about it. I didn't really thrive in the Finland of the seventies. This led me to make fundamental decisions that changed the direction of my life.

I have also said a little about my family, but only reluctantly. I have tried to protect my privacy as far as possible. My family has nevertheless paid a price for my work and the media exposure it has brought. Without the support and understanding of Liisa and our children I wouldn't have achieved anything it would have been worth writing a book about.

I have put my thoughts into words in part orally and in part in writing. Harri Saukkomaa, the other creator of this book, has produced most of the text. I thank everyone who, over the years, has helped make this book possible: the interviewees, the people in the background, and our publishers Otava.

— Jorma Ollila

FOREWORD

By Harri Saukkomaa

WHEN I STARTED WORK ON THE BOOK of Jorma Ollila's life, I literally didn't know what I had taken on. I imagined that the book would be ready in two or three years. Ultimately the book became an adventure that lasted over a decade, during which time I talked to Jorma Ollila about life, leadership, and the future of the world in different surroundings on land, in the air, and at sea. These interviews and conversations spread over hundreds of hours. I also interviewed more than fifty people who knew Jorma Ollila in one way or another. Several of my interviewees sadly died before they could see the book in print.

The book is a life story, in which Jorma Ollila tells his own tale. We decided very early on to tell the story in the first person. This is the most difficult form to use, but it's the only one that ensures that the writer's and the subject's perspectives are aligned, and where there is a single voice. As the writer I was certainly impressed by the book's subject matter and narrative style. I wrote most of the text, which is based on the interviews with Jorma Ollila and others. The book also draws on material in the public domain: books, academic studies, and media reporting.

While the book was being written we lived through the global financial crisis, the dotcom bubble, the 9/11 attacks on the United States, wars, revolutions, and various smaller events in world history.

Nokia saw good periods and bad periods and the crumbling of its dominant market position. In preparing the book I got to know the leaders of Nokia extremely well: their ideas, anxieties, joys, sorrows, and dreams. I learned how Nokia was led and why the company will have a place in the economic history of the world. I also learned why strategies are sometimes impossible to implement, and why success may be impossible, even though all the stars seem to be promisingly aligned. That is why this book is named *Against All Odds*.

I thank Jorma Ollila for some terrific conversations, for enjoyable and memorable moments. I thank everyone I interviewed and all the information sources I used. I thank our Finnish publisher Otava for its patience and strong support. I thank everyone who has read and commented on the manuscript at various stages. In particular I thank Tuukka Hetemäki, who edited and corrected the text during the final stages without sparing either his intellect or energy. And I thank my wife Melek Mazici for support and understanding during this extended project.

— Harri Saukkomaa

PREFACE
TO THE U.S. EDITION

W<small>E HAVE MADE SOME MINOR CHANGES</small> for readers of the U.S. edition. The most significant is that the epilogue now goes up to 2016. It also briefly covers the most recent developments at Nokia and offers American readers some insights into Nokia's achievements in the United States.

We are happy and proud that our book has been published in the United States. We wish to thank our translator Richard Powell, our publishers Jim Pennypacker and Maven House, and our agent Elina Ahlbäck for their outstandingly fruitful collaboration.

— Jorma Ollila
Helsinki
May 8, 2016

PROLOGUE

One Day in January 1992

N O ONE WAS HAPPY when I was chosen as Nokia's CEO on 16 January 1992.

Nokia's share value immediately slumped by ten percent, ending the day four percent down. That told us what investors thought of my prospects. Commentators thought I was too young – I was then forty-one – and too inexperienced to lead a great Finnish company. Nokia's employees feared the worst: a former banker and finance director had been parachuted into the smoldering ruins to salvage what he could and sell it to the highest bidder. My family's view was that I had taken on an impossible task. They expected it would take over my life completely, so that my three children would be lucky to see me late in the evening, if then. Perhaps the next time they saw me would be on our summer holiday. All in all a promising start.

I have to turn this around, make it positive, I thought as I left Nokia's head office that dark evening. I myself was happy, even though others disapproved of my appointment. At least there was an end to the dithering and uncertainty. I had my own ideas on what Nokia's CEO should do. Even so I had barely the faintest idea of what I had let myself in for. This made life easier: I had boarded a roller-coaster whose terrifying swoops, loops, and dips I could never even have imagined. If someone had jumped into the car beside me and told me the success story Nokia would be, I wouldn't have believed them. If someone had asked me what kind of future I expected for Nokia, I'd have replied: "I haven't a clue." If, that is, I'd been compelled to be honest.

If someone could have described just how bad my most difficult times at Nokia would feel, I wouldn't have believed it. Or if I had believed it, I would have revoked my decision to take on leadership of a company sinking under the weight of its financial problems. I was captain of a vessel where only the bridge remained above the waterline: the hull was already submerged, and water was coming into the engine room.

The previous CEO had been sacked after falling out with the chairman, who had then retired. The chairman before him had committed suicide. After that there'd been an attempt to sell Nokia to the Swedish firm Ericsson, which had been wise enough to decline the offer. No wonder then that morale within the company was at rock bottom. My appointment as Nokia's CEO would mark the end of one era in the firm's history, and the start of a new one. I did not, however, yet know that back in 1992. I knew only that the previous generation had tasked me with rebuilding the company they had all but destroyed.

Nor of course could I know that I would lead Nokia for over fourteen years. At that time I didn't dare think as far as six months ahead. When I was offered the top job at Nokia, I had remarked to my wife Liisa that it was a position one could lose at a moment's notice. The shareholders might have had enough, the investors could withdraw their money, or the company's share price could fall so low that it could be snapped up like a tasty snack.

Our competitors perhaps were happy with my appointment. They thought the Nokia story was in its final chapter, otherwise a former finance director would not have been chosen. The company would quickly be sold, either as a whole or in smaller parcels. All our competitors had to do was await Nokia's disintegration and it would be ready for plucking.

My compatriots were scarcely happy with my appointment. I had been a student politician, and after that I had worked in an American bank. These were not plus points. Student politicians were basically unsound, and it would have been more patriotic to have worked in a Finnish bank. Many people in Finland had no idea who I was. My background was unusual for a chief executive: Finns might well ask what this forty-one-year-old engineer and economist knew about factories or the lives of the people who worked in them. It was a good question: in their position I'd have asked it too. I came across as an impatient, smartly dressed banker with a stubborn look and an excellent memory for figures. I had so much self-confidence that I had no idea how many ways there were for me to fail as Nokia's CEO.

I was ready to roll up my sleeves and get down to work. Lots of work. I could do it and I would enjoy it, but on its own it was not enough. I also had to find something that would enable both Nokia and me to survive. I had to find good people who would believe in the company. I had to breathe new life into the company, so that people would believe in themselves. Otherwise we would be lost in that sea where lie so many shipwrecked companies whose names no one remembers.

I and a few other managers of my age at Nokia had a dream. As a dream it was perhaps a little mundane, of the sort one can actually put into effect. We looked around us and saw that Finland and the Finnish economy were close to collapse. We looked at Nokia and we noticed that the company had not been led properly. Nevertheless we knew that Nokia was a fine company. We knew that this company, which had been given to us to lead, could clearly do better than before. We wanted to demonstrate that to the whole world.

This is an account of our time at Nokia during its transformation from an old-fashioned Finnish conglomerate to a global enterprise. It's also the story of how by chance I became CEO of Nokia, though I should have been a physicist or an economist. It's an account of our team, the people of Nokia, who set out to follow an everyday dream. It's a story of exceptional success, but at the same time of the poor judgment we sometimes showed, and the bad decisions and mistakes that we made.

PART I

LIFE BEFORE NOKIA

CHAPTER 1

A Small Town in Finland

M Y JOURNEY BEGAN in southern Ostrobothnia – a rural province on the west side of Finland – in the middle of August 1950. The time and the place are significant. I was an Ostrobothnian on both my mother's and my father's side. My roots went deep into that flat landscape, home for centuries to stubborn farmers, dogged tradesmen, and fanatical preachers.

At the beginning of the 1950s Finland had yet to recover from the war years. We had not been occupied; the country had not been laid waste; and, above all, we had kept our independence. But things were not easy, either. Finland had lost a tenth of its territory; and painful memories of war were still fresh. We had to pay huge war reparations to the Soviet Union. The country was anything but rich, and indeed famine was still a living memory. Industry was developing rapidly, but a large proportion of the population still lived by agriculture and forestry. No one wanted to hang on to the past, rather everyone was looking ahead. There was no room for freeloaders; everyone had do their own share and preferably more. The country's self-esteem still seemed rather shaky. No one could be confident about the future, but every effort went into building it. The war had ended just a short time before, and it was uncertain whether peace would last. Our political leaders were trying to make Finland as secure as possible in a world that was anything but secure.

The whole country was a building site: new houses, flats, little shops, and workshops. Everyone was in a hurry to move forward after the difficult war years and the tedious, lifeless period that came after. The birth rate was high. Poverty coexisted with faith in the future. Everyone was in a tremendous rush so that children were just left to get on with things. There was no television, no computers, no mobile phones, and our days were filled with school, sport, housework, and homework. Our world was small, the size of a village. Everyone knew their place, and life felt secure.

The Ostrobothnian landscape was one of large fields and meadows dotted with barns and divided by riverbanks, as it remains today. In the winter snow would cover the fields, where clumps of trees would stand like black islands. In spring, when the snow melted, the rivers would swell and flood the fields and roads. There wasn't much forest by Finnish standards, but the fields and cows produced enough for expanding families to feed themselves. If you couldn't survive from your smallholding, you had to try something else. For that reason there were many small businesses in Ostrobothnia: in Kurikka where we lived there were a sawmill, a textile works, metalworks, dairies, and various other factories. Around 10,000 people lived in this typical small town, whose center consisted of a church, schools, sports fields, banks, shops, and a factory with a tall chimney. On the short cold winter days grey smoke would rise from this chimney and freeze into little clouds of red against the brilliant sky.

I was born into a family that was not poor, but not rich either. My grandfather Kaarlo (Kalle) Ollila had set up an electrical goods business in Kurikka. His great-grandfather had bought a farm called Hiiripelto – "Mousefield" – in the village of Vähäkyrö. This became the Ollila farmstead. My grandfather's father did not stay to take over the farm, but moved to Copper Cliff, Canada. Two of his three sons died in infancy. The only survivor was my grandfather, who came back to Finland and attended the commercial school in Raahe, a port on the northern coast of the Gulf of Bothnia. He was known as a man who could do complex calculations in his head.

My grandfather was a tall, wiry, headstrong man, who didn't do small talk. He was widowed young and did not marry again. This left its mark on his life. Through a child's eyes granddad seemed a stern and somewhat mysterious man. Kalle fought in three wars: the Civil War, the Winter War, and the Continuation War. He took part in the siege of Tampere in 1918, fighting on the White side. This was the worst battle of the Civil War, and at that time the biggest to have taken place in the Nordic region. But to this day I can't find out anything more about my grandfather's role in these wars. The siege of Tampere was an especially closely guarded secret in our family, and I only learned of it while going through my late father's papers. At my grandfather's funeral we – his grandsons – went through his desk drawers, and in one of them we found a loaded pistol. We had no idea why Kalle Ollila had retained his weapon; but at the very least it posthumously augmented his aura of a man apart.

My father, Oiva Ollila, returned from the war, completed his studies, and graduated in engineering from technical college. He met my mother in Helsinki. Her name was Saima Elisabeth Kallio – she was always called Liisa – and she had studied agriculture and forestry at Helsinki University. They lost no time in starting a family. My mother broke off her studies and returned to Ostrobothnia with my father.

My mother was enchanting, beautiful, and clever. She had large, soft, inquiring eyes, a high forehead, and dark wavy hair. Her bright smile lit up the whole world, though now and then she would gaze yearningly into the distance. She didn't look Finnish: she seemed to have a drop of Italian blood and a dash of Mediterranean warmth. I was the eldest and a boy, so I had no need to compete for my mother's favor: I was always the apple of her eye, the focus of love, and her trusty helper. My sister Leena was born two years later, but I didn't have to compete with her because she was a girl. I was very much my mother's boy, from the beginning and right up until her death.

As the eldest I naturally had responsibilities as well as privileges. I not only had to look after myself, but my younger siblings, too. My parents didn't always have much time to spare for me, and it was assumed I could look after myself. I had family responsibilities: I had to organize the other children to do their chores, and it was assumed I would speak up for them with our parents. And I was expected to set a good example.

Our mother exuded a quiet charisma, which I have come to appreciate more and more over the years. She always made me do my best and expected good results, though these demands were never spoken. I understood them perfectly well from her demeanor and solicitude. I realized I was expected to do well, and I tried to live up to those expectations. My mother accomplished that. She supported me in my studies; she respected knowledge and education, and she had her own reasons for that.

My mother's family was from Isokyrö, not far from my father's family home. Generation after generation had lived in the area. So my entire clan, as far back as the sixteenth century, was of Ostrobothnian farming stock. My mother grew up in modest surroundings with seven brothers and sisters. Her father was Isak Isakinpoika Kallio, a fantastically obstinate farmer who hated the gentry and all its works. He had decided that none of his children should go to secondary school because they would be exposed to bad influences there. My mother was the second youngest child, and her father died before she reached school age. So my mother did after all have the chance of an education. She became the first of her family to graduate from high school. She would certainly have graduated from university had she not met my father and started a family with him.

My father was tall, lean, and hard-working. He was a little unusual because he talked a lot – except about the war, on which he was silent. He was a war hero who had received medals for his part in the battle of Taipale. He had served as a field artillery officer but he never talked much about that time, and certainly never boasted. It wasn't until his grandson – my son – came along that he opened up about his experience of war. For decades after the war it was simply not the done thing to talk about it. And it was not in my father's nature to do so: he had done his duty on the Front, and there was no need to go on about it.

My father worked non-stop, planning and building. He always had many irons in the fire. Through him I became interested in a thousand different things, which caused problems in later life when I had to focus on just one thing at a time. Where we lived men had the right to take an interest in whatever took their fancy, while women were expected to clear up after them. My mother did all the housework, as was usual in Finland in the fifties. When I was born, my mother was twenty-four and my father twenty-eight years old. We all lived at my grandfather's house in Kurikka, where the growing family had to squeeze into two rooms. We shared the ground floor with some other relatives while my grandfather lived upstairs. My father began work in the family electrical business, which my grandfather must have expected him to take over eventually.

There was a real sense of purpose. My home background taught me that one must work, and work hard, if one intends to succeed in life. My grandfather worked very hard in his business, and my father worked seven days a week. My mother toiled at home looking after our growing family, and she taught in the village school as well. As well as his paid work, my father devoted a lot of time to his own projects. He designed the electrical wiring for other people's houses, and built houses and summer cottages. There was enough work to fill every waking moment, and every waking moment was filled with it.

Working was as natural as breathing. Leaving work undone or enjoying moments of creative leisure was considered unnatural. That was laziness, the start of a slippery slope. It might lead to vodka-drinking, which was one of the deadliest sins (village brawls and domestic violence were common to Ostrobothnian life). People were judged by their ability to work. "A good worker" was the finest compliment you could pay someone. Working well

Sitting on my father's lap with my sister Leena in Kurikka 1954.

was linked to another value: autonomy. People should stand on their own two feet and make their own way in life.

The people I grew up with thought you could never do too much work, while leisure time was a potentially fatal menace. It was just this mindset that enabled Finland to become a developed country. There are parallels with the developing economies of Southeast Asia. I see there a mindset familiar from my childhood: work enables one to get on in life, to achieve prosperity, and to educate one's children for a better life. I learned this from my parents. And when life is full of things to be done, at least it isn't dull.

My mother believed in God. Some of her family were Pietists who wore black and sang psalms. I remember as a boy in short trousers taking part in Pietist meetings. God wasn't really mentioned at home, though. We went to church at Christmas, for christenings, and for funerals. My parents were more interested in natural history than in religion. There were many books about geography and natural history on our shelves, and we had encyclopedias and maps and illustrated books of natural wonders, but the family only began to read novels in the 1960s. We read the literary classics, but science books were regarded as a better use of time.

Arithmetic and math were part of everyday life, and our family regarded them as positively virtuous. My parents always assumed their children would have no difficulties with math. They didn't even bother to look at the grades we got for math, for they knew they would always be the top scores. My grandfather's skill with figures had been passed down to my father and then to me and my siblings. And my mother was also known for her mathematical ability. I was keen on mathematics from a very early age, and I demanded high standards of accuracy from myself. Later I demanded them from others. "Surely you know your own numbers," I would say to subordinates who got their figures mixed up when reporting results.

Numbers revealed a much wider world. Numbers meant things, and things could be very important, indeed. If I understood the numbers, I would understand things as well. If I understood things, I could control the world. When the numbers were clear, I could concentrate on the reality they represented. Then I could achieve something new. All this became clear to me much later, but without the respect my father and mother showed for mathematics I would not be the person I am now.

We lived in that small apartment in my grandfather's house until I was four. Then we moved to a bigger space, a flat above a bank in the center of Kurikka. That's where my childhood memories begin. We rented our new home, where we children had our own rooms – there was quite enough space in this old stone apartment block. From home it was a short trip to the shops and schools. This was the first of many moves – I lived in at least seven places before I was seventeen years old.

My own world. That's what I had as a four-year-old in Kurikka. It comprised our new home above the bank, my parents and siblings, and lots of interesting things in the buildings around. Next to the bank building there were wooden buildings in a regular pattern. In our part of the world houses were built in orderly rows. Everything had to be properly organized.

Summer was of course the nicest time. I rode my bike and swam in the river, since there weren't really any lakes where we lived. I also did my bit to feed the family, catching little perch and carp from the river and looking after grandma's cows and sheep. My mother made wonderful sandwiches and buns and the hot chocolate was the best ever.

My mother and father didn't have much time to spare for playing with me, so I could explore in peace. One of the most interesting places was a store a few hundred yards from home. Agricultural machinery was kept there: machines for threshing corn, for shredding straw, for ploughing fields, and for mowing meadows. They were all brand-new, positively gleaming. I found them truly enthralling.

They had red-painted metal parts and bright yellow wooden boards protecting the heart of the machines, where there were motors, blades, belts, and axles – everything that excited me.

Together with my friend Heikki Sillanpää I found one especially fascinating machine. Heikki grabbed the handle. On the other side was a hole through which I could see the blades as sharp as knives shredding straw for the barns. The machine was new and splendid. We must have seen at once how it worked. I decided to look at the mechanism from the other side when Heikki experimented with turning the handle.

The experiment was a roaring success: I thrust my hand inside the machine and Heikki turned the handle. The blades started rotating quite fast and one of the blades cut off the tip of my finger. When I pulled my hand out the end of my finger hung by a thread of skin. The blood spurted all over the place, and I ran toward home, the safest of places, as if possessed. The pain must have been terrific, but oddly enough I don't remember much about it. My sister Leena was in the yard and when she saw blood spurting from my finger she started screaming. Her cries were much louder than mine, since I had managed to control myself. She ran upstairs to get my parents, while I followed up the stairs, bleeding profusely. My blood left permanent traces on the walls of the stairway. Somewhere along the way the tip of my finger had fallen off and couldn't be found even though my parents went out and looked for it.

In the hospital they did the best they could without the missing bit. I will never forget that summer's day in 1955. On that day I learned that while the world may feel safe, it is in fact full of danger. Even curiosity has its limits, if you want to hang on to your hands, fingers, feet, and toes till the end of your natural life.

About that time my father decided to build a new house for his family. Renting the flat above the bank had gone on long enough. Having our own house would tell the world that the Ollilas now lived an independent life, free from undue dependence. Building one's own house was a matter of honor. The previous winter my father had fetched the timber from my mother's family's woodland. The trees had been cut down with handsaws. Then the logs had been dragged out of the forest on a horse-drawn sled and cut down in Kurikka to the right size for building. My father had designed the modern, roomy house himself. He planned every detail meticulously; even the door knobs of cast metal were beautiful examples of craftsmanship. Behind the house was a garden and in winter a skating rink.

I remember carrying bricks and mixing cement when the house was being built. I spent the summer of 1957 on the building site and was proud when I heard passers-by whispering to each other that the Ollila house would be the finest on the whole street. And so it was, and what was best of all was that we children got more space, which was what we needed, for there were now four of us. I would start school in the autumn and would need space for my books and to do my homework. My mother had started work teaching in a middle school, and she too needed room to work at home.

This was the first house that Father built. After that he built one after another and in the end there were seven. He wanted to move to new places and get on in life. He wanted his family to be prosperous and to live a more comfortable life. This meant that we were moving all the time. Just when I'd gotten to know my new classmates, we would move again and I would find myself once more among new faces. I had to build my own world ever more robustly so I could withstand those changes. I turned into a boy who played and studied with others, but who at heart knew he had his own life to lead.

CHAPTER 2

Where Does Self-Confidence Come From?

A SEVEN-YEAR-OLD BOY is perhaps a little young to follow world events. Nevertheless they impinged on the life of every child in Finland in the 1950s. Finland was looking for its place in the world.

Helsinki should have hosted the Olympics in 1940, but war had intervened, and we hosted the 1952 Games instead. They certainly raised Finland's profile. Along with the Games both Coca-Cola and black athletes came to Finland for the first time – the athletes were almost a tourist attraction in themselves. There's even a picture of me, taken a few years later, on the edge of the athletics field, posed in the lap of a black runner. I'm perhaps five years old.

A boatload of Coca-Cola was imported especially for the Olympics and sold in aid of Finnish war veterans. A whole family would often share a single bottle between them. After the Olympics Coca-Cola disappeared for a few years, and it was still a precious beverage when I was a teenager. It was expensive, it came in little bottles, and one sipped it sparingly.

My own self-confidence and self-esteem grew because they had to. Although our home was a secure place to grow up, there was more than enough change to contend with. Just when we had settled into our fine new house, my father decided that we should move to Turku, a city on the Finnish southern coast. He had decided to give up his job in my grandfather's electrical business. This was a disappointment to my grandfather, who closed the shop soon after and found other work. My father got a new job at a larger electrical business in Turku. He wanted bigger challenges and a better standard of living. He was advancing at the same rate as Finland was industrializing. The whole country was a building site. Electricity and electrical equipment were needed more and more. There were still places in Finland waiting for their first electrical cable.

My parents were seeking a new life and a better future, but they also yearned for freedom, to break away from their families and the obligations and preordained future they entailed. My father and mother wanted to create their own life with their own hands, which meant risk, change, and humility. There wasn't much money and every penny had to be earned, so my father worked every day of the week. Mother again looked after the family. We moved to our new home, a wooden house in Turku, in 1959. Our house in Kurikka was sold, and I had to get used to a new school class once again. I left my friends in Kurikka with a heavy heart, and only ever received a couple of letters from them. We didn't waste words, at least not on writing superfluous letters when we were still in primary school.

In Turku I was an ordinary, diligent, well-behaved boy. I was lonely and I wanted to go back to the people and places I knew. I pedaled my bike around the streets of my new home town, trying to make sense of the strange dialect my classmates spoke. The city was much bigger than Kurikka, and my old home seemed a long way away.

My classmates had decided I was a country boy – a yokel – and they let me know all about it. I found it difficult to make friends, not least because I had been to three schools by the time I was ten. I can't regret that I was constantly changing schools. I had to find new friends and conquer my lack of confidence by hard work and good grades. I learned to fit in with all sorts of other people.

Sometimes I look at a school photo from that time. I remember how it was: you had to at least try to smile. The photographer had come to the school with his big camera and a black cloth. He cracked a joke, which should have made the children laugh, and at the same time his flash went off. Everyone sat and looked into the camera. And many did smile, though the teacher remained serious. In the photo I look unsure of myself. My head is sunk into my shoulders and I seem to be seeking reassurance. I had decided to show everyone and be the same as them in the picture. But I didn't begin to smile.

The youngest child in our family, my little sister Sirkku, was born in Turku. Now there were five of us: me (born 1950), Leena (1952), Harri (1954), Yrjö (1956), and Sirkku (1959). My mother's time was spent looking after my siblings, especially when there was a baby in the house. Nevertheless, our home was always spotless. There was always an aroma of freshly baked buns and bread, despite the babies. In our semi-detached house our big family had two rooms and a kitchen and also an attic.

Ollila family Christmas in Vaasa in the mid -1960s (left to right): father Oiva , Sirkku , Leena , Yrjö, mother Liisa , Harri, and I am standing in the back.

The house had been built just after the war, so badly that it seemed about to fall down. Cold water came in and went out again. It was heated with logs. I slept in the attic room with my sister Leena.

We moved to the western part of Turku and this was an improvement. Now we had three rooms and central heating. The rooms were heated by oil, so no one had to fetch logs any more. The windows were no long iced up on cold mornings. The rooms were upstairs; on the ground floor was a dairy. Town and country were still intermingled in 1950s Finland. Our house opened straight on to fields. There we grew spinach, which I helped to pick.

One day when I was about ten I found a little growth on my neck, which required surgery to remove. There was nothing dangerous about the operation, which was a routine matter, and I wasn't scared of blood or hospitals. My parents had just given me a proper, grown-up bike as a present – I kept it for years until it was stolen when I was a student. That morning I packed my rucksack, hopped on the bike, and cycled over the hill and then along narrow streets for a couple of miles to the university hospital, a big white building. I checked in for the operation. It went well and I spent a week convalescing in the hospital. My parents came to see me there once. In the next bed there was a very pleasant girl, who asked me something in her Turku accent that sounded like "ain't it tough?" Only later did I realize that she was asking me if I had any toffee, rather than offering a comment on life.

When I left the hospital a few days later I went home the same way I had come. The experience was vivid, but not particularly scary. Back at the turn of the 1960s it seemed perfectly normal for a ten-year-old boy to go to the hospital on his own.

In spring 1961 my father announced another move. He had already changed employer in Turku, and his new company was transferring him to Vaasa. We were returning to Ostrobothnia.

Because we moved so often I had developed my own interests and activities. One of the most important was tennis. It was a breath of air from a better world. Tennis is more often associated with large towns than with remote villages. It originates in the Anglo-Saxon world, where the more fashionable people play in pure white kit. Finnish sporting life consists of skiing, skating, running, the high jump, baseball, weightlifting, wrestling, and the shot putt – but not tennis. My father, however, was an exception: as well as houses he had decided to build a whole world. He played tennis. I don't know what attracted him, whether it was the sport's image or the technical skill it demanded of its players. Either way, he passed his enthusiasm on to me, and tennis became my lifelong friend, my therapist, and a way to work off the pressures of the day.

When I was eleven I wrote a letter to my mother. She was at home in town; I was spending the summer at my grandmother's farm. My large, carefully formed letters are easy to read. Even so, I nearly put the pen through the paper. I had just learned that we were to move again, to Vaasa. I had done my research and found out that tennis was played in Vaasa. "There's a tennis course for beginners starting today," I wrote. "When I can I am going to join the tennis club, whose name is Tennis-61," I wrote solemnly. I folded the letter into an envelope, wrote mother's address with care, and took the letter to the post office, which was next to the shop. Mother opened the letter the next day, saw my message, and was delighted. Nor was tennis the only reason I was glad to be moving to Vaasa. As I wrote: "It is indeed nice to move back to one's birthplace."

CHAPTER 3

The Birds and the Beatles

M Y SCHOOL – VAASA HIGH SCHOOL – educated the doctors, lawyers, clergymen, and engineers of the future. Many boys went into their fathers' professions, but I had no idea then what my future might hold. We didn't discuss it at home. My father had had enough of electrical installation and had become a factory manager. As for myself, I had made just one decision and I intended to stick to it: there was no way I was going into industry. Factories and workshops seemed dirty, and the work was monotonous. What was more, my father was at work every single day. I doubted whether I wanted such a tough career.

My father never had enough time for me, and everyone else seemed to be in a hurry the whole time, too. Days were full of work and bustle. Everyone was on a journey somewhere, onwards or upwards. No one had time for frivolity, feelings, or fretting. We had a new home on account of my father's new job, a large and light wooden house next to the factory. At home the only thing expected of me was that I would do well at school. This was no problem. Besides, our parents had somehow made me believe that by studying, working, and researching one could meet challenges that at first seemed impossible. By preparation and careful consideration one could get the better of any opponent.

Knowledge was power, by which one could transform one's destiny. With the help of knowledge one could advance and do great things. With knowledge one could compete and never be limited.

I really don't know where this optimistic view of the world came from. Perhaps my parents were drawing on their own disappointments to motivate their children. They had both been compelled to give up studying early. Both had been the first in their family to matriculate from high school, but neither had ever graduated from university. They really wanted their own children to have a chance to study and eventually to graduate.

For my mother the decision to abandon her studies in order to establish a family had been a painful one. It was never openly discussed because it would have hurt my mother too much. It was only by good fortune that she had gone to secondary school after her father's death and fought for a place at university, but she had never had the chance to show how far her intellect and talent would have taken her. I assume she would have gone far. My mother was bitter about her fate, and the bitterness gradually changed to a sort of gray cloud that everyone noticed but no one mentioned. That cloud acted as a silent demand that her children study and take the opportunities denied to her.

My mother's experiences came to mind much later, when I met Chinese president and Party Leader Jiang Zemin in 2002. My mother had died by then, so I couldn't talk to her about my conversation with Jiang. The distinguished chairman and president wanted to know what I thought about setting up a stock exchange in China. My view was that the Chinese could indeed set up a stock exchange, but the most important thing was to take care of education. The country needed good engineers, lawyers, and industrialists in order to remain competitive.

When later in the business world I encountered situations that seemed impossible, I went back to the lessons learned at home. Everything is possible, if only you research, study, and do things right.

Nokia was full of people who thought the same way as me. We couldn't accept that anything was impossible. Everything is possible for those who know what they're doing. But without thorough knowledge, educated humility, and close attentiveness, nothing good will come. I have never been terribly good at improvising. I have always wanted to prepare for everything, both the expected and the unexpected. I am at my best when I know I am well prepared, whether the matter in question is a speech, a deal, or even a routine meeting.

Of course I still knew nothing of this in Vaasa High School at the beginning of the 1960s. There I sat in class with the other boys. Sometimes the teachers were boring and narrow; sometimes they set my thoughts racing. For example, Raimo Teppo's history and social studies lessons were spellbinding, so that every boy listened as quiet as a mouse. Teppo took a keen interest in the economy and in society, and he transmitted his enthusiasm to his pupils. Once we debated which of Finland's banks was best. It was from him that I learned what a stock exchange is and why the value of shares fluctuates.

I was not the sort of boy who would have been voted form captain. I didn't tell anecdotes or jokes, I didn't organize parties, and I didn't experiment with alcohol or tobacco. Girls liked me, but I wasn't a heartthrob who received a constant stream of secret love letters during boring lessons. I had been taught to behave well. At home it was emphasized that everyone was equal and we should all have the chance to develop our talents. No one should need to look up to other people, nor should anyone be allowed to look down.

I was in school to learn, not to enjoy myself. Many of my classmates enjoyed themselves at our teachers' expense. Some of them were fun to tease. Our scripture teacher was so absent-minded that he could never remember where he had left his car; sometimes he even forgot which day it was. Some teachers would find wet mushrooms or sharp tacks on their chairs. I didn't take part in these activities, and I'm sure many of the other boys thought I was a bit of a prig. I certainly seemed more mature than most. Perhaps today I'd be called a geek – nörtti in Finnish.

In those days I often used to cycle to play tennis in the evenings. In the winter it might well be twenty degrees below zero. I took my tennis racket, put on a thick winter jacket and a woolly hat, and rode along Vaasa's dark and slippery streets to the other side of town. The front wheel never seemed to keep straight, and cycling was rather like skating. I would play for hours with my friends in the tennis hall. If I lost I would go home quiet and dejected. Tennis had become a serious contest, like so many other things. But above all I competed with myself, and in myself I encountered a tough opponent.

Besides tennis my recreations were the scouts and a nature club. At that time almost every secondary school in Finland had a nature club. At Vaasa High School it was called Reviiri – the Finnish word for *territory*. It had members from every class in the school and some former pupils as well. I joined when I was about twelve and later I became the chairman of the club. We focused on ornithology because we lay under one of the major avian migration routes. For many a nature club member the hobby was the spark for a career as a biologist or nature photographer.

Through the club I also got to read some fascinating books, such as Rachel Carson's *Silent Spring*. The book's title refers to the dying away of birdsong because the over-use of DDT had disrupted the food chain, and bird populations were in decline.

As the eldest child I was expected to behave better than my brothers and sisters. And we didn't do silly things in our family – we didn't get up to pranks we could all laugh at together. Life wasn't solemn, though, even if it was earnest at times. We didn't broadcast our emotions, either joyful or sad. My mother's family in particular valued silence above great emotional tempests. Everyone in our family kept themselves under control, and our parents were a model for this. I grew up to be a polite, reserved, hard-working, eager-to-please, and ambitious young man.

Global politics intruded on Finland when in November 1963 President Kennedy was assassinated in Dallas. I read this in a newspaper, but many of my fellow students learned about it from television. We had watched television at a neighbor's on a few occasions, but our parents were in no hurry to acquire this new and revolutionary device. In conservative Ostrobothnia television was feared as likely to ruin family life, to destroy children's chances of success at school, and to spread subversive leftist opinions.

We finally got a television in 1964. My schoolmates had convinced me of its advantages. I told my mother that I wouldn't do so well at school if we didn't have one. I really needed to follow world events. My mother told my father, who bought a set the very next day. Television or no television, however, we had to keep order in the family. To do that I gathered all the children and my parents round the table and set out rules in writing for watching television. According to these, we could only watch it at a certain time, only after homework was completed. It would be turned off by ten at the latest. There were exceptions for news and sports, which my father could watch in the middle of the night – for example if a boxing match with Cassius Clay (who had yet to become Muhammed Ali) was broadcast then. Then we boys too would be woken up and would come down and watch. Otherwise the rules I had set out were to be followed.

In 1963 and 1964 something crackled over the airwaves that changed the world for my whole generation. *"All my loving, I will send to you / All my loving, darling I'll be true,"* announced a group of mop-haired Brits. In my mind I bawled the words of "Eight Days a Week," even though I didn't understand them. I was fourteen, it was summer, and I was again in the country, where there were some cows, sheep, and chickens in the barn. It was a long way from Liverpool, the launchpad for the Beatles' attack on the Finnish countryside. Our cows didn't seem in the least bothered by their brilliance.

In my enthusiasm I introduced the Beatles to my mother as well, and she tried to understand them on the radio. My sister had a tape-recorder on which to capture new Beatles recordings. It wasn't only the Beatles' music that inspired the world's youth: their haircuts did, too. The Beatle cut was a novelty and an act of rebellion against the older generation. My own hair remained respectably short, but otherwise the Beatles were part of everyone's life.

The upper floor of our school offered an excellent viewing platform for the yard of the girls' high school. Many of my classmates already had a girlfriend. We both envied and teased the boys who had girlfriends. One of my classmates began going out with a girl when he was fourteen and ended up married to her for many years. But this was an area where I was far from precocious: I was perhaps too shy, too reserved, always in control. Or perhaps I just wasn't sufficiently interested in girls.

CHAPTER 4

The Day that Changed My Life

SCHOOL WAS NOT A PROBLEM FOR ME, so I was pleased to see in the newspaper an announcement that Atlantic College, an international school on the coast of South Wales, intended to recruit some Finnish pupils. I knew at once I wanted to go there. The following day the Rector of the High School, Olavi Niemi, stopped me in the corridor and suggested that I apply. I told him that I'd already sent off for the application forms. I wasn't sure I'd get in because the college required language skills and other qualifications, but I was sure I would do well. In March I submitted the papers to the Finnish Cultural Foundation, which ran the selection process in Finland. In April ten promising candidates were invited to an English-language interview in Helsinki. I spoke stuttering school English. I had never been abroad. I had never used the language anywhere. I had heard people speak English on television, but otherwise I knew nothing of international life.

On the last day of April but one I rang the Finnish Cultural Foundation. I asked if I'd been accepted. The telephone tingled in my hand as I was told that I had. I would leave for the Atlantic coast of Wales the following autumn. My heart jumped for joy. I told my parents the news and they congratulated me. My father slapped my back. My mother conjured up a dinner excelling even her high standards. That meal, which started at five, lasted for hours as we discussed everything that lay ahead. It was one of the happiest days of my life.

I didn't know then that the whole course of my life had changed. But looking back I'm absolutely certain that it did. Some seemingly random events do change the direction of our lives. We don't realize it at the time, only in retrospect. My acceptance at Atlantic College was precisely such an event.

Atlantic College was established to bring together students from different countries to study together for two years. The school was academically ambitious: gifted pupils were chosen on the basis of references and interviews to see how well they would fit in. This year two of us from Finland would go. A stipend from the Cultural Foundation would cover our tuition costs. You could also reach the school by a different route: rich parents could pay the school fees, but their offspring still had to pass the entrance tests. Atlantic College was thus a combination of a high-pressure school and an international organization that was trying in the 1960s to educate the first global generation. The experiment was not a bad one, and in my case at least Atlantic College achieved its goals.

In the summer of 1967 I awaited with mounting excitement the journey to my new school. In Vaasa strange stories were circulating of what the future held for me. The cause of the greatest amazement was that I would not sit my school-leaving exams at the prestigious Vaasa High School, but would move to somewhere in Wales, wherever that was. This seemed to upset everyone's deepest feelings. My mother, too, was in her heart sad that her eldest child would not graduate from high school in his home town.

After a flight on a Finnair Caravelle I arrived in London, where I took the train to the industrial town of Bridgend in Wales and then went by bus to Atlantic College. The school had chosen for its location a gray mediaeval haunted castle that had stood guard for centuries. Around the ramshackle castle there was a sprinkling of new buildings where the students lived and worked. The area was surrounded by fields where sheep grazed. Around the castle was a garden with well-tended slopes sweeping down to the sea. The Atlantic's endless horizon floated above the bright green meadows and dark green trees. Fog rose from the sea and a cold wind blew, though there was nothing new about that for anyone from Finland. The new landscape blew my mind. This was a different world, bigger than Finland. The sea was sea here, too, but it was bigger than the Gulf of Bothnia, which I knew had only Sweden on its other side. Here whole new continents awaited conquest from this strip of shore. Here I could see as far as my eyes would let me.

The library in the arched vaults of the castle took my breath away. So many interesting books, so much to study. My curiosity was already boiling over with the thought that I would get my hands on all this new knowledge because of the great opportunity that by chance – in the form of a newspaper announcement – had come my way.

We Finns were an ambitious crew who had started coming here only the previous year. So we had to show the others that we could handle it. In previous years the Germans had been the best-performing nationality in terms

The Finns at Atlantic College in 1968 (from left) Pentti Kouri, Martti Salomaa, Mika Reinikainen, Eero Nurminen and me.

of academic grades. We decided it was now the Finns' turn. The brightest star in our group was Pentti Kouri. Pentti was two meters tall and brimmed over with self-confidence and a broad general knowledge – his results were the best in Atlantic College's entire history. I saw a good deal of him over the years. He became a brilliant macroeconomics expert, and also a venture capitalist who had varying success. His self-assurance and genius brought him not only friendship but also envy and enmity. Pentti got me ever more interested in macroeconomics. Other students included Martti Salomaa, who became a gifted physicist and mathematician and later professor of theoretical physics at Helsinki University of Technology. And Seppo Honkapohja went on to hold the chair of macroeconomics at Cambridge University and sit on the board of the Bank of Finland.

At Atlantic College no one spoke of a profession they might follow or what the future might hold; but it was clear to all that our future would in some way be academic. Hardly any of us imagined we would become captains of industry, bankers, or leaders of political parties. We were simply enjoying our exploration of the Milky Way of knowledge.

Four boys slept in our dormitory. The metal-framed beds practically touched each other, so we had to learn to put up with the odors and customs of different cultures. I quickly learned who washed their feet and who didn't. I myself was the same conscientious boy I was growing up in Finland.

I wanted the room to be kept straight. When I was sent a food parcel from home, I made sure all my roommates received a share. Some of my new friends came from a similar background to mine, such as my Norwegian roommate. Others came from so far away that I really had to come to grips with a new culture. For example, Lu Pat Ng came from Malaysia, where he belonged to the Chinese minority. If I had not met him when I was young, I would certainly not have gained the understanding I needed later of how things worked in Southeast Asia.

Atlantic College made its students study hard right from the beginning. Every student had to specialize in three subjects: I chose economics, physics, and mathematics. In all three subjects I would be able to use my mathematical gifts. Economics had begun to interest me back in Vaasa – my brilliant teacher Raimo Teppo had made the subject seem fascinating. At Atlantic College it became my passion because there too we had an outstanding teacher, Andrew Maclehose. He made me look at the links between economics and economic policy. He made us put ourselves in the Chancellor of the Exchequer's place. We had to decide: was this the right time to devalue or not? I enjoyed this enormously. My self-confidence grew: I learned that with every piece of knowledge one might influence the world. Knowledge was power.

CHAPTER 5

International School

M Y NEW SCHOOL COMPELLED EVEN ME, a shy country boy, to take a stand on the great issues facing the world. We had to defend our views every day in class, and once a week we had a debate on current events. There you had to be ready to put your arguments forward and give good reasons for them. I remember the heated discussions that events in 1967–68 provoked.

Czechoslovakia was one flashpoint. The Prague Spring in 1968 gave its people greater freedom to express their opinions and greater control over their own lives. In August a surge of Soviet tanks crushed the country's embryonic democracy. There were a couple of boys from Czechoslovakia at Atlantic College, one of whom went on to Harvard. In the school debate we were divided into two camps: those who defended the occupation and those who opposed it. The division was of course artificial: I am sure that none of us really supported the trampling of democracy. But everyone was expected to have a view, and it made for an intense atmosphere.

For my first six months I was the same reserved and rather shy boy who had left Vaasa in Finland on his first foreign trip in order to spend two years here. But then my shyness disappeared and I began to be more assertive. Discipline at Atlantic College was not as strict as in ordinary British boarding schools. It says something of the spirit of the age and the prevailing open-mindedness that we didn't have to wear school uniforms. Jeans were perfectly acceptable as long as they were clean, as was a clean shirt without a tie. For dinner we were expected to don a blazer, tie, and straight trousers.

Atlantic College tried its best to inure us to regular habits. The morning swim took place at a quarter past seven every day until November. The heavy

British breakfast came only after that. The swimming season resumed somewhere around April. You certainly knew you were awake after that morning ritual. The school's other recreations also toughened me up. My studies included life-saving, sculling, and other healthy activities. In my first few months I and another pupil built our own seaworthy boat out of rubber and wood. Apart from a little help from a carpenter the boat was entirely our own work. We also made our own wetsuits from rubber. When I lugged the heavy outfit back to Finland it really gave my brothers and sisters something to marvel at. There was however rather less use for it in Vaasa than on Wales's stormy Atlantic coast.

One of the most important activities throughout my life has been tennis. I'm seen here at Atlantic College, South Wales, in the summer of 1968.

I put a great deal of energy into my schoolwork. In addition to economics I was keen on physics, which was taught by Miss Adams. She was young and beautiful and I always took the seat in class where I could see her figure to best advantage. Despite my rather wandering attention I got top grades in physics, too.

I also did some travelling. In the first Easter holidays I took the boat over to Ireland, from Fishguard to Rosslare. Ireland in those days was by no means the mainstream European country we know today. It wasn't exactly a third-world country, but it didn't feel like part of the first world, either. I took the train up the coast to Dublin and then hitchhiked to the little town of Strabane, which straddles the border between Northern Ireland and the Republic of Ireland. There I stayed for three days with the family of a boy I had met at a scout camp in Finland the previous year. They were a prosperous, middle-class family, but they were Catholics in Northern Ireland where Catholics were treated as second-class citizens. They spoke passionately of their desire to see a "Free Ireland." I could sense from talking to them that something was not right in their lives. I was too polite or too tactful to probe them on the matter, though I knew nothing then of the ancient, almost tribal conflicts that divided Northern Ireland. About six months later the Troubles there ignited.

At Atlantic College I learned to live and work with people from different cultures, which wasn't common for young Finnish men in the 1960s.

There were of course opportunities to go abroad as an exchange student, to Britain or the United States, for example. But this didn't guarantee exposure to the richness of many cultures as Atlantic College did. Finland was a monocultural country in the 1960s, or at least that's how it felt in Ostrobothnia. The generation of corporate executives before mine never learned what real multiculturalism is. On the other hand, for generations younger than mine multiculturalism is one of the necessary conditions for work. Without a multicultural attitude one cannot work in an international company. Atlantic College helped me understand what real multiculturalism is, and why it's essential in a globalized world.

CHAPTER 6

Back to Finland

EVERYTHING COMES TO AN END. My "escape" concluded in the spring of 1969. I graduated from Atlantic College with excellent marks in both the International Baccalaureate and in my A-levels, the British school-leaving exams. I returned to Finland, as did the other Finns. The Finnish Cultural Foundation, which had funded our studies, expected that of us. I suppose, though, that we would have all returned home anyway because a peculiar emotion had developed within us. It would perhaps be too solemn to call it patriotism, while homesickness sounds a little too frivolous. It was something between the two, for which there isn't really a word in either Finnish or English. We had had to represent Finland, which was scarcely known at all in the rest of the world. Now we wanted to come back to our own country and continue our studies and work in Finland.

When I came back to Finland I had to go to the university to sit entrance exams. I was applying for Helsinki University of Technology, which did not recognize the A-levels I had taken at Atlantic College, or indeed give me any credit for them. The university assumed that a student with an international background would sit its tests and so confirm that they would get through the course of study. A week after I'd finished my exams in Wales I once again found myself in the exam hall. It was tedious. Anyone who has ever taken entrance exams for university will know how important it is to prepare properly, and I have always believed in preparing myself thoroughly for everything I do. Now I was sitting exams I hadn't had a single day to prepare for.

I walked across the grass and along the gravel path to the main building of the university. I had to sit the exam in the big auditorium, along with hundreds of other applicants. Apart from the holidays from Atlantic College, it was my first contact in a long time with my Finnish contemporaries. They were hunched over their exam papers, their hair flopping over their ears. Their shirts had wide collars, and a mixture of nylon and tension was making them sweat. The scratching of pencils was the only sound in the room. The tests covered math and physics. Fortunately the grounding I'd received at Atlantic College was so thorough that I knew as soon as it was over that I'd done well. I felt at ease with the way I'd been able to respond to the questions and challenges.

The Finland to which I'd returned had grown economically. Politically, Finland, like other countries, had moved leftwards at the end of the 1960s. The threat of socialism seemed real again, since support for the social democrats and communists was growing, especially among students. In Finland the left-wing student movement was turning into a repugnant form of communism, a species of Stalinism that blindly idealized the Soviet Union. In the early 1970s this strange phenomenon was influential – indeed almost hegemonic – in student organizations and cultural and political life.

Many of my contemporaries were enthusiastic about left-wing or communist thought. Good relations with the Soviet Union were the bedrock of Finnish foreign policy. This meant maintaining good relationships between individuals, and so the closest friends of our strong neighbor also enjoyed the fruits of this policy. The Soviet Union took the lion's share of Finland's foreign trade. For this reason many companies and "capitalist" organizations became participants in Finland's "official" foreign policy. At the same time, of course, Finnish businesses wanted Finland to be open to the west, where Finnish industry's export markets had traditionally been, and where there was real money rather than funny non-convertible rubles. We had traditionally exported tar, butter, and paper and, in recent decades, increasing volumes of machinery and electronics.

In the spring of 1969 I was a very different sort of boy from the one who had left for Atlantic College nearly two years before. I had certainly grown a little taller. I was gangly, long-haired, and fully familiar with the latest pop music from Britain and the States. In the spirit of the age I wore trendy jeans, and my English was fluent, though apart from Finnish and English I didn't really know any other languages. I was still working to fill this gap when I was at Nokia. But the most important thing was that I had grown in self-confidence and self-esteem. I had gone abroad for two years on my first foreign trip. I had survived, indeed flourished, though from time to time I had missed Finland and my family.

Now however I was back home where I spent the summer helping with the hay on my uncle's farm. At the end of the sixties the region was prosperous and lively, although the farm was small and old-fashioned and relatives were the main source of power. Just a little while back at Atlantic College I'd been working with pen and slide-rule; now I was holding a pitchfork or a scythe. That summer was the last extended period I would spend in Ostrobothnia, though I didn't know that as I slogged away in the fields. I felt neither sad nor nostalgic; rather I had a sense of excitement and expectation. When Neil Armstrong and Apollo 11 were approaching the moon, and Armstrong took the first steps on its surface, his progress was continuously monitored from my uncle's traditional little farm.

Atlantic College had made me independent of my parents and cut me free from the place where I grew up. My world was open. My parents were no longer much in my thoughts and I certainly didn't listen to them as I had when I was younger. The self-sufficient child had grown into an independent young man in a single bound. It had been stressful; but it had also been necessary.

While many of my generation interested themselves in Soviet collective farms, the Communist Party, and Five-Year Plans, I had moved west to join the wider European and global conversation. At a key phase of intellectual development, my world view had diverged from many of my contemporaries. I had studied and also seen how the world worked, how capitalism worked. At the same time that many of my friends had cleansed their minds of independent thinking in favor of party propaganda, I had painfully learned to think for myself, to put together my own viewpoints, and to defend them against intelligent criticism. This experience built up my self-esteem, but it also made me an outsider in Finland, where activists in political parties seemed to be gaining the upper hand and taking ever-more-important positions at an ever-younger age.

Leftism – the adoration of the Soviet Union and the German Democratic Republic – had assumed the nature of a group psychosis in Finland. The movement reached its peak in 1970, when universities ground to a halt as students boycotted lectures to go on strike alongside the workers. The student organizations had become party political machines issuing statements on the situation in the Middle East, poverty in Africa, or the dangers Western imperialism posed to the cosmos.

I didn't have a dream profession, but I had a hunch I'd find a niche in academia – I thought I might perhaps be a good professor of physics at a university or polytechnic. I thought, too, that I might continue my civic activities, which I had begun in the inspiring environment of Atlantic College. As a nineteen-year-old I found myself analyzing the Finnish government's economic policies, using the broad experience I had gained from Atlantic College's economics courses and from reading *The Economist* every week. Perhaps a professor of physics could benefit from these activities to some extent? And weren't physics and economics all about calculation and mathematics, which just got easier and easier for me? That was my train of thought as I made hay on holiday that summer.

In August the post brought the sort of letter Finnish families long for: I had been accepted to read applied physics at Helsinki University of Technology. I went with my father to the bank in Vaasa, where I'd had an account since childhood, to apply for a student loan. This was before the state automatically guaranteed such loans. So there we were in our suits and carefully ironed shirts. My father guaranteed the loan, and the following day I received the soothing news that the loan had been approved – my university years could begin.

CHAPTER 7

Engineering Student

THE 1970S HAVE BEEN CALLED THE BROWN DECADE. They began for me on 1 September 1969, when I enrolled at the University of Technology. I went to live in an apartment in a student block next to the university, which had been built to house athletes at the time of the Helsinki Olympics. It can't have changed much since then. The dominant colors were brown and dark blue. During my first year I shared my bedroom with another first-year student. (In the tradition of student banter one could say he hasn't got very far since: Matti Juhala is now professor of vehicle technology at Helsinki University of Technology.) We each had a narrow bed, a desk, a chair, and a wardrobe. There was a basin in the corner for us to brush our teeth and wash our hands, and a communal area with a bathroom, kitchen, and living room. In my second year I had a room to myself in the same block.

Helsinki University of Technology was an almost instinctive choice for me. There have always been lots of engineers in my family, and after me many an Ollila has studied to become a chartered engineer. For my major I chose applied physics, one of the more demanding and theoretical courses on offer. I liked the challenge and hoped the bar would be high enough. My fellow students were clever and had demonstrated as much in their exams. They came from all over Finland, though the Helsinki region was the most strongly represented since that's where the best high schools were. I knew only a handful of the other students beforehand.

The university had moved to its campus in Otaniemi a few years earlier. It was the first American-style campus in Finland, with the whole area given over to university departments and student accommodation. Some of the services left something to be desired, such as the modest shop and post office, but Helsinki was close by.

Study was intensive. There were twenty-five to thirty hours of lectures a week. The rhythm of work I had got used to in Wales continued naturally. In my first two years I only remember studying physics and math. It required work, but Atlantic College had furnished a firm foundation. As well as study the autumn offered new leisure opportunities –social evenings on Tuesdays and dances at weekends. I was especially pleased that meals were provided. I've never been much of a cook, though I can boil potatoes and eggs. I'd been living on packet soups and sandwiches in my room, so a student canteen was a great advance.

The twelve trainee engineers who shared our apartment came from every year of the course. We made a good group and our communal life was very agreeable. Rather than barricade ourselves into our own rooms we spent our free time in the living area, making coffee and discussing current events. The two and a half years I spent in this group were one of the best things about university life. We've often gotten together since.

Engineering students sometimes talk these days of becoming "Otaniemi-fied." This is a particular way of becoming institutionalized, of rarely leaving Otaniemi. It never happened to me. I used to play tennis in downtown Helsinki. I didn't often join in with the organized activities of the other students, though I led an active life. So active, in fact, that even tennis became a seasonal sport. This was the only time in my life I have taken breaks from this important pursuit.

I met my first Stalinists at Otaniemi. They held strong opinions. "The problem for the Social Democrats, the Centre Party, and the Conservatives is that they don't have a society to model themselves on – a pattern for living that would work all over the world, better than Finland. We, on the other hand, have both the GDR and the Soviet Union," they would say.

From today's point of view it's difficult to appreciate just how over-politicized the seventies were. Everything, and I mean everything, was political. I began my political career as a candidate in student elections, which in 1969 had been openly party-political for the first time. I chose to stand as a Conservative. Where I came from we had a two-party system, and everyone I knew voted either for the Conservatives or for the Centre Party. I imagined the Conservatives would be the choice of the thinking person whom socialism didn't attract, in the way it didn't attract me. It rapidly became clear to me that Conservative policy in these elections consisted entirely of opposition to socialism and had no other content. A positive alternative seemed to be lacking: the party's policies seemed entirely negative, with no constructive element. This wasn't enough for me. After the first year I moved to the Centre Party group, where there seemed to be people who could think.

Just as I grew impatient with politics so I began to tire of a wholly technical education. I had no cause for complaint with my studies, but differential equations alone didn't open up the world as much as I wanted. I hankered after a broader education, with a greater focus on social issues. I had studied economics in Wales and I wanted to continue that study at the university level. I had friends in the political science department at Helsinki University, so I applied and was accepted there in 1971. This time I didn't have to sit the entrance exams since to my surprise I was accepted on the basis of my results from Atlantic College.

The economics department was in central Helsinki. I enjoyed it immensely – the atmosphere was agreeable and the discussions and teaching provided a new angle of entry to social issues. The department had some smart people, and I received excellent guidance from them on what I should study. Study was not very sociable, however – I didn't attend a single series of lectures, and just a few seminars. For the most part I had my nose in the books for the examined courses, making up for lost time as fast as I could.

CHAPTER 8

Liisa Changes My Life

ONE FEBRUARY EVENING IN 1970 changed all my plans once more. I was with my friends at a student dance, and so was a young woman with her friends from the Helsinki School of Economics.

I was queuing to buy a beer when my eyes fell on a beautiful, blonde, and clever-looking girl. She seemed to be looking to see who was in the queue. I learned later that this was just a little way she had that didn't really mean anything. Anyway, when I'd bought my beer I asked her to dance. I used my powers of attraction to the full, and later we left together to continue the evening with our friends back at the residence hall. There I asked for her telephone number, which she wrote on a slip of paper.

"Are you sure this number is right?" I asked again at the end of the evening.

"I wouldn't give you a number if it wasn't the right one," she replied. There was decisiveness in her voice, and perhaps a touch of invitation too. I rang her as soon as I could. I thought she might have found me too talkative and eager. My stalking brought a result, however, and I soon met her again.

The girl in question was Liisa Metsola, who had qualified as a nurse and was already working, while I was still studying. We were soon spending a lot of time together. We went to the cinema, to the theatre, to concerts, and to student parties. In other words, we did what young couples do. Liisa came from a family with roots in eastern Finland and Karelia. The eastern Finns are much better at showing and acting on their emotions than we western Finns. Liisa thinks things through for herself in a straightforward way, and isn't afraid to disagree with me.

The first summer we were a couple we had to spend apart, since I had to go back once more to Vaasa. There I had to undertake a placement in an engineering workshop as part of my degree. A place had been arranged in the factory where my father worked, where I did maintenance work and some plumbing jobs. The atmosphere was very different from what I was used to at Atlantic College and the University of Technology, but I got on fine with my workmates. We talked men's talk – of work, of women, of football. (Vaasa FC was then playing in the top division, as I'm proud to say it does today.) My time in that factory taught me some crucial lessons for my future career about the internal dynamics of a workplace and the difference between good and bad line management. I can't exaggerate the importance of one's early work experiences.

Liisa and I were engaged on the May Day holiday in 1971. I approached her father and told him of my intention to marry his daughter. He replied positively to my polite request, although she and I disagreed with him on practically everything else. We argued about politics so furiously that at times it felt like a family feud. He had been an evacuee from Karelia when the Soviet Union had invaded Finland in 1939–40, and his family home had been razed to the ground. His hatred for the Russians wasn't a political stance but something much deeper. He was out of sympathy with the central aim of the Finnish government, which was to achieve friendly relations with the Russians through an active foreign policy. Our arguments were repeated in many Finnish families where memories of the war years were still fresh.

We were married on 25 March 1972 at a little chapel in Otaniemi. The building was surrounded by forest, though it was just a few hundred yards from where I lived on campus. There were about forty guests: a large classroom's worth of relatives, fellow students, and friends. The unique feature of the chapel was its altarpiece. There wasn't one: its place was taken by the Finnish forest landscape, seen through a huge window taking up the entire wall. So it seemed as if the wedding were taking place in a wintry forest. We held our reception in the student restaurant where we had first met. Ostrobothnian weddings are meant to be wild and boisterous, but ours was calm and civilized, with many warm and well-made speeches. The occasion was made in our image.

At the beginning of the 1970s we weren't worried about the future. We were moving so fast that not everybody could keep up. My parents thought we shouldn't have married because I hadn't yet graduated from university nor had I taken my bride to meet my mother. Our marriage was a quick student affair – we didn't have a sound financial base or any clear plans. But I had al-

Liisa and I celebrated our engagement on May Day in 1971.

ready moved on from my family and wanted to live my own life.

Liisa soon noticed she'd married a man whose diary quickly filled up. One day she brought out her own diary. She announced that she didn't intend simply to adapt to whatever plans her new husband happened to make – she had her priorities, and I would have to learn to adapt. "Let's see when we can find a time that suits us both," she said brightly. Her attitude has not changed in forty years, which has helped keep us together. I've tried to be as flexible as I can in my own arrangements, though with varying success.

We were both ambitious people. We were also both self-sufficient: I was the oldest child in my family and used to looking after myself; Liisa was her family's youngest, but her mother had had a serious illness, which had compelled the children to take care of themselves. Although our personalities were different we understood each other *instinctively*. It was easy to build a marriage on this basis. (Well, honestly speaking, I can't say it was always easy, but it was possible because we understood each other.)

We moved to a rented two-bedroom apartment about ten miles west of Helsinki. By that time the brown decade must have been approaching its end, because the walls of our new home were plain white. Ever since then we have wanted to live in houses where the walls are either white or off-white.

There was no Ikea in those days, and our furniture was hand-me-downs from our families or bought secondhand. The area around our home was growing rapidly: new houses, new schools, new shops.

With our modest income we couldn't imagine moving to the center of Helsinki. Many young couples began their married lives as we did, in rapidly-built apartment blocks in new suburbs. During the 60s the old road into the city had been turned into a modern motorway, which was convenient for us. In the mornings we would jump on the bus. The trip took about twenty minutes, though I soon took a break in my studies and went to work in Helsinki.

CHAPTER 9

Student Leader

IN THE AUTUMN OF 1972 I attended the annual conference of the National Union of Students in Finland, the SYL. I was elected to the board and appointed president. We gathered on Friday, held our conference on Saturday, and on Sunday we wondered what on earth we had decided. Formally we were there as representatives of our individual student bodies; I represented the students of the University of Technology. But the elections were nakedly political, as everything was at that time. The talk in the corridors was that a centrist candidate should become president, because neither a conservative nor a leftist would receive broad enough support. The night before the actual elections was key because the crucial politicking took place in the small hours. The search was on for a centrist candidate for president who would be acceptable to everyone. I fitted the bill. Also during that night we drew up an outline program for the coming year, so there were arguments about that as well. It was like drawing up a government program in the space of an evening.

On Sunday I set off on the long journey home knowing my life was about to undergo a major change. I had been elected president of the National Union of Students at the age of twenty-two. I had been the chairman of the National Union of Technology Students, so I had some idea of how to run things. I had for example helped organize boycotts of lectures, intended to encourage the modernizing of university governance. As students we demanded that we should be directly represented on the governing body.

Now I would be advancing students' interests full-time. My new role had a significant international angle, so my studies abroad and language skills certainly helped. When I was appointed I felt the glare of publicity for the first time: the selection of a new student president made the news in the big dailies and even on television. Suddenly I was a figure of national significance. My parents were bemused; they didn't feel this new career path was either desirable or suitable.

Just half a year into our marriage Liisa had to adapt to the fact that her husband was no longer a student. As president I received a small salary, which largely went on rent. The SYL was based on the fifth floor of a fine building in central Helsinki called the New Student House. It opened on to Mannerheimintie, Helsinki's main thoroughfare. For the first time I had my own room to work in.

I went into the office in the morning and came home in the evening, just as in any job. My studies were on hold. I still have two exercise books from that time and the pages are blank: no academic studies for four terms. I wore a suit and tie every day and carried my briefcase to the office and back. Many evenings were taken up with negotiations, meetings, and travel. Everything was in earnest and over-politicized. I took myself very seriously and it seemed as if I were aging very fast in my role. The union was well run, both bureaucratically and financially. The secretaries were highly professional and kept youthful enthusiasm in check, whereas the executive board was of variable ability.

At that time the SYL was seen as a natural springboard to a career in national politics. For example, Tarja Halonen – later president of Finland – had been on the board only a couple of years earlier and later moved via the trade union movement into Parliament.

I wanted to be a student leader, and I enjoyed my work. I often used to travel to universities around the country. I was constantly in meetings with senior officials and government ministers. But I never actually saw myself as a politician, rather as someone whose role was to speak up for students.

I enjoyed working in an organization with a small group of people. I wanted to lead it effectively. Meetings should have an agenda, objectives, and a clear timetable. I wasn't interested in publicity and I didn't seek it, though I did get my first taste of it, which came in handy later. I learned to make speeches entirely spontaneously, which hadn't been among my strong points. I also learned to write long, carefully considered speeches whose official line corresponded with Finnish foreign policy. I have never liked compromises, but as a student politician I had to make them every day – a tedious but also educational side of the job.

Sometimes my impatience rose to the surface. Even on a good day, running the National Union of Students in Finland was a constant defensive operation: the rise of the communists and the growth of their power had to be stopped. Although the Left didn't have a majority, at that time it felt as if there was a real danger that it would take over the entire student world. In many European countries student bodies had become radicalized, and the majority of students were alienated from them. That was what happened in France, for example. Preventing it happening in Finland became a mission for the Centrist group in Finland at the SYL.

As the representative of the Centrists I also had to cooperate with the Conservatives, though many issues were resolved with the Left. The Left and the Centre formed the so-called pan-democratic front, which held power. Even so, while I was its president the SYL never signed the declaration against the Free Trade Agreement with the European Economic Community. There were strident demands for the agreement to be rejected – people who would later hold important positions such as Tarja Halonen (later president of Finland), Erkki Tuomioja (later foreign minister), and Erkki Liikanen (governor of the Bank of Finland) all actively opposed it. In important questions of foreign policy, where relations with the West were at stake, the SYL stayed firmly behind agreed national policy.

I learned the rules of the political game. I had been the agreed choice of the Centrists and the Left for my role. In some issues, after careful deliberation, I voted with the Conservatives to promote what I believed were sensible policies. This irritated the Left and some Centrists too and gave rise to accusations that I was an opportunist and a turncoat.

Learning politics from the inside was an enormous help later on: leading a student organization in Finland in the 1970s certainly taught me what politics, discussions, rhetoric, horse-trading, and opportunism are. A CEO has to understand what politics is all about, otherwise the company will start to misinterpret its environment, which is the society it operates in. The consequences could be fatal to the company because you usually can't change your environment – you have to adapt to it instead.

The main reason the president's job was energy-sapping was the Stalinists. They were self-assured and knew what they wanted. Others piled in behind them. They followed a twin-track policy. On the one hand they took the parliamentary route, actively and aggressively exploiting the SYL's position and resources. On the other hand they were trying to bring about a revolution. This pincer movement was very hard to fend off. Relations with the Soviet Union were ruthlessly exploited as a pretext for change at home. My own attitude took their support as its starting-point. When a group has about 15 percent support, an organization like the SYL has in fairness to give it a hearing.

It's good to remember that the Stalinist movement received more attention than its level of support merited. In parliamentary elections it received only a few percent of the vote, though the figure was higher in student elections.

Finland was led by Urho Kekkonen, who had been in office since 1956. He was the chief architect of the country's foreign policy and the guarantor of Finnish independence vis-à-vis the Soviet Union.

The popularity of his policy was growing in the early seventies, both among the electorate and in political circles. It was largely thanks to Kekkonen that Finland had been able to negotiate a Free Trade Agreement with the EEC; this was important for Finnish export industries. In January 1973 Kekkonen's term of office, due to expire in 1974, had been extended by an exceptional act of parliament to run until 1978. This was no foregone conclusion, since it required five-sixths of the members of parliament to vote for it. It was intimately linked with the EEC Agreement and new laws extending the state's regulatory powers, which the Left in particular supported.

Kekkonen and Finnish foreign policy also enjoyed respect in the West. Finnish neutrality was widely recognized, but many western politicians and journalists never fully understood just what a tightrope Finland had to walk during the Cold War. The president had bitter enemies back home as well, who publicly accused him of kowtowing to Soviet wishes and thus of Finlandization.

I met Kekkonen a number of times. Most of these meetings were formal occasions, but I also went to his official residence to discuss issues such as the reshaping of university governance. We explained the SYL's standpoint to him. Kekkonen's position in Finland was so dominant that people involved him in issues that weren't really his responsibility. He was vigilant and engaged and concerned above all with power politics. How did the parties divide over the issue? How did politicians' public statements reflect their personal goals? These were some of the questions he put to me during our discussions.

My most memorable meeting with him was at the Independence Day reception in December 1973. It was the custom for the Students' Union to present its greetings to the president before the main event. I had prepared a few words requesting the president to focus attention on the serious shortage of student housing. As I walked toward the Presidential Palace it felt as if the damp Helsinki streets were soaking up all the light, despite the Christmas decorations in the shop windows.

We met the president at half past six, half an hour before the official reception started and a stream of guests would flow into the state rooms. Our

Liisa and I at the Independence Day reception in 1973 with Finland's finance minister Johannes Virolainen and his wife Kaarina.

meeting was naturally a terrifying prospect. First there was the age difference: Kekkonen was fifty years older than me – a very fit seventy-three, and he didn't show any sign of the dementia that would afflict him a few years later. Secondly there was Kekkonen's unassailable position, which younger generations find impossible to understand. He had been president since I was five and would carry on until I was thirty-one. It was almost unthinkable that anyone else could be president.

We were a small delegation who arrived at the gates of the Palace and were directed inside. The others, in the spirit of the age, were wearing lounge suits, but I was correctly attired in full evening dress. Frankly, it wasn't all that comfortable. The walls were hung with fine art depicting Finnish forests and wildlife and historical battles, though this wasn't the moment to embark on a course in art history.

We entered the room self-importantly and in line with protocol. The president stood waiting for us with an array of decorations pinned to his chest – Finland, perhaps surprisingly to some, has a flourishing honors system. He looked at us fiercely through his large, intimidating spectacles. He had an adjutant on either side. As one president to another, it was my duty to offer him our salutation. "Mr. President of the Republic, Happy Independence Day," I began. We also offered him a little bouquet of lilies for his wife Sylvi. The president accepted the flowers and I thought I saw the ghost of a smile.

"Thank you, I shall make sure immediately that these reach their intended destination," he replied. It broke the ice. After that I made my little speech.

As the SYL president I had also been invited to the real reception. So after our brief meeting one of the staff guided me around the side of the Palace to join the queue to shake hands with the real president, while he went through the state rooms to the head of the receiving line. There Sylvi, whose health was already starting to fail, was sitting waiting for him. He gave her the flowers and started to shake the hands of his guests for the evening.

CHAPTER 10

East and West

APART FROM OUR DEFENSIVE BATTLES we looked after mundane but nevertheless important matters affecting students. Our responsibilities were greater than those of student leaders elsewhere, since student unions in Finland are property owners on a grand scale. Halls of residence were built. Student health services were developed. University governance was overhauled.

Though my main focus was domestic I spent a lot of my time on international issues. Twice a year there were meetings of Nordic student leaders, for example. Finnish student organizations also had good links to student organizations in the Soviet bloc. As president I travelled many times to Moscow and to Prague, where the headquarters of the Communist student organizations were located. I learned how to operate within the confines of Finnish foreign policy, and that international meetings have their own special usages and rituals.

Home-grown Communists often came along on these excursions. I remember one occasion when we were travelling by train behind the Iron Curtain. The conductor kept a visitors' book, where travelers inscribed their names and a few fraternal words. A select group of Stalinists left this message: "My homeland is Finland, but my Fatherland is the Soviet Union."

I had visited Moscow for the first time in 1970, when we concentrated chiefly on investigating the quality of Soviet beer, which seemed well up to standard. Otherwise I found nothing to celebrate in the Soviet Union because the gap between its super-power status and its level of technological development was clear. But the Russian student politicians we met radiated intelligence and talked readily about international affairs. It was easy to discuss the dollar exchange rate, the oil crisis, or U.S. economic policy. But despite these conversations the Russians remained products of the communist system. They were always aware of the party line, and no one could officially cross it; but in the small hours, after a few vodkas, they might say what they thought. Sadly, genuine friendships were not possible because everyone was stuck with a role. Several of the Russians later found a place in the Gorbachev, Yeltsin, and Putin governments.

The level of education in the Soviet Union was high: student politicians knew mathematics, economics, and international relations. But when, for example, I went on a guided tour of the collective farms in Moldova (then part of the Soviet Union) I saw how the country's logistics let it down. A crop of peaches was left to rot when it should have been sold in Moscow. Their own efforts did not make people richer, and there were no incentives for work. Time after time I returned from the Soviet Union with a feeling of relief: this economic system could never beat a market economy.

The market economy however had problems of its own. Just like communism it contained the seeds of its own destruction. In practicing macroeconomics I had learned to see an economy as a system that moved from disequilibrium to equilibrium and back again. At the beginning of the 1970s it was shifting rapidly toward disequilibrium. At the end of 1973 the oil-producing countries decided to press the western world to change its policy toward Israel. The oil price went up by 70 percent; some oil shipments were sold for ten times or more than what they'd have fetched a year before. The world economy was suddenly hostage to the oil producers, and international recession was a fact.

The world recovered from the oil crisis, but it left an enduring mark on economic thinking. A debate started about energy conservation and alternative energy sources, which is still very much with us today. The Middle East and OPEC became a permanent part of the political agenda. Our whole world changed. In spring 1972, even before the energy crisis, a group of experts and futurists working at the Club of Rome had published a book called *The Limits to Growth,* which warned that the world's resources could no longer sustain constant economic growth. Thus the world's economies had to change: growth had reached its limits. Now the Club of Rome was proposing that zero growth should be the target so that the world with all its natural riches could survive. When the oil crisis burst upon us the warnings given by the Club of Rome were taken seriously. They became the theoretical base for the policies of those political groups, such as my own, that occupied the center ground between the hard Left and the dogmatic Right. While these political groups supported capitalism and the market economy, they also wanted economic development to respect the constraints imposed by nature and natural resources.

I read the Club of Rome report closely; I had, after all, been a member of a nature club at school. I was also a student of macroeconomics and I understood a little about politics. On top of that, technological development interested me even then. I tried to understand the logic of the Club of Rome, but I couldn't believe that they were right. To my mind, zero growth was a superficial target – a figure plucked out of nowhere. I had learned in economics lectures that economic growth was necessary for human well-being in a growing population. I haven't wavered in this belief since.

The Club of Rome didn't take into account technological developments, which enable the same output to be produced using less energy and fewer national resources.

With hindsight the Club of Rome report was far too pessimistic about technology. The report warned that copper or silver might run out by 1990, but nothing will ever run out in a properly functioning market economy. For example, if there were a risk that paper might disappear, new alternatives would become available because paper would become unaffordable. The world's known oil reserves are much greater now than at the beginning of the 1970s, and oil can be extracted in much more difficult conditions than it could then.

The Club of Rome thought in the 1970s that the market economy had an innate tendency to run out of control. But the global economy has shown itself much more flexible than anyone dared imagine.

No one believed in the seventies that the world could adapt to oil crises. The crises of 1973 and 1979 produced a global recession, but they also gave impetus to the technological development that has seen us through. Cars are now much more environmentally friendly, and more nuclear power has come online. Thus the world gained at least thirty years of extra time. None of this would have happened without the oil crises or the Club of Rome's warnings. They asked the right questions, even if they couldn't offer answers.

In the 1970s many young and even older politicians would meet Soviet representatives and visit the Soviet Embassy more often than they went to their corner shop. I went there chiefly for set-piece receptions: my contacts with officials were few and formal. As a counter-balance to the Russians it was important to look westward as well. In May 1973 I travelled to the United States for the first time. There was a U.S. Information Service office in Helsinki, which sent two to four student politicians across the Atlantic each year to get to know the American political system and way of life. Our program took in Washington, Denver, San Francisco, Los Angeles, Las Vegas, New Orleans, and lastly New York. We stayed in hotels, but we met local people in every town we went to, who played the part of host families showing us how Americans lived. Compared to seventies Finland, let alone the Soviet Union, I was struck by the sheer prosperity. There was as much Coca-Cola as you could drink, whereas in my teenage years in Finland it had been sold in parsimonious little bottles. T-bone steaks were the size of children's flippers. Car seats were more comfortable than the sofas in our student rooms. It was a solid introduction to America.

In Washington we visited Congress, where we were given an explanation of the American political system, though there was really only one theme to the discussions: what would happen to the hapless Richard Nixon? During our visit the Watergate scandal was going through one of its most hectic phases and divided America down the middle. The Republicans claimed that the *Washington Post* didn't have the right to humiliate Nixon as they had, while the Democrats were overjoyed that "Tricky Dick" was now on the run. Despite its disagreements over Nixon, the country was by no means as politically polarized as it has since become. We had lively discussions of what was healthy about the whole affair, and what wasn't.

The trip to the United States and the Watergate scandal were an excellent opportunity to study Cold War positions and the Americans' sincere belief that they ruled the world. Many people in Europe, where Social Democratic support was strong, thought it obvious that the United States had had its day.

American leadership had been discredited by Vietnam, the dollar was shaky, and the first oil shock was just around the corner.

There is documentary evidence from those years. One of the better-known treasures from the vaults is a clip from a television program of a grave, longish-haired, gangly, serious student leader on a trip to the World Youth Festival in Berlin. He boldly condemns the growing power of imperialism in the world. Yes, folks, that was me.

CHAPTER 11

Home and Family

O<small>N THE FIRST DAY OF J</small>ULY 1975 Liisa and I received the keys to our new home. We had bought a two-bedroom apartment in a four-story 1950s block in Herttoniemi, a hilly, wooded suburb on the east side of Helsinki. Not much had been done to it: the original bathtub and kitchen cabinets were still there, and it badly needed a makeover. A decorator friend came down from Ostrobothnia to lay new floors and give the place a lick of paint. We got rid of the bath and installed a shower. My parents came for three days to sand down the window frames and kitchen cupboards. I spent six weeks working alongside various workmen. I like carpentry and doing things with my hands; I always got top marks in school for woodwork. I laid a new tile kitchen floor under the decorator's direction. He explained how the tiles were to be laid and what sort of adhesive you should use. I also painted the cupboards my parents had sanded.

I had finished my time as SYL president at the end of the previous year. But in a way I took part in the Conference on Security and Cooperation in Europe (CSCE), which took place in Helsinki in 1975. This was Kekkonen's most visible foreign policy achievement and an important occasion for the world's media. I listened to the speeches on the radio as I painted the cupboards in our new flat. The reports resounded in the empty, echoing rooms. I could follow every twist and turn in the CSCE process long after the conference because I had heard every speech while I was doing up our flat.

Buying our flat had not been entirely straightforward. Liisa had qualified as a nurse, but she was continuing her studies at Helsinki University, majoring in social policy. There was no sign I would ever have a career. We went with these recommendations to see the bank manager, who happened to be an acquaintance. We promised to scrape together a deposit; the rest we would borrow from the bank. My father lent me 3,000 marks (about $3,200 at 2016 prices) which was the only loan my parents ever made to me. We also agreed to use our student loans to increase our share of the capital. The housing market had a growth spurt and house prices rose in its wake. We absolutely wanted to own our own home. Liisa and I were reckless, as were many others, and we believed we would manage. The oil crisis helped us: the Finnish economy had slipped into such a deep bog that rampant inflation seemed to pay off our loan for us very quickly. For once macroeconomic theory was a practical help in our life: we had taken on the loan at just the right time.

I had gone back to studying macroeconomics. I wrote my master's thesis chiefly in the faculty library. I often found myself alongside another student politician who had put his studies aside for a while – Erkki Liikanen, who was my age but had been a member of parliament since 1972. When he became Finland's youngest-ever MP Erkki was a politics student and president of the Teiniliitto – the League of Teenagers. We used to see each other during coffee breaks, where we'd put the world to rights.

I completed my thesis in spring 1976. It was entitled "The Theory of International Trade under Uncertainty" and I received a prize for the best master's thesis in macroeconomics that year. I couldn't have known that, decades on, I would be working on the very same subject in a very practical way. It's probably fair to say that Erkki Liikanen's current work also has a macroeconomic theme, given that he is governor of the Bank of Finland and a member of the board of the European Central Bank.

But even more significant than my graduation was the birth of our first child, our son Jaakko. Liisa and I knew we were ready to be parents, though by present-day standards we were very young.

Becoming a father was a tough job. I was present at the birth and for our son's first ten days at home, when I gave him a bath every day. The birth was also something of a watershed. Life seemed to have become organized: I had my own apartment, I had graduated, I was a husband and father.

Student and housing loans were not enough to keep a family. I had worked as an assistant lecturer in the economics department for a few months and I wanted to continue at the university, but there weren't any openings there. So I accepted more short-term work. The Centre Party and its youth organization needed someone to look after its international affairs. I went to work as International Affairs Secretary at the party office in Helsinki, intending to stay for about half a year.

I looked after international correspondence, I organized visits for delega-
tions and I wrote speeches. From time to time the party chairman would
call and ask me to explain something. I had to take care to respect the party's
foreign policy line, which was pretty easy: it was the same as President Kekkonen's and Finland's. My work did at least provide a salary and a peaceful
place to pursue my studies.

When the office closed for the evening I went to the library to study mathematics. I had decided I would also graduate from the University of Technology, though I did not finally do so until 1981.

I still hadn't the faintest idea what I would do. I had the bright idea that I
should stand for parliament for my home region of Ostrobothnia. I wasn't
at all enthusiastic. I'd had a bellyful of politics, and I doubted I'd get enough
votes to be elected. I've never been a popular favorite, and I would have
hated the electioneering and hand-shaking. The foreign ministry might have
been an interesting alternative, but the life of a civil servant seemed a little
slow for my restless nature. I had to come up with something, though – I
was the twenty-six-year-old father of a family, with a great deal of education
and a certain amount of experience and knowledge of the world, but no idea
what profession I wanted to follow. It's no wonder that my parents were bemused by my activities. They told me it wasn't for this that they'd sent their
son off to study.

CHAPTER 12

Escape from a Troubled Land

By March 1977 I had made my decision. I had talked things through over with Liisa and we decided we would leave Finland.

The intellectual atmosphere in Finland made the decision easier. Kekkonen was still the country's sovereign leader, who sniffed the way the winds were blowing and tailored his skillful rhetoric accordingly. He had recently, in front of television cameras, forced on the country an "emergency government" in which the Communists had a central role. They did not, however, want to accept that responsibility, so the government quickly disintegrated into a minority coalition. The economy was in chaos. For several years inflation galloped at around 15 percent. As a man with a mortgage I benefited from the melting away of my debt, but high inflation was a sign of an unsustainable economic policy. In April 1977 Finland was forced to devalue its currency again. At that time the future of the communist system seemed reasonably promising. Cultural life, the universities, and the intellectual atmosphere were largely in the grip of the Left. There were demonstrations in support of the Soviet Union, Cuba, and the German Democratic Republic, and against capitalist plots, rapprochement with the West, and NATO. In spring 1977 alone over 750,000 wage-earners took part in strikes – about one worker in three.

In the seventies Finnish critics of the Soviet Union did not progress in their careers. At the same time Finnish firms did profitable business with the Soviet Union. Goods that could not be sold on western markets were good enough for the Soviet Union. Finnish products gained a formidable reputation for quality there. Finnish construction companies grew fat on exports over the eastern border, and the sales of Finnish textile and shoe factories were guaranteed. The company chiefs who depended on Soviet trade teamed up with politicians to form a dominant group that didn't bother Soviet politicians with difficult questions – otherwise trade might have suffered.

I respected Kekkonen's achievements and I supported his policy. Nevertheless I felt uneasy about the atmosphere in Finland at the end of the 1970s. I was bothered by the intellectual dishonesty, the rigid resistance to change, and the politicians' ineffectuality. Like many other Finns I feared for my country's future. I saw that Finland had to find a way of moving closer to western Europe: there was no alternative for the Finnish economy if it were ever to thrive. I believed that western democracy and capitalism were practically and morally superior to socialist economics and communist politics. But I wanted to know more about economics; I wanted to learn, so that my thinking would be more firmly grounded and more convincing.

And Helsinki was a dull, gray town. Dining out was grim, with no ethnic food apart from Chinese, or perhaps I should say "Chinese." It was as hard to find a decent bottle of wine in Alko, which had a monopoly on the sale of alcohol, as to find an authentic sauna in Tuscany. The range of clothing in the department stores was very limited, and the fabrics and designs were old-fashioned. The best hotels would have rated perhaps three stars. There wasn't a shred of optimism. And everything was regulated; it seemed as if the state or the local council made all your decisions for you.

In the autumn of 1976 I began to consider new options. At the start of 1977 I saw in a newspaper that the British Council was offering stipends for study in the United Kingdom. It was practically a rerun of the events that had taken me to Atlantic College exactly ten years earlier. Liisa and I sat at the kitchen table in our little flat and talked things through. Staying in Finland might not be the smart thing to do. We planned how Liisa might continue her own studies in London. I decided, after a few seconds' careful consideration, that my new place of study should be The London School of Economics. It was a well-known and highly regarded university that trained economists, social scientists, and philosophers – and rock stars (Mick Jagger is also a graduate). I thought it might suit me well, too. I applied for a grant for postgraduate study at the LSE, and to undertake a doctorate. I was invited to interview and I got the grant. By April I had the funding for my new escape.

My decision caused astonishment, and even amusement. At that time many people abandoned their studies halfway through and became journalists, politicians, or activists. I had already graduated and yet I had decided to continue my studies, and many people found this absurd. Also it was unusual then to study abroad. Those who did went mostly to neighboring Sweden or to the United States. And many leftists wanted to reinforce their faith in the achievements of scientific communism by studying in Moscow, the German Democratic Republic, or even Warsaw.

I told my colleagues in the Centre Party office that I'd be leaving. I sat in a nearby café, where I was joined by two of my colleagues. We ordered pea soup for lunch. "Now, as we discussed earlier, this is a temporary job for me," I began. "At the end of the summer I'll be going to London to study. I've got a grant to complete a doctorate." My colleagues' soup remained untouched. One of them might have dropped a spoon. "So you're really going for a long time? And giving up politics for good?" "Yes, I am. I'm really not sure what I'll do in the long run, but for the moment I'm focusing on an academic career," I replied.

By August 1977 we were back in London. The choice of London was partly a matter of chance and partly a matter of careful deliberation. As a former pupil at Atlantic College I loved British culture, the way of thinking and living. I had gotten to know how British schools worked, and I knew I would adapt well to a British university. The other option would have been the United States, because English was the only language I really knew apart from Finnish. But that would have been much more expensive. It also seemed to me that the LSE was better suited to my perfectionist streak. I wanted to go to a university where expectations were high. And, last but not least, London suited our family life down to the ground. I liked the thought that our son Jaakko, now a year old, would soon become a little Londoner.

In London I would again follow global politics and economics from a splendid vantage point. We socialized with diplomats and dons. Our little boy spent his days at the LSE kindergarten, while Liisa studied Health and Social Policy and Administration. A few years later she would become the first Finnish woman to take a degree at the LSE graduate school. I supported Liisa's studies and believed they would open new doors for her on our return to Finland. Or perhaps we would not return, but would stay and build international academic careers.

London was not at its best in 1977, but it was much livelier and more vibrant and dynamic than Helsinki. The economy was in a mess, and the Labor government found it hard to control the demands of the trade unions. While I spent my time studying the theoretical differences between Keynes and Friedman, Britain was on a crash course in reality. Margaret Thatcher would be elected prime minister in May 1979, against a background of skepticism and hostility. Soon she would become the pre-eminent politician of the western world, so well-known that British psychiatrists had to abandon the question they traditionally used to check if their patients had any grasp of reality at all: "Can you name the prime minister?" Everyone knew who she was.

The LSE really was a return to the classroom. I left home at eight and I was in the university until no later than nine in the evening. I sat in lectures hour after hour. In between we spent time in small groups doing calculation exercises. And of course I did some independent study in the library. The teaching was a preparation for continuing academic study. It was very high-level and intellectually challenging. I was finishing off my M.Sc.; if my studies went well, I would continue to a doctorate. For my specialist field I had chosen the theory of the international monetary economy.

There was strong support in academic circles for ideas that would be implemented in Finland in the 1980s, such as the liberalization of currency markets and the introduction of floating exchange rates. Even in 1977 I had had to fill in a form and send it to the Bank of Finland so I could exchange Finnish markka into pounds before we left for London.

London was also the most important foreign outpost of the Chicago school of neoclassical economics, whose most famous representative was Milton Friedman. He was a stern critic of the prevailing Keynesianism. Friedman and his followers believed that growth in the money supply would revive the economy in the short term, but in the longer term would make itself felt as galloping inflation.

Fiscal policy – that is, demand created by public authorities – was irrelevant to long-term economic success. The role of government in economic policy should be strictly limited. Conversely, central banks had a crucial role regarding the money supply. These views were the opposite of the prevailing wisdom in Finland. I was interested in the Chicago School's research findings, though chiefly as a vehicle for academic reflection. In my mind it had surprisingly little connection with practical economic policy.

Life in London was international, inspiring, and intellectually interesting. We lived in Akehurst Street in southwest London, where we rented a furnished flat on the upper floor of a detached house. We had brought with us from Finland only our stipends and our housing loan. We didn't have the money for any luxuries, and usually we ate our lunch in the student canteen. Sometimes we met up with my friends from Atlantic College from ten years back.

When I had gone to school in the United Kingdom in the sixties, the Beatles had been the big thing, not least for me. Now in the seventies it was the era of heavy rock, such as Led Zeppelin and Deep Purple, whose music wasn't for me at all. Liisa and I started to attend classical concerts instead, for which London offered an inspiring atmosphere.

I studied diligently and with burning ambition. I submitted my final thesis within a year. In August 1978 I received a letter from the university that told me my thesis was good enough for me to move to the doctoral program, which I might complete in two years. My dream of an academic career was coming true. I began to see myself as a professor at Helsinki University or in some respected international institute, as some of my friends from Atlantic College already were. However I still lacked a doctoral dissertation, and the London School of Economics offered a unique opportunity to make that dream a reality.

CHAPTER 13

The Hardest Choice of My Life

I N AUGUST 1978 I REACHED THE AGE OF TWENTY-EIGHT. I had in my hand a letter from the London School of Economics practically guaranteeing me the Ph.D. in economics that would launch me on an international academic career. At just that moment fate or chance intervened and changed my life.

At a lunch given by the Finnish-British Trade Guild I met some executives from Citibank, which was expanding rapidly throughout Europe, setting up new offices as it went. Of course I knew Citibank's operations in London, and I knew that it was a well-run global institution. At the LSE I had familiarized myself with the growth of international capital markets. I knew that the liberalization of the capital markets would have a greater global impact than just about any other conceivable peaceful event.

International banks had a major role in this. Citibank was doing in practice what I had studied in theory.

Citibank offered me a job. I would work first in London, where I would study the workings of the international money markets while also learning how the bank operated. After that I would move to Helsinki, to Citibank's new office there. Citibank offered a salary, real work, and the opportunity to learn new things in an international environment. The bank was recruiting young people from good universities in various countries. I had been picked for the team just as the whistle was blowing for the first match in a new tournament. Citibank reckoned that we young professionals would repay its investment within ten years, though an active system of training brought this down to five or six years. So from the bank's point of view the training system was a profitable investment in the future and in growth in new markets. It also brought Citibank credibility in countries where it was just opening up, such as Finland. Without local expertise the American banking giant could scarcely have competed with the established national banks.

The offer from Citibank compelled me to make the most difficult decision of my life. Many of my contemporaries had already found their niche. They had studied effectively, graduated, and could provide for their families and pay off their mortgages. I wasn't a bohemian – far from it – but I had nevertheless contrived to live my twenty-eight years without serious consideration of what profession I should follow. When I went to London I only knew it would be something in the academic line. It was the same dream I had taken to Atlantic College ten years earlier. That was perhaps part of my nature.

According to one popular analysis people can be divided into four groups: achievers, explorers, socializers, and killers. The names are more or less self-explanatory. Socializers, for example, enjoy doing things together. For them the company is more important than the results; the common good and a feeling of well-being are the most important things. With all due respect one might say that many people from the Mediterranean region belong to this type. I am one of the achievers. Achievers enjoy getting things done. We always want to take on a new project, see it through to its conclusion, and move on to the next. We get enjoyment from working, doing, and studying. Our relationships with other people come through our work. We gather around us the sorts of people we can work with toward common goals. Achievers are always aiming toward something bigger, something better, toward the next project. We relish every success, but our minds are already focusing on something else.

In London back in 1978 I didn't analyze myself in this way. It was only later that I discovered these categories, and Liisa agreed that I was definitely one of the achievers. Of course we all have elements of each personality type; nothing is purely black and white. And fortunately people can take on new qualities.

Although I was only twenty-eight I had already experienced a lot of power games. I had led a student organization, I had negotiated with the Russians, I had become familiar with party politics. I had not, however, enjoyed it; and I was not sociable enough to go out and win votes from strangers. Nor did power structures or power itself interest me enough for me to crave a seat in parliament or a job in the foreign ministry. I simply wanted to achieve things – I wanted good things to happen. I was always delighted when the

National Union of Students won better financial terms or living conditions for its members. If I could say to myself that I had done things right, that was enough for me.

An achiever must always have something to do. Achievers are usually curious about things, because new knowledge makes new achievements possible. An achiever doesn't need too much social life or external recognition – the achievement is its own reward. However, the achiever will be deeply hurt if the value of his or her achievement isn't recognized or if it's disparaged. Achievers keep the promises they make to others, but also the ones they make to themselves. And it's the ones they make to themselves that are the most difficult. In 1978 I had promised myself that I would complete my final dissertation at the University of Technology and then go on to do my doctorate at the LSE. The promise to the British Council weighed on me a little, but not as much as the promise to myself.

Thinking about it now, in my sixties, I think that there may also have been a subconscious debt to my mother, who had never had as much education as she would have liked. I think I wanted to show her that I could become a doctor of economics.

Before the offer from Citibank I had had no experience of business life. I had seen my father's endless and onerous work in the factory, which didn't hold much appeal for me. I had learned how, in theory, businesses should operate in an economy. I was a firm believer in the capitalist system, though I recognized its weaknesses. Finland was dominated by the big banks, the big forestry companies, and a few firms in the metal industry. The power of these enterprises was exerted in a few private dining rooms where the leaders of the banks and insurance companies made decisions on the future of industry – decisions that industrialists should have made.

The Bank of Finland regulated the capital markets, and companies had to apply to it for foreign exchange credit and other financing. The Finnish economy was a club, run by a handful of major companies and closed to new members. But Finland lived by exporting: there was the profitable Soviet trade and the traditional exports of paper, wood products, and machinery to the West. Some Finnish firms had opened up new areas: a company named Nokia had decided at the beginning of the 1970s to start making telephone exchanges, and the firm had also sold some big computers to the banks. I hadn't known anything about this in London.

My understanding of the way companies actually worked, both in general and in Finland, was vague. I had never set up my own company. I had neither bought nor sold. I had never marketed anything and neither had I developed new commercial products. But, in principle, I did have some sort of idea of how businesses operated. I doubted, with good reason, whether I would get along at all in the business world. Though I had learned to make presentations, I was highly analytical and an expert by nature. I loved studying things, especially as part of a larger whole. I rather dreaded joining an organization that existed solely to make money for its shareholders – I wasn't sure if I would find intelligent life there. I looked at the heavyweights among Finnish business leaders, and the question seemed all the more pressing: Did I want one day to be an authoritarian leader who made decisions after five glasses of cognac in some private dining room? Did I want to stop thinking and become a sleek merchant, whose discussions with party hacks from the Soviet Union went on week after week? To that question I certainly knew the answer.

Wasn't there something a little too easy about business life? And wouldn't I have to give up my theoretical musings if I chose "the practical life" in its place? What would I say to all my friends who were advancing in their academic careers? How would I explain all this to myself, if business life turned out just as I feared: mind-numbing, even mindless, profit-making spiced up with opportunistic power games?

The offer from Citibank compelled me to examine closely my dream of an academic career. Did I want to continue my research work on a small salary, when we already had our first child and more would surely follow? Could I endure waiting a decade for my first professorial appointment? And at heart was I really interested in an academic career? Wasn't I rather a practical person who wanted to spend his whole time doing something useful? Was the lonely toil that was part of a scholar's life really for me, when I had always enjoyed the bustle of working with others? Was my academic career a castle in the air, when in reality I wanted something different?

The questions tore me apart. And if I had known then how decisive the conclusion would be as far as my future was concerned, I would have surely deliberated even longer. As it was I considered my options throughout August. My nights were sleepless. I talked it through with Liisa, who doesn't remember ever seeing me so torn by a difficult decision.

Never since have I made a decision that would have such a big impact on my life. On 20 August 1978, five days after my twenty-eighth birthday, and following another sleepless night, I made up my mind – I would accept the Citibank offer. In business life I would perhaps do better on account of all my studying. I would become part of a team and perhaps eventually its captain.

Only much later did I realize how big that decision really was for me. All major decisions demand sacrifices. In making this decision I sacrificed my dream, but I have never regretted that: the coming years showed my decision to have been right, but those August days in London were full only of uncertainty. That, too, is invariably an element of big decisions. You can't plan your life, even if you want to. I'm an instinctive rationalist, but I must nevertheless concede that, without a chain of many random events, I would never have become a chief executive. I could have made a different choice in London, in which case I would now certainly be a professor of economics, perhaps in a world-class university. My life would have been different, at the very least.

Although I had to look at many fundamental factors, there was one practical point that made it easier for me to reach my decision: I still hadn't done my military service, but now I couldn't put it off any longer. I had to join the army before my thirtieth birthday, which would interrupt the writing of my doctoral thesis. Citibank said they would let me take nearly a year's leave of absence for my military service. The following day I told John Quitter, who was responsible for Citibank's Scandinavian affairs, that I would start as a trainee in London just over a week later, at the beginning of September. And I put the LSE's offer concerning my doctorate into a plastic folder and then into an envelope. I would keep it safe against the months and years ahead, in case I came to regret my choice. I had "academic life insurance" if business life disappointed all my expectations and made my nightmares come true. The LSE's letter is still in safekeeping in my personal archive, but I haven't needed to use it.

CHAPTER 14

International Banker

CITIBANK WAS MY UNIVERSITY as far as business life was concerned, and also my first proper place of work. It was a demanding environment for a young economist. I had researched the bank's history. It had been founded in 1812 as the City Bank of New York with an initial capital of $2 million. By 1894 it was the biggest bank in the United States, and by the turn of the century it had started to expand internationally. It operated in Asia, Europe, and India, and its branches stretched from Shanghai to Manila.

Citibank undertook foreign currency transactions earlier and more widely than any other bank in the world. In the year of the Great Crash, 1929, Citibank became the world's largest commercial bank. By World War II it had one hundred offices in twenty-three countries. Citibank was a formidable international financial institution; perhaps that was what interested me most. I knew I could learn from Citibank everything there was to learn about international banking. It was also a prototypical global enterprise, with structures designed for effective international operations. Perhaps only IBM, which also began international operations much earlier than other companies, could compete with it in terms of effectiveness. In fact IBM had been the first company to design its organizational structure rather than let it grow organically. Its ideas were later widely copied.

When I joined the ranks of Citibank it was led by the legendary Walter B Wriston. He ran the bank for seventeen years, first as chief executive, from 1967 to 1970, and then as chairman of the board from 1970 to 1984. Wriston reinvigorated banking. His powerful and far-reaching vision encompassed internationalism and a strong belief in new technology and new services for customers. Some regarded him as too radical; for example, he foresaw the use of automated teller machines and everyday electronic transactions when these ideas must have seemed to belong to the world of science fiction. Back in the 1970s not everyone saw how prescient Wriston's vision was.

I would never have been invited to join Citibank if it hadn't been strongly committed to international expansion – the bank was looking to establish itself in Finland. Until then its London office had taken care of all its Nordic business. Now it was headhunting promising young professionals. There was just one condition: Citibank had promised not to poach people from the big Finnish commercial banks, which didn't want the American giant to pay excessive salaries to young bankers. Citibank politely kept this promise.

I don't know exactly why Citibank approached me. I suppose someone at the Finnish Embassy may have suggested me. I was interviewed by the experienced banker John Quitter, and the interview went well. I was sure I would get into the training program if I wanted to. Citibank was a respected American banking institution. Good manners and a smart appearance were highly regarded there, even if it was more dynamic and aggressive than European banks.

The decision to join the ranks of Citibank changed the direction of my life. But the change also had a more immediate impact: Liisa and I at last had some money. Citibank paid a salary positively ducal compared to student loans. We quickly gave up our student flat in Akehurst Street and moved just half a mile or so to our very own house in Larpent Avenue, baronial in scale to match my new salary. There was plenty of space, and we could entertain. It was our home in London from 1978. We weren't sure that we would find a place equally splendid when we returned to Finland.

I had nothing against a regular monthly income. I had received a small amount as head of the National Union of Students, and when I worked for the Centre Party I had been paid enough to get by. I wasn't a big spender, but I naturally wanted to be sure that our little family would have enough. We started to take in London in great gulps – we met people, went to concerts, made long expeditions on foot. The change in circumstances was welcome. I didn't really own anything, just a debt-laden apartment in Helsinki, and there were some student loans. I didn't own any shares, and I knew nothing about investing because I had never had any money to invest. I hadn't inherited any. When I went to Citibank I started to earn a proper salary. For the first time I felt that my income was in line with my abilities. To be properly rewarded for my efforts was a good feeling and one I have enjoyed ever since.

Shaping the future with one's own hands and through one's own labors was part of my inheritance: my father had built his life and his own house; his father had built his own business; and my mother's father had cleared fields in order to grow food for a large family. My family background, stretching back for hundreds of years, was made up entirely of people who had labored long and hard.

I had many preconceptions about Citibank's work. I had long wondered whether banking could possibly be intellectually stimulating. I also brooded on Citibank's position in Finland. If the head of a Finnish commercial bank had been asked about Citibank, he probably would have said that working for it was a strange choice, possibly even an unpatriotic one. Foreign banks weren't then allowed to disturb the peace of the big Finnish banks.

Only at the beginning of the 1980s did the barriers begin to crumble, when three foreign banks were given full permits to operate in Finland: the French Indosuez; Chase; and Citibank, which received its permit on 27 November 1981. Until then foreign banks had been allowed to practice in Finland only through representative offices that marketed their services. The actual transactions were carried out elsewhere, often in London.

Citibank was my business school. In London I concentrated on studying two things: the analysis of individual firms and how an international bank worked. Once again studying satisfied my ambition. With every atom of my being I soaked up international banking, accounting, analysis, and everything else I imagined I would need in my future work. As well as formal training I also learned how work was done in the bank. Everyone was at their desk by eight at the latest, and we went home at seven or eight in the evening. The office culture was very different from Finland's. We sat in an open-plan office where we heard our colleagues' telephone calls. That too was a new and educational experience.

In Finland the big banks were used to waiting for their customers to come to them, to humbly beg for loans for their projects. Bankers sat on company boards and took care that those companies applied to the right banks for their loans. The banks owned large chunks of industry, and all companies had to live with credit regulation. At Citibank we looked at business cold-bloodedly on the basis of company analysis. I learned the methods for analyzing individual elements of a company, its position relative to its competitors, and its future cash flow and overall prospects. When we concluded from our basic analysis that a project was sound, we started to consider what products we might sell the customer. In the Finnish market the idea of selling banking products to corporate customers was new. Finland's big banks didn't need to waste their time on marketing since their customers were already at their mercy.

Citibank made a salesperson of me. I didn't find it easy at first. I was an analytical person, and through my education and experience I had set out to become the sort of expert who didn't have to worry about customers. And my Finnish and Nordic nature didn't give me a head start in taking on the role of a sleek salesman. But Citibank's global organization was a good teacher. I learned how to approach customers and how to put together proposals that were hard to refuse. I learned, too, how customers should be taken care of at every stage. You must persuade customers that you really care and are ready to do pretty well anything for them. And I learned the subversive truth: businesses, even international banks, live or die by satisfying their customers. If I hadn't learned about customer service at Citibank I could never have succeeded at Nokia, where I always regarded myself as the company's most senior salesperson.

Citibank also became for me the model of a global organization. It had a matrix structure, which worked efficiently and well. A matrix organization is one where management takes place across both functions and business groups, and an individual has more than one reporting line. A matrix structure is seen as the natural and, indeed, only practical model for an international company operating in several areas.

I understood that a strong company must have a strong culture. Back then I had no idea that companies had cultures. But I saw in practice how a strong culture influenced the way Citibank looked after its business and its customers. This hadn't happened overnight. What's more, the bank's culture and its leadership model were interlinked. The head office and the front line had to understand each other, and this required continuous effort. Excellent two-way communication was essential. Citibank wanted to be the front-runner in all forms of new technology and communication. So in 1982 I was already using an email system developed for internal use. I joined Nokia in 1985, but the company used email only from the end of that decade. Citibank developed its internal technical abilities while selling its customers a vision of making money electronic.

My Citibank training turned my own thinking upside down. Only later did I realize how widely what I had learned could be applied. I drew on this new knowledge both consciously and subliminally at Nokia in the late 1980s and early 1990s. When I joined Citibank I was an economist, pure and simple. I knew nothing of balance sheets, for example. Everything I learned about how to analyze a company I learned from Citibank.

I also learned a great deal about how to manage people in large organizations. Earlier I had thought that organization meant a diagram made out of boxes joined to each other by thin lines. I thought that the leader's job was to lead this "organization." At Citibank I learned the revolutionary truth: the leader does not lead boxes or an organization, but people. A leader, even in a big organization, has to be interested in the people whose efforts create the results. Good leaders must know their people. A good leader must also be ready to promote some surprising people within the organization, without regard to the official boxes. At Citibank it was understood that the organization had to be clear but must allow flexibility, for which good internal communications and respect for people were essential.

My role model was John Quitter, a well-informed, civilized, able, and professional American banker. He travelled constantly and knew the Nordic region and its key people well. He was good with figures and was supremely good at asking trainees the sorts of questions that would help them refine their calculations. John was also very gifted socially: he could chat as easily with someone on the shop floor as with the chairman of the board. He was experienced, far-sighted, and cultured. Since then I have met countless captains of industry, and John could bear comparison with any of them, even though he never quite reached the top of the banking world. John became my exemplar, my coach, and my mentor, and I often sought his advice, even after I'd moved to Nokia.

That fertile year in London, from autumn 1978 to autumn 1979, passed quickly, even too quickly. I had made the biggest decision of my life, I had studied, learned a great deal, and become a businessman, or at least a banker. Liisa had completed her dissertation at Helsinki University and also graduated from the LSE. We had both done a great deal of work. Even our little son Jaakko had spent his time in London productively. He had been able to speak Finnish by the time we went to London, then he had stopped speaking altogether, and as a three-year-old he returned to Finland speaking both Finnish and English.

CHAPTER 15

Military Service

My time in London was drawing to a close. I had to come back to Finland for two reasons. First, I had to do my military service. After that I would work at Citibank's Helsinki office, which was still awaiting its official license from the Finnish finance ministry.

In Finland all men had to join the army or begin their civilian service before their thirtieth birthday. They still do. At the end of the 1970s the army was extremely popular. Even extreme communists joined up with enthusiasm, apparently to learn leadership skills in preparation for the revolution and its aftermath. I didn't have strong feelings about the army, for or against. I respected the need for national defense and I wanted to do my duty as a citizen. In going to London I had of course taken the army into account in my plans. It would have made completing my dissertation a little more complicated, but I couldn't do my military service in London, by correspondence course. I would have to spend some time crawling about in the woods, and I would need to come to grips with the basics of Finnish defense strategy.

Liisa had found a job at the Ministry of Social Affairs and Health. She had to be in Finland a few weeks before me to start work, so she and our three-year-old son flew home ahead of me. We had bought our first car in England and wanted to take it to Finland. So when the time came I got behind the wheel of the Audi 100 and drove across Europe. From London I drove to Dover, took a ferry to Oostende, and drove on to Travemünde, where I took the Finnlines ferry to Helsinki. During my journey I crossed the Belgian, Dutch, and German borders. At each border the guards took an interest in me. They understood why my passport was valid for only a couple more days: I was on my way to the army. Whenever I crossed a border I had to put up with taunting: "Ah, you're in a hurry to get home, are you? It's a date you mustn't be late for." I reached Finland on 14 October, and my passport expired the same day. I really had left things to the last moment.

Private Ollila reported for duty at Hyrylä barracks, just north of Helsinki, the following day. Since I had studied physics and math, and so was obviously good with figures, I was dispatched to the air defense regiment. A month earlier I'd been sitting in an office in a pinstripe suit crunching numbers. Now I was in a barracks, in the Finnish army's everyday gray uniform, learning how to dismantle and reassemble an assault rifle. There were twelve men in our hut, most of them between eighteen and twenty years old. Our conversations lacked a certain finesse. The men were from the Helsinki area and seemed a sensible bunch. The barracks block was a sixties box, already in poor shape. The dominant internal features were linoleum, gray concrete, and an endless row of notice boards. Beside the doors the duty officer sat at his desk, controlling the flow of people into the barracks and, more importantly, out.

In the evenings the blue-and-white-checked bedcover had to be folded as neatly as possible into a square and placed on a stool at the foot of the bed. If the bedcover hadn't been folded crisply enough the corporal would notice and it would have to be folded again. My personal diary had been replaced by a schedule pinned to the notice board that told us when we needed to muster for drill, when we needed to be on the firing range, and when we could go to the mess. My life was as tightly timetabled and programmed as that of . . . well . . . the chief executive of Nokia. (Though I had more free time in the army.)

We spent a lot of time out in the open practicing maneuvers. We dug ourselves little foxholes, practiced throwing grenades, and tried to put up our tents as fast as we could. Fortunately the ground hadn't yet frozen for the winter. The contrast with my previous life couldn't have been greater. But I couldn't complain. I had postponed the army as long as I could, and now I had to get it over with. When I had done that I could pick up the threads of my real life. Since I had to spend time in the army I should regard it as a mix of experience and sporting achievement.

Liisa lived in our old home in Herttoniemi. Our stuff had been in storage for two years while we were in England; now we were putting things back in their place. Liisa was delighted with her new role as senior advisor in the Ministry of Social Affairs and Health, from where she recently retired as Deputy Director-General of EU and International Affairs. We adapted with fresh optimism to life in Finland: our feelings were very different from when we had fled the country two years earlier. We had enjoyed a close family life in London, which my time in the army forcibly interrupted, and which wasn't nice for anyone. But I returned to Herttoniemi every few weeks, whenever I had leave.

Within a month of joining the army I'd applied to become an officer. I had graduated, after all, and I wanted to make use of my abilities in the army. A few weeks later I was told I'd been accepted. So after two months at Hyrylä I went straight to the Reserve Officer School in Hamina, on the south coast near the Russian border. I left the sixties barracks behind and went to live in the nineteenth-century main building at Hamina. The atmosphere there was very different from Hyrylä – the officer cadets were ambitious and motivated.

I was elected the chairman of our cohort. The rival candidate was Lauri Kontro, whom I had gotten to know when we were studying, and again later in the Centre Party office, when he had worked in the party's youth organization. Lauri later became a journalist, a diplomat, and a newspaper editor. Since the army and the Reserve Officer School were my point of re-entry into Finnish life, and particularly to ordinary Finnish male life, it felt good to receive a vote of confidence from my peers.

Kontro was elected our secretary and everything ran smoothly. The cadets took care of many of the practical aspects of the course. Social events were important too; indeed for many they seemed to be the high point. In previous years a star performer had sometimes been hired. We decided to dispense with this expensive intrusion into the evening, to widespread relief. Instead the cadets, some of whom were very gifted performers, would take care of everything. We began a new trend.

In Hamina I learned what the Finnish Army's professional officers thought about defense and about society more widely. I met generals and other senior officers, who had to be careful what they said on account of the Cold War but were generally open on their views about the future. The Reserve Officer School was a good experience.

The real world was a more chaotic place than it had been for a long time. Fundamentalists had seized power in Iran. The staff of the U.S. Embassy in Tehran were held hostage and the world was following their fate closely. President Jimmy Carter ordered a rescue attempt, which failed; the American prisoners were not freed until 1981. Finland was still dependent on the Soviet Union and on Soviet trade. The signs of President Kekkonen's illness were becoming apparent and people were starting to discuss who would succeed him. Uncertainty was growing, and many well-educated service-men had to prepare themselves for unemployment, which was something quite new in Finland.

In my last months in the army I held an office job in Helsinki, at the National Board of Economic Defense. I prepared a study of the economics of Finland's defense at a time of crisis. In the evenings I sat in the library and worked on my dissertation for the University of Technology; the subject was "Economic Growth as a Theoretical Problem of Regulation." It applied systems theory to economic growth. I received the best possible grades for it. I suppose it came in useful later on, too, when I had to understand the processes at work in a large enterprise. At least it helped me develop useful ways of thinking.

Both my dissertations had been thought experiments that proved useful later. But the greatest benefit of my time at the University of Technology was practical: I learned how Finnish engineers think, and I gained credibility in their eyes. They saw me as one of themselves, though my qualifications for that status were rather slender. Much later, at Nokia, I desperately needed that credibility.

Thanks to the army I received a crash course in what Finland was all about. Up until then I had lived an elitist life, isolated and insulated from my fellow Finns. As a student leader I had spent my time in agreeable surroundings with other student leaders. Before that, Atlantic College had taken me away from the everyday reality of Finnish life and installed me in a British boarding school. After the students' union I had briefly dabbled in politics. Then we had moved to London, again away from everyday Finland. My employer was an American-owned international bank, which certainly didn't offer a panoramic view of Finland. Without the army I wouldn't have known much about what went on in Finland or how Finns think.

CHAPTER 16

A License to Finance

T HE 1980S BEGAN FOR ME OVER HALF A YEAR LATE, in the autumn when I left the army to return to Citibank and the real world. The atmosphere was now quite different from the over-politicized seventies. New routines and challenges awaited me, and the change was welcome. I became an expert on company finance. I was the new boy in the Helsinki office and naturally I had to deal with the most awkward customers.

These difficult customers were Finland's major companies, who had close links to Finland's big banks. From the forest industry there was Enso-Gutzeit. I also tried to sell our services to Rauma-Repola, Wärtsilä, and Nokia. Finland was still a country where forestry reigned supreme, but in reality there were few investments where Citibank was in a position to add value. State enterprises were out of reach for American banks. We were never the bank of choice for Nokia. Rauma-Repola, for its part, was looked after by the Bank of America. Even so I rolled up my sleeves and got down to work.

I now had to put into practice everything I had learned in London about customer care and negotiation. I mostly dealt with finance directors of my age or a little older. They certainly saw how the world was changing and wanted to know how to change with it. Usually their problem was a fifty-five-year-old finance director, stuck in his ways and unable to manage his ambitious subordinates effectively.

I went assiduously to cocktail parties. I forged links with economic editors, which would stand me in good stead later. Citibank usually got curiously positive publicity because in the Finnish finance world it seemed to have expertise and to be both small and challenging. Citibank could offer a breath of fresh, global thinking to the Finnish banking world, which was just opening up. Three small foreign banks were a modest example of the direction Finnish banks would have to take.

Finland's big banks did their utmost to protect their domestic market from their competitors. The Soviet Union too was interested that American banks were setting up shop in Finland. The Soviet Union had its own banks, which had also set up offices abroad. The Soviet Union would surely expect to receive a license for its own banks to operate in Helsinki to ensure balance. But officials also had many good reasons to open Finland up to international banking competition. The international capital markets still had a slightly vague picture of Finland. We Finns paid a high price for Soviet neighborliness, in a literal sense, because the Soviet Union was known to have an influence on Finnish policy. We had to pay a premium for a political risk that was practically non-existent. But then the markets have never been particularly good at distinguishing details. Besides, the Soviet Union's share of Finland's foreign trade was so great that it posed a risk to Finland's economy as a whole. And Finland was one of those dubious Nordic social democratic countries whose commitment to capitalism seemed a little uncertain, at least in the eyes of American investors. Finnish politicians and officials must certainly have expected American bank offices in Helsinki to send home the right signals about Finland and Finnish companies as a destination for investment, as indeed they did.

Officials also wanted to open up competition and compel Finnish banks to modernize. Foreign banks had less overhead than the big Finnish banks and could offer finance to companies more cheaply. Finnish banks' balance sheets were simply too small for the international credit system. Foreign banks were also more efficient than Finnish banks in foreign exchange dealings and the securities market.

Citibank received permission to begin operating in Finland in November 1981 and started the following year. The conditions of the license were strict: the bank could not establish any additional branches, its share capital was limited to a small sum, competition on interest rates was restricted, and Citibank and the other foreign banks could not get involved in the financing of the lucrative Soviet trade.

Although the foreign banks did not grow very large in Finland, they changed the banking system there for all time. The big Finnish banks were used to financing, owning, and governing Finland's major companies; they burbled happily of their "responsibilities to society." This meant that the banks and their related insurance companies looked after companies' affairs in good times and bad.

The banks lent their favored customers money even when they didn't need it for business purposes.

Company investment policies were decided at board meetings where bank executives sat in. The forestry industry in particular was the banks' special stomping ground: approval for the companies' purchases, sales, and major investments rested with the banks' boards. Young executives at the big Finnish banks quickly learned to flex their muscles in issues of management and finance. They might even imagine that they could run a forestry company better than the company's own CEO.

The foreign banks' arrival in Finland was like a small crack in the wall of a house, a sign of a distant earthquake. But those who looked ahead understood that the relationship between the banks and other businesses in Finland just couldn't carry on as it had. Wise bank directors also foresaw that international competition would reduce the profits and profitability of Finnish banks, which depended on a close relationship with their customers.

I myself had no experience of the Finnish banking system since I had undergone Citibank's American education instead. I thought that a bank's job was to offer effective financial and capital services, often against tough competition, rather than to own, manage, or sell its customers' businesses.

Customers should be able to do that for themselves. If their business went well, our customers would be sure to make money for Citibank, too. At Citibank we believed strongly in banking competition because we were used to operating in the world's most competitive markets. With every Finnish customer we were the competitor, the challenger, and the alternative to the Finnish banks. In Citibank's Helsinki office I built up my own team, responsible for half of Citibank's corporate financing in Finland. I was happy with them. One of my best recruits was a young economist from eastern Finland, Kari Jordan, now the president of Metsä Group, one of Europe's biggest forest industry groups.

I met many interesting senior people at that time, whom I got to know better later on. For example, I met Pekka Herlin of Kone over lunch in the early 1980s. Herlin was a taciturn and grumpy figure, but he conveyed authority and gravitas. It wasn't his role as the owner of a major company that gave weight to his words, but his vision and his grasp of the issues. The gruffness of his persona added its own mystique. There was a lively discussion at the lunch table of the international economic situation, high interest rates, and the sustainability of the finance system. Herlin made sure he was always the hub of the conversation.

Liisa and I had settled down on the coast a few miles west of Helsinki, in a pleasant modern terraced house. We had two more children now: Anna, born in 1981, and her brother Matti, two years younger. I was present at the birth of all three of our children, though I am sorry to say that I was five minutes late for Matti – we had a lively discussion about that. Most of the housework fell to Liisa, even though she was building her own career as a civil servant. But I ironed my own shirts up until the beginning of the 1990s, when we finally started to employ someone to do the cleaning and ironing. Our lives were full with work, family life, and children. Around this time we also acquired a summer cottage in Orivesi, a beautiful small town (or large village) about two hours away – not far from the original Nokia, as it happens. There we did odd jobs, fished, and met our friends. We had an ordinary Finnish life, in short.

Patience has never been my strong suit, and particularly not in the early 1980s. Though I would never go back to being an academic, I had to keep going forward. Or perhaps it was because I had left my academic roots behind me that I wanted to face the next challenge. I was now thirty-four, and as I looked around Citibank I saw lots of eager professionals, many of whom were ten years younger than me. That made me want to accelerate my career. I wanted to get on a faster track, one that offered broader vistas than Citibank's little Helsinki office. I had really enjoyed London, where the world was big, the work international, and I could feel I was developing the whole time. I didn't feel that in Helsinki. Once I had my feet under the desk there, and established my team, it was natural to start looking for the next thing.

Citibank had been my school of leadership. I've noticed since that leaders learn to lead between the ages of twenty-five and thirty-five. It's a critical period, the time when you need a good model of leadership if you're to become a leader yourself. The model sticks in the mind and helps you create your own style of working and also your own expectations of what others can offer. If leaders are bad, lazy, or dishonest, they will pass on the wrong model of leadership to the next generation, who will turn out suspicious, cynical, or downright incompetent. They may become people who are always on the lookout for conspiracies or gratuitously engage in corrosive office politics. If a crooked leader deceives his subordinates, the iron will enter their soul. They will find it difficult to recover or to believe in any leader ever again. So good role models are a matter of life and death for every enterprise. Indeed, I believe that in the worst case a company can die if the model of leadership fails.

Citibank didn't supply a unique model of leadership, but it offered an excellent example of corporate culture. The bank was international and had several sets of values – to the point where some found it chaotic. But it had a large measure of that dynamism that I both valued and had lacked, as well as a strong sense of shared purpose. Its top management were marketers for the bank, who promoted their products and met with clients. Not even Walter Wriston could close the door to his office to enjoy an exalted solitude. The American culture demanded that everyone throw themselves into the job in order to achieve the bank's goals.

I learned this way of thinking at Citibank and took it with me to Nokia. I compelled myself and my senior team to travel the world, meeting customers, learning new things, and selling our products. Perhaps I would have understood all this without Citibank, but I wouldn't have seen how a business culture affects the way one works. Of course Citibank made mistakes, and I tried to learn from those as well.

I wasn't an easy subordinate for anyone. When John Quitter came from London to visit the Helsinki office I arranged a private breakfast with him. I tapped on the table with my fingers, as I sometimes do, and told him I wasn't happy with the way my career was developing. I lacked opportunities to get ahead. Liisa, who was working at the Ministry of Social Affairs and Health, had been offered an international job in Geneva, but Citibank had nothing to offer me there. It was a disappointment for both of us.

John Quitter listened to my outpourings sympathetically but didn't say much in response, because he surely understood that I wouldn't be at Citibank for much longer. I often used to talk things through with him later, after I had left Citibank. I knew that if I stayed there I would be offered the opportunity to gain experience in a larger market – perhaps in another Nordic country, the United States, or Latin America. But in Citibank's structure in Helsinki I was at the third level down. Even if I had gone abroad and returned to Finland, the best I could hope for was to become second-in-command. That wasn't enough for me. I knew my worth and I was impatient to get on. I was already over thirty and had no time to squander.

And there were other things on offer. The powerful chairman of one of Finland's biggest banks and his deputy responsible for international affairs invited me to their bank's head office. In their ceremonious way they announced they had chosen me to lead their daughter bank in Singapore. We discussed the question and I promised to consider the offer. A couple of weeks later I told them I didn't wish to pursue it. One of them told me later that my response had caused great consternation: in the Finland of the early 1980s one didn't lightly refuse such offers.

I received another offer, too. This came from EVA, a think tank established to put the case for the market economy and to counter the simple-minded leftism I mentioned earlier. EVA was politically influential, undertook research, and worked to make public opinion more favorable to business. At that time the head of EVA was Max Jakobson, a former senior ambassador and a foreign policy heavyweight – he came close to becoming the secretary-general of the United Nations, but Kurt Waldheim got the job instead. We had a couple of discussions about a possible move to EVA, which led to a job offer, but again I didn't take it.

Looking back, that was fortunate for me and indeed for EVA, too: I was just about to move into the "right" line of business. That's where my future lay, though I have never ceased to follow politics or try to influence developments in society; it's just that I've done so in my role as a business leader. My path did eventually lead me to EVA: since 2005 I have been chairman of its board.

By my own reckoning I had achieved a great deal at Citibank. The corporate finance portfolio had grown. More and more major Finnish firms came to us. We were trusted; my little team understood the customers. I had learned important things about myself: the world of business really was the place for me.

Though I wasn't entirely happy at Citibank, I had nevertheless made the right decision in London. I still had that yellowing piece of paper, which guaranteed the chance to return to an academic career and to complete my doctoral dissertation. I buried it deeper in my archives.

CHAPTER 17

I Move to Nokia

D EPENDING ON YOUR WORLD VIEW you may see life as a matter of chance or of destiny, or you may even detect the hand of God. My view is that everything affects everything else, although I also believe that people can help shape their own destiny. It was purely by chance that I became a businessman, a banker, and an executive at Citibank. That wouldn't have happened if I'd followed my original plans.

In the autumn of 1984 I intended to spend one more year at Citibank. I wanted to leave the bank with the title of vice president, which would require further arduous training and the achievement of set objectives. I would then leave Citibank and find something else to do. I assumed that would be something to do with corporate finance. No power in the universe could have interested me even then in any opening at a Finnish bank. I could see all too easily that life for the big Finnish banks would soon become rather more problematic.

In September 1984 my phone rang. At the end of the line – it must have been a landline – was the personal assistant to the CEO of Nokia, Kari Kairamo. She had rung to invite me to meet him and his colleague, Simo Vuorilehto, president of Nokia.

A few days later I sat in a private dining room in a Helsinki restaurant with Nokia's two top men. They were well-known figures in Finnish industry, though I didn't know either personally, and both were about twenty years older than me. By the time our chat was over Kari Kairamo was clearly fretting that we'd failed to meet before. Vuorilehto said scarcely a word, while Kairamo talked non-stop. He was a wonderful salesman, and now he was selling me a job at Nokia. He said he'd heard a lot of good things about me. Nokia wanted to hire some promising younger people, to bring new blood and new ideas into the company. Later on we would see just how the company actually made use of those people.

Kari Kairamo was every inch the charismatic leader. His gaze was piercing, but he barely seemed to have the patience to stay in one place. He wore spectacles with large frames, and his hair was receding from his temples, though it had not yet gone gray. He liked to dress tastefully and stylishly, but in a hurry he forgot to tuck his shirt in. He ran Nokia in his shirtsleeves, and he detested all other formalities as well. Kairamo had no need to emphasize his own position: he came from a famous family of Finnish industrialists, which guaranteed a certain degree of self-assurance.

I was interested in his offer, because Citibank's Helsinki office had nothing more to teach me. Until I received Nokia's offer the alternatives facing me were either to go abroad or perhaps to develop investment banking services in Finland. The Finnish capital markets were just opening up. The services offered by banks were changing rapidly, and individual wealth was growing too. But then I would be doing what I had already done for years.

I was ambitious and wanted to go somewhere where I could achieve more. Nokia was just such an enterprise. Although it was a mixed collection of bits of different industries – a conglomerate – it was a Finnish company stepping on to the international stage. Kari Kairamo ran the business briskly.

There was much that needed updating at Nokia, but that would give me the chance to make changes there.

Of course I knew Nokia as a customer. I had studied the company, I had sold it financial services, and I had had frequent discussions with its finance people. I knew its strengths and weaknesses. One friend recalls me banging on about how Nokia could never hope to thrive while it had so many different divisions in such varied fields as mobile telephones and toilet paper. I knew that Nokia had to decide what it wanted to focus on. But that insight was essentially a banker's theoretical musing – I really didn't know what went on inside the company or what its top management thought.

In the early 1980s Nokia had grown to become Finland's most important electronics company. It made televisions, telephone exchanges, mobile phones, and computers. I instinctively thought that its future should lie somewhere other than in making paper, rubber boots, or cables. I genuinely thought that Finns too could conquer the world with new products. And for my own part, which would not initially be a large role, I was ready to join this great adventure. I did not yet see the risks Nokia would later encounter.

Nor did I see that Kari Kairamo himself would become a risk to the company. On the contrary: Kairamo was the most dynamic figure in Finnish business life. His company was the product of his international vision. He tried to fend off the power-hungry Finnish commercial banks. I agreed with him on practically every major issue. And he was regarded as an exceptionally inspiring leader, an assessment I found it easy to agree with after our first meeting.

The more I thought about it, the more attractive a move to Nokia seemed. I signed the contract between Christmas and the New Year. Before that I had told my boss at Citibank about it. I also rang John Quitter in London. John listened calmly, and then he politely but determinedly tried to persuade me to change my mind. He didn't have much to offer, however. I didn't want my future to be up for auction. John was sorry, but he wished me good luck. I promised to keep in touch.

My move from Citibank to Nokia made Nokia my life's work. That move was partly a matter of chance and partly a planned operation. Nokia provided the chance element by getting in touch with me. It might just as easily have been a forestry company, a metals firm, or another conglomerate. But it was Nokia, where I was known because I had handled their account at Citibank. The fact that my friend Pentti Kouri sat on the boards of both Citibank and Nokia might also have had something to do with it, but I don't really know.

Early in February 1985 I started at Nokia, on a journey that would last twenty-five years.

PART II

A CHIEF EXECUTIVE'S
EDUCATION

CHAPTER 18

Fresh and Eager

MY FIRST OFFICE AT NOKIA was in a rather shabby office block opposite Helsinki railway station. I was a young, new, and enthusiastic Nokia man. My fifth-floor room looked out over the station square, one of the largest open spaces in central Helsinki. My first task was to find a desk and chair from somewhere. My arrival seemed to come as a surprise, as the arrival of new workmates often does. "Who on earth is this guy and what on earth are we going to do with him?" seems to be a common reaction.

There were some at Nokia who made it clear that there was no red carpet for me. I must have seemed very fresh and eager, full of myself and what I'd learned at Citibank. As a newcomer I had to show I was useful; only then would I be accepted. There were weaknesses in my CV. I came from a bank, and Nokia had no particular fondness for banks. One of Kari Kairamo's main goals in life had been to win Nokia's independence from the banks, which had been among the company's major shareholders and had thrown their weight around on the board.

In the 1980s Finland was a country governed by banks, and Nokia had declared its own uprising against this system. At least I had not come from either of the main Finnish banks, which were two of Nokia's main shareholders. They kept a close eye on each other at Nokia. The only decisions made were those where the two banks agreed, so decision-making was onerous, complicated, and full of suspicion. The men who ran Finland's banks had little understanding of what it meant to run an international technology company, for they had grown up in a regulated market where they could be confident of their power. For them the customer was servant, not king.

Most major Finnish companies belonged to one of the groups of big banks and insurance companies. This was very different from the United Kingdom or United States, where different financial institutions weren't so closely linked. Perhaps it was more like Japan, which has also effectively been owned and run by financial conglomerates. It's important to know that these groups were held together by more than just ownership. The major Finnish firms were debtors, and the financial groups guided them on the handling of their debt. Directors of banks and insurance companies sat on company boards and often made decisions without the necessary expertise. At the end of the 1980s the two banks where power was concentrated fought a bloody battle between themselves.

The banks naturally got into difficulty, and the whole system changed in the 1990s. The historical irony is that one of the two main banks collapsed and was forced to merge with the other. The merging of the two giants would have been utterly unthinkable in the 1980s.

Nokia's chairman, Kari Kairamo, loathed the Finnish banking system and the banks' power over industry. He thought industrialists should run industry themselves. He gave public speeches demanding laws to restrict the banks' rights of ownership. Kairamo was right. In the Anglo-Saxon world it was industry that made the world go round. The bank's job is to provide the finance, not to wield power within the company. Nevertheless there were many at Nokia who thought Kairamo was gambling. The banks wielded so much power that some of Nokia's board feared the empire might strike back.

Another shortcoming in my CV was an absence of shop-floor experience at Nokia. I hadn't set foot in a factory since my summer job in Vaasa at the end of my first year as a student. I was an engineer, but I didn't design telecommunications networks, mobile phones, or new types of cables. And I had been very active in the field of student politics, which was another black mark. In Finland student politics was often a launch pad for a political career, and that was where my new colleagues thought my ambitions lay. But I've never really spent too long worrying about what other people think of me. I believe in getting things done, in achievements and results. Beyond those, people can think what they like about me.

I had learned how to analyze a company. In my previous job I'd had to assess whether it was worth lending, say, 100 million dollars to some Finnish forestry company. Would the company be able to repay the loan? What was the company's real profitability? Did the managers know their jobs? At Citibank, companies were not analyzed solely on the basis of the figures – the company's management and culture were also factored in. Nokia seemed to employ lots of good people, but the company's management was hidebound and old-fashioned.

The Nokia I joined in 1985 claimed to be an international company. That was certainly the reputation it enjoyed in Finland. It could boast that it operated in twenty-four locations around the world.

Kari Kairamo's stance as an internationalist certainly attracted many young and able people to Nokia, because at least the company wanted to be international. Of those who would be my closest collaborators in the coming years, Sari Baldauf had joined the firm in 1983; Pekka Ala-Pietilä joined in 1984, the same year Matti Alahuhta returned to the company after several years away; Pertti Korhonen joined the company in 1986; and Olli-Pekka Kallasvuo was already there, having started as a lawyer back in 1980.

The company was still dependent on its trade with the Soviet Union, as were many other Finnish firms. It had been agreed within the European cartel that cable trade between Finland and the Soviet Union belonged to Nokia. This guaranteed Nokia a profitable relationship with the Soviet Union – as long as the country continued to exist.

Nokia didn't lack global aspirations. Its wall map of the world map lots of little pins in all sorts of places. The company's leaders had distinguished themselves by the competitive acquisition of large and small enterprises, but no one had ever assembled all the bits into a coherent whole. Some of them were insignificant sales firms – little more than corner shops – while others did sensible things.

My first task at Nokia was to bring some order into this chaos. I sat in my room and collected files that told me about Nokia's international subsidiaries. I tried to work out what they really did and why, and how they fit into the bigger picture. Some of them were complete catastrophes – for example, Nokia had an IT company in England whose losses greatly exceeded its revenue. I asked to see the papers on which Nokia's investment decision had been based; reading them was so sad it was funny.

Files and papers flooded my desk, and I tried to get rid of them as quickly and efficiently as possible. I didn't really have anyone working for me, but I was at the center of power because I answered directly to the company CEO and the president. I was a staff officer whose job was to prepare the company's international projects. I was also expected to consider how the company's leadership structure should be developed. Developing the international side of Nokia's operations was a further apprenticeship for me. In my discussions with Kari Kairamo and Simo Vuorilehto I had been promised a place at the company's front line one day. This was important at Nokia – those who had managed an area of business and brought in money were regarded more highly than those who had stayed at headquarters. This ethos has prevailed at Nokia, and in many other companies, up until today. I lacked front line experience and passionately wished to gain it. I knew, too, that without it I wouldn't get very far at Nokia.

CHAPTER 19

The Last Days of Drowsiness

O NCE AGAIN FATE INTERVENED. When Nokia's lightbulb subsidiary Airam became part of a management buyout, a vacancy for a finance director arose. Simo Vuorilehto wanted me to take it. I knew about finance from Citibank. I was a professional, and Nokia's ambitious European plans demanded a new approach to finance. As well as looking after its acquisitions Nokia needed a higher profile on the stock markets and among investors. I took on this new role with enthusiasm.

At this time – 1986 – Kari Kairamo embarked on a radical restructuring of the company's governance. Powerful figures such as the chairman and deputy chairman of the board had to yield to Kairamo's wishes. The board that had represented the shareholders became the supervisory board. In practice this meant that the actual owners of the company were moved further away from everyday activity.

When this change was made it was stated that the supervisory board would retain the key responsibilities of the previous board. The firm's leading executives would form the board of directors. Kari Kairamo would lead this body in his role as the chairman and CEO.

Kairamo also established an executive committee to oversee Nokia's day-to-day operations. I sat on this in my new capacity as finance director. It was presided over by Simo Vuorilehto, which gave him greater responsibility for operations. Kairamo used his role to concentrate more on making Nokia's influence felt in Finland and more widely in Europe. His most important vehicle for this was the Confederation of Finnish Industry, where Kairamo was chairman from 1985 to 1987.

Nokia's complex governance model turned out to be a millstone around its neck at the end of the 1980s. The company couldn't deal promptly or decisively with the many issues it was facing. The difficulties with this mixed-up management model were among the reasons Nokia's management was made much simpler in the 1990s.

In financial terms Finland was a highly regulated and almost closed economy well into the 1980s. After World War II there had been a dearth of everything. Imports were controlled, as was foreign exchange for decades after the war. Companies couldn't take out long-term foreign loans without permission from the Bank of Finland. Foreign investors could invest in Finnish firms only within strict limits. Capital couldn't move freely either into or out of Finland. The exchange rate of the Finnish markka was administratively determined.

The Bank of Finland also influenced lending in another way: the central bank set the commercial banks' quotas for loans. If the banks exceeded their quotas they had to pay an additional premium to the central bank for their loan capital. The Finnish financial world wasn't subject to conditions set by the market but to those set by the Bank of Finland. Politicians ruled the Bank of Finland, and the governor of the Bank of Finland was one of Finland's most powerful men.

Exchange rate fluctuations were an instrument of economic policy. When Finnish industry, especially the forestry industry, found itself in difficulties abroad and needed help, the cry went up for the Finnish government to devalue the markka. Then industry would gain some breathing space while others had to suffer the negative consequences of devaluation.

Devaluation helped Finnish exporters, which chiefly meant the timber industry. Finnish exports became more competitive on world markets as their prices fell in line with the Finnish markka. Devaluation was paid for by the sectors that relied on imported raw materials and of course by individuals who had to pay more for imported goods.

Finland devalued its currency in 1949, 1957, 1967, 1977, 1978, 1982, and again in 1991. The money markets however began to shake off the hand of regulation in the mid-1980s, when all the rules of the game changed. Major firms had begun to get around the supervision of the Bank of Finland by lending money to each other. Currency controls were abolished. Companies were allowed to import capital to Finland. In 1984 the Bank of Finland opened the floodgates and money started to flow into a country that had been deprived of capital for many decades. Suddenly record amounts of foreign money were sloshing around. Companies invested and individuals consumed: Finland felt as if it was getting richer by the day. In Helsinki shops selling expensive designer goods sprouted overnight, smart and fast new cars appeared on the streets, and hardly a week went by without the opening of a new gourmet restaurant. The media started to talk of "yuppies," whose lives revolved around shameless consumption.

A finance director in a Finnish company could achieve brilliant results by one simple method. All you had to do was borrow foreign currency and invest it in the Finnish markka. Foreign interest rates were much lower than Finnish ones, so even the dimmer finance manager could easily make a good profit. The only threat to this automaticity was the next devaluation. But you could predict this to some degree.

A devaluation was proposed in 1986, but it didn't happen. Instead Finnish monetary policy at last began to be liberalized. Companies were now free to take out long-term loans in foreign currency, and the regulation of commercial bank interest rates was abolished. Genuine international money markets, which would benefit Finnish firms, had at last reached Finland. And with their arrival devaluation disappeared as a reliable option. Now Finnish firms would have to learn to compete by other means.

Finnish companies had done overseas business for many years. The country had lived by its exports: the forestry industry had sent its products abroad for centuries, and strong metals industries had sprung up in the 1950s. Finnish ships and paper-making machines were known the world over. And Nokia, along with many other firms, had started to develop an electronics industry. Foreign trade had taught Finnish companies to look after their foreign exchange skillfully. Forecasting and anticipating the constant devaluations had kept financial managers on their toes. But in many other matters Finnish companies had known very little about how international finance operated. They weren't listed on foreign stock exchanges. The money they borrowed had mostly come from Finnish banks, which also owned and ran the companies. This was barren soil for genuine competition and financial efficiency to take root in.

Nokia wanted to be a different sort of company, free of the influence of the banks. We wanted investors from around the world, from Europe, from Finland, from wherever we operated. From that ownership base we wanted to make Nokia an international company. This was our dream at the end of the 1980s. It became a reality only in the 1990s, when over 90 percent of Nokia was owned by people outside Finland. But we had to start somewhere, and one of our first foreign investors was a man named George Soros.

I didn't know much about George Soros back in 1985. I knew he had fled Nazi-run Hungary at the time of World War II and that he had studied philosophy at the London School of Economics, where I too had been a student.

The book he was writing then, which would appear the following year, was called *The Alchemy of Finance,* and it applied various theories of physics to financial investment. His Quantum Fund was already known for its skillful operations on the markets for foreign exchange, shares, and raw materials.

George Soros's link to Finland was my old friend from Atlantic College, the economist and investment expert Pentti Kouri. Pentti sat on the Nokia board at Kari Kairamo's invitation – Kairamo had been captivated by Pentti's sparkling intellect and also his contacts in the U.S. market. Pentti was a rising star in Finland. He went around telling the leaders of major companies where the world was heading. As a young economist he had already made a theoretical contribution. He had risen via the International Monetary Fund to become a professor at one of America's leading universities. He came from Finnish Lapland, was around six feet, six inches tall, and never really bothered to disguise his own brilliance.

Kouri had recommended some Finnish firms as possible investments for Soros; one of these was Nokia. Kari Kairamo had quickly taken to the idea, because if Soros invested it would help reduce the company's dependence on the banks both as owners and financiers. Kairamo was presumably also looking ahead: if a well-known investor liked the look of Nokia, it would be easier to persuade others to trust the company.

In December 1985 I travelled to New York to sell Nokia shares to Soros and to meet American investment bankers. Soros met me at his office in Columbus Circle, which had a stunning view northward over Central Park. On the streets of downtown Manhattan Christmas carols were already playing in the shops and a queue many yards long wound around FAO Schwarz, the famous toyshop. The carols were fortunately inaudible from the offices of Soros's Quantum Fund. Soros sat with his advisers on one side of the table. I sat with Pentti Kouri facing him.

I had done my homework carefully. Soros looked at me closely from behind large spectacles and fired questions at me in English with a strong Hungarian accent. His aides asked even sharper questions: "Why are you in this business? Will mobile telephones ever be profitable? Why haven't you sold your cable division?" I replied clearly to each question. I knew every figure inside out, for that had always been easy for me. I wasn't tense or nervous, at least not very. I was well prepared for this presentation, what one might now call a road show. On this occasion, however, the road show had an audience of just one investor. After the meeting Pentti Kouri was ecstatic. He told me I'd done rather better than the typical Finnish finance executive.

To me Soros didn't seem to be an especially tough, impressive, or charismatic man. Many bankers I had known at Citibank were much quicker and sharper. I wouldn't have guessed in 1986 that I would encounter Soros's name so often in the 1990s, when the great investor would upset the European exchange rate mechanism, rescue east European culture, and try to improve American society still further.

In Manhattan we tentatively agreed on the price Soros would pay for the Nokia shares. The preliminary agreement was signed at the beginning of January 1986. Everything should have been fine: George Soros would have made a sound investment, and Nokia would have received fresh capital to the sum of 238 million markka ($97 million at 2016 prices). But in a few months nothing was fine. Nokia's shares had begun to rise briskly. We suspected that someone might deliberately try to ramp up Nokia shares. We had agreed with Soros that the two categories of Nokia share he was buying should be priced at 380 and 350 markka ($155 and $143 respectively at 2016 prices). But, given the rise in Nokia's value, the correct prices for these shares were now 473 and 468 markka ($188 and $186 respectively at 2016 prices). Soros the great investor was making an even better deal than we had thought.

The Finnish banks on Nokia's board were furious. They gave notice that they wanted to subscribe for shares at the same price as Soros. The chairman of Nokia's board, Mika Tiivola, said my preliminary agreement with Soros could be revoked at any time. Finally I went to meet George Soros, at his Manhattan residence, on my way to a seminar in Colorado. I sat with him at breakfast, and tried to explain the views of Nokia's Finnish proprietors. Soros appeared seriously irritated when I suggested that we review the price.

"In that case I will have to reconsider all my investments in Finland," Soros announced. He had invested and was investing in about five other companies. His interest had encouraged many other international investors to take an interest in the Helsinki Stock Exchange. Finnish companies could not afford to lose Soros just then.

When I returned to Finland Kari Kairamo informed Soros that the shares had to be repriced. A new price was proposed to him based on Nokia's value in the spring of 1986 reduced by eight percent. Soros accepted the offer, and the planned share issue to the Quantum Fund took place in May 1986. In honor of his investment Soros paid a visit to Finland, where he was accorded the welcome due to a statesman. He met the prime minister, gave a long interview to the country's largest newspaper, and attended a dinner in his honor at Båtvik, a historic seaside villa that Nokia owned. He also saw how mobile phones were made at Nokia's Salo plant.

For me Operation Soros was important. I handled it pretty much by myself from start to finish, and I got Nokia to take a big step toward the community of international investors. If Soros believed in Nokia many other investors were bound to follow. I had gotten to know the big investors' smiling faces, but I had also seen an angry Soros, who believed the Finns had deceived him.

But things turned out satisfactorily for Soros after all. Nokia shares continued their rise in 1986. By September 1986 Soros's investment, made just that spring, already showed a profit of 71.4 percent. If I had been him I would have uncorked the champagne then and there and felt a glow of satisfaction as I looked out over Central Park. George Soros later encapsulated his own philosophy well: "Leave the last 10 percent for the next guy." He has made billions using this recipe. He became famous for knowing when to sell. Deals that stick are those in which both sides benefit. He followed his own advice in our negotiations, too.

CHAPTER 20

Black Monday

I'M AN OSTROBOTHNIAN, FROM WESTERN FINLAND. People from western Finland come across as straightforward but taciturn and a little brusque, but we keep our promises. We tend not to reveal our real feelings: these are hidden below many layers deep down in the soul, and show themselves in deeds rather than in words.

For many years Nokia was a global company run by people from western Finland, with a handful of people from other provincial places. Our bucolic backgrounds greatly amused the Finnish press, while in the wider world no one understood what the fuss might be about – though in every country larger than Luxembourg there are regional differences, and people in the big city always regard themselves as more sophisticated. These things are significant. I strongly identify with my roots. For me people from western Finland are usually the easiest to get along with. I say this with a degree of caution: my wife Liisa's roots are in eastern Finland, and I've been getting on with her for over forty years now.

When I started at Nokia its management was divided into factions that fought each other. I tried to avoid being drawn into these battles. In any case I was hardly part of the inner circle that orbited Kari Kairamo. I kept a little to one side, though I did my job conscientiously, as I have ever since my first class at primary school nearly sixty years ago.

I soon got to know a lawyer in Nokia's legal department named Olli-Pekka Kallasvuo. He stood out from the crowd because his opinions were always analytical and very much his own. In spring 1986 I requested that he be transferred from the legal department to the finance department, which

I had taken charge of. I could discuss finance with him as part of Nokia's broader strategy since he had been closely involved in much of Nokia's acquisitions and financing.

Olli-Pekka Kallasvuo also came from western Finland.

I was a banker by background and very familiar with international finance. But in the mid-1980s no one at Nokia was very interested in that. Olli-Pekka had studied law and had gained practical experience in economics and finance at Nokia. He was a cast-iron finance professional, and I rated his skills highly.

One October Monday back in 1987 Olli-Pekka and I were sitting in my office in Nokia's old headquarters. We were staring at a Reuters computer screen, which nowadays would seem just as clumsy as a 1960s black-and-white television. The terminal displayed green numerals that told us that the New York Stock Exchange was sinking rapidly and inexplicably. The financial panic spread from New York around the world. This was our stock exchange crash, the 1929 of my generation. We stared at the figures, but we didn't understand what was happening. We tried to call people we knew to find out firsthand what was going on, but it wasn't easy to get through to New York.

Nokia wasn't listed on the New York Stock Exchange, but we knew this would impact the company's share price in London and Helsinki, where the company was listed. That spring, with Kari Kairamo's support, we had floated Nokia on the London Stock Exchange, a courageous step for a Finnish company and a vital one if Nokia was to transform itself into a company attractive to international investors. It would guarantee the company access to new finance and make it more independent of the micro-management of the Finnish banks.

Now we stared at the little green numbers darting across the screen and tried to work out whether our dream was over. Were the stock exchanges of the world entering a lasting depression? Was capital fleeing from equities into the credit markets? Had listings and capital operations had their day? Had we gone back to the Stone Age where international finance was concerned? Would small investors ever regain their confidence in the stock market?

Later the great stock market crash of October 1987 would turn out to be much smaller than we had imagined at the time. Shares recovered their previous levels by the following year. Nevertheless Black Monday in October 1987 took its place in history. When the reasons for the crash were investigated, it turned out that programmed trading was responsible. Changes in equity prices had automatically triggered sales on such a massive scale that the market couldn't cope and so it crashed. This happened when both the economy and the stock exchanges were at a very high level. What goes up must come down, and now it was the stock market's turn.

October 1987 was also the first indication that the financial markets had really gone global. The crash in New York affected the stock exchanges in London, Paris, Frankfurt, Stockholm – and Helsinki. The secondary effects would be much greater, but in 1987 we received a foretaste of what was to come ten years later. By then small investors would be using systems that had previously been available only to professional traders.

We sat there late into the night – a hard day's night. It had been a tense day for us, especially since we were both young: I was thirty-seven and Olli-Pekka thirty-four. It left us with a lasting sense of uncertainty, but with the sure knowledge that no rise in a share price could last forever. The work of decades, major investments, and the entire value of companies could be wiped away by the markets in a matter of minutes. Later neither of us ever wanted to invest Nokia's cash reserves in the equity markets. We managed to resist that temptation even when many people regarded us as too conservative.

As the evening went on we wondered what the future held. What would happen to Nokia? Its major acquisitions were just under way. Would the world still provide a market for Nokia's products, or would that melt away? How would things go for us at Nokia? These were the questions going around in my head as I drove home in my Volvo that Monday evening. Outside it was dark, damp, and treacherous and a slushy rain was falling. That October day in 1987 became known as Black Monday. That evening in Helsinki certainly lived up to the name.

CHAPTER 21

The Finance Director Gets Down to Work

A T THE END OF THE 1980s Nokia was a bundle of different activities – tissue paper doesn't have much to do with electrical cables. Nokia had traditionally made rubber boots, but that didn't help much with the mobile phone side of the business.

It was to be my destiny to decide where Nokia should focus in the future. My first job was to work out what we should do with Nokia's paper division. Paper was Nokia's core, Nokia's heart. That was where it had all started.

Nokia had taken its name from a manor house at the confluence of two rivers just west of Tampere, Finland's second city. There had been a house at that spot since as far back as 1270 or thereabouts. The golden age of the Nokia Manor, though, had been the nineteenth century. A town called Nokia later grew up around the house and the factories.

The name "Nokia" has its roots in an old Finnish word for the sable, a small, dark, furry animal that made its home on the banks of the river Nokia, to which the animal gave its name. From there the name passed to the manor house, to the company, and eventually to the whole community. There's something curiously fitting about the name Nokia: the little furry beast was a nimble creature that had to adapt to changes in its environment, just as the company did later. Now the animal has achieved immortality: it appears on the coat of arms of the town of Nokia.

The paper factory was founded by Fredrik Idestam (1838–1916), who was a Finnish government official as well as an entrepreneur. He had heard while travelling abroad that paper could be made from wood. Until then paper had been made from linen rags, but it had been discovered in Germany that paper could be produced more cheaply by adding wood to the pulp. Finland was a land of forests, lakes, and rivers. Wood was the raw material for paper, and water was a source of the energy needed to turn wood into paper.

Idestam set up his first paper mill in 1865. Times were hard: crop failures had led to a devastating famine. Finland was an autonomous part of Russia, dependent on political decisions made in St Petersburg. All in all the economy was weak. Even so, paper consumption appeared to be growing rapidly; Fredrik Idestam had chosen the right area.

Nokia Ltd. was incorporated in 1871, when the company's first general meeting was held in Helsinki. The company developed its paper production at Nokia, while other companies set up mills elsewhere. They laid the foundations for the entire economy of Finland, which became an independent country in 1917.

Nokia's paper division grew and blossomed right up to the end of the 1980s. Domestic competitors had grown up alongside Nokia: companies merged and pooled their resources in the face of ever-fiercer international competition. The paper industry was so important for Finland that many political decisions were made on its terms. When it got into difficulty it expected the government to bail it out. This led to regular devaluations of the Finnish markka to ensure that the paper trade ran smoothly.

And of course other exporting industries benefited from devaluation.

Nokia didn't focus solely on paper production. Indeed, in the 1980s Nokia didn't really focus on anything. It wasn't big enough to succeed as a producer of tissue paper – it had to find new areas or be swallowed up. This was a time of consolidation in the paper industry: Nordic companies were forming alliances in a new way, European firms were buying one another, and American firms were buying European ones.

I had made an early assessment of Nokia when I was a young analyst at Citibank – the company was too diverse. For example, following a reorganization in 1983 it had nine separate divisions, and it owned subsidiaries producing everything from batteries to hunting weapons. The company had to focus on something, fast. I thought it should give up on paper, consumer electronics, and its cable business and concentrate on electronics. But then again, cables produced a healthy cash flow. Of course at that time I wasn't in a position where I could decide Nokia's future direction.

It took a year to get out of paper, and it needed some sticky negotiations and some sweaty journeys to the United States, London, and Italy. It was the first project where I sold part of Nokia. Because the paper division was in a sense sacred I couldn't openly talk about selling it. Instead we talked of alliances, cooperation, and the transfer of operations as part of an international totality. Nokia's top management was divided about giving up paper production. Chairman Kari Kairamo gave an impression that he didn't want to sell anything that belonged to Nokia. He had begun his career in Nokia's paper division. His grandfather had been one of the original subscribers for Nokia shares in 1877. Although Kairamo was forward-looking as Nokia's chairman, he didn't want to be remembered as the man who sold its paper division. The chief executive, Simo Vuorilehto, also had a background in paper production, but he understood that Nokia couldn't compete against larger firms, and he supported the move to cut paper production. On the other hand, the head of the paper division, Janne Simelius, wanted to expand it. And Jaakko Lassila, one of the two dominant figures in the world of Finnish banking, who sat on Nokia's board, was opposed to selling it.

These differences of view on a key strategic question speak volumes about the problems Nokia faced. In the midst of these differences I was given the task of disengaging Nokia from paper, and I saw it as my duty to do so. Nokia had to find an international partner, but where? How could we arrange matters so that the sale would seem a genuine example of cooperation? Who would pay what, and to whom? Would we use shares or money as our means of payment? What did we really want? And what would be good for Finland? If Nokia made the wrong decision the Finnish media and Finnish politicians wouldn't miss the opportunity to attack us the moment the deal was concluded.

Nokia's top management was very short of international expertise. The truth was that the company had lost an entire generation. The company's president, Kari Kairamo, and chief executive, Simo Vuorilehto, were both over fifty. The forty-something board members were either on their way out or otherwise on the sidelines. Whether to end paper production was the first of the big challenges my generation faced at Nokia. It was not of course my personal project. I got to know people with whom I would work very closely later on. One of these acquaintances was the Swedish consultant Per Karlsson, who later became an important advisor and would sit on the Nokia board.

Per Karlsson was an investment banker at the Svenska Enskilda Bank and formerly the head of IKEA in Germany. He was on the small side, bespectacled, cheerful, and courteous. He was soft-spoken but far from soft-headed. He was able to find innovative solutions to difficult strategic problems that others had tried and failed to resolve. He had a thorough knowledge of many industrial sectors. One of his areas of expertise was tissue paper production. I had first met him in London in 1986, at the time of Nokia's listing on the London Stock Exchange. His colleague Roger Gifford had invited us to watch the tennis at Wimbledon. I remember I won a five-pound bet on who would be champion.

Per Karlsson had earlier had discussions with Nokia about our tissue paper division. We had talked about an alliance with Holmen Hygiene, a Swedish firm. We had also made an offer involving the formation of a European company to sell, though the terms weren't clear and wouldn't become clear until we were certain that there was no alternative to selling it. If this sounds confusing, that's because it was.

Sometime in the spring of 1988 Per Karlsson and Roger Gifford came to my office in Nokia's headquarters in the heart of Helsinki. They told me bluntly that Nokia couldn't make a profit as a lone player in the European tissue paper market, so it would be best for Nokia to sell out straight away. Per Karlsson had good contacts in the paper industry, and he reckoned that an American company called James River might be interested in buying out our tissue paper division. At ten o'clock one Swedish spring evening he picked up the phone in Stockholm and rang Brenton Halsey at James River. The switchboard asked Per: "Which Brenton Halsey do you want to talk with?" Per was dumbstruck for a moment – he had forgotten that a father-and-son team ran the company. He chose Brenton Halsey senior, who happened to be the right one.

During this call James River commissioned Per Karlsson to buy Nokia's tissue paper division. He travelled to Richmond, Virginia, where James River Inc. was based. The company was proud of its history and reputation – a cannon from the American Civil War was on display at its headquarters. Brenton Halsey, for his part, assured us that his company was honest and straight in all matters. This I would find out for myself later as the negotiations advanced. These negotiations were not always easy, however. The sale of our paper division became a process that tried my patience intensely. When the negotiations began money wasn't the question uppermost in our minds. But as they continued Nokia's cash reserves dwindled. Now we badly needed the money the sale of the paper division would bring. Selling a company is always difficult. In any such sale there are always a million reasons why one shouldn't be doing it. There's always someone who thinks it's too expensive, or too uncertain, or otherwise a stupid thing to do. And what's more, they're very often right. Someone really has to push for the sale to take place in order for it to happen. On top of that practical matters may turn out to be deal-breakers. In major deals there's always an army of investment bankers, consultants, lawyers, public relations people, and other advisers. In selling our paper division I had for the first time to command this little army of people, all of whom had to do their bit if the deal was to be successful. And even that wasn't enough, because Nokia's divided board would still have to agree to the terms of the deal. For me this was all new and exceedingly instructive.

The negotiations with James River got underway with a meeting with Per Karlsson and Roger Gifford. I took along Olli-Pekka Kallasvuo, who had now moved to the finance department, to work out the practical aspects. The practical aspects meant that every month we flew to London for a couple of days to negotiate the details of the deal.

From time to time Per Karlsson stumbled into my line of fire. I cannot bear delay, foot-dragging, or artificial obstacles in anything that I do. The sale of our tissue paper division was turning into the biggest project of my time as finance director. In the summer of 1988 it seemed to me that the sale wouldn't go ahead. I wanted to make the negotiations go faster, but I didn't know how. I sat in the office late into the night, staring at my papers and talking on the phone. Most often Per Karlsson was at the other end of the line "Per, we need to get this done!" was my simple message. My fingers tapping the desk were so loud they could be heard in London, Per told me later. He was quiet at the other end, listening to my outpourings and saying he would do his best.

In September 1988 the negotiations seemed to be moving forward, though that was just a mirage. Matters had matured to the point where I suggested to Brenton S. Halsey, Sr., that he visit Nokia. He came from Richmond, Virginia, first to Helsinki, where we met him at Nokia's head office. The chairman, Kari Kairamo, was there, with the other directors. After this meeting Halsey flew in Nokia's private aircraft to Nokia, to the birthplace of the entire enterprise and the "sacred" paper factory. Fredrik Idestam's manor house had gone, and in its place stood Nokia's company villa, built of white stone. Many a captain of industry had visited this house before Brenton S. Halsey. The American executives spent a long evening with their Finnish hosts.

Halsey was pretty sharp the following morning. He had come up with three options: sale of the company, time-limited cooperation, or open-ended cooperation.

The Americans wanted to conclude the deal. I wanted to conclude the deal. Nokia's CEO wanted to conclude the deal. Nevertheless the negotiations ground to a halt: Nokia's chairman, Kari Kairamo, didn't want to conclude the deal.

The process was logjammed for several months. It resumed again only in December 1988, when Kairamo's views were no longer decisive and a preliminary agreement was signed in London. It says a lot about Nokia's company culture at the time that the board member who signed it, Harry Mildh, had played no part at all in the negotiations. He just happened to occupy the right seat on the board.

Olli-Pekka and I knew very little about paper production or, to be honest, about the paper industry in general. We were technocrats, and it was our job to see this operation through to the end because we believed it was a matter of necessity for Nokia. When we presented the deal to the board I explained the background, which showed that the tissue paper division was profitable but the outlook for growth was weak. Also, Nokia was less profitable than its international competitors in this sector. The aim of these explanations was of course to build up the case for the deal.

Such deals never run according to the timetable. Unexpected problems cropped up in this project, too. The ownership arrangements became ever more complex. Olli-Pekka kept an eye on the legal aspects, and we also engaged the services of Tomas Lindholm at one of the top Helsinki law firms. He described the deal as the most complex of his career. He became my trusted lawyer, whom I called on again later when I was in a tight corner.

Nokia's board agreed to the sale of the paper division in 1989. In the final stages the Italian firm, Montedison, part of the Ferruzzi group, joined James River as Nokia's partner in the new joint company. At the decisive meeting of the board one of the directors gave an ill-tempered speech in which he said the sale was a mistake. It would have been better to sell off Nokia's consumer electronics division instead. He was both right and wrong. The consumer electronics arm had to be sold in any case. Selling it would be the next long and arduous process we had to go through. But we were also right to sell the paper division. Our keenness to sell it was sharpened by the knowledge that Nokia was hemorrhaging cash. According to its interim results that spring, the company's profit was 100 million markka ($36 million in 2016 money), less than budgeted for. The previous year the profit had shrunk by 130 million markka ($47 million). Nokia's descent into the abyss had begun.

The arrival of the Italians at the negotiating table brought new color to the deal. I later became a board member of the joint company established by Nokia, James River, and Montedison. I added Milan to my frequent-flyer program, though the preliminary discussions on the role of the Italians were held in London. The investment bankers and consultants relished that. The Swedish investment banker Bengt Hammar announced pompously at one stage that his client was "Raoul Gardinia himself, the Chairman of Ferruzzi, whom I am representing personally." "Then not the Pope himself," I whispered to Olli-Pekka, who was sitting beside me. He had great difficulty in containing his fit of laughter – but if he hadn't it would have done immense damage to his reputation for stone-faced imperturbability.

The new joint venture became Europe's biggest tissue paper company. Nokia announced in its press release that it was passing to the new company "all its activities in the field of paper, or that part of the firm from which Nokia began 125 years ago." Later, in January 1991, Nokia would sell its share in the company. Thus Nokia had taken its first big step in moving toward a new age and a new scene of operations. The deal was financially sound for Nokia: by my calculations Nokia profited from the sale of its paper division to the tune of about $148 million at 2016 rates.

The deal included some terms very favorable to Nokia regarding exchange rates: the price would rise to Nokia's advantage right up to the very day the deal became binding.

I don't know what Fredrik Idestam would have made of our deal. His brainchild had survived and turned a profit for 125 years. In that time Nokia had fortunately had new ideas and moved into new fields. Perhaps he would have been pleased that we had at least achieved a good price for our paper division. He was a true cosmopolitan who did much to bring European ideas to Finland. So our international operations, which had produced a much larger and more vigorous enterprise, would certainly have pleased him. Perhaps Fredrik Enestam would have wished us bon voyage into the new millennium, when Nokia would once again be an entirely new company. What else is there of Idestam's legacy? The manor house is still owned by Nokia and still stands in the town of that name. The mills on Tehdassaari – factory island – are still working, though now under the name of SCA – Svenska Cellulosa Aktiebolaget.

I was now a more experienced business leader, and I understood better how big organizations were run. The deal I had just concluded didn't make me a great enthusiast for mergers or acquisitions. At the same time I sensed that we still had to divest ourselves of consumer electronics, rubber products, and cables. That would provide work for the coming years.

When I later became chief executive of Nokia I wouldn't do much in that line. Nokia would concentrate on organic growth in a growing market. There are always so many risks in M&A. It's not worth buying a failing business, and a successful one is never for sale at an affordable price. And acquisitions are dangerous for corporate culture. By one estimate, 70 percent of them don't meet the targets set when done. I don't find that surprising. Deals always look easier on paper than they turn out to be in the real world, which has real people, institutions, emotions, and history. So I've tried to resist the temptation of acquisitions, and in this I've succeeded rather well.

CHAPTER 22

Spend, Spend, Spend

I N THE 1980S WELLINGTON BOOTS were still Nokia's best-known product. They were in very wide use. In Finland's challenging climate there's a use for a pair of decent wellies all year round: for working or walking in the forests, fields, and bogs – and even on the lakes or sea when they're frozen in winter. Nokia had produced its first rubber footwear back in 1898, when it started making galoshes. Then it moved into bicycle tires, car tires, and industrial rubber. It started to produce its classic Wellingtons in 1934. The Finnish army had them as part of its regular kit and wore them in key campaigns. I had worn them myself during my military service.

In 1988 Nokia was still Europe's largest producer of rubber boots. But a couple of years later the company exited the business when there was a management buyout of this traditional sector. In the early 1990s Nokia divested all of its traditional basic industries, which was when it finally started to look like an electronics company. It was looking for areas of growth – capturing new markets lay at the heart of Nokia's long-term strategy. The company had developed its capability in telephone networks and switchboards. Now it tried to grow through direct sales to consumers. Nokia had embarked on an adventure that would put its entire future at stake.

There was plenty for Nokia's finance director to do in the 1980s when the company set off on its European spending spree. The most important part of my job was ensuring that we could pay the bills for the chairman's shopping.

Kari Kairamo believed that the secret of growth lay in some combination of consumer electronics, computers, and mobile phones. He thought the company needed to be active in all three sectors to be certain of success.

My views didn't diverge from Kairamo's, but I, and many others, understood that Nokia was taking some hair-raising risks.

In 1987 Nokia decided to take many serious risks simultaneously. The atmosphere was competitive: who could bring to the board the most interesting international project? In the spring the company bought the French television producer Oceanic from the Swedish firm Electrolux. That made Nokia Europe's third-biggest maker of televisions. That was the starter. For the main course Nokia was eyeing a really big fish: the German company Standard Elektrik Lorenz (SEL).

Antti Lagerroos was in charge of this. He was an ambitious, self-assured, and purposeful member of Nokia's board, whose dream was one day to take Kari Kairamo's place as the company's chairman. He was assisted by the exceptionally gifted and much-loved Timo Koski, who had joined Nokia from Siemens in 1983 and had become head of Nokia electronics and a member of the board. He was one of the few people in Nokia with real international experience and a vision to match. At the time Koski had less than a year to live, though none of us knew that then.

These two men drove Nokia to make a series of acquisitions that turned it into the king of European television production. According to them SEL was the last company in Europe it would be possible to buy. They were not disturbed by the fact that Sony had looked at the company and decided not to buy it. During the planning of these deals there was a buzz on the fifth floor of Nokia's headquarters, where the top management had their offices. I didn't have anything to do either with the calculations or with making the decisions. I kept to myself the thought that the market for televisions was quite unknown to Nokia, and that it was full of pitfalls.

The purchase of SEL was announced in the middle of December 1987. It was a major deal, but there was more to come. All autumn Nokia had been negotiating with its arch-rival, the Swedish company Ericsson, over the acquisition of its computer division. The discussions reached their conclusion at the same time as the SEL deal. Nokia was becoming a formidable player in the European television market, and the largest computer firm in the Nordic region.

We held a press conference in the ballroom of the Marski Hotel in Helsinki to announce our purchase of Ericsson Data. As we were getting ready for that I chatted with my Nokia colleagues. I was quite sure that the journalists would attack our ambitious strategy. I was certain that someone would ask: "How can you be sure these deals will ever succeed?" But this question didn't come up.

That was just as well, because it was a question that Nokia's board hadn't even asked each other before concluding the deals. Silence reigned: no critics of the deals came forward, even though Kari Kairamo was said to have had doubts about the purchase of SEL right up to the evening before the deal was signed. He had asked some executives to come to his office and had asked them: "Will this sink Nokia?" No one had been able to offer an answer. Silence filled the room.

The head of the Dutch television company Philips, Jan Timmer, made a striking observation when Nokia acquired its television factories in 1988. Timmer had visited Helsinki to get to know his new competitor. During his trip back to the airport he was deep in thought. He told the Nokia director accompanying him exactly what he thought after their day of discussions: "It's dangerous to find ourselves in an area where a new player comes along knowing nothing about making televisions." This was Dutch directness at its sharpest. Those wrong decisions and those managers' silence cost Nokia dearly, right up until 1996. Kari Kairamo asked just once whether Nokia could afford this expansion program. He ought to have asked a dozen times a day. SEL and Ericsson Data cost Nokia 3.75 billion markka in all (about $1.6 billion at 2016 prices). At the end of the 1980s that figure represented a serious threat.

My answer to Kairamo was clear. "Nokia's balance sheet is under strain on account of these deals. Both of them – televisions and computers – have to work if Nokia is to stay solvent," was what I told him. Kairamo listened to my explanation. He looked at me through the transparent screen of his large spectacles and went on to the next thing. He was a small man, restless and mercurial, who took people on trust. He had a brilliant intellect and a compelling vision. He had good intuition and the ability to inspire people. He was a charismatic leader in the fullest sense. But he wasn't always able to accept hard facts if they challenged his own vision. Or perhaps he just thought Nokia had to go forward and any problems could be solved one at a time. Or that the company's future growth would take care of any financing problems. I'm still not quite sure what he could have thought. Neither do I know how much he really believed his plans could succeed.

Although Kairamo had added me to the payroll, I wasn't one of his inner circle. Officially I reported to the president, Simo Vuorilehto, not to Kairamo. Also, we were very different people. Kairamo wanted everything to be fun. He was quite capable of gathering his secretaries and whoever else happened to be around for a quick game of ice hockey on a nearby rink. He loved long evenings that went on far into the night, long after the invited guests had departed. Once, on the way to an island Nokia owned, Kairamo dangled from the door of his helicopter, to the delight of his friends making the journey by boat below.

Kairamo was a perpetual schoolboy, always surrounded by fun, even when things weren't very funny. He kept those around him busy day and night. It wasn't my job to write the speeches he gave several times a week in Finland and abroad. Matti Saarinen, then head of information at Nokia, worked two floors above Kairamo. He might be summoned by the chairman five or ten times a day. Eventually a new phone was installed for Saarinen – a hot line for Kairamo's sole use. In this way Saarinen could hurtle downstairs, putting life and limb at risk, to see the chairman, for whom issues of presentation and PR took precedence over all else. Saarinen could not take the lift to see Kairamo, because it was too slow and nothing could be done about that.

Mobira Cityman

Kari Kairamo always had his sleeves rolled up and was always in a hurry to be somewhere else. His helicopter waited just around the corner. Or some project had to be kicked off today, in order to be ready by yesterday. Kairamo really wasn't a man for long-term planning. Everything happened here and now, quickly and intuitively. Even Kairamo's personal possessions were not always in order. He was always leaving wallets, briefcases, and even clothes in various locations. His habit of piling up papers and press cuttings in his office drove his secretaries and subordinates to despair.

Now and again Kairamo managed to annoy people other than his own staff. When Nokia succeeded in making its first workable mobile phone, Kairamo became the best possible salesperson for them. This model, the Mobira Cityman, weighed about as much as a brick, but Kairamo took it everywhere. Meaningfully and with great ceremony he would place it front of him at the dinner table. He would wait for it to ring, and when it did he would reply with engaged enthusiasm. His hosts at Helsinki's finest restaurants didn't always appreciate this new sign of the times.

Sometime in 1988 I travelled with Kairamo to an investment seminar in the United States. He boarded the plane with a briefcase and three plastic carrier bags full of foreign newspapers a couple of weeks old. When the plane had taken off he dug out scissors and a pen, with which he annotated the items that interested him, to dispatch to his underlings when we reached the other end. He wanted his organization to take care of things and follow new developments. He wanted Nokia to move forward and to remain intellectually alert. Kairamo was a generator who never seemed to run short of energy – a perpetual motion machine. But as anyone who has ever studied physics knows, such a device cannot exist.

Kari Kairamo could be the world's most irritating manager. He would change his plans without telling anyone. His work rate was manic; he drove himself to the edge and seemed to enjoy it. And he assumed that his younger staff members were ready to work at the same rate. As for me, I tried to live as regular a life as I could. I didn't really like going out in the evenings, and Liisa liked it even less. Generally I got home sometime after eight, but always by half past, when the television evening news began. On Sundays I would play tennis in the afternoon, after which I often drove to work and got ready for the following week.

CHAPTER 23

Annus horribilis

E VERYTHING STILL LOOKED GOOD IN THE SPRING OF 1988. Nokia had become a major Nordic and European company. But danger signs had already begun to appear. Senior executives were jostling for position, and in the corridors of the head office no one worried anymore about what would be good for the company, but only what would be good for themselves in the next chapter of the Nokia story.

As summer approached the worst year in Nokia's history began. Its opening act was a human tragedy. One of our senior executives, Timo Koski, was returning to Finland from a holiday in London. As the plane taxied along the runway at Heathrow airport he suffered a stroke. Before he lost consciousness he managed to speak to the air crew. He was rushed to a hospital in Wimbledon specializing in such emergencies. Finnish and British doctors consulted each other, but there was nothing they could do. Timo H. A. Koski died as the result of a stroke at the age of forty.

Koski's death was of course a great shock to us all. But the death of one key manager doesn't derail an entire company. It was nevertheless a grim reminder that overwork may lead to exhaustion and worse. But Nokia was already beginning to slow down by then.

A sickness, a cancer, had taken hold of Nokia, and it was eating up the time of those who should have been running the company. The head office spent its days in plots and power struggles, even as the cash flow was drying up. Nokia had made major acquisitions in television and computer manufacturing, and now it was time to combine them as efficiently as possible into an integral whole.

There would be some difficult decisions ahead concerning redundancies and relocations to countries where manufacturing costs were lower. Nokia's computers were doing markedly better than televisions – computer production had been effectively restructured earlier that year and the results were beginning to show.

It was in the television division that the dismal truth began to reveal itself. European television makers were in ever-worse difficulties – color televisions hadn't sold as well as expected. The major European companies, Thomson and Philips, were scaling back their production or moving it to the Far East, where costs were lower. Europe was simply making too many televisions for a saturated market that was weakening along with the wider economy.

Nokia's total revenue was over 22 billion markka in 1988 ($8.2 billion at 2016 prices). Consumer electronics accounted for about 6 billion markka ($2.3 million) – and employed over 13,000 people. That was far too many: restructuring had started too late. At the beginning of August Nokia's senior management all knew we had bitten off more than we could chew. Antti Lagerroos had lost Kari Kairamo's confidence and had been removed as head of consumer electronics. In his place Kairamo had installed a Frenchman, Jacques Noels. The necessary restructuring had stalled. Noels based his office in Geneva, where he seemed remote from the company's Finland-based leadership.

Noels was too slow in delivering the necessary efficiencies when his division needed decisive leadership to simplify its technology base. We made far too many different models of television and needed to do some pruning if we were to be competitive. We also had too many people working on product development, scattered across too many locations. We should have shed workers from our German factories, but this wasn't done because Kairamo had promised there would be no redundancies. Inevitable but painful decisions were not made, which meant we had to make them later when they were more difficult and expensive.

Nokia's top man, Chairman Kari Kairamo, seemed to devote his time to almost everything except running his own company. He had been invited to join the European Round Table, which gathered the continent's most important business leaders together in various locations to discuss the issues of the day. This was of course highly prestigious from Nokia's point of view, except that the company was in danger of collapse.

In August Kari Kairamo held a crayfish party in honor of the president of the European Commission, Jacques Delors. Nokia's crayfish parties were legendary. They took place in the historic Båtvik manor at Kirkkonummi, about twenty miles west of Helsinki. It was in the area known as the Pork-kala peninsula, which the Finnish government had been forced to lease to the Soviet Union after World War II, and which had been returned to Finland in 1956 in poor condition. The area was a living reminder of the war between Finland and the Soviet Union, when Finland fought heroically for its independence, which it retained but at great cost in men and money. So it was perhaps a fitting irony that in the 1970s and 1980s Båtvik saw many long and liquid evenings where Soviet politicians were encouraged to increase their purchases of Nokia products.

Now Nokia's guests were no longer from the Soviet Union, but from Brussels. Times had changed – Nokia was a major player in the Nordic region and in Western Europe. That was why the top man at the European Commission was learning how to eat crayfish Finnish-style. Nokia's chairman helped Delors tie the ribbons of his bib before the sacred ritual of opening his crayfish. Kairamo later received a beautiful thank-you letter from his distinguished guest. Nokia didn't skimp on its crayfish parties or its other amusements, though the company's business results were declining rapidly in the autumn of 1988. A fleeting and deceptive sense of hopefulness had taken root in the company the previous year, which had been the best in the company's history to date – its profits had exceeded a billion markka for the first time – just over $411 million in 2016 money. Nokia would not achieve as good a result again until 1994.

CHAPTER 24

The Leader Departs

I REMEMBER TRYING TO GET CHAIRMAN KARI KAIRAMO to take an interest in the company's finances. I was frustrated and fearful for the future of the firm, which was looking ever more dismal. One day in the autumn I met Kairamo outside his office, where I tried to tell him about either our latest results or some financial details, I don't recall which, but neither would have made for happy listening. Kairamo stopped for a minute, then continued on his way, because somewhere a gaggle of journalists or others who might promote his public image was waiting.

In the course of 1988 Nokia's relations with the Finnish banks had become strained as its financial results had deteriorated. It didn't help that Nokia had stealthily begun to use its cash reserves to buy back the Nokia shares that the banks owned. This suited Kairamo's aim of gaining independence for Nokia, but the company's weakening position was pushing matters in the other direction. The two main Finnish banks were compelled to intervene in Nokia's affairs more frequently. Kairamo may even have feared that his own position was in danger. Later I heard rumors that the banks had been planning to force him out, but nothing I knew at the time suggested that his days might be numbered.

For investors Nokia's deteriorating results were a cold shower. The company's stock price had fallen by about 40 percent in the course of a year. Chairman Kairamo received hate mail from individual investors in various parts of the world. Next in line was the press, which began to criticize Nokia's plans to conquer the world. Until then Kairamo had been regarded as Finland's best business leader, and his reputation had begun to spread well beyond Finland. In 1988 there wasn't a European newspaper whose request for an interview he would turn down. And there were requests aplenty.

Chairman Kairamo began to live more and more through the media, and the media always creates its own reality. The more one appears in the media, the more its artificial reality diverges from real life and the real world. The media is like a treacherous goblin, which promises a million beautiful things when all is well. But when the luck runs out it finds vengeance all the sweeter.

I organized a Christmas drinks party at my home for staff in the finance department on 8 December 1988. About twenty-five guests came to our terraced house, and we had fun. We sang Christmas carols, ate Christmas food, and drank glögi – something between punch and mulled wine. I had invited Kari Kairamo to drop by, though this was something one could never be sure of: his plans could change at the last moment. So it was all the more delightful when he turned up at our front door as happy and lively as ever. He didn't stay long, because he was having dinner with the board of a major bank. And the following day, a Friday, would be the meeting of Nokia's board's executive committee. Kairamo seemed to be running at full speed, or perhaps even faster.

The following Sunday – 11 December 1988 – I went as usual to the tennis court and after the match to my office, as I often did. I liked to have a peaceful period to focus on my work for the coming week. I sat in my office, studied my papers, and thought about the week ahead, when Nokia's board would address the company's situation. I rang my secretary, who wasn't always delighted to hear from me on Sundays, but who promised to do everything I asked. When I had done all I could I gathered my papers and my tennis bag, went down in the lift to the garage, and left for home. I had seen a light in the boardroom, and I wondered what might be up. I rang Olli-Pekka Kallasvuo, my closest colleague and the second-in-command in the finance department, but he hadn't heard anything out of the ordinary.

I started my Volvo and set off to drive home to Espoo through the dark December night. When I had driven about a hundred yards my car phone rang. The head of communications, Matti Saarinen, was on the line. I could tell from his voice that something was wrong.

"Listen, Kari Kairamo is dead. He has committed suicide," said Saarinen. I was silent for a long time. "Well, well," I eventually managed to say.

I continued on my way home, but I just couldn't concentrate on driving. On either side of the road it was dark. The ice on the sea round the coast of Helsinki seemed extraordinarily black. I felt powerless and a little betrayed.

Had Kairamo left us to take care of this mess? Was that just and fair to us?

I knew at once that suicide was Kairamo's personal solution. There weren't any other skeletons in Nokia's cupboard: as the finance director I was certain of that. Everything would change the following day, but life had to go on, and we had to save what we could of Nokia. After Kairamo's suicide that would be no easier than before.

The last time I met Kairamo was at that Christmas drinks party at my house, on the Thursday evening. On the Saturday he had set out alone for his place in the country, and on the Sunday he had hanged himself there. In the past he had suffered from depression and bipolar disorder. Now he left a suicide note, signed "Sick." But the situation at Nokia had certainly influenced his decision – the pressures on him were stacking up from every direction. And his troubled mind probably added to his problems by inventing other pressures out of thin air.

I was a different generation from Kairamo and also too serious and earnest for his inner circle. I lacked that sense of fun and spontaneity that Kairamo valued above all else, apart from intelligence in those close to him. So I had no feelings other than a great sense of emptiness when Matti Saarinen gave me the news of Kairamo's death. Besides, I tried to push all my feelings to one side because we would all have such an overwhelming amount to do in the following days.

A photo-shoot at Nokia's head office had been arranged for the following morning with the French magazine *Dynasteurs*. The interviews for the story had been done a while back. Now the photographer wanted to immortalize Kari Kairamo, some other senior figure, and me. While the photographer was setting up his lights and cameras in our head office, our press office was trying to write a press release, in all the major languages of the world, announcing that our chairman was dead. But no one could let the photographer know because it was still inside information. Only around midday did Nokia's press officer tell the photographer that one of his subjects had passed away.

"Our Chairman Kari Kairamo died suddenly at home as the consequence of a stroke in the early hours of Sunday morning. Despite this grievous loss we are continuing to work normally." This sanitized message, signed by the chief executive, Simo Vuorilehto, was sent to all Nokia's employees. But Finland's leading newspaper, *Helsingin Sanomat*, decided to release the news that Kari Kairamo's death was suicide. The private tragedy was now very public.

I sat for the photographer at 9 a.m., wearing a dark suit and a subdued tie. I looked more serious than I had ever looked before. My skin was gray. But

I sat for my portrait because it had been arranged – once again I performed the task I had been given. Inside my dark suit and my gray skin, however, I was trying to keep myself together. The picture appeared later in the French magazine; in it I appear to be smiling. I still don't understand how I could have contorted my features into a smile that day.

Altogether I worked with Kairamo for just under four years. His energy and his vigor made Nokia a special company, a place that attracted many talented people. The people Kairamo had brought into the organization made Nokia the company it became later.

Kairamo was not in any sense a business leader or a captain of industry. He was a leader, who could easily have led a political party, or become president of Finland or the head of some international organization. He knew how to bring people with him, and how to inspire and motivate them. Kari Kairamo was a great leader. He immersed himself deeply in key issues. He followed things through. He had a vision of Nokia's role in Europe. And although it didn't work out in practice, his vision was clear and correct. Kairamo believed in globalization and in specialization in high technology, which was rare in Finland in the 1980s.

Kairamo's legacy was a great help when Nokia became a global corporation in the 1990s. When he died my generation had to take enormous responsibility for the company. Our outlook was more international than our predecessors', but we didn't have much experience. These days I would scarcely allow such inexperienced individuals to make decisions on such big issues, as we had to.

A good leader has to have at least three qualities: competence, willpower, and a desire to work hard. Kari Kairamo had all these. I wasn't present at his funeral, which was a private affair, but I was told that a storm covered the mourners' cars with a thick white layer of snow, blew people's hats off, and made it almost impossible to walk. The whole church went dark with the force of the storm. That's the sort of man Kari Kairamo was – a snowstorm from Finland.

CHAPTER 25

Preparing to Lead

Simo Vuorilehto took over as chairman following Kairamo's death. It fell to him to lead Nokia through one of the most difficult periods in its history. The recession that was just beginning, and Nokia's overambitious program of acquisitions, threatened to engulf the company. Vuorilehto had to restructure Nokia ruthlessly in order to ensure that the company would survive.

The dramatic departure of Nokia's most senior figure left its mark on the company's workforce. It was a constant presence during Vuorilehto's three years at the helm. Kairamo's decision to commit suicide was the elephant in the meeting room, the cruel fact that everyone knew but no one would talk about. Vuorilehto's role was itself a daily reminder of it.

Suicide is ultimately a private human tragedy. The job of a chair or a chief executive is one of the loneliest the world can offer. I understood that only when I experienced it. Of course, Kairamo was pretty remote from most of us in his everyday routine at Nokia. But that didn't stop us silently asking ourselves questions: Could we have spotted something? Could we have done something?

I have often discussed the issue with my colleagues. Many of them felt that the atmosphere in the company took a turn for the better somewhere around 1992 or 1993. By then Nokia had an entirely new management team that wasn't so connected to the Kairamo era. Perhaps the regeneration of Nokia also demonstrated the company's strong internal culture. A weaker company could have lost its way completely after the suicide of a charismatic chairman.

The end of the 1980s saw me carrying out my daily agenda in Nokia's finance department. Companies were bought and sold, and there was also plenty to do in managing and organizing processes. Ambitious people in the 1980s ensured that they ticked the right boxes by managing profit centers and factories. The finance department was necessary, but not very interesting. Those who didn't make, sell, or invest anything might thrive there, but it wasn't regarded as a particularly exciting place.

When I became the finance director I decided to change things. I wanted the people in my department to value their work, and I wanted the best possible people to come and work there. And later I tried to help them take their careers forward, at Nokia and in the world beyond. At Citibank I had managed a few groups of finance specialists. Before that I had had no leadership experience to speak of. The finance department was my first real managerial position: twenty-five people answered to me. After my time in Nokia's finance department I was in charge of 2,000 people. And six years after that I was responsible for 50,000.

Leadership is largely a matter of communication, and the methods and channels one uses depend very much on the number of people you're managing. If you have lots of subordinates you have to consider how you can be certain of getting your message across to the whole organization. In the finance department I could tell everyone directly what was on my mind, and they could give me feedback directly. You can't do that with 50,000 people. So communication must be clear and carefully planned. This is the CEO's most important task: communication, communication, communication. The second important task is personnel policy: the CEO is always a company's most senior personnel manager. These two matters cannot be delegated to anyone.

It was with these two matters that I wanted to begin as Nokia's finance director. I explained to people that much would be expected from them, but also that good results would be rewarded. I put new people in new positions. Many of my appointments came as a surprise and caused a great deal of discussion within the company. I began to spring these surprises in Nokia's finance department, then in Nokia Mobile Phones, and I have followed the same policy as head of Nokia.

I enjoyed both the surprises and the discussion they caused. I seriously believe that an organization needs a regular shake-up in order to stay fresh and lively. One should give lots of responsibility and power to good people, perhaps three times more than they could imagine in their wildest dreams.

People who are trying their best shouldn't be punished for the odd mistake, but they must learn from every mistake they make. Every failure or error is a formidable packet of information that the company should be able to profit from. Not everyone is fond of my habit of regularly turning the organization upside down. For me, though, it's an instrument of leadership. It offers a means for as many people as possible to use as many of their skills as possible, and to learn many new ones. New tasks should be genuinely new. Individuals' learning processes enrich the whole company, but they enrich the individuals themselves even more.

I didn't know all this when I became finance director. Much of it I learned only much later. I have also sometimes made mistakes when recruiting people and appointing them to new positions, but I've tried to learn from that. In the finance department I wanted to extract from people as much energy for Nokia as I could. Because we needed to save money I couldn't take on many new people, but I concocted other ways of making us more effective. I decided to offer everyone in the department a home computer, paid for by the firm. In this way we were no longer tied to normal working hours. Parents who wanted to leave early to look after their children could work later at home. In those days the concept of remote working had hardly been invented, so our department was truly ahead of its time.

I started to transform Nokia's financial management in other respects. Together with my fellow director Kari Haavisto, I persuaded Nokia to adopt international accounting standards – the IAS. At that time this was an object of wonder, and we frequently found ourselves justifying it to our colleagues. We had agreed that, from that moment, Nokia would really be an international company. We had to comply with international accounting standards if international investors were to read our accounts and compare them with those of other firms. The old guard had a fit of the horrors, but Kari Kairamo was enthusiastic about it. By some inexplicable instinct he always chose the international alternative, if one was open to Nokia.

I have never had any time for conservative people. They dwell in the bureaucracies and on the boards of many a major enterprise. They believe that every little change threatens the entire heritage of the firm or, perhaps more to the point, their own desire for a comfortable life. Indeed, they often organize things so that the company serves them rather better than they serve it. Meeting such people can easily throw me into a rage. They simply can't comprehend that if the company does something new, it learns something new as well. After that every new thing becomes a little easier. Every company has its share of these intransigent people who do all they can to prevent every change or reform. But by adopting the international accounting standards Nokia moved up a league and also learned to think in a new way.

I set other reforms in motion, which rapidly brought financial results. Nokia's old system had channeled money to all the banks Nokia dealt with. As a former banker I decided to make the banks compete for our custom and so save money for Nokia. We created a system of strict financial controls whereby the different parts of the company had to take instructions from the head office. In this way we prevented Nokia from repeating the foreign exchange losses it had suffered in the early 1980s, when the dollar collapsed.

We established a finance company in Geneva whose function was to control all Nokia cash streams. This was a new idea that reduced the power of Nokia's business units but also made things simpler. It was just the sort of idea worth pushing forward when reorganizing a company. So of course it too met with vigorous opposition. The business units thought that Nokia's head office was grabbing power – they would no longer be able to lend or invest their own money freely. But it was exactly this freedom that had cost Nokia so dearly in payments to its bankers. I wanted to restrict that freedom and keep the money for Nokia. We thought our plans through very thoroughly, again with Kari Kairamo's support, before we moved the entire company's financial management to Geneva.

At the same time we focused our banking relationships on our main bankers, and we adopted the net principle: the net effect of each foreign exchange transaction was taken into account. In this way we no longer had to pay the banks interest on accounts that were in the red if on the same day another account was in the black. All Nokia's cash transactions were simplified and focused. In the finance department we were building a new Nokia: international, well-run, clear in its reports to international investors.

New ways of doing things call for new people to do them. I churned through staff in the finance department rather fast because I wanted the most talented people. Little by little I succeeded in my goal. When Olli-Pekka Kallasvuo came to us, other stars were not far behind. I wanted "my" stars to continue their trajectory way beyond my department. When I was transferred to a new job at Nokia, Olli-Pekka was promoted to be finance director. The role fitted him like a glove.

I constantly preached to people in the finance department about lifelong learning, new challenges, and new opportunities in Nokia. Pii Kotilainen was an excellent example. She had joined us a couple of years earlier, when she was about twenty-five years old, to work as a corporate dealer. Rather grandiosely I called her cubicle our dealing room. There might have been a couple of people working with her. But it was our nerve center, where we learned the business of the money markets. For me it was an important place because of my background in banking. I had learned to follow the markets, and I got energy from their rapid movement. I would disturb the work of the corporate dealers by phoning them and asking questions, which they would painfully attempt to answer. Pii was one of them; she told me later that I always rang when she was least ready to respond to anything.

When Pii had worked eight years in the finance department I summoned her to the CEO's office. She must have thought that Nokia's foreign exchange positions had collapsed, that her trades had failed, or that the final reckoning was due for some other reason. She couldn't have been more wrong. When she sat down on the dark brown sofa I asked her how much longer she intended to spend in the finance department. I proposed that she might become the head of training for the whole of Nokia. Her look of amazement was truly worth seeing. She didn't have a single day's experience of personnel matters, but she was a brilliant example of the ability to learn new things. She was one of many who moved from the finance department to other work and new challenges. That was my goal, and I was happy when I could achieve my goals.

CHAPTER 26

The Finance Director Hits the Shop Floor

UNTIL 1990 I WAS NOKIA'S MONEY MAN. I ran the firm's capital operations, I looked after the investors, the finance, and the company's head office, and I was also in charge of strategic planning. I watched over Nokia from the bridge, but I didn't know much about what life was like below deck. I knew very little about how the company developed, made, or marketed its products.

The new CEO, Simo Vuorilehto, tried to stop Nokia drifting and put it back on the right track. He was a very different leader from Kairamo: cautious, realistic, and stiff. He tried to simplify our corporate governance, for example, by doing away with internal committees, which he regarded as pointless.

One night in January 1990 Vuorilehto rang me at home and asked whether I would like to manage Nokia's mobile phone division. He must not have expected me to sign up there and then, because when I did he repeated his question in case I had misunderstood: was I sure I wanted to bring some order into that chaos? I told him I was up for it.

The mobile phone division had previously been run by Antti Lagerroos, who had long been another of Nokia's rising stars and a strong candidate to be the company's next CEO. But Lagerroos found himself on a collision course with Vuorilehto. In February 1990 Lagerroos left the company, and Kalle Isokallio was promoted to Nokia's second-in-command at Vuorilehto's suggestion. In April 1990 Nokia's supervisory board, which would soon become the board, chose Isokallio as the new president of Nokia. The deputy chairman, Jaakko Lassila, made the proposal because the chairman, Mika

Tiivola, was Isokallio's father-in-law and could be seen as having a conflict of interest.

Although I had spent my time at Nokia in the head office I knew a little about our mobile phone operation. I had had to chair a working group whose task was to rationalize Nokia's television and mobile phone manufacturing. We worked on this for about five months and suggested some restructuring and ways of improving productivity.

Nokia's mobile phones were manufactured in Salo in southwest Finland and Korea. There were historical reasons for this. Salo had long been a center for electronics, with Salora, which made televisions, the dominant company there. Nokia had set up a joint venture with Salora, called Mobira, back in 1979. The ethos at our plant in Salo was very different from that at the head office in Helsinki, where we wondered if we would ever get a grip on television production. We planned savings and new targets, but these never seemed to be met. When visitors to Salo from the head office left the factory to return to Helsinki, everything lapsed back to business, or lack of it, as usual. I suppose the new CEO wanted someone to straighten Salo out.

Nokia had made mobile phones since the 1970s. At its peak in the 1980s the Nokia-Mobira share of the world market had been 13 percent. Nokia had been particularly successful in the United States with the goods it sold using the Tandy brand name. But by the end of the 1980s Motorola dominated the market. In 1990 Motorola had 22 percent of the market, Nokia just 10 percent. It was clear who we had to beat in the mobile phone market.

Motorola had started a complex and time-consuming patent infringement case against Nokia in 1988. Motorola's aim seemed to be to prevent Nokia from entering the U.S. market (a commonly used competitive tactic). We settled the dispute and had to pay hefty damages in December 1989, just before I started in the mobile phone division. The damages, over ten million dollars, now seems pocket money compared to the amounts involved in such disputes today. But at the time it was a substantial sum, especially compared with the size and profitability of the mobile phone division. The incident didn't imbue us with friendly feelings toward Motorola.

Motorola was arrogant with good reason. They had good product development, a good brand, and the necessary capital. Nokia's mobile phone brand didn't exist then. The Nokia trademark had a long history, stretching back to the beginning of the 1900s, but it had nothing to do with mobile phones. At the end of the 1980s Nokia owned seven makes of television and two of mobile phones, all sporting national trademarks, but not one of them was "Nokia." Something had to be done about that.

In taking responsibility for the mobile phone division I was taking on a small unit that had three years of financial losses behind it, from 1987 to 1989. The mobile phone division's share of the company's total revenue was just one tenth in 1990. Nokia Mobile Phones was then like the start-ups of the 2010s – it had passion, intelligence, expertise, and gifted, hard-working people. But it wasn't systematic or efficient. Within the unit there were constant problems with both product development and production. My job was to establish whether mobile phones could become a profitable, productive area of activity.

Deep within Finnish society lurks a belief in heavy industry. The belief in the value of mobile phones was nowhere near universal, even within Nokia. Many believed that mobile phones were like televisions, in that only the Japanese were capable of manufacturing them profitably.

I drove the seventy miles from Helsinki to Salo, out toward the western coast. The road wandered through the Finnish countryside: woods, fields, water, and prosperous farmsteads. There was time to think on the hour's journey, but I also had to concentrate on the driving because traffic was heavy on that constricted road. I felt uneasy. There were some tough decisions to be made, which the workers at the factory wouldn't like at all. Even then Nokia's plant was among the largest in the small town of Salo. The boxy buildings housed labyrinthine production lines, which were not designed in the most efficient way, in so far as they were designed at all.

My appointment as manager of the mobile phone group gave the people at Salo every reason to fear the worst. I was the fourth manager in three years. If I had been a worker at Salo, I would have started to look for a new job as soon as I heard that finance director Jorma Ollila had been put in charge.

For me the factory was almost unearthly, although my father had worked in industry. As a boy I had told the world that factories would play no part in my future. As a student I had spent one summer in a factory, but since then about twenty years had passed, during which I had had nothing to do with industrial production. But now I was as involved as it was possible to be. I was a thirty-nine-year-old chartered engineer, an economist, a banker, and a former finance director who now had to learn how to run product development, manufacturing, and marketing. And if I didn't learn, there wouldn't be much of a future for me at Nokia.

I encountered considerable suspicion about the motives of Nokia's top management. It didn't reveal itself directly – no one said anything, there were no signs of rebellion. It was more dangerous than that – it took the form of a deep and icy silence. Finnish silence is famous, perhaps notorious

– but this went far beyond our famed reticence. When I went for the first time to address the employees at the plant, you could have heard a feather drop. They stared at the floor. They didn't ask any questions or offer any comment. But their fear was so palpable and real and so dense and overwhelming that I felt the factory could collapse into nothing, like a star falling in upon itself to form a black hole.

I had called a meeting in the largest room I could find. I talked, talked, talked, and talked some more. I used every positive word I honestly could. I told them this outfit would be knocked into shape and made to grow. I was open about Nokia's failings and admitted that the company had handled this area of its operations badly. "No one deserves to have four bosses in three years," I said. All this did little to reassure the employees – my employees. I kept on talking in the midst of a dismal silence.

"From this day on there is the prospect of growth and an attractive future. Now we must roll up our sleeves and get down to work," I concluded my speech. I believed what I had told my employees.

But I couldn't promise anything. It could all turn sourer still. Motorola might take over what was left of the market. A shortage of parts might cause our production to collapse. Or marketing mistakes could kill us. Nokia could decide to stop throwing good money after bad. And if anyone knew the state of Nokia's finances it was the company's former finance director – me.

I ascended from the factory floor to my office at the top floor of the building. I looked out on the western Finnish landscape and on the blocks built on the fields in the 1970s. The spring sun shone with unyielding clarity. My fingers drummed on my desk as I focused all my powers on getting to grips with this new job. I pondered briefly whether leaving the head office had been a mistake. I sighed from the bottom of my heart, but I'm glad to say there was no one to hear.

Within Nokia's mobile phone division there were of course various functions. The most important were product development, production, marketing, and human resources. Now Nokia's new products had to be better than its competitors'. And we had to make them more efficiently than our competitors made theirs. The whole division had to internationalize.

And we had to create a brand, Nokia's own brand. To succeed in this I needed the best people I could get for my own unit. Matti Alahuhta, a brilliant and highly analytical young manager, was going to look after product development. I had gotten to know Matti before the other key leaders in Nokia. We had gone to Vaasa High School at the same time, though Matti was a couple of years below me and I had only known him slightly.

The next time I met Matti was in 1985, when I started at Nokia. It was a joyful reunion. He worked in Nokia's telecommunications group and in the middle of the 1980s was promoted to leader of the Dedicated Networks business, which had been spun off from Mobira. Matti had begun his career in Nokia as a research engineer even before he graduated from the University of Technology in 1975. He had made a sideways move and become a sales director at Rank Xerox from 1982 to 1984, but had then come back to Nokia.

Matti had become an extremely reliable and results-oriented executive. You could put him into any situation and his analytical mind would not be flustered in the least. He combined the best aspects of a researcher and a business leader. And his sangfroid would never let you down. Matti joined the Nokia executive board in 1993 and continued there until 2004. In 2005 he moved to the elevator company Kone as CEO.

When I started in the mobile phone unit Matti was writing a dissertation at one of the world's best business schools, IMD in Switzerland. We had already agreed in principle that he would be my deputy in the mobile phone group. But the president of Nokia Telecommunications, Sakari Salminen, who had been coaching his designated successor in the telecommunications group, wasn't willing to let Matti go.

When I moved to the mobile phone unit I noticed that support from the head office was even more modest than had been agreed upon and promised beforehand. One day Nokia's resident eccentric, the usually good-humored Kalle Isokallio, called me to his office. There he moved about agitatedly and beat about the bush before he reached his point. He didn't make any of his characteristic wisecracks. "The way things are now, you'll have to cope there on your own," he finally managed to say. No apology, nothing about the breaking of a promise, no indication of support. I felt betrayed, but I kept my feelings to myself. I decided to roll up my sleeves and do the best I could with the hand I had been dealt.

I grabbed the young and gifted people I found at Salo. They would have key roles in the success story of Nokia mobile phones in the 1990s. Kaj Linden would be in charge of product development. The Global System for Mobile Communications (GSM) project was fragmented, and I gave Reijo Paajanen responsibility for sorting it out. Markku Alasaari had quietly moved from the telecommunications group to take charge of manufacturing. In addition I brought on board a quiet, balding man who wore round glasses. He was a thirty-three-year-old business graduate from Helsinki School of Economics, where he had been a researcher before coming to Nokia in 1984. Now he was in charge of Nokia's U.S. production. His name was Pekka Ala-Pietilä.

Pekka Ala-Pietilä comes from a small town north of Helsinki. He was born into a family of entrepreneurs and saw the joys and sorrows of business life from an early age. His grandfather was a timber carrier on one of Finland's largest lakes, and his father imported medical supplies to Finland. The roller-coaster that was the life of the small business owner convinced Pekka that a large firm might be a better place to work than a small one. He came to Nokia and stayed there. He started by selling Nokia's computer systems, but mobile phones were something quite new, and they attracted him as they attracted other forward-looking people at Nokia.

In the mobile phone division, then called Mobira, Pekka rapidly encountered new challenges. He went on study visits to possible new markets, travelling to post-Pinochet Chile and to Argentina, which was still a police state. Pekka brought calm analysis to the table. When I thumped my fist on the desk, demanded everything immediately and showed how impatient I could be, Pekka behaved like the tranquil surface of a Finnish lake. A stone might break the surface, but once the ripples had radiated away it would soon be calm and peaceful again.

Pekka is an analytical manager. We worked extremely well together – we were sufficiently different from one another, but we respected each other. Pekka is more philosophical in his approach. I, on the other hand, am always focused on practical achievement: I want quick results. We were united by our desire to achieve results and also a certain conceptual way of thinking: Pekka's analyses weren't the most rapid, but they usually hit the right spot. In meetings other people put their opinions forward before Pekka did, but things were usually done the way he thought they should be.

CHAPTER 27

Taking Production Seriously

A T NOKIA NO ONE SEEMED VERY INTERESTED IN PRODUCTION, at least it certainly didn't seem to interest Nokia's senior personages. These individuals would stay in a factory only for the moment it took to open a new production line in the glare of the cameras. Production had something dirty about it – it was physical work that didn't demand much attention, there was nothing dramatic about it, and you were hardly likely to get the press interested in a rearrangement of the production lines or the acquisition of new machinery. Business editors glazed over if you tried to talk to them about the details of production; they didn't want to understand. Nor were consumers interested in how their phones were manufactured as long as they worked. And if the phones didn't work, it was the chair or the marketing chief who got it in the neck, not the production manager.

I started by reading, as I always did. I read books, reports, descriptions of processes. I read at home in the evening, in the office in the mornings, and on Sunday nights in Nokia's Helsinki headquarters. In Salo, at the factory, I called Markku Alasaari, the production manager, to my room. I asked him to explain how the factory worked, how mobile phones were made. After that I asked all the key production people to talk me through the same things, one by one. I tried to ask simple questions. I learned about the role of material resource planning in production, about operations management. I learned what impact a certain machine made by Panasonic would have on our production line. (And I still understand it today.) I wanted to learn the language that production people spoke. It helped that I had an excellent memory, which would be extremely useful later on as well. I find it easy to remember numbers, names, abbreviations . . . everything, in fact, whether I need to or not.

Perhaps the most difficult issue, which I had to address pretty much as soon as I started the job, was to introduce a three-shift system. At Salo in 1990 all the work was still carried out in a single shift, and moving to a shift system aroused fierce opposition. I ran the project personally. Markku Alasaari held meetings where we were clear about what we were doing and why. Our competitors, such as Motorola, already operated a shift system at their most productive factories. We had to work more efficiently, too. I held frequent and informal meetings with the supervisor and trade union representatives. Through patient discussions we brought about a complete change in less than half a year.

Production was important in Salo because we had to bring our goods to market quickly, preferably according to a clear timetable, and faster than our competitors. We also had to design phones that we could be confident we could actually make. Our product development had risen to the challenge posed by Motorola: we developed a model with features that would ensure that we would beat our American competitors. It was an excellent piece of work, but we couldn't make it efficiently or profitably. My most important job now was to ensure that the demands of production were factored in at the planning stage.

Product development has always been one of Nokia's strengths. Nokia engineers were always proud of their ability to develop new ideas and apply them without preconceptions. There has always been a dash of madness in Nokia's genes – we believed that we could do things if other people could do them. This has never been too big a challenge for Nokia, but for some reason it was just this characteristic that got us completely bogged down at the factory. When Motorola announced its new model, Nokia's engineers were all over the place. We tried to respond in half a year, but our production lines weren't up to it and we sank even deeper into a quagmire. Not all Motorola's products were successful, but they were successful enough to drive us to the brink of panic. The production people were always the lowest caste in a thriving company, and at Nokia they were often regarded as failed product developers. So when senior management started to take production seriously the impact was immediate.

I went on to the shop floor once a month and the production line was stopped. I gathered the employees together to listen and tried to explain as openly as I could how things were going both in the company as a whole and at Salo. I listened to their complaints and considered their suggestions. I kept up my factory visits even when I became CEO and then chairman. The key thing was to develop relationships of trust with the local shop stewards. Lilja Laakso, the chief shop steward at the Salo plant, was especially supportive. Her rigorous but reasonable approach solved many problems as the factory grew and changes were set in motion.

I reached the age of forty in August 1990. I organized a small party at our home in Espoo, near Helsinki. I felt good. Liisa, my wife, regretted that Nokia was taking up ever more of my time. But we raised a glass of champagne to each other to mark the big day.

It seemed to me that I was a success in my new job. People had regained their self-confidence. The company's management was in good shape. Product development and production were marching in step. I had been driving to Salo several days a week, and during the journey I had time to think of everything I could possibly do to make things run better there. I must have seemed enviably, almost absurdly fit, and I made my staff feel guilty by advertising that I played tennis at seven in the morning before setting off for Salo.

We needed to move faster at Salo. Motorola was ahead of us all the time. Our acquisition of the British firm Technophone in March 1991 gave us a boost. Technophone was an important player in the U.S. car phone market. So with this acquisition we stealthily installed a tank on Motorola's front lawn. For some years customers bought phones under the brand name Technophone. It wasn't until 1995 that we started selling phones under the brand name Nokia in the United States.

The acquisition of Technophone was among Nokia's more important deals. Discussions had begun in 1990. The company was registered in the United Kingdom, but its founder was Nils Mårtenson, a Swede. Again I called on my Swedish friend Per Karlsson, who had helped me sell our tissue paper business. Per had visited our Salo plant in October 1990. After that visit Per organized a meeting in Stockholm for Kari-Pekka Wilska and me with Technophone's owners. The discussions were painfully slow. At some point in the evening Per said in his polite way that he would have been delighted to continue these gentlemanly discussions, but that very same evening he had to attend a meeting in Italy of the new board of the tissue paper company, Jamont. The discussions were suspended for thirty-six hours, but when they resumed we promptly reached an agreement.

We also had to get Nokia's senior management and board to give their blessing to the acquisition of Technophone. Per Karlsson and I went to discuss it with Kalle Isokallio. The asking price was 238 million markka ($76 million at 2016 prices). Isokallio stared for a moment at the calculations.

"OK," said Isokallio, "Jorma has made roughly this much for Nokia. So he has every right to spend the money." The deal had been accepted.

By buying Technophone Nokia gained a stronger position in the U.S. market: a larger market share, increased revenue, and a strong mobile phone brand. We would find out later what else we had taken on. Technophone's production capabilities were first rate. Behind them lay one man – Frank McGovern, who had made millions upon millions of dollars for Technophone's owners. This stocky, lively, Scottish engineer knew how to organize production lines and work processes to manufacture mobile phones with world-class efficiency. He wasn't a marketing man, he wasn't a product developer, but he knew how to run a plant to best effect.

Another major leap was our move to the English language. When we bought the British company Technophone, our middle managers had had to learn a new language and a new culture. In a small town factory this was a major change, even if the market had always been international. We prepared our presentations in English, we practiced thinking in English, and we tried to work out what our English-speaking customers were thinking.

In Salo the meetings held by my predecessors had been very long. Managers had spent days agonizing over strategy. I wanted an orderly and efficient management group whose members were keen to take personal responsibility for the areas they ran. I wanted to put the right people in the right places. In addition to production I wanted to focus on personnel.

For the important jobs I looked for people who radiated a quiet charisma. By that I don't mean brashness, bumptiousness, or self-centeredness, but some intangible quality that will win people over without their noticing it. And this quality includes a strong work ethic, a vision, and an ability to think.

There were very few European companies where young and inexperienced managers could rise so quickly to positions of responsibility; Nokia in the 1990s was one of these. Our employees in Finland developed a healthy self-respect. I used an overhead projector to show a slide to our management group comparing us to Motorola and announced that in the future we would be *Dynamic Champion.* We would beat Motorola. We started to speak openly about our strategy and objectives.

I wanted every single one of our workers to understand what these were. We didn't delude ourselves that each and every worker would become a true believer in our objectives. Sometimes I wasn't even sure myself where we might end up. But fortunately things started to happen. We were bringing products to market that would at last make us a serious challenger. The first of these was the mobile phone Nokia 101.

CHAPTER 28

The Miracle of the Mobile

IN 1991 OUR BIGGEST PROBLEM was to create a phone that would enable us to increase our market share globally. We wanted a mobile phone that would be light, functional, and that you could take anywhere. And if it looked good and was easy to use, then so much the better. At the beginning of the year we didn't have such a phone, but we would need to have a new phone on the market by the following January if we intended to survive. Everyone knew the company would stand or fall by the success or failure of its new phone.

A new and wonderful product doesn't spring into being overnight, or even over the course of twelve months. Behind its development, design, and testing lie many years and many people. Those people must have dedicated their lives to product development, technology, and innovation. For this they need the right sort of education to transform raw talent into ability. Fortunately Finland had the right sort of people with a good basic technical education.

Genius is the property of individuals, of course, but it shows itself best in a group that must meet a formidable challenge in a given time. The story of our new phone is an example of this. But to understand its development it's necessary to go back in time to its beginning, over forty years, and to the village of Meltaus, north of the Arctic Circle in Finnish Lapland, six hundred miles or more from Helsinki. The village has a school, a library, shops, and a bank. Two rivers converge there, which is presumably why people settled there in the distant past. The inhabitants make a living from agriculture, fishing, and tourism. In the summer the sun shines round the clock. In winter the days are very short – the sun just glimmers briefly on the horizon. Meltaus is cold, dark, and to many minds dreary.

Back in the 1970s the library in Meltaus was its cultural center. Day after day a ten-year-old boy went there, avid for every book on technology he could lay his hands on. He read the *Inventor's Handbook* a dozen times. He read every issue of the magazine *Technical World* until it was in shreds. Eventually he had read all the books in Meltaus library, at least all the reference books.

The boy's father had died when he was three. His mother was a teacher. He went to primary school in Meltaus and then to the sixth-form college in Rovaniemi, the capital of Lapland nearly fifty miles away. He dismantled and rebuilt every possible thing that ran on electricity. He constructed his own steam engine and electric guitar. In his hands every tool was made to work, and he understood mathematically how each device and mechanism worked. So it was the simplest thing in the world for him to go and study at Oulu University. Oulu is south of Rovaniemi, but even from there it's nearly four hundred miles to Helsinki. From the boy's viewpoint Helsinki, London, and New York were way over the horizon.

The young man rapidly mastered technology at Oulu University. He became interested in mobile phones because they contained new and exciting technologies. The students at Oulu University were enthusiastic about this small, new, and perhaps growing field. The young man got a place as a research assistant at Nokia, but before that he still had to complete his military service. Life is full of random events, he thought: a couple of years earlier he had tried to get a summer job at Nokia, but he hadn't been taken on then.

The young man, Pertti Korhonen, was Nokia's tenth employee in Oulu. First he completed his diploma work and then he became an expert on product development. He lived for his work. Sometimes his research team continued its work until two in the morning because in northern Finland the spring and summer evenings are so light. They couldn't bear to leave their work halfway through. And so they continued into the small hours because everything was new, interesting, and had something about it that they thought might change the world. When they did stop working they went to the sauna, did some more thinking, and then started again early in the morning.

The twenty-five-year-old Pertti Korhonen exuded expertise, even though he had only just graduated as an engineer. He was given the task of designing the integrated circuit systems for the base stations, even though he had never even seen an integrated circuit for a base station for a mobile phone network. He worked with the same enthusiasm as that little boy who had made himself an electric guitar and a steam engine.

Korhonen didn't know he was solving impossible problems. He only learned that later when one of the component manufacturers told him that he had thought the problem in question was insoluble.

Korhonen's solution was taken into production and stayed there for over ten years. Hundreds of millions of calls on mobile phones in different corners of the world went smoothly and reliably through the integrated circuits Korhonen had designed.

Success in this first project was an important lesson for Pertti Korhonen and his team. And it was a very simple lesson: nothing is impossible. People are the only animals that build themselves cages. Once something has been pronounced impossible, that's how it's likely to stay. Pertti Korhonen personified Nokia's core values in the 1990s – we did impossible things. We decided to change the path of history and to challenge those adversaries who seemed to us impossibly big and powerful.

In 1989 Pertti Korhonen encountered an adversary whom most people would have thought invincible. He held in his hand Motorola's new model of mobile phone. It was the first flip phone, which opened neatly to reveal its keypad. It was small, functional, and beautiful. Korhonen took the Motorola phone in his hand and swore. "Voi perkeleen perkele, voi helevetin helevetti!" he shouted once he was alone in his own office in the Oulu research unit – and Finnish swear words are at least as strong as English ones, and you can imagine a translation for yourself. His northern accent added something to his words, which already contained a lot of determination and much else besides. "And then when Motorola has its Iridium [a plan for a satellite phone offering global coverage] they will have everything sewn up . . . It's a tough job for a northern lad, if we want to get something done about it.

"What on earth can we do about it?"

Korhonen talked it through with himself. After that he took Motorola's wonder phone to bits and examined every component and circuit. He had to admit that Nokia's big American competitor had indeed made a marvelous phone.

Pertti Korhonen and his team decided to make an even finer phone. Its catalog number was the Nokia 101. All Nokia's best talents – in product development, in production, in design, and in marketing – were focused on this new product. It would establish Nokia as a brand. We bet Nokia's entire future on this new model of phone.

In January 1989 the project outline for the new 101 was agreed upon. Pertti Korhonen was in charge of the systems design. The European football championship was on in Italy. The star players were the Argentinian Diego

Maradona, England's Gary Lineker, and Italy's Salvatore Schillaci. I watch all sports avidly. At half-time I rang Korhonen, who was on holiday in Spain. I left a message on his answering machine and after a short while he called me back.

"Could you take over as product development manager?" I asked him.

"Bloody hell! Do you really think I'm up to it? Can you give me some time to think?" he asked.

"Of course I can. You can have until the end of this match," I said and hung up. Up till then I had met Korhonen just once, but I was sure he was the best possible person for the job. He decided to take it on. Later I got into the habit of asking him to take on difficult tasks.

Things didn't all run smoothly, however. The years 1990–91 were extremely difficult in financial terms. Nokia's cash reserves drained away. We had to save money everywhere. Product development was reorganized again. We cut back on foreign trips. Development of the new model was put on ice for the moment, but Pertti Korhonen seemed to take that in his stride. Later he told me he designed a phone in secret and on his own time after the order had come to suspend work.

Nothing would hold Korhonen back. His goal was to make the lightest mobile phone possible. He also wanted to double the length of time it could be used. Once again his engineers said it was an impossible challenge. He put the circuit diagram for Nokia's current model, the Cityman 100, under the microscope and reached the only possible conclusion: the number of components had to be halved. The engineers tore their hair out and declared that Korhonen was mad. But one summer night Korhonen and his team had an inspiration – they suddenly realized how the phone needed to be designed in order to meet all the requirements. It was like a religious experience: a thunderbolt from heaven. The problem had been solved.

Korhonen ordered components from subcontractors. ST Microelectronics made microcircuits; Korhonen recklessly asked for quotes for 100,000 or 200,000 at a time. The subcontractor thought he must be over-estimating. A few years later Korhonen received a souvenir from the subcontractor – because Nokia had ordered 10 million microcircuits for its phones.

Nokia's new phone was developed in the middle of a crisis in the market. In the past we had managed to sell moderately expensive phones to customers in the Nordic region. Car phones and the Cityman 100 were among our successes, but we hadn't gotten very far with cheaper models. Our phones were aimed at just a few market segments. We were still not a global operator, but now we had to become one. Motorola was bringing down its prices in the

United States. The Japanese had already arrived in Europe. Panasonic, NEC, and a gaggle of other companies were conquering markets where Nokia should have been dominant. The markets, and business activity in general, were in such a state of crisis that Nokia's future was in danger. Nokia might well have been a footnote in history: a company that made mobile phones for a brief moment before shrinking and dying. We all understood this, if only subconsciously, and it gave us the strength to go on living on the edge.

Microcircuits or technical properties were not enough to ensure the success of our phone. It also needed to look good, to be marketed brilliantly, and to be what the customers wanted. For the first time we were creating a product that would be bought by individuals all over the world, so we had to find out quickly what they really wanted. This job fell to Juha Pinomaa, a young product manager. He tried feverishly to learn what people hoped to get from their mobile phones.

Was the market really for such a miniature item? Was the timing right? How would customers react to a family of products with different models for consumer and for business use? Was our product development fast enough to respond to the hopes and expectations that our customer research revealed?

Pinomaa tried his best. He noticed that while we were designing our phone our competitors had changed the antennas of their phones. Now they were retractable, rather than built into the body of the device. We made a rapid shift, which must have given our engineers grey hairs. But our new phone got its retractable antenna because that was what the consumers seemed to want. For the first time our product development process had responded to signals coming directly from the market.

We developed a six-stage process for the introduction of a new product. At each stage we assessed how things looked: if they were satisfactory, we moved on to the next stage. For the first time this brought together product development, sourcing of components, and marketing. For the first time everyone involved was at the same table looking at the same product.

This was a revolutionary process for Nokia at the beginning of the 1990s. The same process, the same way of thinking, in stages from zero to five, became part of our way of doing things for many years. When I met the engineers designing our new phones in Salo they were using the same process. It was one of the most important factors in Nokia's success.

Once the Technophone deal was in the bag we needed to consolidate all our production and other European activities in the United Kingdom and Finland. One Sunday in September I rang Pertti Korhonen in Oulu.

"Do you want to move to England? To manage the next phase of product development?" I asked him.

"Can I have some time to think about it?" Korhonen replied. I said he had until the next day. He took up my offer, and from that November on Pertti Korhonen was responsible for everything to do with linking up our U.K. operations with those in Finland. Before that Pertti Korhonen had never worked abroad and had never managed a factory. He was twenty-nine when he started and he spent a year and a half in England. After that he was in charge of European production, and with his team made the Nokia 2110 phone a mass-production item. His work was excellent and he began to win a reputation as Nokia's finest problem solver.

CHAPTER 29

The Nokia Brand Is Born

I'M NOT A NATURAL PRODUCT DEVELOPMENT ENGINEER. On my own I'm not particularly creative, but I try to bring creativity into organizations and to provide opportunities for people who are creative. Nor am I especially skilled at marketing, so I decided I would also leave that to the experts. Kari-Pekka Wilska, head of sales and marketing, looked after all the marketing activities around the world better than anyone. But we needed some fresh energy as well if we were to turn Nokia into a global brand.

In autumn 1990 I invited three of the most important members of my staff to a meeting. Our organization needed more oomph. We needed to renew ourselves, to internationalize, and to generate some fresh ideas. I told the three men that I hoped they would take on staff more intelligent than themselves. These new managers might come from within Nokia, but it would be better if they were recruited externally. "Make sure that they're better than you at one thing, at the very least. Better still, at two," I said and looked at the startled managers. Two of them did start an enthusiastic hunt for "people smarter than themselves." That was how we found Anssi Vanjoki, who came to Nokia from his position as second-in-command at 3M's Finnish operation.

Six and a half feet tall, fair-haired, and with a booming voice, Anssi impressed me in a matter of minutes. He had a brilliant knack for bringing together the rational and the emotional sides of marketing. He had an analytical mind, but he also understood what might entice a customer to buy our products.

For some reason most of Nokia's successful managers came from Finland's smaller towns, and many from western Finland. More than a few came from an entrepreneurial background, or at least from a middle-class home. Many were active in the scouts or cadets during their school years.

Anssi Vanjoki met only some of these criteria. He had grown up in the suburbs of Finland's only major city, Helsinki. His father had spent his whole working life in Volkswagen's Finnish operation, where he had risen from humble general duties to become managing director. Anssi had not been top of the class at school, but he had spent all his time in the scouts and playing basketball. After graduating from Helsinki School of Economics in 1981 Anssi received four job offers; he accepted 3M's. In ten years he had risen to the number two position in Finland and had Europe-wide responsibilities.

In 1990 Anssi Vanjoki took a phone call from a headhunter, who wanted him to meet Kari-Pekka Wilska from Nokia to discuss a possible change of job. The two men met. Wilska asked Vanjoki how he could set about making him angry. Anssi Vanjoki must have succeeded in answering the question brilliantly, because Wilska offered him a job on the spot.

I met Anssi Vanjoki at Nokia's head office, on Helsinki's central Esplanade. I explained our alternatives to him: either we made something big out of mobile phones, or we sold them off. My own suggestion was that we should try to make something big from them. Vanjoki seemed convinced and decided to take up the new job at the beginning of January 1991.

Vanjoki made a circuit of Nokia's production facilities. Every day of his tour delivered new shocks to his system. He walked around inside our Salo plant. He compared Nokia's electronics manufacturing methods with 3M's and was clearly horrified. Something was badly wrong.

Production was dreadfully organized, the workers lolling around amid complete chaos, cigarettes drooping from their mouths. When the agitated Vanjoki left this factory, he rang his wife.

"I have made a terrible mistake. I should never have left 3M for this mess," he sighed into his Cityman 100, which resembled nothing more than a brick.

Anssi decided to stay with Nokia, however. He knocked sales and marketing into shape. But his greatest contribution lay in building Nokia as a brand. I asked him to arrange a "branding afternoon" – a brainstorming session to discuss how Nokia might be built up as a brand. This fired him up at once: this was one of the areas where he was expert, and one where he had self-confidence, which in later years we really came to appreciate. Anssi had become interested in brands as a student. He had studied Mercedes-Benz, Marlboro, and Nike and their history as brands. Each was the leader in its field. Finland didn't have a single internationally recognized brand to its name, with the possible exception of Marimekko. But even Marimekko was known only to a few select groups of discerning consumers.

Finnish industry was focused on the production of capital goods, intended not for individual consumers but for businesses. Indeed, one leading Finnish industrialist said that in Finland it wasn't worth producing anything smaller than a horse or that couldn't be bolted to the floor. Paper-making machinery certainly met these criteria; mobile phones, on the other hand, did not. Even so we were convinced it was worth giving phones a go. And if we didn't succeed in creating a strong brand there was no future for us in the world market.

At our branding afternoon Anssi Vanjoki explained that it would be better for Nokia to focus on a single brand name rather than the plethora of trademarks then in use. Some people thought the only hope for Nokia would be to design and manufacture mobile phones as a sub-contractor to other manufacturers: Nokia didn't have what it took to create its own brand. That would have been the easy way out. Surprisingly many people at Nokia wanted to take it. If we had Nokia would have ultimately become the same sort of manufacturer as many Chinese and Taiwanese firms are today – they make products anonymously for Nokia and other brands.

The people at that meeting sat on the edge of their seats as Anssi ran through his presentation. Many were gripped by dread. They thought Ollila and Vanjoki must be mad. Nokia, which had only recently emerged from the Finnish forests, could surely never become something that one might mention in the same breath as Mercedes-Benz. But in true Finnish style those dissidents were silent and waited to see how we would stumble in implementing our megalomaniac ideas.

After our seminar I asked Anssi Vanjoki to develop Nokia's first brand strategy. He also opened tendering discussions with international advertising agencies.

We decided that from now on our brand would be simply "Nokia." The only exception would be the British mobile phone company Technophone, which we had bought. But apart from that we would use no name other than Nokia. Anssi argued forcefully for this decision. When it had been made Anssi became the key strategist of the Nokia brand, which had five dimensions: high technology, Nordic touch, individuality, freedom, and lasting quality.

But what should the new phone look like? What shape should it be? What sort of phone would customers be eager to buy? Could a mobile phone be some color other than black? We found ourselves in a world where everything was possible, but where we didn't know what would work. Fortunately we found Frank Nuovo.

The designer Frank Nuovo had worked for Nokia since 1987 through the company Designworks. It was Pekka Ala-Pietilä who "found" him. Our new mobile phone was the first that Frank Nuovo designed. After that there would be many more. We took design seriously. We believed that a phone's external appearance and the user's experience of using it would be critical in the consumer market. The Finns also had a good sense of design. We were known for our architecture, our glassware, Marimekko textiles, and other classics of industrial design. We tended to take design seriously, both as a matter of natural professionalism and because it had brought us our earlier success and helped put us on the map.

Frank Nuovo's family was originally Italian, but he himself was thoroughly American, a child of the West Coast. He was born in Monterey, California. His approach brought sun, a sea breeze, and warmth to our projects, which were born almost literally in our time of kaamos – the long winter night when the sun doesn't rise for weeks in northern Finland. Nuovo gained his inspiration from the play of the waves of the warm Pacific Ocean on the rocky shores of the West Coast. Finnish snow, ice, darkness, and coldness must have been a culture shock for him, though one that he politely kept to himself.

We didn't of course want design for design's sake. We were going head-to-head with Motorola over which of us would produce the iconic mobile phone. Fortunately, Anssi Vanjoki, of our marketing group, and Jyrki Salminen, our head of marketing, understood the nature of this battle. They had seen how Motorola had already succeeded in making its flip phone an iconic product. We couldn't take that away from Motorola, so we had to come up with something new. We wanted to plant in consumers' minds the idea that Nokia made the iconic mobile, that a Nokia is what a mobile should be.

In winter 1991 Frank Nuovo travelled from balmy California to Salo, which was up to its knees in snow, slush, and ice. In his summer clothes he waded across the snowy yard to the meeting room. He had with him a large and interesting travelling bag, and he spread its contents out over the meeting room table. Juha Pinomaa, the product manager, gazed at them dumbstruck. He invited the others to take a look at what Frank had brought. The table was a sea of color, every possible color: violets, reds, bright greens, whites. They were colored casings, the first colored casings ever made for mobile phones.

The realization that mobile phones need not all be black had struck our team in a meeting a short time earlier. They had been standing around a table on which they had all put their phones down. Suddenly someone's phone started to ring, and no one knew whose phone was. After all, there had probably never been so many mobile phones in one place before.

"If only there was a way of telling them apart. If only there was a way of seeing which one was yours," someone said. "Aha," Pekka Ala-Pietilä replied. Everybody knew that when Pekka said "aha" he was on to something. Usually, too, his ideas were pretty good. He realized now that mobile phones might be different colors.

Our marketing people had quite an argument about the colors, to the point where discussion broke down. No one had a clue which colors might work. Nuovo gathered up the colorful models and put them back in his bag. Anssi Vanjoki asked Juha Pinomaa to choose just a few examples for the next meeting, which would take place in Helsinki in the summer. There the discussion continued. Many customers had said they would like a white phone, but fortunately we were on our guard: white phones had already appeared in the shops, but customers hadn't bought them. We wanted more women customers, but a white phone combined with lipstick stains wasn't really part of our design.

Finally Anssi Vanjoki, our master of branding, decided that our new phone would be made available in two colors, green and grey. The back of the phone would always be charcoal gray, so all our phones could be switched between two colors by removing one colored casing and replacing it with the other.

A new era had begun – the mobile phone was black no more. The customer could choose. The mobile phone was no longer merely a dull utensil but a way to show your individuality and to send out messages about yourself. After this nothing would ever be the same in the development of mobile phones.

Anssi Vanjoki began work on a revolutionary marketing operation. We didn't have much money to spend, however, at least not compared to our competitors. One of Anssi's most brilliant ideas was to buy little advertisements on the most boring pages of the financial press. Readers of the *Wall Street Journal* who turned to the stock exchange reports suddenly found themselves staring at a strange new phenomenon: the Nokia name and brand. American readers had a ready explanation for this: yet another Japanese company was trying to infiltrate the consciousness of American consumers. That didn't bother us at all.

An international PR agency had recommended that Nokia carry out a huge advertising campaign to take its products direct to the consumer. Anssi

Vanjoki, stubborn as ever, had kept his head and concentrated on the quality press and CNN, which was a favorite of business leaders. There Nokia's adverts hit decision-makers in the morning, just after they had woken up. Anssi Vanjoki loved to gamble, and he had placed Nokia's modest marketing money on the winning number.

Nokia's market share began to rise, especially among consumers with high incomes. From them the news about our phone began to spread to people who aspired to high incomes. The result was brilliant: our share grew in all market segments. Then the news began to spread by word of mouth. After that we needed much less money for marketing. We did all this against the advice of every advertising and media agency.

Earlier our products had been packed into off-putting brown boxes, whose only embellishment was a bar code on the bright yellow base. Every other manufacturer's phones were packed "bloody colorfully" as Anssi put it. All the others had understood years before us what would work with customers.

Anssi Vanjoki made a study of the cosmetics shelves of shops. He found a shampoo that was called simply "Extremely Fine Finnish Shampoo" (in Finnish, of course). It came in a plain and simple blue bottle, but nonetheless it practically jumped off the shelf. Anssi decided that Nokia would have two colors, blue and green. They were the colors Nokia used for its packaging for over a decade.

As well as Finnish cosmetics shelves Anssi studied Japanese cameras. For many years these had had a "quality mark" – a little sticker that said "passed." Our marketing people wondered what we might be able to come up with. We briefly considered the word *Suomi* (*Finland*), but at that time the signal it sent out seemed more negative than positive. So we decided to stick a little label with "Nordic" on it on to our phones, because Nordic values seemed good. They embodied clarity, naturalness, good design. But we quickly realized that the "Nordic sticker" didn't do much to improve our sales or our brand, let alone help us create an identity. We were ready to stand on our own two feet as simply Nokia.

We had a very simple goal for our television advertising: we wanted the viewers to think "Nokia" whenever there was any mention of a mobile phone. We ran a campaign showing life before and after Nokia. Life before was really grim – a despondent figure reminiscent of James Dean wandered gloomy streets in search of adventure. In the next sequence the same young man talked into a Nokia phone, smiled, and the whole world turned bright. We wanted to touch everyone on earth, we wanted everyone to talk to one another, and to smile.

I tried my best to spur people along. I gave good people plenty of space. Because our budgets were so small compared to our competitors', I had to encourage people to take risks and use their imaginations. I regularly took part in the meetings of the project group. There I emphasized that phones had to be easy to make. I wanted to get rid of the silo mentality of marketing, product development, production, and the procurement of components. Every member of the project group should be ready to talk about the issues that worried them. I learned a great deal from this. Our group was committed to a common goal and a common timetable.

CHAPTER 30

A Telephone in an Envelope

THE OUTLOOK FOR THE MOBILE PHONE GROUP seemed much brighter than when I'd taken it over at the beginning of 1990. But Nokia Mobile Phones was not in a position of great strength within the larger company.

The highly respected Boston Consulting Group had carried out a study in the early autumn of 1991 in which it tried to analyze which business areas Nokia should focus on and which it should withdraw from. The study had been commissioned by Tapio Hintikka, the head of planning, and Kalle Iso-kallio, the chief executive. The consultants visited us and interviewed many of my key executives, though they didn't interview me.

The result was a very broadly based report, a great pile of useless paper-work, to be frank. The consultants affirmed that mobile phones were a prom-ising area of business. But Nokia didn't have the capacity to compete effec-tively with Motorola or Japanese manufacturers. Nor were the mobile phone division's leadership resources adequate. This wasn't a particularly comfort-ing assessment, since those resources consisted of me and my management team. The consultants' view of Nokia's future was generally dire: the company could not hope to succeed globally in any of the areas where it was active.

This report didn't generate any follow-up activity at Nokia. The situation at the head office was inflamed, with the double-headed leadership scarcely on speaking terms. I don't know much more than that about the background. I understand the report was buried because the cautious chairman Simo Vuorilehto didn't accept the consultants' views.

About ten years later I received a visitor from the United States, the chief executive of the Boston Consulting Group. I have rarely had a conversation with an individual so ready to admit that his firm had got things wrong. The apology just came flooding out; the man who made it must have spent the whole long flight over the Atlantic working out what to say.

This example shows that one cannot run a company by blindly trusting what consultants have to say. Though it can be useful to have external opinions, either for or against, senior managers must have their own clear policies.

Meanwhile at Salo the product development experts were preoccupied with more concrete matters. Could a telephone fit into an envelope? Could a telephone fit into a pocket, really? Could the battery of a telephone last several hours without recharging? We had to bring a winning product to market.

By the end of 1991 we knew we were on to a winner. The new phone, the 101, had wonderful features. It was small, much smaller than our earlier models. The world's

The Nokia 101

first GSM call was made on 1 July 1991, when former Prime Minister Harri Holkeri rang the deputy mayor of Tampere, Kaarina Suonio. The 101 was an analog phone, operating according to three different mobile phone standards: NMT, AMPS, and TACS. That gave us immediate access to the US, European, and Asian markets. And the TACS standard also opened the door to the U.K. market. (The phone's digital sister was launched in autumn 1992.)

The 101 was ready at the end of 1991, and we decided to announce it on 9 January at Nokia's Helsinki headquarters. We invited about ten economic journalists from Finnish newspapers. Our publicity department had worked far into the night and had come up with an inspired idea. They had made little cardboard mock-ups of the new phone and popped them into envelopes. The bemused journalists each had in front of them a cup of coffee, a bun, and an envelope. When I told them they could, the journalists opened the packet and saw for themselves that a phone could fit inside an envelope – for the first time in the history of the world. We made the impression we wanted: the journalists were amazed, even if they'd have found it difficult to make a call on a cardboard phone.

The original 101 came in just two colors: graphite gray and green. Its buttons didn't twinkle in the dark like the lights of Las Vegas. It didn't have a radio, thermometer, or camera. But it was an effective and reliable mobile phone that sold well everywhere. It weighed just 9.7 ounces, which made it the lightest you could buy. Its batteries were the best available and the longest-lasting. And it looked good. Without it we would never have achieved our great successes later in the 1990s. The 101 was the Model T Ford of our time: it took mobile phone production out of the workshop and into the factory. It was a mobile phone that we could churn out in vast quantities and so gain the advantages of mass production. And it gave a foretaste of Nokia's design language.

I did well at the press conference. I had all the facts and details at my fingertips, as I usually do. Fortunately none of the journalists asked aggressive questions about Nokia's future leadership. At that press conference I knew that six days later my appointment as chief executive would be announced, so my head was already spinning with all sorts of issues above and beyond the launch of the latest mobile. A couple of days before the press conference I had jotted down on a couple of sheets of paper my ideas on how we could save Nokia. The plan was audacious, very short, and, should the worst happen, wrong. But I believed in it completely.

Nokia had drifted into ever more troubled waters for the whole of the year just gone by: the banks had turned off the taps as far as further credit was concerned and revoked their existing credit limits. The finance director, Olli-Pekka Kallasvuo, had travelled the world to get more capital wherever it was to be had, but every time he came back to Finland he was grayer and more depressed.

After the Helsinki press conference I flew to Stockholm to talk about our new model there. The Swedish journalists were aggressive in their usual way. They asked why Nokia wanted to launch an old-fashioned NMT phone when Ericsson's forthcoming model would use the new GSM technology. This grilling didn't feel good, for I sensed an undercurrent of Finnish-Swedish rivalry.

Somehow I got through the press conference, but it was an uncomfortable experience. The fact was that Ericsson was far too early in trying to exploit the new technology. Nokia sold its "old-fashioned" phones at least until 1994. Model 101 kept our factories going through our darkest years. And I learned that you should never offer people new technology before they're ready for it. It's not worth it: you can't teach your customers; what you have to do is listen to them very carefully. I understood, though, that we had to be in a position to launch a good GSM phone as soon as we could.

We had now brought Nokia's mobile phone business back into the black after three years of losses. But there was still a long journey ahead before we achieved real growth. The 101 was a great help in this, and it was a success story for many years. This one phone carried our entire business a long way. In 1992 its share of our total mobile phone sales was 28 percent and the following year 22 percent. This one product in its various versions was Nokia's bread and butter just then.

One of my last duties while I was in charge of the mobile phone division, just four days or so before my new appointment was announced, was to host a visit by the local press to the Salo factory. We had arranged to give the chief editors and other journalists a presentation on the mobile phone market. This would be followed by drinks, a sauna, and supper. In those days Finns often looked after our communications and marketing in the sauna, and Nokia was no exception. Indeed, in earlier times executives would often go to the sauna during the day, but happily those times were already behind us.

On this occasion I didn't have time to linger in the sauna. Instead I would set out my thoughts on the mobile phone industry in a series of slides using an overhead projector. But the projector wasn't working because our communications chief, Lauri Kivinen, had forgotten to check it beforehand. "Doesn't anything work around here?" I shouted at the terrified Kivinen. After that he learned to check the equipment in advance. The local newspaper editor who happened to be in the room was a little startled at my volcanic reaction. My new duties were already pressing down on me.

Nokia's board asked me who should succeed me as the manager of the mobile phone division. I told them that wasn't an easy question and that I would need at least two months to mull it over. I thought hard and long, until the answer was clear to me. March 1992 Pekka Ala-Pietilä would take charge of Nokia's mobile phone operations. Pekka, who was then thirty-five, didn't really have any experience of running a major operation. He wasn't overly bubbly or full of himself. His appointment was one of my bigger risks. But I was used to trusting my intuition, and that now told me that Pekka could grow into the job. The first six months were difficult, but after that everyone saw I had been right. The choice was of course a surprise; some people in the mobile phone group imagined they had a right to that job. But it was perhaps Pekka who was the most surprised. I heard it in his voice when I called him.

"Can you give me till the morning to think it over?" Pekka replied. Later he told me he had spent a sleepless night and had talked it through with Tiina, his wife. In the morning he took on the biggest challenge of his life.

My time in charge of mobile phones had been difficult but rewarding. We had played as a team and made a crucial breakthrough. We had shown that mobile phones could be designed and manufactured profitably in Finland. We had created new ways of working, which Nokia would exploit in the future. Now the role of chief executive awaited me. It would be full of solitude, responsibility, and unrelenting publicity that would often be exaggerated and unfair.

CHAPTER 31

An Offer and a Reply

I WAS FORTY-ONE, HAPPILY MARRIED, AND A FATHER OF THREE. I had learned my own strengths and weaknesses. I knew I could run a company. Now I had been offered the role of Nokia's chief executive, and I wouldn't get a second chance like this at Nokia. The company was a catastrophe. There were only two ways it could go: either it would be knocked into shape, or it would be sold off bit by bit. And that would be the end of over a hundred years of Finnish industrial history and expertise.

For a year or more before I took over there had been speculation that Nokia might be sold. Informal discussions had begun in March 1991 with a view to preparing Nokia for sale to Ericsson. The banks that owned most of Nokia led the way. But they too were in a bad way because Finland faced the worst recession of any western European country in more than forty years.

In practice, preparations for Nokia's sale to Ericsson were in the hands of a small group of corporate investors. The man who was behind it was Casimir Ehrnrooth, one of Finland's most influential industrialists and also a member of the Nokia board of directors. He was well known to Ericsson's Swedish owners and would play an important role at Nokia in the next few years.

In spring 1991 it seemed practically certain that Nokia would be sold to Ericsson. Discussions took place in a positive spirit. The aim was to conclude the matter by the autumn; the Finnish banks had a great deal to worry about at that time and would welcome having one of their burdens lifted.

The tenth of October was the deadline for Ericsson to reply to the group that had prepared the sale of Nokia. I was told that they gathered in the offices of an insurance company in the center of Helsinki. There they waited around the table for the conference call bringing final confirmation from Stockholm. But when the call came it brought bad news: while Ericsson had been interested in Nokia, it had decided that the consumer electronics division, which was losing money, posed too great a risk. The price was too high to cover the risk, so Ericsson would not buy Nokia after all. The investment bankers were first stunned and then deeply disappointed.

Ericsson made its decision for sound reasons. But the company's top management clearly didn't understand the impact their decision would have on the telecommunications industry, or indeed on their own position. There's nothing unusual about that: such decisions are often made pretty much by chance, and only later are reasons found to justify them.

I personally took no part in these discussions since I was still running the mobile phone division in Salo. My enthusiasm had proved infectious: people now tried to beat their previous achievements and our growth targets. Nokia was still a small player in the mobile phone market compared to, say, Motorola, but our fighting spirit was on the march, fortified by our results so far.

It must have been around late October that discussions started on whether I would be a suitable candidate for the job of Nokia's chief executive. These mostly took place in the private dining room of Yhdyspankki, one of Finland's two big banks. I don't know exactly who came up with my name, but certainly Casimir Ehrnrooth, the bank's chairman Ahti Hirvonen, and its senior banker Björn Wahlroos were involved. Later I was told that no other internal candidates were discussed.

My boss, Nokia's CEO Simo Vuorilehto, summoned me to his office one day in November to tell me I was in the frame to be Nokia's new chief executive. He was ready to retire before his contract came to an end; his relationship with the company president, Kalle Isokallio, was poor. Vuorilehto wanted Isokallio to step down as Nokia's second-in-command.

I reported this conversation to Liisa. Her reaction was horror rather than delight, but she was ready to support me. Taking on this new role was a personal risk. When I asked Liisa if I should accept the challenge, her answer was clear: "Of course you should." But we both knew that if things went badly my fall would be precipitous. Failure as Nokia's chief executive would have been a very black mark at a time when Finland's job market had all but closed down.

Things went forward. I had a meeting with a bank chairman, who asked me what I thought should be done with Nokia. I told him, and he made a note of my thoughts on a large notepad. I also discussed my future with Per Karlsson. I had gotten to know Per well, and I trusted his analytical abilities.

We met in London in mid-December and had an English breakfast at the Capitol Hotel, which was my favorite, when I told him that I'd been invited to take over at Nokia. He was stunned.

"Well, that's something that only happens once in a lifetime. You have to take it, of course. But you must also discuss things very carefully with Liisa," Per said seriously.

After breakfast I walked from the hotel to my car. I had to drive to Camberley, where we had a mobile phone factory. As I drove I thought that nobody would say to me: "Don't take that job!" I had to take it. That's certainly what I thought myself, but I also wanted to think through all the less appealing options. There weren't many people I could discuss these with, but the conversations I did have made me all the more determined to take the new job.

There were some skeptical views. I discussed the offer with my old friend Pentti Kouri. He understood the state Nokia was in since he had joined the board a year before. Kouri kicked the idea around and analyzed Nokia's situation and the risks associated with becoming its chief executive in a very personal way. "Is there anything in this for you?" was the question that summed up his view.

At the end of November I took a call from Casimir Ehrnrooth. We had met very briefly on a few occasions, but I couldn't really say I knew him. He suggested a meeting, which started a collaboration at Nokia that lasted nearly a decade. Ehrnrooth wanted to know whether I was interested in becoming the chief executive of Nokia and what I thought should be done with the company. We met on 30 December in an office overlooking Helsinki's Old Church. There was still no snow in the churchyard. The tombstones of the plague victims buried there appeared as dark shadows against the ground, while the trees seemed even darker and more threatening. The impression was radiant in a way only a deep Finnish winter can be.

Casimir Ehrnrooth was accompanied by another board member, the chief executive of the Pohjola insurance company Yrjö Niskanen. My two bosses-to-be presented me officially with the question: "Are you ready to accept the position of chief executive of Nokia?" When I had officially answered that I was, our conversation began. In breaks between drinking coffee we discussed how Nokia had gotten into its current state and what might be done about it. We agreed that I would do some serious thinking about Nokia's future. I promised to prepare a presentation for them in the New Year.

I did have some thoughts, or rather one thought. While my discussions over the new job were going on I was also working on my vision with Olli-Pekka Kallasvuo. We sat around in the New Year and drafted a short paper, which was extremely simple. The message was clear: Nokia had to focus on mobile phones, telecommunications, and cables, and it had to add value for its shareholders.

Everything else should follow from that. In practice this meant that Nokia had to move out of many areas. It was a radical but simple idea. Such ideas are often the best.

When I look again at that two-page report, I am still unashamedly proud of it. Of course I didn't predict the entire future correctly –some of the details came closer to reality than others. But I could put something very similar forward again with a clear conscience.

My view was that the company should examine at once whether it could sell off the whole consumer electronics operation. If that wasn't possible, I put forward a model for a joint venture that would guarantee it could be sold later.

Cable manufacture was one of Nokia's oldest areas of business and very much part of its history. Nokia had made cables since the 1920s, and until 1991 that had been its most profitable division. It didn't make a profit in 1992, but at least it brought in more money than the budget forecast. I thought the cable business was worth pursuing, though this turned out to be a misjudgment. The cable industry was languishing across Europe, and we sold the division later in the decade.

Finland was sinking into an economic depression. The Soviet Union was crumbling; indeed it had formally ceased to exist four days before I accepted the new job. It had been an important trading partner for Nokia, a stable and lucrative source of income. The break-up had a serious effect on the telecommunications and cable divisions in particular.

Between January and May 1992 Nokia's losses amounted to around 200 million markka (about $62 million at 2016 prices). Only its mobile phones and basic industry divisions were clearly making a profit. The losses had worsened from the previous year, and revenue was down compared to both the previous year and the budget. The figures confirmed the impression that the whole company was in a tailspin.

In my report I suggested that mobile phone networks would be the investment of the future. I didn't, however, believe that Nokia could go it alone; I thought that it needed to consider alliances with other companies. On mobile phones I wrote the following sentences, which I'm still proud of: "Mobile phones are a central focus, which there is no reason even to consider relinquishing. At the very least our aim should be to maintain the group's current position globally."

I had myself been in charge of the mobile phone division from 1990 to 1992, and I knew that we could achieve results. I knew the employees at our Salo development center and plant were motivated and keen to make a world champion of Nokia. I didn't of course know that ten years after I wrote that paper Nokia would command 40 percent of the global mobile market – or indeed how big that market would be. That could scarcely have been predicted. Nor would I have dared put a bet on it myself back in 1992.

If the Nokia of 1992 had a core business it was tire production. We had given up paper manufacture some time earlier, and I had been actively involved in that decision. In my own report I proposed divesting ourselves of our core business as well. And we did, though not until 1994, when Nokia Tyres was sold off and listed on the Helsinki Stock Exchange. It's become an extremely successful company.

The report was ready for 3 January, when I met Casimir Ehrnrooth and Yrjö Niskanen again. At that meeting I learned how much I would be offered to take on the role of CEO. We also dealt with some other practical matters. I had one request for my new bosses: I wanted complete freedom in choosing my staff. Ehrnrooth and Niskanen agreed without demur. My report was put into final form a few days later and Nokia's board discussed it when they met on 16 January.

Even now I don't really know how I found the self-confidence to write that two-page report. I only knew that something had to be done. Money should flow from companies to their owners, not the other way round. Lines of responsibility should be simple. The company's values and a new leadership team should be established on that basis. And there wasn't a moment to waste.

The day before the crucial meeting I met the investment banker Björn Wahlroos. He told me all about the previous year's discussions on the ownership of the company. When the proposed sale to Ericsson had collapsed, one bank's shareholder group had come up with an alternative. The idea was that some of the shareholders would have Nokia delisted from the stock exchange by buying out its shares. The debt arising from this purchase would have been passed to Nokia for payment. In this way Nokia would have become a private company. I had no experience with private companies. I had only worked in Citibank, which was a big firm listed on the stock exchange. After that I had moved to Nokia, also a listed company, though not one that brought much joy to its shareholders in the difficult years at the end of the 1980s and beginning of the 1990s.

Ultimately Nokia's auditors refused to allow this arrangement. It's hard to say if Nokia would have survived as a private company owned by one banking group. It was much easier to measure Nokia against its targets if it were a listed company. The markets are merciless and put a price on our capabilities every single day. I'm not sure if a private owner would have been ready for that enormous changes we were compelled to make in order for our value on the stock exchange to rise. These are difficult questions to which there really is no final answer. At the beginning of 1992 we knew only that Nokia was a public company and would stay that way.

The board made the formal decision to appoint me at its meeting on 16 January. The company would now have just one leader. Kalle Isokallio left Nokia at once, and Simo Vuorilehto would stand down from his roles as chief executive and chairman of the executive board as of 1 June, when I would take on the latter role as well. Chairman of the Board Mika Tiivola also submitted his resignation, and Casimir Ehrnrooth was elected in his place at a general meeting on 2 April.

Rumors that Nokia would be broken up continued after my appointment. Indeed in some parts of the media the rumors intensified. My banking background was used against me in their stories. Because I crunched numbers and determined what the company was worth, it followed that my job was to slice Nokia up and sell the bits off to the highest bidders. And there would be those who understood Nokia's value and would want to buy.

And there were those who sold. Around that time one of Finland's two big banks made the worst trades in its history by selling its shares in Nokia. Ten years later those shares were worth many times what the bank had sold them for.

PART III

MASTERS
OF THE UNIVERSE

CHAPTER 32

Life as a Chief Executive

MY JOB AS NOKIA'S CHIEF EXECUTIVE demanded absolute commitment. I always had Nokia's latest model of mobile phone, and it was always switched on, even at night. You may, if you wished, detect a dark irony in the fact that I dedicated my career to promoting products that ensure that senior business executives, myself included, are never off duty.

Wireless communications have also made senior executives lives much easier, made work more efficient, and enabled the freedom of movement that executives have always aimed for. The evolution of working habits that began in the early 1990s and is still going on today is truly remarkable. These days you don't need to go the office to get your work done.

When I accepted the job, I knew what was coming. For summer holidays I would snatch a few days or maybe a week; around Christmas and the New Year I might even take ten days. I tried to keep Saturdays for my family, and we'd often spend time together at our summer cottage in Orivesi. By Sunday morning it was back to my desk to start preparing my agenda for the following week.

My diary filled up several months ahead. If I wanted time for free discussion or an unscheduled meeting with my senior managers the options were seven o'clock in the morning, late in the evening, or on Sunday. I usually went into the office between three and five on Sunday afternoons and stayed there long into the evening. Often on Sunday evenings I'd set off on a business trip. Conference calls and other forms of remote working that would later make life easier were still in their infancy.

In my first few months I carried out my duties as my secretaries programmed me to do. My diary was full of meetings with investors and banks and with the company's obligatory internal meetings. Days quickly fill up with such meetings unless you take care to avoid them. Time is the most valuable resource of all, and you can waste it on all the wrong things. I still didn't have any experience of what it really meant to work as a company's chief executive. Every incoming CEO has to start with the processes and projects inherited from his predecessor.

Only in June 1992 did I start to run according to my own timetable and bring my own teams together. I started to actively influence Nokia's strategy. My feet were now back firmly on the ground after months when I had struggled just to keep things going one day at a time. I gave myself body and soul so that Nokia would stay alive. While I managed to sleep at night, when summer 1992 finally arrived I was utterly exhausted. The company's board were worried about me, and the following year they compelled me to take a proper holiday.

Back in 1992 Nokia suffered a lack of self-confidence, though by Finnish standards the company was pretty lively internationally. Its success however had remained modest. Its major European acquisitions were losing money: Nokia was withdrawing from international markets like a defeated army leaving the battlefield to tend its wounds. Battle-weariness was all around, and we had to rebuild our self-confidence from scratch.

Because we didn't have much confidence in ourselves, other people didn't have much confidence in us. Nokia was not in complete crisis, but the company's cash reserves were dwindling. Our business activity was shrinking, and losses were mounting, especially in consumer electronics. We had to build trust with everyone we dealt with: the banks, who were reluctant to finance us; the shareholders, who didn't trust Nokia as a sound investment; and the customers, who were losing faith in our products. More to the point, perhaps, our competitors' products, especially Motorola's, dominated the market overwhelmingly. On top of all that, the media doubted our ability: they thought that Nokia should be sliced up and the bits sold off to the highest bidders among its competitors. When I began as chief executive in 1992, rebuilding trust was the most important task facing me. I would also need to assemble a new team, just as I had when I took charge of mobile phones.

Apart from appointing people I spent that spring firefighting, trying to prevent the company from going under and morale from crumbling completely. My diary from that time shows that I met many bankers around Europe and the United States. Olli-Pekka Kallasvuo, our finance director, and I used to travel to try to persuade people that Nokia did indeed have a future and to patiently try to rebuild trust. Every banker wanted to know what we intended to do with the unprofitable consumer electronics operation. In March 1992 bankers from Kommerzbank came to our head office in Helsinki. We all sat in our conference room and I told the bemused bankers that the entire European consumer electronics industry was badly run. "Now is the time for some real businessmen to come in," I said as I tried to convince my listeners with some carefully chosen words.

The German bankers seemed to believe me, because they continued to finance Nokia after that meeting. I have never been sure where my own self-confidence came from. Consumer electronics was our big problem, and back in 1992 I had no idea how long it would take and how difficult it would be to solve it. But my own self-confidence was infectious and persuaded others to trust us.

A few months later Olli-Pekka and I were on the banking circuit in Zurich, where we stayed at the Baur au Lac Hotel. The doormen there were amazed when a car from Credit Suisse took us to the airport. "Those men must be really rich if the bank ferries them around in a limo," they whispered to one another. The truth was completely the opposite: Nokia owed so much to Credit Suisse that the bank wanted to do everything within its power to ensure that its debtors wouldn't disappear before they could catch their flight back to Finland.

Much later I took a closer look at my travels between 1992 and 2006. On average I was travelling 115 days each year. This is roughly half the working days in a year, and nearly one in three of all days. Most of my trips were abroad; I used to go five or six times a year to Asia and seven or eight times to the United States. Between 1988 and 2006 I went to China fifty-two times. The chief executive of a major company can't travel more than this, otherwise the company will start to suffer from a lack of leadership. A leader has to be present. Modern communications do indeed help, but all the blogging or tweeting in the world can't substitute for a physical presence.

I don't remember many of the details of that spring. My diary says that as well as bankers I met many shareholders and staff, that I held numerous internal meetings, and that I always travelled to see customers when they wanted me to. I worked from morning to night and into the small hours so that Nokia could be saved – it was truly a battle for survival. The company had to regain trust by every possible means, both internally and externally.

In April I received another visitor from Germany. The second-in-command at Siemens, Dr. Herman Franz, came to our head office in Helsinki. He informed me that Siemens wished to buy our cellular systems unit, which was just then becoming a key element of our strategy for developing mobile phone networks. Siemens knew that Nokia had difficulties in the area of consumer electronics. The Germans thought we would be ready to sell the very unit on which our future would be based. (Siemens would eventually withdraw from the mobile phone business.) I listened politely, promised to reply in due course, and bade farewell to the distinguished German.

I discussed Siemens' offer a couple of times with Olli-Pekka Kallasvuo and Sari Baldauf, then in charge of networks. Dr. Franz came back to Finland on the afternoon of 16 June. We had prepared a little cup of coffee for him in the dark-paneled meeting room next to my office. I told him we were not interested in selling our network business. The German stiffened. "Mr. Ollila, I do hope you understand that you are making a great mistake," he managed to say when he had recovered from his surprise. He rose from the table halfway through his coffee. "You will be hearing more from us," said the representative of Siemens just before the door slammed shut.

I sat down again. We had avoided a major trap, but I have to say I felt rather more isolated as a result. Nevertheless we felt that we had made the right decision, Olli-Pekka Kallasvuo, Sari Baldauf, and I. We were on our own now. We would have to be even faster and more agile if we were to topple the Goliaths. I took full responsibility for my decision, which in truth was based on nothing more than my self-confidence and my trust in Nokia's capabilities. So I didn't tell the board about the visit of the man from Siemens. The chairman of the board, Casimir Ehrnrooth, heard about it only a year later, but he didn't complain. The outcome was the right one.

I got on extremely well with the new chairman from day one. It says something about Casimir Ehrnrooth's career in Finnish business that he had first sat on the board of a listed company as far back as 1954, when he was just twenty-three. He was a highly cultivated and skilled manager and businessman. He had not spent his career in technology companies, but in forestry. He was a highly conscientious member of Nokia's board and briefed himself thoroughly on our fields of activity and our figures. Whenever I talked to him and asked his opinion I received a clear reply. He did not defer matters to unnecessary meetings or working groups, and this was crucial when the changes in Nokia were so rapid. He was especially interested in corporate governance. He was absolutely clear about the division between the roles of the CEO, the board of directors, and the board chairman. Within this framework he allowed those of us with day-to-day responsibility a great deal of freedom and room for movement.

At that time the boards of companies listed on the Finnish stock exchange often had working committees. At Nokia this committee comprised the chief executive, the board chair, and the deputy chair, at that time Yrjö Niskanen.

The working committee met once a month, and we spoke for about an hour and a half about the current situation in the company and in the markets. When necessary an outside expert might be invited to give a presentation on a selected subject. I made these meetings very brief. At Casimir Ehrnrooth's suggestion we abolished the working committee in 1997 since there was no real point to it.

Ehrnrooth was extremely consistent in carrying out his duties. When things were difficult, as they often were, he showed understanding and gave us support. In 2006 I became chairman of the board; in pondering this role I took the way Casimir Ehrnrooth had carried it out as my reference point.

Although I had confidence both in Nokia's management and in myself, I wasn't entirely hopeful. I didn't know whether we could be sure of surviving, even if we did as well as we possibly could. The consumer electronics division was still hemorrhaging cash. Spring 1992 didn't bring Nokia back into the black. We published our results for the first four months of the year in June, just before the whole of Finland went on holiday at midsummer. The bottom line was a heavy loss, heavier than ever before. At the same point in the previous year we had made 119 million markka ($39 million at 2016 prices). Now our losses were 178 million markka ($58 million). For tactical reasons we released the results at a time when most Finns had other things than economic news to think about. But after midsummer the headlines were bigger than before. The press wondered if Nokia could ever rise to the surface and whether the company's CEO had any credibility. The media's silence during the spring had turned into a furious onslaught.

I drove Liisa and the children to our summer place at Orivesi, but my holiday wasn't long. By 3 July I was already at a meeting in the United Kingdom. There, after a meeting of the board of Jamont, the paper company, I met my trusted adviser, Per Karlsson. We sat together in the great hall of a country house, while outside the sun shone on the English countryside. "Per, could you do me a favor? Could you help me get us out of consumer electronics? The figures are just dreadful. I need help fast," I said. "I can try," he replied. Olli-Pekka Kallasvuo and I had agreed we should ask Per to discuss with Philips, the electronics company, whether there was the possibility for a joint venture or even the sale of the money-losing division. These talks with Per helped a little at least. July 1992 was one of the most difficult times in my entire career. While many matters were progressing reasonably well, we still didn't know whether Nokia was safe.

The collapse of consumer electronics – a grand title for various television assembly plants scattered around Europe – was dragging down Nokia's profitable and growing sectors even though the figures for mobile phones and telecommunications networks had improved. So our share price also sank lower. Nokia was becoming an interesting purchasing prospect for those most familiar with the firm's affairs. Companies other than Siemens were starting to understand Nokia's potential for growth.

Would we sink before we really started to grow, or would we soon reach the surface and break through into profitable growth? That was the only question on my mind in July 1992. The following months would surely answer it, I thought.

CHAPTER 33

New Plans

IN THE AUTUMN OF 1992 Nokia's executive committee made a decision that had a more lasting impact than most in the company's history – we chose a slogan for Nokia. I had asked the head of communications, Matti Saarinen, to come up with a phrase that captured what we were trying to do.

Saarinen presented us with a long list of ideas. We had a discussion, based on the list, that took less than half an hour. We crossed out all but five of Matti's suggestions, all of which were linked in some way with the themes of "Human Technology" or "Connecting People." Then we took a time-out and agreed that we would come back to the question at our next meeting a month later. There we affirmed with one voice that "Connecting People" was our guiding principle. At that time the field of wireless communication was still young, so we were in the happy position that we could make our choice freely because not all the best slogans had yet been snapped up. Boards and committees are not always the strongest links in the creative process, but "Connecting People" has shown its staying power.

In 1992 we had at last decided that Nokia would concentrate on telecommunications. The decision was clear, brave, and final. I believed in it myself, knowing that my whole career depended on getting this decision right.

I communicated the decision at workplace meetings, typically to about a hundred people at a time. Of these perhaps twenty would find a place at the Nokia of the future that I believed in; the other eighty belonged to the parts of the company we had decided to sacrifice. The sacrifices were needed for two reasons: we needed to concentrate on an area where we would be one of the world's best, and it had to be in a growing market. Only this combination could save us. It was clear that both making our decision and explaining it caused people pain, distress, and anxiety about their own future. In many cases the anxiety proved well-founded. But things were going so badly at Nokia in 1992 that almost everyone knew that the company was fighting for its very existence.

Nokia had never been a homogeneous company. For its entire history it had been made up of individual units or subsidiaries that often competed with each other. In 1992 Nokia still had separate units responsible for mobile phones, telecommunications networks, cables, consumer electronics, and basic industry. These units, or rather the people working in them, often didn't have the faintest idea of what people in the other units did. People didn't feel they were working for Nokia, but only for their own unit.

My vision of Nokia's future crystallized around four key concepts, which I expressed in English because that was the language in which we needed to do business. They were: focused, global, telecommunications-oriented, and high value-added. These words encapsulate a decade of activity at Nokia. Back in 1992 they were aspirations, but by the end of the decade they were also achievements. Each of the four concepts had its own story to tell. The number of concepts wasn't a matter of chance – I believe that people can absorb no more than four concepts at a time. Three is often too few, and five is already too many to remember. Over the years people working under me have learned my way of doing things. I expect them to simplify even complex matters to enable us to communicate our goals clearly.

Focused meant that Nokia really would concentrate on those areas we believed in. It's also, however, an instruction on how to work. We had neither time nor money to waste on the wrong things. In 1992 we were a challenger in almost every market. We had to devote all our resources to narrow, clear aims. We had to find exactly those areas where our competitors were weakest, or those areas where we had budding know-how that we could quickly nurture and spread. And we expected all our managers at Nokia to focus on their own working methods and time management and to concentrate on what was essential.

Global was, back in 1992, an as yet-unrealized ambition for Nokia. Of course we had our international activities. Nokia had factories, sales subsidiaries, and representatives around the world, but we didn't really function on a global scale. We lacked global logistics, marketing, and a global brand. We were used to comparing ourselves to the Swedes and to Ericsson, but that was no longer enough. I announced that we had to fly beyond Stockholm airport and engage with more distant parts of the world. Our entire mode of operation had to go global. We had a great deal to do: our organizational structure, our attitudes, and our communication and marketing methods had to change.

When did Nokia become a global company? I think we started to work in a global way in 1994–95. That was when the GSM mobile phone standard spread as far as Asia. We were listed on the New York Stock Exchange in 1994, which compelled us to work according to the conditions set by the international capital markets. Also in 1994 English became our working language.

Telecommunications-oriented was a relatively clear and simple aim. It did however contain a strategic risk. If we didn't succeed in telecoms, we wouldn't succeed in anything. But our expertise was rooted in this area – we didn't pluck our goals from the air. Many other areas of our business had come up against barriers to growth or encountered other difficulties. Our cable division had lost its Soviet market, while in western Europe the profitable cartel had been dismantled. There was clearly a future in telecommunications – you could see the market growing in front of your eyes – but no one could have predicted that global growth would be as impressive as it was by the end of the decade. In fact it was only in 1994 that Nokia's board, meeting in Hong Kong, decided that we would sell everything except telecommunications. The struggle to sell consumer electronics went on for another two years. Our "simple" goal was by no means easy to realize.

High value-added meant we should concentrate on the most profitable products, where the margins were highest, so that the profitability of the entire company would reach a new level. We needed to develop products that could command high prices. That demanded strong design, a strong brand, and a strong technological capability. We had to get money flowing back to the shareholders at last – an increase in shareholder value became one of our fundamental goals. At the beginning of the 1990s many of Finland's institutional investors didn't believe Nokia had a future. They voted with their money and withdrew from the ranks of our shareholders. Investors, the government, and my fellow chief executives were all fixated on "my harsh fate" back in 1992.

Once the company's basic objectives had been set out, the organization seemed to get down to work. Stating the objectives worked like an electric shock of just the right intensity. People woke up and stirred themselves, and the company began to pull itself together. These basic aims needed to be repeated and repeated all the time and everywhere. Everyone had to learn what Nokia was about. If one of Nokia's employees were to be awoken in his own bed in the middle of the night, he should be able to describe the Nokia he wanted to create. This provided an altogether new sense of self-assurance and clarity for everything we did.

Where did my own self-confidence come from? I don't exactly know. I had put together my own short vision of Nokia's future when I was asked to take over as CEO. I believed in that vision, which would turn Nokia into a telecommunications company. Everything else was, in principle, for sale. It's part of my nature that if I internalize a vision I'll be ready to do everything I can to make it a reality.

Although my colleagues and I understood the opportunities open to Nokia, the vultures were already circling what they took for Nokia's dying body. At least three investment banks were circulating calculations of how Nokia might best be split up and sold. My first year as CEO had been diffi-cult, even bleak. After the spring of 1992 I didn't know if Nokia would make it. I have never been deeply depressed, but my darkest moments were during that summer.

CHAPTER 34

Values Underlie Everything

I DEMANDED A GREAT DEAL FROM THE PEOPLE AT NOKIA, but every chief executive expects a lot from his or her employees. It's like saying that a swimming teacher makes her pupils go in the water. It's essential for getting the job done.

As chief executive I expected everyone in a position of responsibility to have their facts and figures straight. Senior executives don't generally lay their pens down on their desks at quarter past four in the afternoon, as happens in most of Finland's offices. I worked evenings and weekends and so did many others at Nokia. It must often have seemed to them and their families tedious and unreasonable.

No one can know what a chief executive's job is like until they do it themselves. I had observed closely how Kari Kairamo and Simo Vuorilehto set about their duties, but it was only when I took over that I really grasped how wretchedly difficult and onerous it could sometimes be.

The chief executive's position at Nokia in the early 1990s sometimes felt especially hard. The company's statistics were dismal, the banks were breathing down our necks, and in the backs of our minds was the fear that one of our competitors would buy us out. I knew too that among my closest colleagues were people who were waiting for me to fail and wanted to step into my shoes. I had no guarantee that the company I was leading would take wing. Conditions in the early 1990s were difficult and sometimes my feelings boiled over. I raised my voice, too often, but I also tried to support my management team. Eventually we got the struggling company back on its feet, and this lifted the spirits of the people running it. Our success made us feel we were all in it together and gave us the energy to go on.

As a management tool I sometimes deliberately gave meetings an adrenalin boost. We can all imagine the torpid atmosphere in regular, two-hour meetings where the work of a business unit is minutely examined. Tedium and a lack of meaningful activity are dangerous for a company. They're soporific and they turn the company's management into a bloated Politburo. I wanted to fight this, and so I raised my own levels of energy and intensity. Some people regarded this as ranting.

Leadership is a skill that can be learned, and experience is the foundation on which one can start to build a management style. I grew as a leader in perhaps the most visible position in Finnish business life, and my management style has evolved over the years – the rough edges have become smoother. "There's no need to make a fuss about those explosions from Jorma anymore, since they don't often happen now," said Matti Alahuhta, one of my closest colleagues, sometime at the beginning of the 2000s.

Many people completely misunderstand how an enterprise the size of Nokia is run. They imagine that the chief executive personally intervenes in every little issue where there might be a problem. That would be neither possible nor reasonable. When I took over as chief executive, Nokia employed roughly 25,000 people. The successful leadership of such a large group demands shared values. In the early 1990s value leadership was still a relatively new concept. In the 2010s the discussion has moved on and values have shifted in significance. Now we talk, for example, of the significance of work. In any case it's generally understood that employees are not solely motivated by external incentives such as pay.

In 1992–93 we didn't have a clue how a global company should be run. We didn't even need to know, because at that stage Nokia hadn't really become a global company. Nokia's top management was a group of young managers who were extremely ambitious but inexperienced. We had to learn to trust each other completely in all circumstances, in good times as well as bad.

I had encapsulated Nokia's objectives in four key concepts. But objectives and values are not the same thing. Our values needed to be something that people genuinely wanted to be committed to but also something that Nokia wanted them to commit themselves to. We needed a value system that would hold up well should the company succeed. A company's values will often see it through the hard times, because then people have to pull together and trust one another. But the significance of values will be called into question if the company does well. Sudden and unexpected success is one of the greatest risks to a business. Then the company acquires the wrong sort of arrogance, the customer is forgotten, self-satisfaction increases, and sensitiveness to change diminishes.

The roots of the work on values lay years back in Telenokia, our telecommunications network unit. I kicked off our wider discussion of Nokia's values in spring 1992. I set up a working group to consider Nokia's core values and mission. The group identified and affirmed three Nokia values.

These values were implicit in the way the company operated, but they needed to be clarified. They were *Customer Orientation, Achievement,* and *Continuous Learning.* The group discovered one new value they felt it important to add to the list *–Respecting the Individual.*

In September 1992 we gathered at Båtvik, Nokia's traditional representational villa. Our top leaders were all there – 25 key individuals. Nokia's success was by no means assured, and I delivered a rather long and gloomy monologue, straight from my heart. We also had a long discussion about our values, our mission, and our working methods. Our gaze was very much focused on the present, which still presented many threats, but we also glanced toward the future.

It helped that there was no one there who hankered after a golden past. Our meeting managed to convince Nokia's senior management that we needed a statement of shared values. Some of them regarded the whole process as an utter waste of time that should have been spent on sales or product development. But just a few months later everyone agreed that without our discussion of values we wouldn't have gotten through.

At that meeting we gained an insight that swept Nokia forward by ten years. After our lengthy discussions we understood that two factors would determine whether Nokia succeeded. On the one hand our products, technology, and design had to be first class. But all our competitors had exactly the same aim. How could Nokia offer more? What did our customers really want? By pondering these questions we came up with *The Nokia Way.* This was a package that contained our firm's values, working methods, processes, and mission. We explained our core values everywhere we could. For example, in the course of a year our head of strategy, Mikko Kosonen, spoke about Nokia's values and working methods over a hundred times in different places in different parts of the world. This was mainly in internal engagements but also included outside events.

Customer Orientation meant that we would correctly identify the customers' needs, we would add value for our customers through our products, and we would take trouble and care over our customers. We wanted our customers to guide everything we did. We declared the customer, not Nokia, to be our employer.

Respecting the Individual strengthened our mutual trust, but also made Nokia a good and attractive employer. We wanted people to be treated honestly, openly, and fairly. But we also wanted to stress that we all depended on each other. We needed one another. We had to learn to trust one another. I also wanted Nokia to be a multicultural workplace, where we valued diversity, whether that arose from gender, nationality, skin color, or religion. This is conventional wisdom now, but in the Finland of 1992 it was revolutionary.

Achievement is rather an obvious value in a company. Every company wants to meet its objectives. A company should also want its employees to achieve their own goals along with the company's goals. Nokia no longer had resources to spare for vested interests or internal battles over our goals. Everything had to be shared, perhaps even to the point where our customers could sign on to our goals. We emphasized the urge to win, which was already high on the list of Nokia's corporate values. We also wanted to make it clear to our employees that those who achieved their goals would be valued. We wanted to demonstrate that we would reward people for their achievements, not their presence. This goal was indeed realized later, when our revenue and profits grew so spectacularly. Many people at Nokia became millionaires because of the way our incentives were structured.

Continuous Learning was perhaps the value closest to my heart. I believe that a company whose leaders and employees have stopped learning is condemned to an early grave. In Nokia, learning – continuous learning – is one of the highest values. That means learning on the job, in negotiations, in relations with customers, and in developing processes. Sometimes it also means that the company's managers continue their studies and complete dissertations. It's not a matter of one-off achievements, but an attitude toward the whole of work and life. It's the attitude of an organization as well as the people within the organization. It cannot be measured by qualifications gained or some financial metric, but if a company loses its ability to learn, one will soon see the results in red on the balance sheet. At Nokia learning means innovation and bold decisions. The company wanted to enable its employees to grow as people through their own jobs.

We accepted that mistakes and failures happen. Indeed, we wanted the right number of them to occur, for every mistake and failure brings a huge amount of information that can be put to good use.

Success often provides less in the way of new information. At its best failure leads to a thorough rethink and overhaul of the company's processes.

Over the years people working for me have learned to recognize my catch-phrase, which is that everyone in the company has the right to make mistakes, but never the same mistake twice.

The concept of a humble and open mind is also linked to these values. I'm always afraid I'll be misunderstood when I talk of humility. Humility doesn't mean humiliation, timidity, or excessive caution, nor does it mean a lack of self-esteem. It means such strong self-esteem that an individual or a company has the strength to show humility in the face of difficult or unfamiliar facts and fresh challenges. I also mean humility toward competitors, when they have succeeded in doing something special. In my view Pertti Korhonen showed exemplary humility when he picked up Motorola's new phone in 1991. He recognized that Motorola had come up with a brilliant product, though even then he was sure that Nokia could do even better. That belief took us a long way, for it led to the creation of our success story, the Nokia 101.

As well as establishing our core values, we agreed how Nokia would be run. We decided that our structures should be as flat and decentralized as possible. They should also be as efficient as possible, and everything should be based on teamwork. Managers should set clear goals for the operations they supervised. Managers and foremen should work primarily as coaches, who would enable those working for them to realize their potential. And the organization should do all that it could to promote the mobility of the labor force. Nokia was constructing a company that believed in free and active global mobility for people. It would have been mind-boggling if we hadn't believed in mobility within our own company.

We identified three processes that we saw as the most important in the new Nokia. They were strategic planning, financial control, and human resource management. But even more important than the processes were the values, which preceded everything. The processes were there only to enable the company to realize the goals based on its values. The example of Nokia in the 1990s shows how a company can be run on the basis of values. We called this "value-based management," which may not have been very imaginative but made it clear what we were about. Senior managers often imagine that once the values have been identified and communicated to the staff, things will be fine. But from my own experience I would say that if value-based management is taken seriously, communicating the values is only the first stage.

At Nokia we started by explaining our values to our hundred most important managers in January 1993. That spring we organized further events.

We disseminated Nokia's new values and guiding principles throughout our global organization. Later in the spring we considered what the values would mean for our human resource management. Our values and guiding principles would have no meaning unless they were incorporated into the everyday activities in the company. Personnel management was the most important area of all, because the company was beginning to grow, which meant hiring new people, selecting new managers, and increasing mobility inside Nokia. The global energy firm Enron, which collapsed into wrongdoing and criminality, had a fine set of values, better than those of many companies, but they weren't incorporated into the everyday activities of the company.

I remember well the time we first outlined our new values to senior managers. Some of my colleagues were enthusiastic, some were indifferent, and some showed openly that they thought the new chief executive's speech was just for show and had nothing at all to do with everyday life. On the one hand, the values raised many expectations, while on the other, people were skeptical about whether they would actually lead to anything.

I had thrown myself behind the new values and the idea of value-based leadership. I spoke about values in hundreds of meetings. Other senior managers were required to discuss them with their own subordinates. No one was allowed to let the discussion of values slip off the agenda. *The Nokia Way* was just as important as the manufacture and marketing of mobile phones, the purchasing of components, or putting together the company's business plan. It was even more important, really. I don't think we could actually have gotten the business going until we had worked out what we all fundamentally believed in and how we wanted to run Nokia together.

In every meeting and board discussion I made it clear how much I myself believed in our work on values. I made sure that the company would meet its financial targets. Of course every day I made decisions, small and large. But I knew that only a common culture and common values could bring Nokia back to growth and a new resurgence where the company would endure the pains and dangers of success. Only then would its real ethos be tested.

Nokia's personnel people often said that "even big boys can cry." They were referring to our staff appraisal process, which looked each year at what individuals had achieved, how they had developed, and their character. Many companies hold development discussions with their staff, but by the early 1990s Nokia already had a system where superiors, subordinates, and peers all evaluated each other. I believe in the power of example. So at Nokia we extended these discussions to include executive board members, right up to the chief executive. Thus I too received an annual appraisal of my development in accordance with Nokia's values. It was sometimes hard, but necessary.

Nokia's core values were knitted into these development discussions: everything was measured in relation to those values. There were years when we focused on just one out of the four core values. We might want, for example, to do better in *Respecting the Individual.* Then all our discussions would stress just that value. Our personnel department also laid stress on understanding people's own values, if for example a manager or expert was posted into an unfamiliar culture. Our company's values were not intended to contain even the slightest hint of cultural superiority. So we created a method to help us check out the values held by key employees, before they were posted.

When our personnel department was given value-related objectives, we gained several additional tools for changing the organization. The personnel department's job was to ensure that *The Nokia Way* was the crucial principle in recruitment, managerial appointments, and team-building. From now on those values would form the sole basis for the development of our workforce. It would ensure continuity, real security, dynamism, and consistency. It would also differentiate Nokia from other employers. We would be able to say very simply what we believed in and how we saw ourselves.

We believed it would make Nokia an attractive company on the international job market.

Trust was the password that would open everything up. The executive committee needed to learn to trust me as chief executive: that was another reason we needed values to which everyone was publicly signed on. My leadership style should have come as no surprise to my colleagues: it was all there between the covers of *The Nokia Way.*

Several of my senior colleagues helped lead the discussion on values. They expended a great deal of valuable management time on it. People below them continued the discussion, which fortunately began to focus on practical issues, which was not always easy. "What if my supervisor asks to me to do something for a customer at six o'clock on a Friday when my family is expecting me for a special dinner?" might be a typical question. It was certainly a concrete and realistic question, and even now I'm not quite sure what the right answer might be. But that makes it just the sort of matter you need to discuss.

CHAPTER 35

A Black Hole

MY GREATEST HEADACHE IN THE EARLY 1990S was consumer electronics. At the beginning of the decade, when I was in charge of mobile phones, there had been a brief moment of optimism when there suddenly seemed to be golden opportunities for television production in Europe.

To understand why, we have to go back a little in time. In November 1989, Günter Schabowksi, a member of the Central Committee of the Communist Party of the German Democratic Republic, held a press conference in what was then East Berlin. At the close of this event Schabowski read out a statement he had received only hours before. It said, in the complex language of communist bureaucracy, that restrictions on travel by the East Germans were to be relaxed. A journalist asked when the change would come into effect. The confused party official replied with the words that would change the course of history: "sofrot, unverzüglich" – "immediately, without delay." In fact it was intended that travel was to be made easier only on the following day.

People interpreted the decision in their own way: before an hour had passed thousands of people thronged in front of the Berlin Wall, clamoring to exchange communist dictatorship for the freedoms of the West. The border was opened, and the Wall, which had kept the two Germanys apart for nearly 30 years, was torn down. World history had changed as the result of a mistake, and certainly not for the first time.

A little later Germany was unified. East German marks were exchanged for the Deutschmark. The impoverished East Germans suddenly had money to buy the goods they had dreamed about for decades. They travelled to the

West in their little Trabant cars to buy bigger western vehicles, fridges, and, of course, televisions. They wanted well-known German makes, which they had seen advertised for decades in the press or on the West German television channels they secretly watched. Nokia happened to own some of these.

This caused a spike in demand, which obscured the real future of the television market. More experienced television makers, such as Philips, pointed out that this sudden growth in demand was a one-off. It might last six months, but after that production would fall back to its old depressed and depressing level. But at Nokia we were desperately short of good news just then, so such warnings from our Dutch competitors were not taken seriously.

On the contrary: Nokia's then-president, Kalle Isokallio, used television production as an example of how Nokia could do well in the wider market. And things looked good for those first four months. After that there was an appalling slide, which at times looked as if it might bring down the whole of Nokia.

In 1991 Philips had wanted to buy our television manufacturing division and was ready to pay real money – 500 million markkas, as I remember ($159 million at 2016 prices). But German demand was at its peak, televisions were selling well, and Nokia's directors were seized with a joyful optimism and didn't want to sell. Electronics would make the company a global player. The company's double-headed leadership was in open disagreement, which made all decision-making difficult. There was also the fear that Nokia would shrink too much in the course of a single year if the company sold off both its computer and its television production.

We had succeeded in selling our computer division at an excellent price and at just the right time to the British company ICL. Just six months later we would have gotten virtually nothing for Nokia Data. The deal on the computer division was a combination of good luck and of Isokallio's skill. While Nokia's other directors wondered whether we would get as much as £150 million for our computer division, Isokallio sent off a fax to London suggesting a price tag of £320 million ($715 million in 2016 money), a figure plucked from the air based on nothing more than his intuition and eye for the game.

We should undoubtedly have accepted the Philips offer. Nokia would have been relieved of its millstone, and money would have been freed up for the expanding new fields of mobile phones and networks. It would also have cleared the way for Ericsson to buy Nokia in October 1991 since it wouldn't have had to worry about the risks associated with our money-losing television production. The major consumer electronics deals of the 1980s had been a colossal mistake. Paradoxically, it was probably those mistakes that ensured that Nokia remained an independent company.

This mess became my responsibility in 1992. Consumer electronics was run from Geneva by the Frenchman Jacques Noels, who was known as a good strategic planner but not, to be frank, for his successful management of operations. In February 1992 I wanted to know for myself exactly what was going on. I asked our strategic planning director Tapio Hintikka to tell me, so he came to my office one February evening. I must have looked exhausted: I was working fifteen-hour days at least six days a week. Hintikka was very critical of the way the consumer electronics operation was run.

The following morning I flew to Geneva and heard what Jacques Noels and his team had to say. Their plans sounded good to me. So the following day I called Hintikka back into my office. "What you told me was complete rubbish. They have all the plans they need to put things right," I said. He gently contradicted me. (Hintikka is eight years senior to me, a calm and strong-willed manager who was not afraid to disagree with me.) He told me that the same plans had been presented in a beautiful leather-bound file four years earlier, but nothing had come of them. I looked at the matter again, and two weeks later Jacques Noel was replaced as head of consumer electronics by Nokia's Finnish finance director, Hannu Bergholm.

Our consumer electronics arm caused me great anxiety in my first years as chief executive. We hadn't sold the division, though we had identified opportunities to do so. It lost almost as much money in 1993 as in the previous year. In 1992–93 the losses from consumer electronics were greater than the whole of Nokia's net profit for 1993.

We were sinking ever deeper, because the market for televisions showed no signs of growing. Nokia produced cathode ray tubes and also complete televisions, and both areas were in serious difficulty. Our tube factory at Esslingen in Germany was a major financial loser. We hadn't been able to bring production up to a profitable level because we effectively faced a cartel formed by Philips and Thomson. We were feverishly looking for an escape route from the whole consumer electronics field. We were perhaps fortunate not to know that this millstone would remain around our neck for another four years.

The spectrum of opinion in Nokia ranged from strong optimism, on the part of those who made the televisions, to grave doubts about the future of the operation – a view that Olli-Pekka Kallasvuo and I held strongly. When we discussed consumer electronics together we wondered whether it could ever be a profitable part of Nokia. "You must be joking," was our conclusion.

On the other hand I trusted Hannu Bergholm. If he couldn't knock things into shape, no one could. His second-in-command was Heikki Koskinen, who knew the television business better than anyone.

Bergholm told Nokia's board in a memorandum that without investment the Esslingen television tube factory would have to be shut down. If our plans for a joint venture were to get anywhere, we had to show the world that we believed we had a future in this area. I agreed to the investments Bergholm proposed at the outset, because they seemed unavoidable. Without them we wouldn't have any credibility.

Nokia made television tubes and used them in making its own televisions. Nokia made about 2 million of the 22 million television tubes sold in Europe each year. Now Nokia was looking for an ally to help it boost production to 3 million annually. We could have closed the whole factory, but that would have had disastrous implications for Nokia's balance sheet, which in 1992 was as robust as the first thin film of ice on a Finnish lake after a September frost. We couldn't afford to do anything apart from pump more money into making televisions. We had no guarantees that that would work; we could only hope for the best.

Consumer electronics became the company's black hole – it sucked so much time and energy out of us. I must have spent half my waking hours thinking about, talking about, and planning what to do with our consumer electronics division. Sometimes the black hole shrank a little, when demand for televisions seemed to be rising. But then the black hole would grow bigger still, no matter how hard we tried – and the consumer electronics managers certainly did their best. Both publicly and inside the company I had to defend my belief that our consumer electronics division could be made to prosper. I adopted my most confident manner, straightened my back and my tie, and issued statements to the effect that we would knock this side of our business into shape.

Sometimes I didn't succeed in disguising the reality. In 1993 Olli-Pekka Kallasvuo and I flew to Boston for a meeting at Fidelity, the major international finance house. Twenty-four sharp and attentive analysts listened to our presentations, trying to find any cracks they might exploit for investment purposes. Nokia was still relatively unknown then. Most people in the United States still thought we were a Japanese company because of our strange name. Compared to Motorola we really hadn't achieved any profile, and we weren't yet listed on the New York Stock Exchange.

I started my presentation by saying that mobile phones were our real success story, but of course we did have a few little problems with consumer electronics. I thought that "little problems" was just within the bounds of honesty, though our problems were hardly the smallest possible. Before I had finished my sentence a hand shot up in the front row. It belonged to the sharpest analyst of all, and I think it held a gold-plated Cross pen. The analyst asked just one question throughout the whole presentation. When I said "consumer electronics" the analyst asked: "Can it be saved?" "Indeed it can, though I doubt if it will ever be really profitable," I answered, though I didn't believe it myself. And I also had to ask myself why we should keep going in an area that would never be profitable enough. How could I explain that to the board, to the shareholders, to the analysts – and to myself?

We had recently installed a new management team at consumer electronics, which I had chosen myself. I had to support those executives, as CEOs must always support the executives they've appointed, until they cease to be managers. Also thousands of people depended on consumer electronics for their jobs. Most of them were working in Germany, where a strong trade union movement watched out for factory closures, and politicians vigilantly followed what international companies did. What was more, those thousands of people were certainly working hard, because they too knew that times weren't easy. Fairness demanded that I should support the managers, the workers, and everyone else who was trying to make a go of television production.

Honesty and fairness were in conflict. I let fairness win, so honesty lost out on this occasion. I don't mean that I knew for sure that we would fail, but all the facts were against us. On top of that my instinct told me that we had to concentrate all our energies on mobile phones and mobile phone networks. If half my time and that of my colleagues was spent on contemplating the black hole of television production, there was a risk it would swallow us up altogether.

There were many reasons why television production couldn't succeed. Some of these were common to all the European companies that made televisions. Some were particular to Nokia. Television production in Europe was growing at 10 to 15 percent annually. It wasn't that new companies were coming into the field, but that all the producers were increasing their efficiency, while the market wasn't growing. The European market for televisions was mature – about the same number were sold every year. The only exception was the spike in demand following German unification.

Also, manufacturers in the Far East made televisions much more cheaply than the Europeans did. In Japan televisions could be found in the supermarkets somewhere between the beer and the noodles. Occasionally a television would be thrown in free if a customer bought enough groceries. The Europeans couldn't compete with such aggressive pricing and marketing. Small and cheap Japanese brands had broken into the European market, and customers had responded enthusiastically.

Nokia's problem was that it had acquired a varied collection of television factories and brands, and it simply produced too many models in a complicated and expensive production process. Our models would have filled a sizeable room. In 1992 we made 102 different models, with a total of 407 variants. Later we cut back to 37 models, with "only" 235 variants. We had to reduce the number of models further, but we couldn't do it in time. We should have weeded out the redundant models back in 1988–92, but the managers then couldn't do it. When we did start to slim down our catalog we were too late and could do nothing about it.

As a purchaser of components Nokia was altogether too small a player in the market. We learned later, when manufacturing mobile phones, that one of the most important factors in our competitiveness was to get the right quantity of the right components at the right time. We couldn't do anything to affect the price or the availability of television components.

In Germany we had decided to sell our televisions through 6,000 outlets. Our thinking was that we should team up with small market traders, which would set us apart from Philips and our other competitors. The concept was good, but facts got in the way again and did in our wishful thinking. Small traders weren't interested in our brand or our marketing. They just wanted to sell televisions at whatever price they could.

We made many other mistakes, many of which I didn't even hear about. I tried to believe, to hope, to support and sustain, and to say good things in public about our brilliant future on the European television market. Nor was I alone in my public optimism. The European Union was investing huge amounts of money in its high-definition TV system, a revolutionary television that would stimulate the torpid television market. The money, the enthusiasm, and the fine speeches were all wasted. European taxpayers paid the bill for this attempt to launch a technology the customers had no need for. But if we hadn't invested in television production, or showed our belief in its future, we would have spoiled what chances we had either of selling it or of collaborating with others in this area.

CHAPTER 36

The Future and the Past

A T THE BEGINNING OF THE 1990s Nokia was divided in two: mobile telephones and mobile telephone networks. We knew what the company
should focus on. We had decided that Nokia would be a telecommunications company, but there was still a long way to go.

According to the company accounts for 1992, telecoms and mobile phones
brought the company 864 million markka ($270 million at 2016 prices),
while consumer electronics lost us 783 million markka ($245 million). In
other words, consumer electronics lost us almost as much money as our core
business of telecoms made. Fortunately cables, cable machinery, and rubber
products were all profitable, so Nokia as a whole showed profits for 1992 of
288 million marks ($90 million). Compared with the previous year this was
a major achievement, since in 1991 our losses had amounted to 96 million
markka ($31 million).

We knew that growth would come from mobile phones and telecommunications networks, and also that these were what we did best. We did many
things in different ways from our competitors. We were without preconceptions, because we had no alternative. We had no history as a significant
player in international telecommunications, so all our decisions had to be
new and fresh and sometimes improvised.

Improvisation had long been part of life at Nokia. My predecessors as CEO
had always encouraged flowers to bloom wherever they could. Engineers
were encouraged to develop their ideas freely and "privately." If an idea looked
like it might fly, Nokia was always keen to invest in it. The engineers had developed a spirit of enterprise, which included a willingness to accept failure.

The birth of the Nokia mobile phone was an example of that spirit. The company had begun to design and manufacture mobile phones as far back as the 1970s. This was very much a cottage industry at the time; the methods in operation could never have been scaled up to allow global production or distribution. Even so that first phase was important: without such bold experimentation Nokia could never have become a global enterprise. Nokia phones were marketed in Finland in the 1990s using the slogan "Nokia's engineers do it all."

The Nokia 1011

The first generation of mobile phones often only worked in a car. Analogue "portables" were so big that you had to have a special pocket sewn into the jacket of your suit to carry one around. Our competitors, especially Motorola, did however offer much smaller models. Nokia felt compelled to meet the challenge, which was how we came to create the 101 and its digital sister the 1011, launched in 1992.

In the early 1990s mobiles were aimed at corporate executives and senior government officials. Motorola's background was in army and police equipment. People thought then that mobiles would remain the preserve of people who "really" needed them. Nokia overturned such thinking. When Anssi Vanjoki began to develop Nokia as a brand, our goal was to sell mobiles to everyone.

The change was rapid. To give an example, when the digital model 1011 was launched in 1992 it cost 8,250 marks ($2,577 at 2016 prices). At the time that was well over half a substantial month's salary. When the 6110 came on to the market in 1998 it cost 3250 marks ($943 at 2016 prices). Nowadays the cheapest models cost a few tens of dollars, if that. Competition brought new products and special offers to the customers, so prices fell. The mobile phone was less and less the tool of senior managers, police officers, and salesmen and more and more a universal means of personal communication. This didn't happen overnight: we couldn't have guessed what a phenomenon the mobile phone would become. We didn't know that it would surpass every previous consumer or electronic product in the speed at which it was adopted.

We had started a revolution, and we still didn't understand the consequences. Indeed, at that time even we didn't realize that we had started a revolution. We knew that the market would grow. And we had lots of luck on our side: we had chosen the right technology. We were geared up for the digital age. When GSM phones took off we were ready to make them for every market.

We had changed the rules of the game in three ways: we wanted to bring mobile phones within reach of everyone; we wanted through marketing to make Nokia the leading brand; and we had focused on the right technology. All this kept us busy between 1992 and 1994. We saw the results of our labors, for the first years of explosive growth had begun. Our mobile phone revenue grew by over 50 percent per year, and profits grew at about the same rate. The Nokia ringtone was heard more and more often all over the world.

At the beginning of the 1990s the world changed in ways that were very helpful to Nokia. The European Single Market was declared complete in 1992. That meant that capital, people, and production could move freely inside Europe. Earlier every market had needed its own factory run by a subsidiary registered there, doing things in different ways from the factory in the country next door. A global concern can't operate in different ways in different countries. In order to gain the benefits of global production and distribution, a company must work on the same basis everywhere. Materials and components need to move freely across borders. The finished products need to reach their markets without customs barriers. Europe was moving in just this direction, and Nokia benefited greatly from these changes.

In the United States Bill Clinton took over from George H. W. Bush. The challenger had defeated the incumbent. The country's economy was showing signs of growth based on a belief in information technology. People were starting to talk of the Internet, the linking of computers into a network that could quickly share information and send messages almost instantaneously. Economists argued over whether it would have any effect on the world economy. That debate was eventually resolved.

People's desire to communicate with each other has surely been constant. Smoke signals, carrier pigeons, papyri, even wood chips in a fast-flowing river have all been used to relay messages. Later on, newspapers, radio, and television communicated with a mass audience. But all these were tied to a particular place or a particular time. People had to fit their lives and their businesses around the message and the medium; by and large, messages didn't follow people around. You had to light the bonfire at the appointed time and place if the people of the next village were to see the smoke. You had to collect post from the postbox. You ordered your newspaper and it was delivered at a certain time each morning, or you bought it from a newspaper vendor on the way to work. Only small, commercial radio stations were really adapted to people on the move, but radio didn't become a me-

dium of personal communication. You couldn't use it
to chat with your partner or ask your children where
they were.

Mobile phones changed all that. If you had one you
were no longer tied to the office, or to home, or to
your car, or to telephone kiosks, or to the country
you lived in. Mobile phones facilitated mobility, but
they also happened to come on the market just when
a new, more mobile generation was growing up. The
younger generation moved around more than ever
before. Whole nations were on the move. A mobile
workforce needed mobile communications that were
personal and easy and pleasant to use. Mobile media not only changed the way people spoke and exchanged information, it changed their entire way of
life, fashion, and culture.

The Nokia 6110

I am neither a sociologist nor a philosopher. I can't
say how this change will look fifty or a hundred years from now. I wasn't one
of the first to use text messages or all the many other services our phones
offer. But the mobile phone is now an integral part of everyday life and I suspect it has changed forever how we do our work, how we conduct our family
life, and how we pursue our interests.

Finns eagerly adopted Nokia's new products in the early 1990s, though by
1992 about 56 percent of Nokia's revenue already came from other parts of
Europe. Finland's share of revenue was around 20 percent, though this figure
rapidly started to decline as markets grew beyond Finland and Europe. By
the mid-1990s Finland was already much more dependent on Nokia than
Nokia was on Finland, but Nokia had certainly gained from the rapid development of the Finnish market at the beginning of the decade.

In 1993 we could start to breathe a little easier. By 1994 we knew that in
mobile phones we had found an area that would propel Nokia to the very
top of the world league.

CHAPTER 37

Markets in the West

NOKIA HAD MADE TELEPHONE EXCHANGES BACK IN THE 1970S. This was an example of the boldness of Finnish engineers. Nokia engineers had risen to a challenge knowing nothing of its difficulty. Nokia's competitors in the great wide world assumed that a little outfit like the Telenokia of those days wouldn't get anywhere in designing a telephone exchange.

Nokia's engineers saw things differently. They grasped one key fact: old-style engineering logic, where you did everything yourself, wasn't suited to industrial production, let alone global dominance. The thing to do was to use ready-made components to create something new and valuable. This concept might have gone against the grain of the way things had been done, but it was the reason Nokia could make telephone exchanges quicker and more cheaply than its competitors.

The first strategic decision was made in 1987, when Nokia realized that the mobile phone business was bound to grow. Nokia had succeeded in developing a digital telephone exchange to which it gave the model number DX 800. It was a profitable line, with the Soviet Union its main market. And it was a good platform for a digital mobile phone exchange.

Trade with the Soviet Union ended when the whole Soviet Union disappeared into the fog of history, so Telenokia had to look west. With the sudden loss of the Soviet market Telenokia had to fight for its existence. In August 1991 we saw that our Soviet sales were 400 million marks ($128 million at 2016 prices), less than budgeted for, but sales to western Europe and beyond Europe were growing briskly. Telenokia was successful in opening up new markets, though the collapse of the Soviet Union cost it over a billion marks ($319 million).

At the beginning of my time as chief executive we reorganized our mobile telephone network group: Matti Alahuhta was put in charge while Sari Baldauf took over Cellular Systems, which focused particularly on mobile phone networks. It helped Nokia that in Finland the mobile phone operator Radiolinja inaugurated its own GSM network in 1991. A new era had dawned. So we were ready when markets based on the GSM standard began to grow in other countries.

Sari Baldauf (née Niiranen) was born in Kotka, a maritime town in southeast Finland, but her family soon moved to central Finland. Sari went to high school in the industrial town of Lahti and graduated from the Helsinki School of Economics. In the early 1980s Sari went with her then-husband to work in Abu Dhabi; she joined Nokia in 1983, the year before I did. I got to know her as soon as I started at the head office. Three years later she wanted to take on some practical responsibilities for a business unit, and she was given a real challenge. She started as the first head of the mobile phone network division in 1988, at the age of thirty-two, when the division's sales were 1.5 billion marks ($566 million at 2016 values). In 2004, her final year as head of the division, its worldwide sales were worth $8.5 billion. Nokia Cellular Networks is a global growth story almost without compare.

All of us in Nokia's core team had different approaches as leaders, and Sari had the strongest spirit of entrepreneurship of any of us. She was notably independent, inspiring, and empowering in her role as head of mobile phone networks. She listened to her customers and understood their concerns. As chief executive I could trust her to look after her patch. And more. "Life is a series of projects" was her unofficial motto. One of her more unusual projects was the sabbatical she took in 1995. "I made fish soup and studied Roman history," she commented later. Since she left Nokia Sari has followed a successful international career in corporate governance.

In 1992 I knew that our network business would grow and improve its profitability. All the indications were good, and I trusted Matti Alahuhta and Sari Baldauf, who were both part of my core team. Later on it was easy to transfer our success to the theory of business leadership. In his famous book *The Innovator's Dilemma* (1997), the American Clayton M Christensen described innovations that led to what he termed *disruptive competition*. The victims of this were usually large companies that dominated their markets and had become complacent about themselves and their aging products.

Major companies that produced telecommunications networks had a great deal to lose. Siemens, for example, held sway over markets that Nokia could only dream about. But Nokia decided to concentrate on one narrow area: telephone networks, which would provide a digital platform for mobile phones. We chose a narrow area because we wanted to break into the western market. The choice wasn't particularly bold or strategic. We made it because it was the only way we could see of breaking into the markets that major companies had divided up between them. We played a single card, which happened to scoop the pool.

Not everything at Nokia was based just on luck or intuition. Matti Ala-huhta had written a dissertation on the globalization of technology companies. A key factor in their success was early entry into important markets, where changes in consumers' expectations and in technology were apparent. Our director of strategy, Mikko Kosonen, had written his dissertation on the same theme. They both observed that when markets opened and globalized, companies structured themselves in a new way. Earlier every country had its own subsidiary that carried out a full range of functions. We understood, in theory and practice, that the world was changing. We were still not a global firm, so we could structure our activities differently from the established companies we were competing against. We didn't set up a product development department or even a manufacturing capacity in every country. We developed our products where the quality was best. We made them where it was most efficient to do so.

Our old Swedish rival Ericsson had done everything differently. The company had established a top-heavy organization in many countries. This drove up costs and slowed things down. If every country had its own CEO, the company would quickly be paralyzed by a combination of self-adminis-tration and turf battles. Nokia managed to avoid this danger. Ericsson found itself with 2,000 people in Thailand, but that didn't stop Nokia winning a key network contract there, though we had just 20 people there.

The network business is completely different from selling mobile phones to consumers. In the whole world there were only a few thousand cus-tomers for networks, whereas our mobile phone customers soon num-bered in the millions. In networks the essential thing was to target the key decision-makers. In different countries these were different sorts of people: in one country decisions were made for political reasons, while in another they were based entirely on commercial factors. Nokia had to adapt to both situations while bearing in mind that our values prohibited us from com-peting by dishonest or unethical means. If our products, prices, or services weren't good enough, we had to accept the customer's decision. Nokia didn't bribe its customers or use political influence.

In the mid-1990s the mobile phone division ran into problems caused by rapid growth, and the group's results were rather weak for a time. Networks, however, produced consistently good results and were Nokia's second pillar. When crisis struck it was networks that kept Nokia alive.

Nokia's network and mobile phone divisions functioned completely separately. They had separate subsidiaries and even separate locations around the world. For example, in Brazil they had separate offices in Sao Paulo and Rio de Janeiro. They also had different cultures, though both did things *The Nokia Way*. And they did work together in certain areas, such as customer orientation and technology.

The importance of networks is sometimes overlooked in the Nokia story because the growth of mobile phones was so spectacular. As the new millennium approached networks provided roughly a quarter of Nokia's income, while mobile phones accounted for three-quarters.

I want to emphasize, however, that the story of networks is exceptional from two standpoints. Throughout Nokia's history the company has developed a unique and deep expertise in telecommunications networks. The company was internationalized in the 1990s on the basis of that world-class expertise. The story of networks is one of both innovation and internationalization. Thanks are due to Sari Baldauf, Matti Alahuhta, and their teams.

CHAPTER 38

Sums on Scrap Paper

B Y THE BEGINNING OF 1993 I knew that Nokia would survive. All of us
at Nokia had already come a long way together, and at last we started
to feel solid ground beneath our feet. Although the profits for 1992 had not
been very large, we were at least in the black – Nokia was a profitable company once more. In the spring I saw that our profits were clearly on an up-
ward curve. I took the risk of saying so in the foreword to our annual report.
Our profits for 1993 eventually turned out to be more than four times those
of the previous year. Mobile phones and telecommunications networks
showed a doubling of profits. Cables too showed the most profitable year
in the company's history. In percentage terms, the leap in our profits – from
$89 million in 1992 (in 2016 money) to $446 million in 1993 – was the greatest ever: growth of over 500 percent. Five years later our profits would be
ten times greater than in 1993, but the annual growth figures were smaller.

Nevertheless I still had a lot to worry about – I feared that Nokia might become a target for a hostile takeover. We had quietly built up the profitability
of our mobile phones and telecommunications networks. The press wasn't
particularly interested in us because, to put it bluntly, we weren't expected
to succeed. But we understood our position and we believed in our future.
In any case, any company whose profits grow five times over in a single year
may become a target for a takeover, as long as its shares are undervalued.

In 1993 Nokia began to transform itself into an international company,
both economically and psychologically. Finland had protected its own industries by placing restrictions on foreign share ownership, but at the beginning of 1993 these restrictions were swept away. Ownership of Nokia began

to shift from Finnish banks, insurance companies, and other institutions into American hands.

We made two issues of shares to international investors in 1993 and 1994, because we wanted an international ownership base. It gave us the opportunity to raise new capital for our investments. We didn't want to take on debt, but rather to finance our investments with our own cash flow or capital. The share issues brought us fresh capital of 3.5 billion marks ($1 billion at 2016 values).

Successful conglomerates do exist. The world's biggest company, General Electric, does well from one year to the next. In Europe the only feature many of Siemens' activities had in common was the name they bore. Conglomerates often have a gentle time during turbulent periods because their different areas of activity don't all rise or fall in unison.

But neither the Siemens model nor the General Electric model were the Nokia model. Nokia had become a conglomerate by chance, and many of its sectors were too small to be viable on a global scale. In many of its traditional areas the markets had already been divided up among larger players, or they were threatened by new and even bigger competitors from the Far East who offered lower prices. Nokia couldn't afford to compete in every area where we were active. We had to focus product development where the prospects for growth looked best. We needed to choose those areas of technology where we could set the global standard.

I respect conglomerates. They work especially well when they have good cash reserves behind them. But if a technology company focuses very clearly on one or two areas, it's much better placed to challenge the established players than a conglomerate could ever be. A highly focused company doesn't carry passengers: it doesn't have an indulgent parent in another part of the company who will cover up and pay the bills for its mistakes. Everyone must try their very best in a company that has decided to focus on its greatest strength and to succeed in its chosen market. In general, life is more exciting in a company that's concentrating on one area.

Conglomerates and closely focused companies call for very different leadership styles. The chief executive of a conglomerate can concentrate on running his or her company as if it were a portfolio of investments. The company's head office has investments in various industries, and it tries to nurture, cultivate, and develop these investments, and to sell them when the time comes. The chair must be neutral; if he favors one sector it will look as if he's neglecting others. The company's managers will feel that its resources aren't being shared evenly, and the best of them will leave for companies that look after their own areas of expertise better than the conglomerate does. The best people thrive in those companies that know exactly what they're doing, companies where they're allowed to concentrate on what they do best. It's the responsibility of a good company to give them the opportunities to do that.

In a company that's focused on particular sectors and products, the chief executive needs to know what the company is doing and why. He doesn't have the time to lead a finance company or develop a leadership culture. He must know the basic facts about the company's products, the technologies they use, and how and why they're marketed as they are. Professor Clayton M. Christensen believes that many major companies are led by their customers, not their executives. He's right, and the only chief executive who can discuss things with the customers is one who understands what his or her company does. On the other hand, the head of a conglomerate will be hard put to understand everything the company produces, how it works, and how it's marketed. Technological development, global competition, and evolving markets ensure that chief executives have their work cut out to remain masters of just one sector.

So I support specialization. It has suited Nokia well and fits my own style of leadership. The decision in the 1990s ultimately to focus on two areas – mobile phones and mobile phone networks – was one for which I was largely responsible. But the path we followed in turning Nokia from a conglomerate into a specialized technology company wasn't logical, easy, or short.

In 1993 I sat once more with Olli-Pekka Kallasvuo pondering the company's future. In these meetings we spoke of big things and small things alike. We considered Nokia's strategy, its investors, and also little practical matters. I came up with what I thought was a good idea. I asked Olli-Pekka what the value of our various sectors was. If Nokia's value on the stock exchange – the total market value of its shares – were distributed across the various sectors, what would their value be?

Olli-Pekka couldn't answer that straight away, but he promised to work it out.

We came back to the matter a couple of weeks later. Once again we sat in my office while Olli-Pekka went through some calculations he had done in pencil on some scrap paper. He concluded that our mobile phone and network businesses had a positive value. The cable business was slightly positive, while consumer electronics was negative to roughly the same degree. We stared at the figures for a moment and pondered what they signified. They meant that Nokia was worth what its mobile phones and networks were worth. Everything else – that is, consumer electronics and cables – should be sold off. But this should be done in such a way that the company could be sure of its ability to generate an income in the short term. The company's value in the eyes of investors is often a rather different matter from the company's ability to generate revenue over the next few months or years.

I took Olli-Pekka's piece of paper. I kept it in my leather briefcase, where it was with me for at least two years. It became an important reminder of what Nokia had to do. It was on the basis of those calculations that we finally decided where Nokia's future should lie. But such decisions were not made during the course of my conversations with Olli-Pekka. The next step was to speak to the board's executive committee, on which the chairman, Casimir Ehrnrooth, and his deputy, Yrjö Niskanen, also sat. "The rationale sounds good. But the board needs to consider whether Nokia is preparing too big a bang. . . . Perhaps we need a third opinion."

We decided that the consulting firm McKinsey should conduct an independent examination of Nokia's options, a strategic appraisal of whether our plans to focus solely on mobile phones and networks were overly bold. Their study would be ready for the board's strategy meeting in Hong Kong in May 1994. The consultants decided to support our recommendations. We estimated that Nokia could have a 25 percent global market share in 2000, compared with 20 percent in 1994. McKinsey's comment on this was simply "good luck." Our market share in 2000 turned out to be 32 percent.

We also set out our own vision of Nokia's future. We said that we believed in organic growth in mobile phones and mobile phone networks. We also proposed that after 1995 our strategy should find a way of exploiting our home electronics expertise in multimedia products, even though the growth strategy demanded withdrawal from the actual production of consumer electronics and cables.

Once the strategic direction was clear we got down to work. Our cable business was sold to international investors in 1995–96. Nokia Tyres, which was very successful, was launched on the Helsinki Stock Exchange in 1995, though Nokia kept hold of some shares, which it sold in 2003. In October 1993 the board agreed that the chief objective should be to sell the whole of our consumer electronics business, but the operations needed to be restructured before we had any hope of selling it. In March 2004 the decision was made to close the cathode ray tube factory at Esslingen. Our position was starting to look a little brighter, because our success with mobile phones and telecoms had strengthened our balance sheet to the point where it could bear the costs associated with getting out of televisions.

At the board meeting in June 1994 we set out a future for Nokia right up to 2001. We estimated that the new strategy could achieve a profit of $819 million in 2001, when our revenue would be $10.6 billion. The figures show how none of us could imagine the developments of the next few years. We didn't know, nor did anyone else, how Nokia was about to find itself at the very eye of a tornado. In 2000 our profits were $5.9 billion, and our revenue $31.1 billion. The figures show how I at least was not very good at forecasting the growth prospects for mobile phones back in 1994. All Nokia's directors had learned their lessons, however – none of us wanted to promise more than we could be sure of delivering. In Finnish style our estimates were more cautious than those of our competitors. Sometimes, during the years of explosive growth, that left investors and investment analysts bemused.

The tornado had already started to form in the mobile phone sector. It would pluck Nokia from the ground and lift it to dazzling heights. Later it would dash the company back down again, when the company would feel as if it were breaking up on re-entry. Exciting times were in store for us; exciting times that no one could imagine in Hong Kong in 1994.

My idea that we should concentrate on what we did best and what we most believed in was now signed and sealed. In this sense Nokia's fate was settled in Hong Kong in 1994 for the coming years and indeed decades. I felt that I bore the responsibility, but my joy was boundless. Now Nokia was becoming the sort of company that I believed in and that I wanted to lead. But Nokia was still very much in a growth phase and still had growing pains to endure.

CHAPTER 39

Turning Off the Televisions

W E WERE FEVERISHLY TRYING TO FIND A WAY to extract ourselves from consumer electronics. I had given my trusted friend Per Karlsson the task of finding a possible partner and an escape route. Per met many people, heard what investment bankers had to say, and reported it back to me. But not even he was a wizard or the master of the universe – he couldn't find a quick way out. Ultimately Hannu Bergholm was let go as head of consumer electronics, and all responsibility passed on to Tapio Hintikka. This wasn't an easy decision, because Hannu had done all he could to make a go of the television business. He had been a respected chief controller before his current job, but not even he was up to the impossible task of making a go of consumer electronics.

Tapio's job was to sell, to end Nokia's involvement, and to tie up the loose ends. He opened discussions with every conceivable television manufacturer. We spoke to Philips, Grundig, Sharp, Samsung, and Daewoo. I really can't remember now how many television manufacturers we tried to make a deal with. Week by week, month by month, the situation seemed ever less hopeful.

In the autumn of 1995 Tapio got to know Nobuyuki Idei, the chairman of Sony. The two men had discussed a possible partnership between Sony and Nokia. Sony's joint venture with Siemens had failed, and the company was looking for a new European partner. Tapio set up a meeting in Japan at the end of January 1996. Our director who covered trade policy, Veli Sundbäck, came with us. We met the Sony team at two o'clock and we continued the discussions over a Japanese dinner table.

Everything flowed very politely. Idei proposed that collaboration should go wider than the sale of our consumer electronics division to Sony. He was seeking a new pattern of cooperation, to include mobile phones as well as televisions. This would have brought a new brand into being: Sony-Nokia. The Japanese presumably realized that January 1996 wasn't our finest hour in any sphere of activity, since our mobile phone division was in the middle of a logistical crisis. Sony saw a chance to grab a slice of our success with mobile phones. My polite reply to Mr. Idei was an unconditional refusal of his offer. Mobile phones were not up for discussion. Nokia would stand or fall on the strength of its own brand.

We had spent many months preparing for cooperation with Sony. We set up working groups and held serious discussions. European television manufacturers chiefly wanted to ensure that we would fail, whatever we did, since they wanted to reduce television production capacity in Europe. It suited them for Nokia to do the dirty work and close its factories and let them have its brand names. They weren't interested in continuing production because there were too many televisions chasing too few customers. For its part Sony was seeking a strategic partner, but I wasn't interested in that. Idei looked disappointed, but he remained polite. Years later Sony used the same tactics with more success, though the pseudo-Japanese Sony Ericsson that resulted never became a major player in the global mobile phone market.

Our negotiations with Sony didn't help us solve our problems with television production. Tapio Hintikka continued work and met nearly every one of the world's television makers. He went to South Korea, Turkey, Taiwan, Japan, and many European countries. He returned empty-handed from every trip: we were still stuck with those money-losing factories. Finally we decided that we had to do something different. We had to announce our intentions. Unless we told the world we were closing our factories we would never find the partners we were looking for. In our position that was the only thing we could do.

In November Tapio went to Bochum in Germany to announce our decision to close the factory there. He had been warned there would be a large-scale demonstration, and he tried to avoid this by arranging an early flight. But the flight was delayed, and he came face-to-face with a couple of thousand angry workers. He was warned that he needed to make a convincing presentation to make the German trade unions understand how serious things were, but the gruff and taciturn Tapio wasn't a man for presentations. He stood in front of his audience and spoke in clear and simple Finnish for about a quarter of an hour. There wasn't a single protest or a single aggressive question. He had achieved what he set out to do.

When news spread of the closure at Bochum, a possible purchaser appeared. The Hong Kong-owned Semi-Tech wanted to lift our burdens from us. Negotiations began, facilitated by an agent from New York. We wanted Semi-Tech to take over our production lines in Germany, and we wanted the deal to include our long-established television factory at Turku in Finland. Semi-Tech wanted to transfer production to China.

Semi-Tech was the creation of a Mr. Ting. James Henry Ting Wei had founded the company in Canada at the beginning of the 1980s. The company's methods were pretty crude: it acquired established trademarks and then produced the goods bearing those names wherever it was cheapest. Semi-Tech didn't bother to develop its own products but instead sucked a stream of cash from its acquisitions as efficiently as possible. The company had already taken over the famous Singer sewing machine brand name, for example.

After we checked out Mr. Ting, we pressed on with the negotiations. They were tense. We had to give cash to cover the losses of the Turku factory in Finland. We also had to surrender our production capacity and our trademarks. It was a strange deal: we were selling something, but the net result was a loss of around 600 million marks ($181 million in 2016 prices). It wasn't an especially smart deal, but we didn't have any other options. We wanted to give up television production once and for all.

The negotiations went on through the spring and into the summer of 1996. At the beginning of July Tapio Hintikka, who was on his boat, received a forty-five-page fax concerning preliminary negotiations. Hintikka marveled at the development of communications technology, because the fax had arrived wirelessly.

The concluding negotiations with Semi-Tech began on 12 July 1996. They lasted nearly five days. At around five in the morning on 17 July we had thrashed out an agreement acceptable to both sides. In those final early morning hours the negotiators were at their limits of endurance. One young Dutch lawyer dramatically passed out at the table. In any event, we concluded a chapter in Nokia's history.

At the next meeting of the board I offered special thanks to Tapio Hintikka, who had fought hard until the very last moment of the negotiations. Having sold practically everything Nokia had to sell, he moved that autumn to become chief executive of Hackman, a prominent kitchenware company. He will best be remembered as the chairman of Sonera and later TeliaSonera.

Semi-Tech and Mr. Ting had permission to use the Nokia name on their products until 1999. With minor restrictions they also used the Luxor, Salora, Finlux, Schaub-Lorenz, Oceanic, and Guestlink trademarks. Many Finns had one of those brands of television. Semi-Tech twice asked for an extension in the use of the Nokia name, but I didn't agree to that. It would be bad enough to come across adverts for Nokia when I turned on the television in hotels over the next three years; I didn't want it to go on after that. Our marketing people were trying with some success to make Nokia a globally recognized name in mobile phones and mobile communications, and we didn't want the public to be confused by other product ranges bearing the Nokia name. Later things went wrong for Semi-Tech – the company went bankrupt and Mr. Ting must have lost his money. But that wasn't our problem anymore. We had lost quite enough of our own money already: over seven billion marks of it, over the years, or $2.2 billion at 2016 prices.

I had promised investors the previous autumn that television production would no longer be a problem in 1996. I had kept this promise and I was proud of it. Perhaps we should have made the tough decisions earlier. Still, it was right to give the people who ran the division the chance to make it work, even if it were up for sale. The situation had been difficult since we had conflicting aims, and this causes stress. I was greatly relieved when this unhealthy phase ended. But I often asked myself if I could have done something quicker or better.

It wasn't just the money. Our adventure with televisions had wasted a huge amount of time, skill, and nervous energy among our top management, our planning staff, our experts, and our employees. If that energy could have been directed toward more productive areas, Nokia could have done even better. I can't blame the people who had decided to make Nokia one of Europe's largest producers of televisions, but I wish they'd had the pleasure of seeing the trap they'd set for the generation of managers who succeeded them.

CHAPTER 40

The Five
A Different Way to Lead

NOKIA'S NEW SENIOR MANAGEMENT and management methods took shape only gradually. At the end of 1994 we had assembled a management team with much more in common than a shared workplace. We shared our value system, our intuitions, our vision of the company's future, and an exceptional commitment to making that vision a reality.

This leadership model was unusual, perhaps unique. At the core were five individuals, though in all there were around a dozen people in the senior management team. But in terms of leadership there were five key people – The Five – who drove the company forward, with little in the way of formal structures but much in the way of trust and information sharing.

I had met Olli-Pekka Kallasvuo in my first few weeks at Nokia back in 1985. Among his strengths were his feel for legal and financial issues and a solid understanding of commercial law. Olli-Pekka always had the company's interests uppermost in his mind, and he looked continually for ways of developing synergies between networks and mobile phones. He had a greater tendency toward pessimism than the others and thus often had the least to say.

Sari Baldauf was also known to me from my time at the head office in the 1980s. She had been the first head of mobile phone networks. Sari had a business education, a gentle approach to management, and an extraordinary ability to inspire people. She was close to the mobile network operating companies, and the customers' needs were her bread and butter.

Matti Alahuhta became head of the telecommunications group in 1993. Matti was a representative of Finland's strong engineering heritage and the only one in our group who was really academically oriented. His dissertation had been on the growth dynamics of small engineering firms. He was our technology whiz who systematically assessed technical trends in both networks and phones.

Pekka Ala-Pietilä had begun at Nokia Data in the 1980s working on computer software. I met him for the first time at the mobile phone division in Salo in the 1990s, which he later managed. Pekka brought the consumer's voice to our discussions because he had internalized mobile phone users' everyday reactions to our products and operations.

Without clear planning or a single deliberate decision our group ran Nokia from 1994 to 2004. All five of us had a similar background: we were all Finns who had grown up in the provinces, studied in Helsinki, and come to work at Nokia. More significant, however, were the differences between us in the ways we approached issues, both theoretically and practically. Our group had immense cognitive diversity. This really showed when we had problems to solve. As chief executive I usually found it anything but easy to find an agreed line. The disputes, however, demonstrated creativity and forced us to consider all sides of a question.

Why five of us? Why not four or seven? It may have been a question of chance – The Five were there and that was that. But later I came across a study by an American psychologist; one of its conclusions was that the optimal size for a group was 4.7. Chance, then, sure enough.

The Five wasn't a sort of military junta that had usurped legitimate power within the company. An executive committee of about a dozen people scrutinized all important matters on a monthly basis. I don't remember ever deviating from the correct procedures. We took great care over major decisions and they were only implemented with the approval of the board. But before that stage was reached The Five would have done the basic planning and discussion. Usually a few phone calls were enough to shape the issue to the point where it could be decided. Because the group was completely open-form, proper meetings were very rare.

Only when we needed a closer examination, such as a question of a new strategic policy or a change in the company's procedures, did we all gather around the table. This would typically happen on Sunday evening or at seven o'clock on a weekday morning – these were the only times our diaries would allow. We would usually meet in my conference room, but sometimes we would retreat to Båtvik, to the Nokia villa outside Helsinki. We never made a transcript or formal record of these or other meetings. I often had one-on-one meetings with the other members of The Five as well.

The famous Dream Team represented the United States in basketball at the Barcelona Olympics in 1992. Professional players from the NBA were part of the team for the first time, which meant that the team was overwhelming on the basketball court. The media started to call the Nokia Five the Dream Team too – though, with the exception of Anssi Vanjoki, there wasn't much interest in basketball at Nokia. And within the company we certainly didn't talk of the Dream Team, though the phrase took on a life of its own in the wider world, having as many different meanings as there were people who used it.

How was it possible for such an extraordinary group and management style to come about? There were a number of factors. The most important was our common conception of the direction Nokia should take and how high it was possible for us to rise. This had been formed over the course of the years through experience. It meant a shared vision of the way the company should be led and the organization built up.

Behind everything was our shared value system. This meant loyalty to and trust in what was best for the company. Our practical methods included an intellectual honesty, a willingness to take responsibility, an ability to listen, and a refusal to play office politics. We tried to avoid decisions that merely papered over the cracks. We allowed contradictions to flourish, since this was healthier than an artificial unanimity. A good example was the ongoing tension between the network and phone divisions. We let this continue unresolved, unlike our competitors who all came down in favor of one or the other. This approach led to a real collegiality – anyone could challenge anybody in an argument over facts, but arguments about authority were not allowed to see the light of day.

Value leadership was the basis of Nokia's procedures. It may have helped that when we started we weren't particularly close. None of us had been close friends before The Five got together. Our mutual regard was based on the knowledge that we each cared for the company in the same way, and that we cared for people in the company even more, above almost anything else. This created such a strong commitment to our shared project that it's not easy to find a comparison. Our daily work was characterized by communication and openness – crucial issues were shared between us. So problems didn't become surprises, because everyone was working on the basis of the same information. In this way we maintained trust despite the long absences forced on us by the need to spend time travelling.

Over the years we developed a silent, internalized trust. On this basis we could take risks and make rapid decisions, acting in the company's name without formal processes and rituals of rubber-stamping. Factories weren't built without proper approval, but individual members of The Five were able to make big but routine decisions independently. We weren't in the habit of querying decisions retrospectively, either. Everyone understood that if Sari, Pekka, Matti, or Olli-Pekka had made a decision, it must have been on a sound basis with the company's best interests clearly in mind. One can see this growing trust as a form of human capital, which in Nokia grew by example.

One might describe Nokia's leadership over these ten years as a free-form model typical of businesses in their growth phase. Aside from the official hierarchy one can discern four levels: the chief executive, The Five, the executive committee, and two hundred key individuals. The four levels were nested, and they communicated intensively the whole time.

The two hundred or so key individuals were the group through which routine operations were managed on a global scale. As chief executive I found that I could speak directly to them, and so did the other members of The Five. In the 1990s it was still usual to call, since email wasn't yet in general use. Bearing in mind Nokia's area of activity, the phone was indeed a pretty good way of exchanging thoughts. The other members of The Five didn't mind when I got in touch directly with their subordinates. It was part of Nokia's culture for its chief executive to speak to those who knew most about an issue. This was central to the way I worked and ensured a rapid response.

Our management team worked together for an exceptionally long time, over ten years. Such a long period is unusual in a major global company because the pressures are unrelenting and the physical strains severe. At the same time one must try to be an inspiring leader to one's own staff. I believe there were a number of factors behind our especially long tenure. Top of the list is naturally the rapid change and break with the past and the excitement it brought – we were living in extraordinary times. Every one of us was faced with some very difficult issues, and resolving them only increased our confidence in each other. Our productivity brought great personal satisfaction to us all and added to our motivation.

Another factor is certainly to be found in the rotation of responsibilities that every one of the group experienced during those ten years. Matti Alahuhta was at first responsible for networks and later for mobile phones. After running the mobile phone unit Pekka Ala-Pietilä took over new business activities and strategy. As well as her responsibilities for mobile networks Sari Baldauf spent two years on Nokia's business operations in Asia. The rotation allowed us to examine matters from new perspectives and helped us maintain the group's dynamism and creativity.

There was another reason for The Five's practical creativity. Because our values were so closely aligned we had an exceptional ability to work together – dynamic teamwork at its finest. In particular I mean the way in which expressions of feelings and sheer passion powered our discussions. Personal weaknesses and strengths are present in every group working intensively together. We knew this and tried to channel them for the company's benefit.

This was a group in which personal concern for each other was exceptionally strong. If you were exhausted you got support and were encouraged to take a break. Losing your temper and other human weaknesses were understood. I have often characterized Nokia as a total experience that was more than a place to work – it was an emotional journey. In part this comes from the positive experience that The Five shared.

All good things come to end. It was natural that at the start of the 2000s we had to face different pressures. Between 1998 and 2001 our workforce grew by around 40,000 people to 60,000. This in itself brought about pressure for change – a growing global organization calls for a more formal mode of leadership. Nokia's approach to leadership was refreshed through the early 2000s.

But time did its work and certainly the whole concept and its allure began to fade. No free-form structure – if that isn't a contradiction in terms – can last forever. It's always a child of its time. Perhaps the announcement of my departure from Nokia, made well in advance of that event, caused a degree of restlessness and allowed little shortcuts in the way things were done. These were few, however, and in 2004 a handful of critical problems were taken care of in the usual way in an exceptional spirit.

One may ask whether The Five model could be adopted elsewhere. Yes and no, is my answer. The basic principles of our leadership method – trust, openness, and so on – are suited to any organization and thus can be recommended for adaptation. On the other hand The Five's personal working methods can't simply be copied. This way of working is clearly best suited to a fast-growing company where a nimble and responsive entrepreneurial approach is needed. The ability to make rapid decisions brought Nokia competitive advantages. The more mature the business environment and the larger the company, the less appropriate our free-form model would be.

CHAPTER 41

The Nokia Miracle?

IN JUNE 1994 FINLAND'S EQUIVALENT OF *NEWSWEEK* published a cover story headlined "The Miracle of Nokia." This stated that Nokia had "retired from public life" in 1992 to put its affairs in order. Now the company was ready to conquer the world. The cover told its readers that "Jorma Ollila has turned the company's death spiral to an energetic ascent." The magazine also explained that 43 percent of Nokia was now in foreign ownership and that this figure would rise: the company was just being listed on the New York Stock Exchange.

The headline shows how little had been expected of Nokia in 1992–94. The mere fact that we had survived and grown was in itself cause for wonder, at least to outsiders. It goes against the grain for me to use the word *miracle,* though we certainly enjoyed a run of luck, which we desperately needed. But it was more than luck – we owed our survival to hard work, careful planning, personal enthusiasm, and concentration on the essentials. We had had to make sacrifices to focus on the things we did best.

I am a strong believer in the views of American professor Jim Collins on how a company should set its strategy. It must identify three key areas: what the company is best in the world at; what it's passionate about; and what it can do to have the greatest economic impact – in other words, how it can produce the greatest profits. The optimal results will emerge from the point where these three criteria intersect. That was just how Nokia worked in 1994–95, though Collins' excellent theory had yet to be published.

Our listing on the New York Stock Exchange in July 1994 increased Nokia's visibility. It also forced the company to improve its messaging to investors as we quickly acquired new and demanding shareholders, especially in the United States. We began to report our results quarterly rather than three times a year, which was the Finnish practice. We began to hold conference calls with our investors whenever we published our quarterly or annual results. We reported the results for each business division separately.

The New York Stock Exchange became the measure whereby our performance in global markets was assessed mercilessly, every second of every day. The listing also had an impact on Nokia's internal workings. It became easier for me to demand results from my employees because I could use the investors' reactions both as a carrot and a stick. Investors and investment analysts responded rapidly to both our successes and our mistakes. Our share price and Nokia's market value became the key measure of our success.

At the same time we became far less a Finnish company. The share of foreign ownership grew from 43 percent in 1994 to 70 percent in 1997. It's worth noting that at that time Nokia had two series of shares. The K-shares had greater voting strength, and foreign investors owned just 16 percent of them in 1997, so domestic shareholders still had the decisive voting power. The two series were combined in 1999. Thus Nokia became an internationally owned company. Finnish banks, which in the 1980s had held sovereign power at Nokia, were in the forefront of those who scaled back their holdings of our shares. Those Finnish investors who had shown faith in Nokia and hung on to their shares through the early 1990s saw their value grow tenfold by 1994. But that was only the beginning.

Although the Nokia "miracle" was already a reality back in 1994, we still hadn't conquered the world. Indeed, the world didn't know who we were. In challenging Motorola or Siemens we enjoyed the benefits of anonymity. In the United States Motorola was still seen as the home team, and the media often acted as its cheerleaders. For example, *Fortune* magazine extolled it as "the world's best-run company" in its April 1994 issue. The magazine said it was hard to find a runner-up to compare to the genius of Motorola. In the article experts and Motorola's top managers extolled Motorola's company culture, its use of technology, and its new ventures such as the Iridium satellite phone. It forecast that by 2013 Motorola would have grown into a giant with a revenue of $270 billion a year. The article concluded that there was only one serpent in this Eden: Motorola could fail if it became overconfident.

Fortune magazine's rosiest dreams of Motorola's future weren't realized. Nokia overtook Motorola's share of the mobile phone market in 1998. The Iridium project was buried after immense losses. The biggest company in its field is usually the least agile and can't react quickly enough to new technology or to the opening of new markets. The battle is endless, and every company and every chief executive have to determine the opportunities for growth and renewal for themselves. It's extremely difficult.

The year 1994 was a wonderful time for Nokia. Our future was becoming clearer, and our growth was at record levels. We were a nimble opponent who could land our blows without difficulty because the bigger players had hardly begun to notice that we were encroaching on their markets. And we were also developing new markets that were entirely our own. Finland's significance as a market was diminishing steadily. In 1994 it accounted for only 11 percent of our revenue. Europe's share was 59 percent, North America's 13 percent and Asia's 12 percent. The European share would continue to remain high while our North American and Asian sales grew strongly.

By 1994 it seemed to me that, little by little, we had also succeeded in transforming Nokia's mindset. Senior managers – all of us – had championed our values, held frequent discussions with our employees, and carried on dialogues about how Nokia should develop. We knew what we were doing. For 1994 I had chosen the theme "Excellence in Execution." After our discussion of values it was time to develop our practical side. We needed to put our decisions into effect, and we had to develop better structures to support all our processes.

Every leader knows that rapid growth brings dangers. If we grew too fast we would lose control and be unable to plan our activities as thoroughly and effectively as we needed to. But there were few critical voices to be heard. The black years, with all their worries about our survival and their obsessive but essential cost-cutting, were at last behind us. We had won that contest. Even the bankers on whose doors we had knocked with trepidation a couple of years earlier now came knocking on our door instead. For some reason they now wanted to offer us money, whereas just a short time before we had represented a significant risk. For me, a former banker, that felt especially good.

CHAPTER 42

An Unforgettable Year

I N 1994 WE ENJOYED THE FRUITS OF GREAT SUCCESS for the first time. The markets for mobile phones were booming, our profitability had improved, and our production was growing at over 100 percent a year.

Like the rest of Nokia's top management I had no experience of great success. We knew what hard times were, although we had had times of optimism and growth, too. We had lived through periods when it seemed that our company could never become as big and strong as competitors such as Motorola and Ericsson. We had also had some dreadful days when we thought everything would collapse, and all the risks taken on by the previous generation of managers would come crashing down on our heads. And we had known moments of jubilation when everything we did had come together, when the Nokia spirit and the Nokia team were at their very best.

We didn't know how Nokia would operate as a global company in what was probably the fastest growing area of the century. No one knew anything about that. Even so Nokia became a global company in just two years, 1994 and 1995. It had to be transformed; we knew that because in the mid-1990s we had driven at full speed into a brick wall.

On 16 June 1995 Nokia published its results for the first quarter. Things had gone as well as could have been predicted on the basis of the previous year. First quarter profits had grown from 970 million markka in 1994 ($298 million at 2016 prices) to 1.8 billion markka in 1995 ($548 million). Investment analysts had predicted a figure of 1.5 billion markka ($456 million). Naturally our share price shot up even before Finland's summer reached its greatest glory. I was taking my summer holiday in my usual way, travelling to meet our customers in Tokyo, Hong Kong, and Kuala Lumpur. I was back in the office for a week in July.

I took some more holiday at the end of the month. I wanted to spend my short break in peace at our summer cottage in the forest at Orivesi. We fished, had barbecues, and met our friends – as all Finns do. It seemed to me that that summer I really deserved it. Most things in the company were on the right track. I was still troubled by the need to resolve the problems with consumer electronics, but I knew we could find a way out of our difficult situation.

In Finland 1995 was a year of change as well. The after-effects of the economic crisis the country had suffered in the early 1990s were still working through the system. At the beginning of the year the country had joined the European Union, which would have been unthinkable even five years earlier when the Soviet Union still existed. That made us part of the European Single Market and more open to foreign investment. The fresh winds of competition blew into every corner of Finland.

Companies had to adapt or die: the two biggest banks, formerly deadly enemies, now merged to form a single bank, which before long became part of the pan-Nordic Nordea. It also gave a further push to changes already underway in Finnish society. The small farms of my childhood were becoming a thing of the past, while urbanization grew rapidly.

Elsewhere the peoples of the former Yugoslavia were bloodily fighting each other. News of ethnic cleansing started to reach every home from a country that had been part of old Europe. Suddenly war was again at the heart of the continent. In the Caucasus, Russia was razing Chechnya to the ground. In the Middle East it was a relatively peaceful year – at least until November when Yitzak Rabin was assassinated in the middle of Tel Aviv. That began a new cycle of violence.

Also there was talk of the Internet, which would revolutionize the way business was done. As yet it hardly touched most people's lives. But scientists and researchers, businesses and officials were finding uses for this network that seemed to be joining up large numbers of computers to chat together. It seemed revolutionary, and Nokia too had to consider its possible uses. Sadly, not even Nokia's imagination was up to forecasting the full impact of the Internet. Besides, we had our hands full manufacturing all those mobile phones that the world wished to buy. Everyone wanted to talk to each other, and soon they would want to send text messages as well.

In 1995 the world was exciting, risky, changing, and also full of new opportunities we hoped Nokia could exploit. Now the company just had to

In November 1995, I traveled to Johannesburg , where I met Nelson Mandela, who gladly listened to business leaders.

grow out of its homespun Finnish garb and don the garments of global success. That gave us plenty to think about and do.

These ideas were certainly revolving in my head as I lounged beside the lake at Orivesi. That summer was exceptionally warm. We left the cottage only for a trip to the opera in the medieval castle at Savonlinna.

I returned to work on the last day of July. Summer ends abruptly in Finland, and by the end of July you can sense that autumn is on its way. August may be warm, and its evenings fine; but already it's autumn. And when autumn comes, companies sharpen up. Before the holidays everything seems to be sweetness and light, but things change over the summer. Sales may have fallen. Marketing may have soaked up too much money. Products may have failed to find customers. Perhaps plans haven't been completed in time. The moment of truth always dawns in August. Then there's still time to make things better, enough time before the end of the year to put many things straight. But if a complete collapse is on the way August is already too late to avoid it.

Different types of business run according to different timetables. At Nokia we had learned that November was the decisive month, when the mobile network operating companies and the retail outlets stocked their shelves for Christmas. If there weren't enough phones to meet demand in November, or if we didn't have orders for those we had produced, the game was up.

Ultimately the outcome for the whole year depended on sales at Christmas, especially in developed markets. That was why in August the right sorts of phones needed to be ready.

Nokia had a top-quality product ready for the market. Its catalog number was 2110. It had a large screen, bigger than any of our earlier mobile phones. It was completely digital. It had many new functions. There was also something quite new about its design: our new phone was a real beauty, created by our chief designer, Frank Nuovo.

The design was completely different from anything we were used to. Some of its more striking features – its organic, rounded shape and the strong dark band around the screen – made us hesitate.

When Nuovo first showed the phone to Pekka Ala-Pietilä, Pekka had to think long and hard whether such a radical and innovative model would really sell.

"Are you sure?" Pekka asked Frank.

"Damn sure," replied Frank. And so the decision was made.

We desperately needed a successful new product, for we had spent the whole of the early 1990s living off the old 101 model and its descendants. This phone that Pertti Korhonen and his team had designed had been a global success. In 1995 we were still selling about 4.5 million of them a year, 42 percent of our total sales of mobile phones. But it was more than three years since this phone had begun to conquer the markets, and now we really needed a new model to open a new chapter in the Nokia story, which was progressing so well.

The more we tested the new model, the surer we were that it would be a success. "These are bloody fantastic. We'll sell more of them than we can count, beyond our wildest dreams," said Anssi Vanjoki in his typical way. So I had good reasons to relax in August 1995. The world's mobile phone markets were growing fast, and this new model was our response to that. All in all the year seemed to be proceeding in line with the positive forecasts I had made in June, when I presented the results from the first reporting period to international investors and the media.

On my first day back from holiday I watched the television news. The main economic story was that the Disney Corporation had bought Capital Cities, a media conglomerate that owned the ABC Corporation. Disney thereby became the biggest media and communications company in the United States. I was happy that in our own area there was no need to spend money on expensive acquisitions. Our growth and profitability seemed to be enough for our investors as things were. Disney's acquisition cost it $19 billion. Earning so much money back wasn't going to be easy in the fickle and fast-moving media market. I didn't envy Michael Eisner, Disney's chief executive, who would have to spend the next decade fighting for profitability and growth.

Things were different in the mobile phone market. In 1994, 26.2 million mobile phones were sold worldwide. The following year the figure was 43.1 million, which was still less than one for every hundred people. If Nokia kept growing in parallel with the market it would grow faster than anyone could have predicted. It looked easy. Altogether too easy.

We were expecting vigorous growth in 1995. If we increased our volumes and produced enough phones to meet demand, we could make record profits. We reckoned that the markets would grow faster in 1995 than anyone else would predict. And we had an attractive product in our hands. We were ready to make a tiger's leap. We were ready to more than double our production, though we really had no inkling of what impact that would have on our organization or our human capacities.

Every company should have a proper system for following results, profitability, procurement, and logistics. Nokia did indeed have such a system. It generated information, but it had been designed for a much smaller enterprise. It had grown along with Nokia, but we had grown so fast that no system could have kept up.

The previous year we had planned to adopt the German SAP system, which would bring together our production, stock control, and logistics. We wanted to bind together all those little threads of information that we needed to make, market, and sell phones, and to follow cash flows and profits. It was only the Germans who had succeeded in designing a system that was systematic and reliable enough. But as often happens the project had been delayed by half a year. Our fine new reporting system wasn't yet in use in the autumn of 1995. We had no time to lament this delay, for we had our work cut out in sourcing components, making our phones, and selling them. Still, everything seemed to be in order. August's results would be in line with expectations.

I quietly celebrated my forty-fifth birthday in mid-August and went to crayfish parties, a traditional way of relaxing with friends in Finland at that time of year. I was receiving ever more invitations on account of Nokia's success, and having to turn down ever more of them. I was also receiving more invitations to go on hunting expeditions, not all of which I declined. At the end of September I drove with my family to our summer cottage at Orivesi, heated the sauna, threw the fishing nets into the lake, and enjoyed the Finnish autumn.

Nokia's results at this time were still reported three times a year; the next report was due at the end of August. The results still seemed good – we would reach those targets we had promised to reach over the whole year. The investors and the media could hardly ask for more. We were increasingly satisfied with our progress.

At the beginning of October Pekka Ala-Pietilä presented me with the preliminary results for September. They were somewhat disappointing: sales weren't in line with our targets, and our costs had increased. The result was that we had broken even, which was far from what we had expected.

"September wasn't good. But I'm confident that October and November will go well," Pekka said. A little flicker of doubt crossed my mind, but I decided to take Pekka's word for it. Really I didn't have much choice: our reporting system seemed to work, and I knew there had been problems in procuring particular components in September and that our costs had risen.

I knew all about the problems with components. We relied on an Israeli subcontractor, ATS, which was the only company that could produce the key components for our wonderful new phone. The ATS factory in Austria produced those components, and they were absolutely essential. But in August we had received only 20 or 30 percent of the components we needed to meet our targets. It was a catastrophe – usually we received over 90 percent of our requirements by then. Pekka Ala-Pietilä and I flew to Austria, where I gave the subcontractor some very direct feedback. But we also discussed how we could resolve matters.

We knew that we would face gigantic problems, because by mid-September phone production would be delayed and could come to a complete halt. But I assumed that the problem would be a one-off, which could be quickly put right. How wrong I was.

Later I learned that good news and bad news always come in waves. A stream of good news is self-generating. Things go well and move forward as if they had a momentum of their own. Markets grow, people make the right decisions, success breeds fresh success. By the time you hear the third item of good news in a row you should start to be suspicious. Somewhere a fire has broken out, but the smoke hasn't yet reached the company's upper floors. Somewhere one of your tens of thousands of employees has made a seriously wrong decision whose consequences will take time to make themselves felt. Or somewhere your subcontractors have changed their working methods just a little, but just enough for your entire product line to fail and for your customers to feel permanently let down. All this we were about to learn.

CHAPTER 43

Toward Baden-Baden

THE RESULTS FOR NOVEMBER WOULD BE CLEAR in early December. We had to have a lot of phones ready in November if we were to meet the demands of the Christmas market.

Pekka Ala-Pietilä came to present the November figures. I saw from his serious expression that they were bad. As I listened to his presentation I realized that they were not bad; they were calamitous.

My fingers drummed on the table top, and I looked Pekka straight in the eye. Nokia's entire profit for 1995 would be wiped out by those figures. We would have to give a profit warning the following week. This was not just because of the results for mobile phones, but also because our consumer electronics division had entered an even deeper phase of its downward spiral.

Pekka left my room, despondent. I took a deep breath. I looked out over Helsinki's central boulevard: Christmas decorations had appeared in the shop windows, there was a Christmas tree in the park below, and red tents were selling Christmas items for all sorts of good causes. This would be a different sort of Christmas from previous ones. I stared at the figures showing our results, but I still couldn't take them in. That was odd, because I was in charge of this company, after all. Had a successful company turned into a company in crisis without its chief executive noticing anything?

What figures and forecasts could I trust? And what would happen to Nokia and to me?

In the midst of all these questions there were a few clear facts: my basic view of Nokia's success and future wasn't altered at all. We would survive this too, but how long would it take and how would we do it? It would give

me something to ponder during the Christmas holidays, I thought rueful-
ly. Meanwhile I started to prepare for the board meeting on 14 December.
That meeting would not, after all, be the celebration of growing profits that
Nokia's board had become used to in recent years. My stomach was in turmoil, my body was trembling. The profit warning would not be easy for me.
And why should it be? I would be answerable for all this in my own name
and in person when the media fireworks began.

On 14 December I issued a profit warning that stated that Nokia consumer electronics "will continue to lose money this year." "The downward
trend in the television business accelerated toward the end of the year. All
television makers are in difficulty, not just Nokia," was how Olli-Pekka Kallasvuo explained the news to the press. He told them that both the growth
in mobile phones and our revenue had been "to some degree weaker than
expected." He could scarcely have said more: we had no comprehension of
how we had ended up with the results we had in 1995. We simply didn't
know how serious the crisis was.

When I had given the profit warning I got into the car to go to the airport.
At 4:30 p.m. I boarded the plane to fly to Baden-Baden, the German spa
town whose sparkling spring waters had been known from Roman times,
and which had been named after its baths in the middle ages. After World
War II the town was the headquarters of French troops on German territory.
I had been told that Nokia had gotten a special rate at the hotel because our
conference was taking place off-season.

The flight lasted two and a half hours. I looked down on the Baltic Sea
far below and at the forests sparkling with their first snow. I leafed distract-
edly through my papers. My stomach was still uneasy. I had given the profit
warning, but I didn't know yet what effect it had had on the stock markets.
When I reached Baden-Baden and the Max Grundig Foundation's spa hotel
I heard that Nokia's share value on the Helsinki Stock Exchange had fallen
about 30 percent. Nothing like that had been seen in Helsinki since the international crash in 1987. On the New York Stock Exchange Nokia's value
had fallen 25 percent in the course of the day.

About a hundred of the most important people in Nokia's mobile phone
group were awaiting my arrival in the pleasant but wintry spa town. The
three-day meeting in Baden-Baden was a kick-off event to help us get off to
a flying start in 1996. I entered the conference room just as Intel's managing director, Andy Grove, appeared on a video link. Andy's book, *Only the
Paranoid Survive,* had just been published. Its title should have been some
comfort to me just then.

The conference timetable was tight, though there was room for good food: the dinner menu included venison pie. Some of the participants had brought their partners. There was also the chance to play roulette, but I suppose that buying Nokia shares that evening would have been a better bet.

And many people certainly did buy shares then and did well out of them.

My turn came the following morning. I had gone through the issues with Pekka and the other senior managers late into the night. At dinner news of the profit warning and the consequent fall in the share price had spread from table to table like a small bush fire. In the morning everyone in the hall could see from my expression that I was not at my breeziest.

I began my speech to the silent audience. The atmosphere was tense, expectant, and perhaps a little fearful. I don't remember exactly what I said. I didn't smile, but I did make clear what I expected from those responsible for the mess we were in, which was all of us. We had failed together. "Now it's important to analyze why this happened. We can't keep on having to publicly revise our expected results," I said. I listed all our problems, or rather I listed all the problems that Pekka and I had identified.

"Our forecasts for U.S. sales are going through the floor. The best product we've ever designed isn't reaching the shelves because we can't get the components to make it. Our financial management systems might as well use Roman numerals for all the good they are. We have to find a better balance between our rush for growth and our ability to satisfy it."

The silence continued. We all knew it was unfair for Nokia, and for all of us as individuals, that this should happen now when the outlook was so promising. But nobody had seen that promising outlook because everything was in such a mess. In fact our affairs were in such a mess that our reporting systems were unable to tell us how deep a mess we were in. Serious faces, nodding heads, tired expressions. But nothing about the audience suggested that anyone thought the war would be lost.

After my presentation I left straight for the airport and for Finland. The participants at the kick-off event stayed to ponder Nokia's future a little longer. Anssi Vanjoki, with his grasp of marketing, summed things up brilliantly. When Pekka Ala-Pietilä invited Anssi to conclude the meeting, he pushed a cassette of *Monty Python's Life of Brian* into the video machine and started to play the film's final scene. In this scene practically the entire cast of the movie, suspended on crosses, sings "Always Look on the Bright Side of Life." Anssi had asked the participants to join in. And so they did.

"We're not going to get anywhere by tickling anyone's balls. What we have to do is create a real can-do approach," said Anssi. He was spot on.

CHAPTER 44

A Year of Hell

T HE INVESTORS WERE FURIOUS WITH NOKIA and with me. Some Finnish investment bankers told the press anonymously that just a day earlier I had boasted about how well Nokia was doing in the United States. Olli-Pekka Kallasvuo was also said to have been upbeat. So now Finnish investors felt they had been deceived, and international investors were nervous. We had managed to build up a valuable stock of confidence following our listing in New York, but now that confidence was in jeopardy. That meant that our future operations were also endangered. Once more we needed additional capital. Our cash flow was negative, and disposing of our consumer electronics operation was costing us a hefty sum. We had to get the investors – both Finnish and international – to calm down.

"As if God had stumbled," read the headline in *Helsingin Sanomat*, Finland's largest daily newspaper, in its story about Nokia and its PR. There were other headlines: "The Great Deception," "A Strange Affair," and "Communications Catastrophe." Finnish investors were particularly angry because the profit warning had been given after trading on the Helsinki Stock Exchange had ended for the day, just as it was beginning in New York. But we wanted to look after our international investors, because they were becoming ever more important to us. I couldn't help smiling at the worst headlines, when I remembered the enthusiasm with which Finnish investors had tried to shed their investments in Nokia even before the good years of 1993–95. Now they seemed even keener to do the same thing. And that was the worst mistake an investor could have made in December 1995.

Nokia was now on sale at a reduced price. Those who bought shares would do well when real profits resumed. I knew we would soon be back on track.

I couldn't say for sure how long that would take, but we would get things straight. It was just a pity that on that gloomy day, 15 December 1995, I found it hard to find anyone to believe me. The media had attacked me with a sledgehammer, and the investors were demanding better explanations than they had so far received. I either had to give new explanations or to repeat my earlier ones.

We decided to set up a conference call with international investors that Friday evening. It was one of the most difficult phone conversations of my career. I tried to be as clear and consistent as I could be. I said I had warned of a weakening in the market for televisions in Europe back in October. At that time Nokia had published its results for the first eight months. I said that precise information on the market's impact on Nokia had become available only on Thursday. That was when the company's board had discussed the matter before agreeing that I should issue the profit warning. We had told the investors as soon as possible. I explained that the consumer electronics management team had changed. I promised also that consumer electronics would cause no further disappointments for investors the following year. I told investors that our earlier forecasts for the U.S. market for mobile phones had in fact been rather more pessimistic than our current ones. Our difficulties were the result of growing pains. We hadn't received all the components we had needed when and where we needed them, which was why growth and profitability hadn't developed as we had hoped.

I felt that I had managed to extinguish the worst fires at least. Nevertheless, the honesty, or at least the consistency, of the information I had given out was called into question, for the first time. That seemed to me unfair, wrong, and even repugnant. But I had to admit that I would have thought the same way if I had been an international investor. "Ollila goes on and on explaining, but what he says is quite different from what he said a month ago. Perhaps he doesn't know where his company is heading? Can we really trust him as chief executive?" is what I might have said. There would have been many good reasons for saying it.

We found out that the mobile phone components had been travelling the world over, more or less at random. For example, we had ordered 500,000 parts from one supplier in Hong Kong, but it turned out that they were in Korea and weren't what we were looking for anyway. When we tried to buy a further batch of half a million the price rose astronomically, production slowed down, and our budgeting fell to bits. We had stealthily grown into a global company, but we lacked a global company's logistics and efficiency. No company, and least of all a major global company, can operate without proper processes. It may have the cleverest and most wonderful people on earth: but it needs processes. If it grows rapidly those processes must grow with it. In major companies at least three things are in circulation: money, materials, and information. If they don't circulate at the same pace, the company is at risk, as Nokia was in 1995.

About a week after the profit warning Pekka Ala-Pietilä and I discussed things in my office. Christmas was just a few days away, but we hadn't spent much time on our Christmas preparations.

"Do you have any idea what the results for December will be like?" I asked Pekka.

"They could even be slightly worse than November's – though not much worse," Pekka replied a little uncertainly. In November we had just made a profit, though not much.

"Look, we've got two or three months coming up where we'll make a loss. Have you had a chance to consider that at all?" I said. Pekka was quiet for a moment and looked at his papers.

"Yes, that could happen. But I haven't really thought about it," he said.

My information was in no way better than Pekka's. We were in the same boat as far as real figures and real profit forecasts were concerned. Perhaps my uncompromising nature made me wonder what the worst that could happen would be. When things start to go badly you don't want to think how they could get worse. It's natural: accepting a loss is psychologically difficult, especially when things have gone well. After just one month of losing money almost every chief executive will try to find at least some positive signals that say the next month will be better.

Over the Christmas break I thought hard about everything we needed to do. The most difficult decisions of my career on Nokia's internal organization awaited me. And it seemed to us that Nokia faced at least one full year of hell.

CHAPTER 45

Who Is To Blame?

T HERE WERE MANY REASONS THAT NOKIA COLLIDED with a brick wall. The complete picture took several months to become clear, during which my pessimistic prediction of further losses was borne out. The Five tried to discover what the real problems were, sitting far into the night in the gloomy head office. We often began our meetings at eight o'clock on Sunday evenings and carried on until we ran out of steam. The picture began to become clearer.

We couldn't discuss everything in that group. As Nokia's chief executive it was my job to determine who had been responsible for this mess; then I had to decide what to do next. These are matters that a company chief can never delegate or avoid. The organization expects someone to make the decisions and set the direction, while showing how the company deals with failure. As I ran through the alternatives I knew that my decisions would set a precedent. Never before had we failed as badly as we did in the autumn of 1995. Of course, Nokia had failed even more dramatically in making the investments it did in the 1980s, but an earlier generation of leaders had been responsible then. Now we had to be pathologically precise in investigating the causes of our failure, learning from it, and putting the company back on track. On this we were all agreed.

A managing director or a chief executive can never run a company over the heads of the next most senior people, because that would damage the credibility of both the individuals and the organization. The people in charge of divisions have to gain experience of the freedom and responsibility that make an inseparable pair in developing the business. Chief executives must

trust the senior managers they work with in all circumstances, because ultimately those executives are responsible for the company's results.

They're responsible to investors, to the board, to the media, to the employees, and of course to themselves. One of the more difficult elements of
the chief executive's job is to be responsible for everything while lacking
the practical power essential to run the company. The chief executive runs
the company through its senior managers, by being an example, creating
processes, making appointments, and developing a leadership culture. On
top of all that a chief executive has to know as much as possible about the
company, its products and its prospects, the good news, and, especially, the
bad news.

There were certainly some strong individuals in Nokia's management
team. All of them had been used to success since their earliest years. I had
personally selected each and every member of my senior team because that's
one of the key tasks of a chief executive. Thus I was responsible to the people
to whom I answered for what those team members did. If one of them was
criticized, it was a criticism of me too.

That was only fair. I couldn't explain to the board that it was someone else's
fault that the company had failed – the board would only ask me why that
person was in that position. Who was responsible for that appointment?
That would have been easy to answer.

Direct responsibility for mobile phones actually sat with Pekka Ala-Pietilä. He took the responsibility for the failure of his sector. Now I had to
decide how that responsibility should be discharged in practice. I had myself
put Pekka in charge of mobile phones: Pekka was my man. I had taken great
risks in trusting to Pekka's abilities, but those risks had shown themselves to
be justified. Also, I needed Pekka to help develop my own ideas. He comple-
mented my thinking with his analytical approach and his optimism. Pekka
believed the best about people, even when I wasn't quite so sure myself. We
had grown together, becoming exceptionally close colleagues along the way.

If Nokia had been an American company the decision would have been
clear. Pekka would have had to pack his bags and clear his desk in the middle
of December, after the first profit warning. In the United States the chief executive is responsible to the investors for everything and in every respect. If
the company fails, someone's head must be offered up, both as a warning to
other executives and as a sacrifice to the investors. Conversely, in European
companies managers are allowed to carry on regardless of how many failures happen on their watch. Now I had to decide which road Nokia would
take and thereby what its leadership culture would be. The board, the inves-

tors, the workforce, and the media all awaited my decision. It was one of the most important of my career. I spent December thinking it through. I also discussed things at home with Liisa, who worried how much of all this I could take.

The external pressures were tremendous. Nokia had many international shareholders, who were used to seeing a company's senior managers in person when there was trouble. The media would certainly doubt my decision-making capacity if nothing happened. The media onslaught had begun already, and in the New Year it would only become more intense. Some people thought that the chief executive should resign.

After Christmas I made up my mind – Pekka Ala-Pietilä would keep his job. His most important task was about to begin: he would spend the next few months sorting out the mess Nokia had got itself into. I also decided that Olli-Pekka Kallasvuo would become a temporary member of the team that ran our mobile phone operations. His job was to monitor product development and to provide financial acumen. From above it must have looked as if he were acting as my eyes and ears in Pekka's team. In fact I trusted Pekka's reporting, but I also wanted to ensure that his unit would get everything straight.

I decided that the responsibility for all this would rest with Pekka and me. When we met after Christmas we agreed that Pekka would withdraw from all public activities. He would scrub from his calendar everything unconnected with this firefighting. He would be given the chance to raise his unit from the ashes. We agreed that I would accept any and all public criticism for as long as it took to put things straight. That would give Pekka the breathing space he needed to get things back into shape.

It was important to send two signals to Nokia internally. Earlier I said that you could make mistakes in Nokia, though no one was to make the same mistake twice. If I had gotten rid of Pekka I would have gone against my own principles of leadership. Mistakes are for learning from. Very few people in a company will make mistakes consciously or from bad faith. We made this mistake because we didn't understand what our rate of growth demanded from the company and from us.

My message to everyone working for Nokia was that we had indeed made a mistake but that we weren't playing a blame game. It was a message that the next eight months were a serious test of how Pekka's organization could be knocked back into shape. If Pekka and his team didn't succeed I would have to look at things afresh, but I was confident that Pekka and his team would get things straight. I really didn't have much choice when I made my decision. I couldn't give special attention to running one particular unit because that would have been a misuse of a chief executive's position and time. I gave the responsibility to the people whose responsibility it was, but that didn't mean I was indifferent as to the outcome.

I had intensive conversations with Pekka. We met one-on-one and as part of the management team. I spoke to him at great length. I know that period was very difficult for Pekka. I was certainly partly guilty of making it so: I wanted to use every possible means to ensure that this mistake would not be fatal to us or to Nokia. I was paranoid in my search for weak points in Pekka's plans, and I continually demanded additional information from him. I was hard on him, just as I was hard on myself, too. I was demanding the impossible, but Pekka already knew to expect that – he knew me.

But I never criticized him publicly. We discussed things together, and I wanted him to know that I wouldn't let go of the matter until I knew we were back in calm waters.

In January 1996 we agreed that there was really only one person who could ensure that we did reach those calm waters – Pertti Korhonen. He was the best person to extricate Nokia from its difficulties. His powers of organization, experience, and optimism were an absolutely unbeatable combination. Pertti's task would be to create a mechanism robust enough to withstand the fastest growth, which would bring everything together into one chain of processes. Everything would be integrated: from product development and design, through the procurement of components, and on to manufacturing and even marketing. This was no small challenge, and Pertti wanted a little time to think. He had some difficulties with the idea. He had run an organization of three to four thousand people, but now he would become some peculiar one-man band. It wouldn't look very good, either inside Nokia or in the press. It would look as if a successful young manager had been pushed to the sidelines. There was another problem, too, which made Pertti hesitate – he didn't understand anything at all about logistics. But that wasn't a big worry for Pekka or me. Good Nokia people that we were, we believed that Pertti would soon learn all he needed to.

We had set up a reliable process for manufacturing mobile phones and we could make large batches efficiently. But that wasn't enough. We still lacked control systems that could tell our factories what they should produce and by when, what components were needed, and in what numbers and where. The stage was set for an internal battle: the production people said that the marketing people should be able to forecast what sorts of phones would be needed. The marketing people said what they thought demand would be,

Liisa and me with Intel president and CEO Craig Barret and his wife Barbara in Sun Valley in 2003. Intel was a Nokia supplier as early as the 1980s. Barbara later became the U.S. ambassador to Finland.

but the phones stayed in the warehouse when demand shifted to another model. But that other phone, the one customers did want to buy, wasn't in the warehouse. It was a big mess. Its roots didn't lie in the company's stratified structure so much as at its very center. It sat at the center of every western company.

For decades now every company has believed in organization by function. A company will have a production division, a sales division, and many other divisions, and each has its own job to do. That's why it's called organization by function. This system works splendidly when development is proceeding smoothly. When the markets for your product aren't growing too fast, everyone knows what their job is. Also, the company can make it clear what it expects each division to do – otherwise, individual divisions will start to pursue their own interests. For example, using machinery at full capacity was the most important thing for one of our production managers, who had been trained in Japan. That made production efficient because it minimized the unit cost of every mobile phone, the essence of efficiency. But the manager in question wasn't at all interested in whether he was making phones that would sell or phones that would stay on the shelves. From Nokia's viewpoint it was better for the sorts of phones that stay on the shelves to remain unmade.

These were points that Pertti quickly identified. But the full picture of the catastrophe only became clear a little at a time. We understood that the problem lay with our processes, though we had also suffered from problems with the supply of components and from unreliable business partners. Before Christmas 1995 it was clear to us there were problems with chargers provided by a Norwegian company. Most of them functioned perfectly well, but some of them caused a short circuit when you tried to use them. The casing turned into a hot grey mass of plastic. Eventually you would be left with two pins sticking out of the wall socket, ready to electrocute any passing adult, child, or pet. It was no wonder that U.S. officials responsible for product safety demanded that we do something. We were ever more dependent on our suppliers – although they made the parts, we bore the responsibility if anything went wrong. (Later we learned more about this dependence.) We also had to work with our suppliers to improve our processes.

Our entire organization was running at full throttle. Pekka Ala-Pietilä hardly slept at night. He spent a great deal of time travelling to sort out our problems. Pertti Korhonen put all his energy into working out what we had gotten ourselves into and how we could get out again. He too shuttled between our factories, our suppliers, and our sales units. I had at least managed to instill the feeling that Nokia faced a crisis.

After he shuttled around the world Pertti began to understand where our problems lay. Nokia's distribution centers around the world were full of stock that had failed to sell. Pertti had seen vast reserves of phones on his trip. We wondered what we could have gotten for the money tied up in these phones. How many miles of motorway? How many jumbo jets would we have been able to buy?

Had we tied up all the money from our listing on the New York Stock Exchange the previous year in these phones that no one wanted? We had indeed done just that. As I listened to Pertti's account, an impotent fury coursed through my veins once more. I wanted to rage at someone, but the only rightful target for my wrath was me.

Pertti Korhonen was working without preconceptions because he wasn't familiar with our old working methods. He knew only that it was his job to save Nokia, so he could look at Nokia's logistics with a clear eye. First he had to establish in his own mind what exactly lay at the heart of the problem. When he had made things clear to himself it would be easy for him to talk to others about them.

CHAPTER 46

Turning Weakness into Strength

B EFORE 1995 I HADN'T ENCOUNTERED FAILURE on a massive scale at Nokia. I had been a success in the finance department, although the entire company was in ruins. I had created the conditions for success when I was in charge of mobile phones. Later I had taken charge of Nokia when the company faced formidable risks and failure was a real possibility. I was unsure how to set about turning the whole of Nokia around in the spring of 1992, but I succeeded nonetheless.

The events of 1995 were like a bad dream, a nightmare even, that should never have occurred. In fact the nightmare seemed to go on and on, getting scarier all the time. I had given Pekka, Pertti, and their teams eight to nine months to sort things out. I had steeled myself to consider Pekka's position again after six months – if he didn't succeed I would have to remove him. That would be hard but unavoidable.

I put pressure on Pekka, I kept him up to the mark, and I spurred him on. And I supported him. I used every means at my disposal. Some of these were agreeable enough, but I kept on at him like an angry dog that wouldn't let go. I trusted him, but I also wanted to be sure I was doing my own bit. I did everything I could for him, and of course for Nokia and for myself. We owed that to the company and to all our 30,000 employees. We couldn't let them down. We couldn't be allowed to fail.

As far as the press was concerned we had pretty much failed already, and they had good reasons to think that. At the end of February we issued our results for the whole of 1995. Our profits had grown by 39 percent, but they were smaller than the analysts had forecast. All the growth was down to our telecommunications division, which had generated over half our profits. The profit from mobile phones stayed much as it had been, and consumer electronics did little to make the figures look better. We also announced that we were finally getting out of television production altogether. I warned that our results for 1996 would be weaker. I explained that competition in telecommunications would reduce our profits and would also affect our profits from mobile phones. My profit warning didn't please the investors – our share value sank like a stone. In the course of six months Nokia shares lost nearly half their value. It wasn't an achievement I'm going to boast about in these memoirs.

Growth in our profits stalled in 1996 and ended up 15 percent lower than in the previous year.

Even so, Nokia's results were the best in its history: they had grown by nearly 40 percent in a year. Our share of the mobile phone market had risen from 20 percent to 24 percent. We had almost doubled our sales of mobile phones from 5.5 million to 10.5 million, but that was still 1.6 million less than our budget had forecast. The world was becoming an extraordinary place, I reflected. I couldn't think of any precedents for the sort of business we were doing. We had failed, but we were still growing at an immense speed. The pace of change was so fast that we could never have predicted how it would change, even if we had dared to try.

Besides, the press brought us back to earth. On Friday, 1 March, the *Financial Times*, which I have always held in high regard, published a story that hit home harder than anything before. I had become inured to the comments of the Finnish press, which were often weak on analysis; I had a thick skin as far as they were concerned. Nokia was already too big for Finland. It was an excellent target for journalists who wanted to let their feelings spill out as long as they could find a little material on which to base a story. I found the criticisms of the international press much more to the point. The *Financial Times* had published a story under the headline "Nokia says Goodbye to the Golden Days." It pointed out that I had issued two profit warnings in the course of three months and that the company's share value had fallen by 50 percent. In light of these facts it said, "Nokia's sensational run as one of the best technology shares" seemed to be coming to an end. The paper said that the latest profit warning confirmed the view that, at the very least, the company faced some intractable problems. "The big question is whether Nokia can return to form this year," it wrote.

I received the paper at the office that Friday morning. I felt gloomy as I read it. Apart from everything else the question touched on my reputation, my pride, my ability. I decided to show the *Financial Times* that we would succeed again, and better than before.

That year, 1996, was surely one of the most important in Nokia's history. It looked to me as if we were fighting on every front. At first we seemed to be sustaining losses in every battle, but as the year's end approached we began to see glimpses of victory.

Pekka Ala-Pietilä, Pertti Korhonen, and their teams succeeded – Nokia's production and distribution had been reconfigured. Earlier our factories had made products for which we had to find customers. Now we made only those products for which we knew there was a demand. The whole organization knew that Nokia held far too much stock, which tied up far too much money. Now our wares wouldn't lie around in warehouses; they would be sold much more quickly and efficiently.

One of Nokia's working methods crystallized during this rescue operation – people had to move out of their comfort zones. Taking an external viewpoint doesn't mean amateurishness, because every outsider should learn how to do things properly. Ultimately the question is down to the individual: if people are endowed with boldness, curiosity, and the right degree of responsibility, they can move from one area to another without serious problems.

The change is always difficult. It's difficult to move out of areas where you've experienced clear success. It's difficult to let go of people and structures that have served you well. It's difficult to risk failure when things are going so well. But there are at least two reasons that a company must push people to take risk to its limits. When the company is in crisis, solutions are hardly likely to emerge from inside the comfort zone, but will by definition be high risk. And the organization has to recognize and understand that the company is indeed in crisis. This knowledge shouldn't lead people to despair, it should act as a powerful motivator for change. Between these two – despair and a desire for transformation – the difference is only a hair's breadth. But it's dramatically important. If senior management signals despair, the game is lost. Besides, a company crisis is never the fault of single individuals. Blaming people for a crisis will paralyze the company and make the crisis still deeper.

Apart from crises people should be pushed to take risks, because at the risk boundary you'll often find growth, new business areas, and new thinking. When people are dealing with risk they learn how to handle and reduce it; put another way, they learn from their new experiences. That's always good for the company. Unfamiliar areas become familiar. The risk boundary is pushed back and the unknown region shrinks. The company has learned something valuable, which it can exploit in the future.

Nokia's logistics crisis in 1995–96 happened at just the "right time," even if it didn't feel that way just then. We managed to put things straight over the course of nine months. We rebuilt our logistics chains, and we renewed our methods of production and the ways we worked with our partners. From now on our sales and our production would work seamlessly together. Components would reach the right factories at the right time. And all this would show up promptly and in the right form in our financial reports. Earlier our sales people always accused those in charge of production of making the wrong products. And the production people blamed our sales force for their failure to sell the goods they had ordered. When everything was overhauled Nokia's production machinery was better than that of any of its competitors. It was the most efficient in the entire industry. The crisis had compelled us to create something we desperately needed when sales of mobile phones started their explosive growth. After the crisis Nokia's machinery was in such good shape that it could withstand any conceivable demands made on it.

"Platform thinking" was a central part of our improvement in production efficiency. This means that several different phones can be mounted on the same technical base. We were able to extend the range of models we made while keeping production simple and efficient. The concept has also become part of Nokia's internal language. Many a friend or relative has heard talk of "platforms" in all sorts of situations. One of our employees reportedly urged his relatives to come to his wedding reception by saying "it's a wonderful platform for having a great time." At Nokia we would find nothing strange in that, but the wedding guests would disagree.

CHAPTER 47

The World Becomes a Web

THE CRISIS COMPELLED NOKIA TO RECONFIGURE its most important processes. The crisis also compelled us to consider what the company should really focus on. We discussed that in the corridors, in strategy groups, and among senior management. Many of us doubted that growth in our mobile phone business was sustainable. Creating one's own brand was becoming more difficult and expensive. Even so, our network business was growing and turning in impressive profits. Perhaps we should focus more on joint ventures with mobile network operating companies than on developing new consumer products. That might be the best way to safeguard our future.

Nokia's network business and its mobile phone business had long been separate. But in practice this wasn't a black-and-white distinction. We had to understand our customers, whether they were individuals who wanted to buy a mobile phone or operating companies that bought major networks from us. Operating companies were also customers for our phones. In the 1990s we sold over half our output to the operators, who sold them on to retail customers through their own sales channels. We tried to make our brands and products enticing so that consumers would want to buy them and the operators would have to stock them.

The winner in our internal discussions was often the division that happened to be performing best, so our mobile phone operations had to respond to internal criticism. At the heart of the discussion was Nokia's future direction. Sometime in March The Five met one Sunday evening to examine that question. Nokia Mobile Phones, led by Pekka Ala-Pietilä, was very much in the position of defendant. "None of the rest of you apart from Jorma knows enough about this business. And even Jorma's experience doesn't go back very far," said Pekka rather indignantly, which was unusual for him.

These discussions never became part of Nokia's formal strategic planning. Even so they say something about the uncertainty that the year 1996 brought us and about the real quest that was under way. We couldn't produce mobile phones without regard to the operators' wishes or empathy for their concerns. But in no circumstance would we give up our own brand to become solely a manufacturer of generic products with some operator's label stuck on the casing. We had succeeded in growing the value of our brand on the global market. We weren't at the top yet, but we were well on the way. We believed we would be able to exploit technical advances to make better phones that did innovative things. We had a chance to become the world's leading mobile phone company. For that we needed the will, hard work, good decisions, and, it must be said, a certain degree of good luck.

We did draw on outside help in developing our own thinking. For example, in 1995 we organized a "future seminar" on mobile phones. We invited the highly regarded Gary Hamel, a management guru whose name is known to every business student. The seminar generated a fat file of new ideas that we drew on for years afterwards.

My own decision was that we should continue our twin-track approach. We would continue to develop our own brand, our own technology, and better mobile products aimed directly at our customers. Nokia would also become a company that developed both industrial production and software. We would listen very closely to our customers among the operating companies, because so much of our turnover depended on them. Thus ended this phase of introspection at Nokia. But I knew that what I had decided was easier said than done.

We soon had other reasons for introspection. The world was changing without asking Nokia's permission. We had to evolve rapidly, but in which direction? In many respects Nokia was at the eye of a storm. If we made the right decisions we would get wind in our sails, but if we failed the storm would consign us to the deep along with other forgotten shipwrecked companies. There wasn't much time to make the right decisions, and no one had enough information about what the future might have in store for technology companies in the 2000s. Nor did we know how our customers would behave, whether they were in Europe, Asia, or North America. But we would have to find out if we were to survive the coming onslaught.

We also had to create our own momentum to carry us forward. The new generation of GSM-standard mobile phones provided some impetus. GSM

(Global System for Mobile Communications) was the world's most important standard, thanks to the combined might of Nokia and Ericsson. We wanted it to be the global standard for new digital phones. In the United States operators were free to select their own standards, whereas in Europe the view was that the standard should be universal. After that it was up to the operators to compete by offering the best possible service. So a Swedish girl could call home as easily from a holiday in Spain as when she had popped out to the shops in Stockholm. In the United States she might not be able to speak to someone in the next state.

In the spring of 1994 the U.S. government held an auction of licenses for mobile phone operators. It was up to the operators which standard they adopted. Nokia's chief technology officer, Yrjö Neuvo, and I went around to many American operators and tried to persuade them of the excellence of the GSM standard. I can't say we were very successful. GSM became only the third most popular of the standards on offer. That was why the United States lagged far behind Europe and Japan when new mobile services were developed at the end of the 1990s.

In Europe GSM was already an important standard, which suited Nokia completely. We wanted the next generation of mobile phones to take GSM as its starting point. A battle began in 1996 that the press later characterized as "Nokia's First World War." Our goal was ambitious: we wanted the world to adopt a mobile phone standard that would put our own products in a strong position. And of course we also believed that such a standard would be best for consumers.

In Europe we decided to form a Nordic alliance with our Swedish competitor Ericsson. In the opposite corner stood the Franco-German alliance of Siemens and Alcatel. At the end of October 1997 I travelled to Brussels with two colleagues to meet the president of the European Commission, Jacques Santer. This crisis meeting, however, didn't lead to agreement on the future of the European mobile phone industry. The Nordic front needed additional support. In November 1997 the president of Finland, Martti Ahtisaari, told the British prime minister, Tony Blair, that he thought the standard proposed by Nokia and Ericsson would be the best for the United Kingdom as well. A couple of weeks later British Telecom weighed in on our side. Our global shuttling went on since we needed more supporters from the network operators both in Europe and in Asia.

At the end of November I again found myself in Brussels. E.U. Commissioner Martin Bangemann was now having a go at solving the European dispute, though without success. Finally the European Telecommunications Standards Institute (ETSI) took the first vote in its history to decide which of the competing standards was better and should be adopted. The Nokia-Ericsson proposal received 58.3 percent of the votes. This ultimate victory was ratified at a conference in Paris in January 1998.

We had opened negotiations on future standards with the Japanese back in September 1996. We wanted to avoid a situation where European and Japanese companies competed in Asian markets on the basis of different standards. We took the Japanese delegation go-karting and magnanimously allowed them to win. Later the Japanese negotiators enjoyed Nokia's hospitality at Båtvik manor, where the evening culminated in a musical solo by a senior Japanese director. We were sure that the evening had been a success. At the end of August the Japanese told us confidentially that they favored European technology for the next generation of networks.

In the United States the battle continued even after the Paris agreement. The American company Qualcomm accused European companies of reaching an unfair agreement. At the end of 1998 the U.S. government made a formal accusation of unfair competition against the European Union in a deposition signed by the U.S. secretary of state, Madeleine Albright. The battle eased off only in March 1999, when Europe and the United States agreed to end their public dispute over standards. At the same time Qualcomm sold its network business and its product development arm to Ericsson. The final flames of the Great Standards War had been extinguished.

At Nokia we started to believe that the future was digital much earlier than our competitors did. We did so because we were the challengers and also because Finnish engineers were keen to try something new. From our point of view it was well worth investing all our efforts in something that could transform the entire market. While Nokia was pushing digital phones, Motorola was still living in the analog era. Nokia surpassed Motorola partly because we were early adopters of digital technology.

With hindsight it's always easy to say that you were in the right place at the right time. This is as true of companies as it is of individuals. At the time of the technological tornado of the late 1990s no one knew for sure that they were in the right place at the right time. The years 1996 to 1999 were a time of explosive growth for all the world's technology companies, and the most important task their leaders faced was to keep their wits about them. As history relates, we didn't all succeed in that.

The Internet generated a tremendous wave of new companies, stupendous profits, a share price bubble, and the rise and fall of an entire generation of investors seeking riches. For an instant the Internet resembled the oil industry or U.S. railroads in their early days: unscrupulous entrepreneurs who could sense a quick opportunity made astronomical profits. The Internet was like those industries in another way: it changed the way things were done. It changed the way companies communicated, marketed their products, planned, and made things. The real impact of the Internet only started to become clear after the bubble burst at the beginning of the 2000s.

At Nokia we understood that the Internet would change many things forever. But we weren't sure exactly which things would change. We watched with our hair standing on end – at least those of us who still had hair – as tiny companies found their capital value growing to Nokia proportions. In our own minds, however, we were a serious and profitable company that made tangible things. Many consultants came to us recommending business models that would raise our share value to the skies, if only we could get our heads around the idea of a virtual company. I understood later that Enron must have listened to consultants like these before starting down the road to perdition.

The Internet also affected Nokia through changes in people's behavior. People wanted perfect mobility. At least that's what we believed at Nokia. We saw people's lives as divided into three: their personal life, their domestic life, and their working life. In all these an individual – our customer – needed perfect mobile services. These services were surely to be Internet-based.

CHAPTER 48

Discussions of Public Policy

FINLAND WAS HIT HARD BY AN ECONOMIC DEPRESSION at the beginning of the 1990s. Trade with the Soviet Union had collapsed, revealing the inefficiency of much of Finnish industry. An asset price bubble burst. We had to face a hefty dose of reality. GDP shrank by 30 percent and the stock market lost half its value. This compelled Finland to overhaul its structures and its thinking. I often exchanged thoughts with the prime ministers of the time – Esko Aho, who belonged to the Centre Party, and Paavo Lipponen, who was a Social Democrat – and their respective finance ministers. I met Aho in January 1992, immediately after my appointment as chief executive of Nokia. I told him that the company had had difficulties, which we would overcome because the core business was sound. We could build our future using our own resources: Nokia would never ask the government for money. What we wanted was for the government to create a business environment where companies like ours could thrive. I also stressed that I would do my best to support him, because a thriving Finland was absolutely crucial for Nokia.

At this time there was a vigorous debate on increasing the resources devoted to research and development. The government proposed a target of 3 percent of GDP by the end of the decade. This was confirmed by the Science and Technology Policy Council for Finland, which included representatives from businesses, universities, and research institutes as well as the key ministries. The government undertook to provide a 40-percent share, with the private sector covering the remaining 60 percent. They both had to sharply increase their investment in research and development, and we weren't talking of small sums of money. There was much skepticism in official circles but overall the target was reached by 1999. The private sector's share was 68 percent, and the state's contribution was also significantly higher than forecast in cash terms, since growth in GDP had exceeded all predictions. The increased R&D spending revitalized many universities, which were then able to contribute to Nokia's need for able graduates. Universities also became good research partners for Nokia and other high-tech companies.

In the early autumn of 1996 Nokia's long logistical crisis seemed to be coming to its end, but an entirely new sort of problem was now on the agenda. Would Finland continue to be the right place for Nokia to have its head office or indeed for Nokia in general? The question had been floating around since the late 1980s, but not in any very serious way. In the early 1990s, when Nokia was rapidly becoming more international, there had been lots of little practical issues that might have been resolved more easily elsewhere, and discussions over the location of the head office gathered pace. Many people thought that if Nokia did indeed become a successful major international company, it was inevitable that the head office and perhaps other functions would have to relocate. Speculation always seemed to heighten, in the media as well as within the company, when results and growth rates were good, and it would fall back once again when everyday problems pressed down or results didn't live up to expectations.

At the end of October 1996 I summoned The Five for a short meeting. First we ran through current issues as we usually did; a snapshot of activity showed that the company as a whole was performing well. Then without any particular preparation I brought up the question of where the head office should be sited. I noted that even though we had survived our recent logistical crisis in mobile phones, it was likely even in the best-case scenario that in the next five years we would find ourselves in a storm similar to the one we had just weathered. If we were to emerge victorious from our current phase of growth we needed to develop our leadership significantly, to recruit new key individuals and specialists, to strengthen our global organization, and above all to create a more stable environment for development and renewal, as we had done at the beginning of the decade. All this was already well in hand, but my message was that our efforts needed more oomph.

At the same time Finland seemed to be emerging from its own economic problems. Its economic policy was steady, pragmatic, and successful. Nokia had a lot to do in the coming years in terms of its internal development. There would be no benefit for the company if its senior management spent its time niggling over where to site its head office or other peripheral questions. We had had quite enough of those in recent years – both external and self-inflicted.

I proposed to my colleagues that we should not add the question of the location of our head office to our agenda, but should tersely note that Nokia would remain in Finland and develop its operations on that assumption. We could come back to the matter if there were significant new factors to consider and we needed to check our basic approach. I also proposed that I would tell the prime minister and finance minister, but otherwise we should remain silent on the issue.

To my surprise this didn't give rise to much discussion, and my view received a clear endorsement. For my colleagues it seemed a natural line to follow, which apparently didn't even need this much consideration, for without this discussion we would simply have followed this line anyway – it was the default position. Because there had been so little discussion I checked later with each of the others that they really were happy with what we'd agreed.

I told both the prime minister and finance minister toward the end of 1996 that we'd decided to keep our head office in Finland. I added that we also intended to raise the proportion of the product development that we conducted in Finland – it was already 75 percent. We had no demands to make or conditions to impose, and we never would. There were just two things we hoped to see. First, that Nokia would not be "punished" for this decision and that the government for its part would sincerely try to look after the environment for international companies operating in Finland.

When they had recovered from their initial surprise, both party leaders, as they then were, grasped the magnitude of the request. We then had an exceptionally open discussion of what was needed if Finland was to become an attractive destination for investment and business was to be successful. I hadn't brought a wish-list along – and I wouldn't have wanted that sort of discussion since it would have gone against the grain of my principles. I brought up only one crucial point: the high level of personal taxation in Finland. This didn't have much direct impact on Nokia, but it had a greater indirect impact because it affected the dynamism of the economy.

In Finland the high marginal rates of taxation had long been a problem for those moving from middle incomes into higher tax brackets. When I discussed the issue with Finnish engineers at Nokia in 1999 there was clearly growing dissatisfaction with the punitive tax progression. I did some simple sums, based on an engineer at Salo who had a wife and two children. These showed that when a recently qualified engineer's salary was doubled, his take-home pay rose by only 15 percent. The higher tax rates were not the only reason for this; other benefits such as housing support were removed as the salary increased.

The message was clear: it was difficult in Finland to motivate engineers to achieve results or aim for more senior positions because taxes would take almost all the increase in salary just when they were trying to start a family. For the best engineers this was an additional reason for seeking work overseas. I discussed this several times with the prime minister, finance minister, and cabinet secretary. These long conversations brought results. At the start of January 2000, at a breakfast meeting at the prime minister's official residence, I received confirmation that the tax progression scale would be revised and a more rational system of banding introduced. These changes would be introduced over several years, as indeed they were. This process showed that the Finnish establishment was working toward sensible structural change. It also brought the incentive effects of taxation on to the political agenda.

The possible relocation of our head office remained a focus of interest at the highest levels of government. In 2005 President Tarja Halonen asked me privately what Nokia intended to do regarding its domicile. The president sounded very concerned. "My understanding is that the head office will remain in Finland," I replied. "But it's not out of the question that an individual division might relocate abroad. The latest software trends come chiefly from the United States, so we really have to be there in some way. We will be very pragmatic on this point."

I have always followed broader developments in society, taking part in public discussions where they touch on the challenges of business life and the problems that companies face. I have also taken a close interest in public education at all levels. Many people in Finland have interpreted this as a desire to one day take part in politics as an elected representative. (I have never shown any wish to do so, not even as a remote possibility.) When I went to study at the London School of Economics in 1977 I left behind an over-politicized country with an emergency government. Though it felt good to come back to Finland, my decision was clear: I had returned to pursue a business career. Life in political circles had absolutely no appeal.

In May 1999 the finance minister wanted to have a confidential talk with me, and we met in a private room at the Palace restaurant. I recall a fine view over the Helsinki market square and the onion domes of the Orthodox cathedral. The minister hoped I would consider becoming the Conservative candidate for president. His idea was that the Centre Party might also put its weight behind me and that I would emerge as an unbeatable "bourgeois" candidate. (In Finland presidential candidates stand as individuals, but with support from political parties.) I explained that I was not available, because the previous year I had undertaken to lead Nokia well into the following decade. I couldn't imagine reneging on that obligation.

In November 2003 Prime Minister Matti Vanhanen invited Liisa and me to dinner at his home in his constituency about thirty miles from Helsinki. His wife had prepared a delicious meal and we all got on very well together, even if the décor wasn't entirely to our taste. Over the dinner table we spoke mostly about international politics. Vanhanen was fascinating to talk to, and both knowledgeable and passionate about the European Union and the other issues we discussed. As the evening drew to a close he unexpectedly raised the forthcoming presidential elections. He noted that the Centre Party didn't have a strong candidate and that I ought to think very seriously about standing. I hadn't expected the question but my answer was ready. It was a clear "no." Although I was already thinking of standing down from the role of chief executive, I wasn't ready even to think about becoming a presidential candidate. This time I didn't have a follow-up conversation.

CHAPTER 49

What Do People Want?

IN 1996 NOKIA DEMONSTRATED A NEW PRODUCT, which we proudly called the Communicator. It wasn't simply a phone; it also had an Internet browser, a fax, email, and a calendar. It could have been called the first smartphone long before that term was invented.

The Communicator was the creation of one man. Reijo Paajanen, who worked in Tampere, drove his idea through regardless of all opposition. Thanks to his perseverance one of Nokia's technological icons saw the light of day.

The Communicator wasn't quite ready when it was first launched – its software didn't work as well as it should, and it didn't have all the applications necessary for all its features to be fully functional. It was quite a large device, and many people found it clumsy. It wasn't especially significant as far as Nokia's revenue was concerned. But its impact on our public image as a company at the cutting edge of technology was immeasurable. The Communicator soon occupied the prime position on the financial pages of the *New York Times* under the headline: "Made in Finland, Sold Just About All Over." That's the sort of advertising money can't buy.

The Communicator was a product designed for professionals. It was an implement that salespeople, stockbrokers, estate agents, and even truck drivers might use. It could fit in a pocket, even if it needed to be a large pocket. With the Communicator we were announcing that we were targeting business customers who wanted to work efficiently when they were on the move. From then on Nokia would make products that weren't just telephones, but wireless devices for business use.

The Communicator didn't so much belong in an office as it was an office. Finnish diplomats who attended E.U. meetings in Brussels on a daily basis equipped themselves with Communicators so they could go through their email and hold conversations with the Finnish foreign ministry during breaks in the meetings or even, undetected, while they were in progress.

Even though the Communicator wasn't our greatest commercial success, it did give us a real edge over our competitors. Our achievements began to be noticed more widely. People began to mention Nokia in the same breath as other leading companies such as Microsoft, Intel, and Sony. We were world class now, and this could be measured. The *Financial Times* and the consulting firm Price Waterhouse put together a list of Europe's most highly regarded companies: we came nineteenth. In electronics we came third, just after Siemens and Electrolux. Later we improved our rankings.

Though these were only lists, they did boost our self-esteem. Years of hard work had begun to pay off: at last we were among the big players, which is where we had wanted to be ever since we had asked ourselves, five years earlier, what our goals should be. We were also moving into a further phase of spectacular growth.

In 1997 we had to think about what was going on around us and how Nokia should change to reflect that. We held a few meetings of The Five at Båtvik. I wanted us to take seriously what was going on the world. Wireless technology was exploding in front of our eyes, the Internet was creating a technological revolution, and digital technology was changing everything. What did we believe in? In which areas did we want to grow? What should we think about all this? How should Nokia be structured to face these challenges?

We also had a debate on whether Nokia's future lay in mobile phones or in networks. We encouraged and challenged each other. Some thought that concentrating on networks would suit Nokia best. They saw no need for Nokia to focus either on media or on multimedia; the company should stay in those areas it did best. That wasn't my opinion. I thought we should at least play a more active role in developing Internet technology. I decided that we would abandon one of our old principles, that Nokia should not seek growth through acquisitions. I had it noted in the board minutes in September 1997 that "acquisitions are a possible (but not prioritized) means of enhancing Nokia's structure."

Nokia would be divided into three parts: its highly profitable and expanding mobile phone and network businesses, and a little Internet unit to give us experience and something to learn from. So we established Nokia Ventures

Nokia 9000 Communicator (1996) beside the smaller Nokia E7 (2010). Kryštof Korb photo, GNU Free Documentation 1.2, Wikimedia Commons.

Organization, which bought small but capable Internet technology companies, most of them American. They never became a large part of Nokia: in 2000 they accounted for just three percent of revenue.

These discussions about Nokia's future direction were important. The people in my core group had clear opinions influenced by their backgrounds and personalities. Pekka Ala-Pietilä and Sari Baldauf were particularly good at seeing beyond their own narrow areas and also at picking up even faint signals. They were also the most ready to embrace new ways of working and changes in organization. So Pekka was the most natural choice to manage the new Internet unit.

In 1997 we also set ourselves the objective of stabilizing our mobile phone division. This meant that we never wanted to have another nightmare like the one we lived through in 1995. I wanted to ensure that our processes were in such good shape that the right components would always be available to make the right phones available to consumers at the right time. I was now quite paranoid about this and I didn't want to leave anything to chance.

Our results in 1997 were extraordinary – our profits grew by 98 percent. I started to feel that I had carried out the task I'd been assigned. Five years had passed since I became Nokia's chief executive. Now our position was stronger than ever before and also stronger than we could have imagined five years earlier.

But despite my delight I still saw causes for concern when I looked around: I knew that the most dangerous was success. I saw all sorts of things that we understood absolutely nothing about. We weren't an Internet company and didn't want to become one. But had we perhaps defined ourselves a little too narrowly, identified ourselves too closely with mobile phones? Many types of new wireless networks began to sprout toward the end of the 1990s. In the United States people were starting to use palmtop computers and wireless local area networks.

We needed to do some more fundamental thinking and establish what people wanted. What did New York financiers, Tokyo teenagers, Istanbul shopkeepers, and cattle farmers in Brazil want? They weren't interested in GSM technology, WLAN, UMTS, 3G, or any other technical gobbledygook. They were only interested in services that would actually help them. In a mobile world they wanted to find new ways of working; and they would want to use the products and services we offered as long as they were reliable, affordable, and visually attractive. Customer satisfaction would be the key success factor in the future, too.

Nokia was stepping into a new era, where success would be determined by customer satisfaction. But our customers were everywhere, and everywhere they were slightly different. And lots of things had an impact on them, apart from our wonderful products. Perhaps we should place customer needs center stage and move technical concerns to the wings. If we believed only in established technologies we would soon find ourselves in the wings when customers found something that met their needs better than our products did.

In 1997 my journey to work became significantly shorter when we opened our new head office in Espoo, about five miles to the west of Helsinki. The length of my commute, however, hadn't been a criterion in the choice of location, particularly since I spent more and more time globetrotting on Nokia business. Relocation at Keilahti had been under consideration as far back as 1982. Pekka Helin and Tuomo Siitonen had won the architectural competition with a design they called *Kide,* which means *crystal,* and this design was the basis for our fine new offices.

CHAPTER 50

How to Lead a Global Nokia?

W E REALIZED IN 1996 that at Nokia we didn't know enough about the world. We had grown by accident into a global company that was now being compared to other global companies. We were like a little local team that suddenly finds itself playing in the big leagues.

I concluded that the firm's top leadership should monitor and study our most important markets. Thus Olli-Pekka Kallasvuo took responsibility for North America, and Sari Baldauf for Asia, which meant Japan, South Korea, China, Hong Kong, and Taiwan. I wanted us to know what was going on in these key markets. I also wanted regional viewpoints to play a more prominent role in our decision-making.

I wanted to create a matrix system for Nokia that would ensure that a subsidiary wouldn't find itself buried out of sight in China or America. I wanted information to flow from these markets back to Finland; and, conversely, for Nokia's strategy to take root in those areas. I'm not sure how well all this actually worked, because Sari Baldauf and Olli-Pekka Kallasvuo had only a couple of years before I reconfigured the organization again. But I do know that Nokia would never have gained a strong position in China if Sari hadn't introduced new ways of doing things there.

Changes in the markets, our own growth, and technological development combined to force us to consider our future strategy more closely. One of the hardest things was to communicate our strategy to our staff, whose numbers were growing by several thousand a year. We had 31,766 employees in 1996, and 35,430 a year later. The following year nearly 10,000 people joined Nokia: we had 44,543 employees altogether. How was some twenty-five-year-old Australian computer expert going to learn anything about Nokia's values or strategy in his very first proper job? I had no ready answer to this, but we tried to construct processes that would project both our values and our strategy. And projection on its own wasn't enough: we also had to bring our employees along with us so that they would feel that they could influence our strategy and values in their turn.

We opened our annual strategy discussion by bringing together our four hundred most important managers. These meetings had originally had two hundred participants, but we expanded that number to reflect the company's growth. We ran through all the most important challenges facing us. These weren't occasions for self-congratulation or self-satisfied speeches. In line with Nokia's finest traditions these meetings were held so that the company's leadership could hear in plain English exactly what people thought. We spoke of our successes and how we had achieved them, of course, but we also homed in on things we needed to do better. On these occasions Finns were over-represented, but the proportion of non-Finns was growing rapidly.

I'm not a believer in great strategic theories or consultants. For me strategic thinking is very mundane work. It's a matter of operational planning, which has to include a clear idea of where we want to be and how we'll get there. A good strategy should pretty well update itself automatically. A strategy should also allow room to make continuous adjustments and corrections. When Nokia was growing fast at the end of the 1990s, we simply didn't have time to commit ourselves to a single rigid strategy; we had to set off without knowing where we would end up. We could work out the exact route when we were on our way.

Although strategic thinking is routine work, you still have to create structures where it can flourish. We set up a strategy panel at Nokia that met once a month. It consisted of the executive committee augmented by a few other senior managers. An outsider sitting in on a meeting of the strategy panel might be bewildered. The discussion might take some great issue as its theme, but it would be equally likely to focus on small details. The most important thing was that no decisions were reached at the meetings. There was no agenda, and no minutes were kept. Sometimes discussion was heated, sometimes everyone was lost in thought. The meetings usually lasted about three hours. Mikko Kosonen, who was responsible for corporate planning, usually proposed a theme, or occasionally I would make suggestions for discussion. I liked to use the strategy panel to test out my own ideas and to find answers to those questions at the forefront of my mind.

Over the years the strategy panel demonstrated its usefulness as a discussion forum. I enjoy group discussions but I'm not sure they bring out the best in me. I suppose I've had my best strategy discussions with individuals, on a one-on-one basis. Often I took away one or two key thoughts from the strategy panel, which I would later discuss with the relevant colleague. My leadership style was based on The Five and also on direct connections to the two hundred or so key individuals within Nokia.

I believe that wisdom doesn't reside in the head of some great leader but is diffused throughout the workforce. Companies usually don't listen enough to alternative strategies. If someone has ended up as a chief executive or executive committee member, he has almost certainly lost not only his hair but his capacity for fresh ideas. But even experienced managers can revitalize themselves if they really want to. Organizations should encourage this renewal, because otherwise their strategy cannot be renewed. But even more than that, organizations must find a way for new and dissident ideas to make themselves heard. A company must be able to question its own objectives and working methods, otherwise it won't thrive in the real world, the one we all live in.

In our discussions we disagreed over only a few matters. We argued vigorously about how we should work with mobile network operators and to what extent we should tailor our products to please them. We had divergent opinions about that for at least a decade. The question is one of principle and goes to the heart of Nokia. Nokia always had to balance the conflicting demands of its own brand and the needs of its customers among the mobile network operators, whose negotiating power varied over time. Highly competitive auctions of future telephone bandwidth drove many of them to the brink of bankruptcy. Then Nokia and others had to keep them afloat financially so that business could carry on. Conversely, as in 1995, our sales of mobile phones were so poor at times that sales of networks to the operators were the only thing that kept our business afloat.

But even within Nokia there were extreme differences of view on fundamental questions. One of our directors might think that you should never throw in your lot with the operators but should aim to shake them off eventually in favor of dealing directly with individual consumers. Another might say that the operators were among our most important customers and we should do things exactly as they want. It would be nice if one could find a clear answer to this question, but there's no such thing. So Nokia will always have to navigate this passageway as best it can.

It may be that Nokia focused too much on technologies associated with mobile phones – cellular technologies, in other words. It may be that Nokia should have learned more about other wireless technologies. If we had been quicker off the mark we might have developed new areas of business that would have flourished in the difficult new decade of the 2000s. But over-hauling a company's entire strategy is no longer a simple matter if it's grown to become the global leader in its field. The degree of difficulty becomes many times greater.

The worst that can happen to a company is to run out of money and be forced into bankruptcy. Enormous success is perhaps the next worst. It dazzles you and creates the notion that history will repeat itself. Impressive growth figures or the opening of new markets make you believe that there exists a path paved with gold, and that if only you can find the secret of success you'll soon find your way back to it. If the company has been successful in the past, that's where you'll probably look to find this secret. If the company has grown and become successful it can no longer make its own decisions. Investment analysts and investors follow its every move at every nanosecond.

The worst news an investor can hear is that the company has made a new and unexpected strategic choice that will lead it away from the golden path, with its guarantee of success and security. It's pointless to expect investors to have a long-term perspective. A company has to show growth in its share price in the short-term, over the next reporting period. A company has to do what it promised. Just the idea of a company taking a new direction or adopting a new strategy is enough to scare people off. The share price might fall, and the company may have less room to maneuver. Its most important managers will lose any bonuses linked to the share price. It won't be able to use its shares as collateral as it once did. The media will use its share price performance as a reason to condemn its change in direction.

If a company's leaders are to push through a new strategy or a complete renewal of the company, they must either have immense willpower or face a crisis. If you set out to renew a company that has successfully launched itself on the stock exchange you may even put your own financial position at risk. That makes it very difficult to revitalize a successful global public company. Even so, some succeed: for example, I admire enormously Lou Gerstner's work at IBM. He changed a company that made things into one that sold software and services, at the same time maintaining the company's position in the world.

Nokia didn't become a major Internet company at the end of the 1990s. Its board meeting in Beijing in 1998 looked at the alternatives facing the company: either remain as a significant force in wireless technology or try to establish itself in the new markets opened up by the Internet. That would have necessitated major acquisitions, especially in the United States, at the time

I'm shown here with Georg Ehrnrooth, member of the Nokia board of directors.

the Internet bubble was expanding. Nokia's profitability and its share price would have dipped for a few years, and the company could well have become the target for a hostile takeover. Nobody knows where we would have been by, say, 2005. It's possible that Nokia would have been in a stronger position. But it's also possible that Nokia would no longer have an independent existence, that some other company would have swallowed us up. No one can offer a certain answer to a counter-factual question.

My own role at Nokia changed as the end of the millennium approached. My boss, Chairman of the Board Casimir Ehrnrooth, invited me to his manor house in July 1997. I had gotten on very well with Ehrnrooth. We had dealt with each other directly; no fussing around, just discussion and agreement on major issues when we needed it, such as after board meetings. So I guessed there must be some special reason for this visit, but I didn't know what that might be beforehand.

We took a sauna and were eating supper when Ehrnrooth explained why he had invited me. "I've been discussing with the owners who should be chairman of the board. We're all agreed that no one already on the board is really suited to the job. We've thought about it and I wondered whether you might take on this responsibility, given that operational responsibility would continue to rest with you?"

The arrangement that Ehrnrooth proposed, which combined the jobs of chair and chief executive, was common in U.S. companies but less so in

Europe. Nokia had gradually been approaching the U.S. model in its internal structures, and against that background the proposal wasn't unprecedented. Studies had been made of which sort of company worked better: those where the chair had operational responsibility, or those where the chair and the chief executive were different people. No significant differences had been identified across a wide range of companies or over both long and short time frames.

But in 1997 Finnish company law didn't allow the two roles to be combined, so we needed to do some work on the legal basis for the decision. In such a case the company would appoint a new chief executive, who would be responsible for the company's operations in the sense demanded by the law, though it would be agreed that I would be ultimately responsible for the company's operations.

The proposal had been presented. I promised to think about it over several months, because there was clearly no great hurry. We would revisit the issue the following autumn. "I'm ready to take on this arrangement, though in Finland it's a little unusual. But we have to make sure the legal aspects are properly worked out," was my answer to Ehrnrooth.

The company secretary and director of legal affairs, Ursula Ranin, drew up a long and thorough memorandum, which she submitted in December 1997. As well as the legal aspects it summarized international experience. The advantage of the dual role was the opportunity it gave for decisive advancement of the company's vision and chosen focus. The dual role was risky in so far as the board might no longer be independent of the executive committee. There would be an exceptional risk if the board's members were linked to or dependent on the company or its executive committee. The board's ability to carry out its supervisory duties would be weakened, and it was likely to be too slow to respond if, for example, there was a need to remove board members.

Around this time we carried out another restructuring. Pekka Ala-Pietilä was no longer in charge of the mobile phone division but was now responsible for strategic planning and projects linked with Nokia's future. We had set up the New Ventures Organization to identify suitable companies for Nokia to buy. Pekka was in charge of this unit and he also continued as director of Nokia Communications Products. He was also appointed deputy chief executive, which foreshadowed his appointment as president. Matti Alahuhta became head of the mobile phone division. Starting at the beginning of 1999 the president of the network division would be Sari Baldauf, who had been running our operations in Asia.

Pekka Ala-Pietilä was thus appointed president of Nokia. Pekka also became the natural candidate to take over from me when I eventually stood down as chairman. Why Pekka Ala-Pietilä? I knew all my closest colleagues extremely well. Pekka seemed very well prepared for the job. He was good at managing people and had a strong strategic grasp. He was also a brilliant change manager and very good at picking up signals. His background as leader of the mobile phone division also influenced the decision. At that time we believed that mobile phones were even more central to Nokia's future than networks.

My conversations with Sari Baldauf also formed part of the background. Sari had told me that she didn't intend to spend many more years with the company. She had already been in charge of networks for nearly a decade. "This has been a wonderful project, but there must be something more to life than Nokia," was how she put it. Her original intention had been to leave Nokia in 2001, but the combination of the changed circumstances and some arm-twisting from me persuaded her to stay until the beginning of 2005.

The official decisions were made at the annual general meeting in 1999. Casimir Ehrnrooth stepped down from the role of chairman of the board after seven years. There was no drama about this: Ehrnrooth was sixty-eight. Pekka Ala-Pietilä became president of Nokia and I was appointed chairman and chief executive.

The media didn't find the changes particularly significant. "Only the job titles change," wrote the business weekly *Talouselämä*. I emphasized at the press conference that in the last resort operational responsibility remained with me.

Of course everyone should have a boss. As far as I was concerned it was the deputy chair of the board who fulfilled this role. From spring 1999 until spring 2000 Iiro Viinanen, who had joined the board in 1996, occupied the slot. Paul J. Collins, who had joined the board in 1998, took over in 2000. Robert F. W. van Oordt had also joined the board in 1998, which was when we had made English our operational language. After that there were numerous board members from outside Finland. The change from the Nokia of old, where the board had been a wrestling mat for Finnish bankers, couldn't have been starker.

Collins's background was the world of finance: he was deputy chairman of Citibank. He took quite an active role and spoke to me even more frequently and intensively than Casimir Ehrnrooth. He lived in London, so we spoke on the telephone and met at board meetings. We had a very American-style dialogue, unstructured and direct. Collins's role at the beginning of the 2000s was notably bigger and more important than it appeared in public.

CHAPTER 51

Meeting the Media

A CHIEF EXECUTIVE'S RELATIONS WITH THE MEDIA are so important they deserve a chapter to themselves. While what I write here is obviously based on my experience in Finland, the lessons I learned are applicable much more widely, perhaps universally.

Even when I was at school I actively followed both the Finnish and the international media. My interest deepened when I was at Atlantic College in Wales: our economics teacher Andrew Maclehose spiced up his lessons with the *Economist* and the *Financial Times*, which was my favorite paper for decades. Maclehose taught us that carefully argued articles make an impact, that the media may describe an issue in different ways, and that it's essential to crystallize one's arguments if one is to get a message across.

Another eye-opening, or perhaps I should say ear-opening, experience was the radio editing course I attended in Vaasa in 1966, run by two veteran broadcasters. In that course I learned my first lessons in how journalism simplifies issues, trivializes arguments, and insists on having the last word.

The first time I was the subject of media interest was during my time as president of the National Union of University Students in Finland between 1972 and 1974. The first media profile of me appeared in 1972 in Finland's leading newspaper, *Helsingin Sanomat*. The over-politicized atmosphere of the 1970s was not conducive to good journalism. Everything was seen through a political party lens. The culture of journalism was weak and its integrity left much to be desired. It was yet another factor contributing to our decision to move to London for a while.

As finance director of Nokia I met many investors but fewer media representatives, because they focused their attention on the charismatic chairman, Kari Kairamo. During his time the main objective of Nokia's media strategy was to generate international coverage of its fascinating chairman. I remember Kari once sighing: "I have to meet every little parish magazine in Europe that has any interest in us at all." During the course of a day Kairamo might meet four or even five different editors, even though there might be nothing much happening at the time. This was long before there were celebrity CEOs. Kairamo's passing left a vacuum in Nokia's publicity.

Kairamo's successor as chairman, Simo Vuorilehto, was an altogether more cautious figure. The man in charge of our corporate communications, Matti Saarinen, described his media strategy as "low profile, dim lights." Vuorilehto didn't give wide-ranging interviews because of Nokia's financial problems and internal power battles. Instead a steady stream of gossip and rumor issued from the company, which then had to try to explain it away. It would have been best for Nokia not to appear in the press.

At that time I was in charge of mobile phones and I had to give more attention to the media than I had previously. In the small town of Salo what Nokia said was important. The mobile phone unit had financial problems, and I made a real effort with internal communications. I had to bring my team along with me in the battle for survival. From time to time I met the chief editor of the local paper to keep him up to date on what was really happening. I would call him on my way to Salo and drop in for morning coffee before my real working day began. I believe these background conversations helped us both. I learned a lot about local feeling and managed to soften the general impression in Salo of Nokia as "the great unknown."

When I marched into the first-floor auditorium at Nokia's head office in Helsinki on 16 January 1992, my first day as chief executive, I was unprepared for the media storm I met there. In those days strategies to communicate such major changes weren't prepared as thoroughly as they are now. It was seen as just a matter of clarification. The chief executive's "megaphone" came as a surprise: matters I had inconsequentially talked about earlier were suddenly interesting and newsworthy. I also learned that I couldn't use such vigorous and direct language as I had done earlier; I had to soften my messages so that the wave of news wouldn't break with unwarranted force. Big headlines often caused concern among the staff. Anyone in a serious position of authority soon learns this lesson, often the hard way.

According to many accounts, new chief executives of major companies are surprised at how much of their time is taken up with the media. And becoming accustomed to the media's working methods isn't a simple matter. At least there's plenty of advice: it's better to say nothing than to tell part of the truth; you should never talk about work in progress; you should never comment on your competitors; you shouldn't discuss internal matters in public; you should guard against complacency; you should keep a clear head in a crisis.

Some of the best advice I ever received came from Marjorie Scardino, our long-time deputy chair, about ten years ago. Scardino had been a journalist and was for a long time the chief executive of Pearson, which owns the *Financial Times*. "When your company is in crisis and you feel weak and lack energy, don't bother with what journalists write. When things are going well and your ears are ringing with praise, don't yield to the temptation to read the press. In both cases take a break." This seems very wise to me.

In January 1992 Nokia's position was so serious that we had to implement a lot of major changes at once, which took up all our time. So our communications strategy wasn't very high on the list of priorities of the new executive committee. It may have helped that Finland's domestic media didn't believe Nokia had any chance of success. During the economic depression of that time there were more than enough horrors to go around without seeking them out, so we were left in peace for a couple of years to build the future.

I did however set out a simple policy. We would appear in the press when it would advance Nokia's interests, and we wouldn't "sell" stories using the chief executive. The difference from Kari Kairamo's time was evident. The new policy was possible because mobile phones were entering general use little by little, and we were becoming more interesting as a result. Building the Nokia brand had started in earnest.

In spring 1996 The Five discussed the form our communications should take. It seemed that my colleagues all had their hands full with other work and woe. They suggested that I should take more explicit responsibility for communications and relieve them of pressure from the media. I went along with this, but I told them that their turn would come. In interviews I took the line that I was strictly focused on my job and I would give interviews only when I had something new and interesting to say. Chief executives can easily fall in love with PR to the point where the job is forgotten and only their visibility and image are important. In extreme cases they begin to live through their publicity. I decided to avoid that. Usually in interviews I concentrated on the most important matters from Nokia's standpoint, though occasionally I took a position on issues of broader interest to society. I refused to do interviews on personal topics. I found myself best suited to longer, themed interviews that allowed me to go deeper into the subject.

A cover story in *Business Week*, then highly regarded, had long been one of our goals. It was finally achieved in August 1998, though stories about us

Nokia's success made me the desired interviewee of the world's media. I was on the cover of *BusinessWeek* for the first time in 1998.

had been published earlier. We didn't pursue the cover story for its intrinsic value but because it would confirm that Nokia had at last become a globally important firm. A similar article appeared in *Forbes* in May 2000. These two treatments of Nokia's progress through the 1990s were in a class of their own. No other articles succeeded so well in capturing the essence of Nokia's company culture. It was perplexing and astonishing that no Finnish journalist even tried to do so.

The American specialist media was in a supreme position for grabbing international attention. Stories spread at the speed of light to the media elsewhere, so they had a powerful impact on the way the company was perceived globally. I'd go so far as to say that our listing on the New York Stock Exchange in 1994 and the simultaneous breakthrough of GSM technology were the turning points as far as the Nokia brand was concerned.

When products are launched it's customary to arrange group interviews, or to stage them around the production line. I was never very keen on these, though I did them from time to time. Fortunately at Nokia we had a large group of media-trained experts, which widened the pool of company spokespeople. We always used to consider very carefully who would best represent us at any given interview.

In Anglo-Saxon style we had delegated some of the spokesperson's role to our press office even in Kairamo's day. This had long been standard practice in major companies, but it was relatively new to Finland and gave rise to a lively discussion among editors. For us it was a question of the best use of the executive committee's time. The committee needed to focus on developing the company and meeting customers, staff, and other stakeholders. The press office, on the other hand, was always ready and available, so Nokia could meet the media's needs without delay.

We had also followed major international companies in insisting that someone from the press office accompanied senior figures at interviews. This too was unpopular with the Finnish media, though it had been standard practice elsewhere for decades. I used to maintain close links with our communications director so that our press office knew what was going on at Nokia – and also so I would know what interested the media at any given time.

At Nokia I had the chance to work with first-class media professionals, which changed my understanding of the media for good. Each member of our media team had their own independent understanding of what the communications director's role should be, and they acted as key advisers and sparring partners for the chief executive.

As Nokia's position became stronger and it became a Fortune 500 company, I received more and more requests for interviews. I stuck fast to the line that the most publicity is not the best publicity. I did indeed do more interviews, but I tried to limit my media work so that I would appear often enough, but not too often, in the international media. Otherwise the press office covered most of our publicity. At the end of the 1990s and even at the beginning of the 2000s there were many chief executives in the United States who had a high profile. I regarded this as a dangerous strategy from the viewpoint of both the company and the chief executive.

I had always enjoyed background interviews with editors more than traditional interviews. These conversations were rewarding for both parties. I gained a lot from them and they gave me the chance to explain what was going on at Nokia without the distortions of the chief executive's megaphone. When you don't have to plan every word in advance you can concentrate better on what you're actually saying and have an exchange of views. The journalists for their part can benefit from the conversation in the ways that they want – if they want.

Ever since Atlantic College I had admired the Anglo-Saxon culture of debate, though it isn't well suited to an interview situation. On the other hand, in background conversations one can approach issues in a more provocative way from different standpoints, which I believe should interest editors as well. The Finnish and the international media reacted differently to this. International journalists liked wide-ranging background briefings, from which they could pluck a few nuggets to quote. Finnish editors, on the other hand, prized the question-and-answer format and liked to make recordings – though to my delight I found that a few of them enjoyed a free-form dialogue. Many editors have the ability to see all sides of an issue and to analyze and shape them.

Our relationship with the Finnish press wasn't always problem-free. And no wonder, given Nokia's position as a large global company in a relatively small economy. On the other hand I was a blunt-speaking Finn deeply committed to my job and my company; at times I was very direct.

Because we were such a big company in such an interesting field, investors were quick to calculate the cash value of every little story. A single mistake could have a significant impact on our share price, which is always a problem for listed companies. Errors are never beneficial to a company, nor is the rumor mill. They hamper normal activity and speculators make money from them.

I remember a number of articles where I disagreed with the editor. My policy was to say so because I found it hard to take criticism based on misinformation or misleading assertions. All editors claim to want feedback, but my experience suggests differently. The media's appreciation of dialogue has sometimes been limited, though things have improved over time.

When in 2006 I stepped down from the position of chief executive to become part-time chairman of the board, I tried to draw a clear distinction between the public faces of the two roles. As a young chief executive I had enjoyed exceptional support from the chairman of the board, Casimir Ehrnrooth. He defined his role very clearly while also strongly supporting me. In the same way I wanted to withdraw from Nokia's PR work and give strong background support to Olli-Pekka Kallasvuo and the rest of the executive committee. In some cultures, such as Sweden and the United Kingdom, the board chair is expected to be appreciably more visible, but I like the Finnish model.

CHAPTER 52

The Biggest

IN JUNE 1998 I WAS SITTING IN MY NEW OFFICE when my mobile phone rang. At the other end was Pekka Ala-Pietilä, head of the mobile phone division. "Jorma, listen . . . it's happened!" "What's that?" "We are the biggest, beyond question. Our June sales have overtaken Motorola's." Pekka sounded relaxed as always.

We had achieved the objective I had set out at our Salo plant back in 1990. For the first time we had beaten Motorola on their home turf. That year, 1998, was the year we broke through in the United States: our market share grew by 15 percentage points to 36 percent, while Motorola's share fell to 26 percent.

"Well, what next?" I asked. We were a little nonplussed and simply agreed we would carry on as we had. Pekka likes champagne a little more than I do, so a few weeks later when we were on a business trip we raised a glass at the airport to mark our achievement. And that was the extent of our celebrations. At Nokia we were famously bad at saluting our own success.

We had survived the 1995 crisis, and by 1997 phone production was going at a fair pace, though our market share had fallen a little. That year the global market for mobile telephones passed the 100-million mark for the first time. Mobile phones were becoming by far the most important consumer electronics item, way ahead of personal computers, watches, and other products. Nobody could forecast the growth figures. Between 1997 and 1999 the global number of mobile phones almost trebled: by the end of 1999 there were estimated to be 278 million in use, nearly half of them in Europe.

In October 1998 we announced that Nokia had become the largest mobile phone manufacturer, with about a quarter of the global market. I told the press that this was only an interim target. Of course, it meant more than that to me and to everyone else at Nokia. More than ten years of hard work had not been wasted. The decisions we had made back in 1992 had been vindicated. Nokia had focused on areas with a future, and that future was brighter than any of us could have imagined in our wildest dreams. The price of that future was hard work, which many people regarded not so much as work but as drudgery. The days were long, the breaks were brief, and often the weekends were taken up with work.

Becoming the world's biggest mobile phone company meant many things. It meant we had overtaken Motorola, which didn't really take us seriously before the middle of the 1990s. We had beaten our eternal competitor Ericsson, which had intended to buy Nokia in 1991 until the Swedes decided we were too feeble to bother with and so withdrew their offer. We had overtaken Siemens, which in 1992 had been eager to buy our network business. We had surpassed all of our competitors.

We had also shown that we knew how to get out of the crisis that the media had portrayed as the beginning of the end for Nokia. The crisis had made us stronger as the markets grew. Our logistics were performing brilliantly, our factories were turning out phones for the right places at the right time, and the markets were growing ever faster. In 1998 we sold 40.8 million phones, compared to 21.3 million the previous year. By the measure of the total number of phones we made, our growth was nearly 100 percent. And the trend in our market share had also reversed itself: in 1997 it was 19 percent and a year later 24 percent. Our revenue grew by 51 percent in 1998, and our trading profit by 75 percent. In one year our share value rose 220 percent.

For Nokia the early 1990s had been hard, but after some difficult years the company began to grow at an unprecedented rate. We didn't understand why it grew so fast. During the decade the number of employees doubled, revenue grew tenfold, and profits grew more than a hundredfold. Our share value went up by a factor of 312. Our brand, which at the beginning of the decade was associated with rubber boots, was now one of the world's most valuable.

The rise in share price was driven by expectations of future success. At the end of the 1990s and in the early 2000s we succeeded magnificently, though shares in technology companies were generally highly valued at that time. The value of companies on stock exchanges was becoming detached from solid business success. Share values also fluctuated wildly. Later people would talk of the dotcom bubble. Nokia shares reached their all-time peak when their price on 20 June 2000 touched $66.

During the 1990s we completely reorganized our incentive structures. We introduced the first share option scheme in 1994, covering about 50 employees. New schemes followed in 1995 (about 350 people), 1997 (about 2,000 people), and 1999 (nearly 5,000 people). Participation in these schemes was exceptionally wide.

Options from the first scheme began to be worth selling when their value rose at the end of the 1990s as the company's results improved and the dotcom bubble inflated. The peak years for options in Finland were 1999 and 2000, when many Nokia employees became millionaires. Many of them didn't live or work in Finland. It's also important to remember that options packages and the circumstances in which they could be redeemed were different for different employees. And it wasn't a choice between nothing and ten million marks, rather that the sums earned through options rose in stages.

Finns enjoy a risky undertaking. Now hundreds of senior managers received a sum comparable to a lottery win in the middle of their careers. Getting rich quickly naturally tended to throw people off course, and some were unable to deal with it. They simply ran out of motivation. In the Salo plant, for example, a small group of fifty-something engineers decided to take early retirement.

My own closest colleagues didn't find that options made any difference – work days were no shorter and their lifestyles didn't change. Their colleagues in similar positions elsewhere in the world earned even more than they did. About five years later some of Nokia's key staff did leave the company, but they did so because they wanted to do something different with their lives, not just because they had been granted economic freedom. This was clear in the choices they made: most of them went on to leadership roles in other major companies rather than head for the golf course. When Nokia was expanding so rapidly, job satisfaction was the main motivator for senior managers.

In American culture it's natural to talk about money. "What's your net worth?" is a perfectly ordinary question. But in Finland we're silent on the subject, and the question wasn't broached in Nokia's business units. But the popular press unofficially took care of internal communication by reporting our salaries, down to the last mark, by examining our tax returns, which are a matter of public record in Finland.

CHAPTER 53

Nokia in Finland, Finland in Nokia

THE LOBBY AT NOKIA HEADQUARTERS was one of the most international places in Finland around the turn of the millennium. Each morning travelers would arrive there, with their luggage, from almost every country in the world: our partners in joint ventures, software designers, strategic planners, investment bankers, stock market analysts, journalists, and of course Nokia's own employees. They all looked around them with curiosity and reverence, and many clutched their mobiles and immortalized the scene and the works of art. The atmosphere was more international than at Helsinki airport. Many of them knew more about the company than the country where Nokia was located. The people who used our phones around the world of course knew even less about the country where they were made.

Nokia's "Finnishness" had begun to arouse interest back when the company started to grow and become international. Foreign analysts asked whether the company or its managers were "too Finnish." For many it was a miracle that Nokia had transcended its Finnish origins to become a global company in a business centered on growing markets in the Far East, but where innovations took place mostly in Silicon Valley on the U.S. West Coast.

Nokia's leaders had to review the company's relationship with Finland. Was Finland too remote a place for Nokia to develop and grow? Did Finland and Finnishness distort its management's perceptions of global markets? Ought we to go and set up in one of the world's real centers of activity? Could Finland satisfy our needs for creativity and expertise? Was our small domestic market an advantage or a nuisance? These were just a few of our questions. We also had to consider how we could attract top talent to Finland when the country could offer little in the way of sunshine or low taxes. Helsinki was not a great metropolis, and it wouldn't become one even with Nokia's help.

On the other hand we knew well that Finns weren't short of ambition or a desire to impress – that was how the company's ascent had begun, after all. Finnish engineers did excellent work and wanted to make the world's best products. Finland had always been an early adopter of new technologies, such as the bicycle, electricity, and the telephone.

Despite these deliberations Nokia was part of Finland's destiny, and Finland was part of Nokia's destiny.

The figures showed this clearly at the end of the 1990s: Nokia's share of Finland's exports was nearly a quarter, and the company accounted for over 5 percent of the country's GDP. Nokia had a huge impact, at times even greater than these figures indicate. Nokia brought a fresh self-confidence and boldness to a country recovering from economic depression. Nokia gave hope to companies and individuals who wanted to become world leaders in their field. "It's possible to do great things in Finland, because here there are fewer hierarchical structures and internal brakes on activity then in many other societies," the orchestral conductor Esa-Pekka Salonen has said of his own experiences.

This encapsulates one of Finland's strengths. It certainly helped us.

In the early 1990s two global phenomena occurred that were of great benefit to us: a technological leap forward in telecommunications and the liberalization of trade. These presented an immense opportunity to a company with its origins in a small country, and we were quick to seize it.

Finland too needed to break with its past. The landscape was bleak following a round of bankruptcies and failure. Finland's adjustment to liberalized financial markets and European competition had not been painless. Finland needed a new spirit of enterprise and business-mindedness. The example of Nokia's success was crucial in changing attitudes. There was a virtuous circle: Finland became more visible, and influential people started to take an interest in what was happening there and what they could learn from it.

Finland's economic growth after 1993 was exceptional. Changes in the tax system helped things along, while attitudes toward enterprise and wealth creation became much healthier as Finland developed into a modern market economy, assisted by Nokia. Nokia brought wealth to Finland by creating good taxpayers concentrated in the regions where the company operated. Finland's new wealth sometimes inspired admiration, sometimes envy. Ultimately it showed that success enriches those who have thrown themselves into creating it. We had created an example in Finland that many have followed since.

No winning streak lasts forever. Nokia and Finland were the leaders in technological development in telecommunications in the 1990s, but their roles changed during the Internet revolution in the following decade. The United States was now where new content, services, and applications originated, and the Finns didn't really understand the new world, let alone master it. This naturally affected Nokia. We should have drawn on global expertise better and faster.

Finland had its limitations. Nokia was a major company in a Finnish environment, and this was reflected in discussions about the company. Nokia's importance was sometimes exaggerated, sometimes undervalued. Finns were slow to learn that despite Nokia's Finnishness all the company's decisions were made in the face of worldwide competition. Nokia's growth also made national figures of its senior people. Some of us liked this, but for many it was just a nuisance. Basking in the limelight really wasn't part of Nokia's culture, and in any case we had more than enough to do. Members of the executive committee ran divisions that, if they had been individual companies, would have been among the largest in Finland.

I was always proud of Nokia's Finnishness. If Nokia's success helped Finland, that was the best psychological salary of all. But I also knew that the company couldn't remain the prisoner of Finland's position or size, because that would be a defeat for Finland.

Over the years our own attitude toward Nokia's domicile changed in a positive way. As China became more important to us, it became clear that there was nothing to complain about in being just seven and a half hours away from both New York and Beijing. Helsinki was suddenly not such a bad place to be based.

CHAPTER 54

Toward the New Millennium

ONE MEETING IN 1999 STICKS IN MY MIND. In June I took part in a conference organized by Allen & Company in Sun Valley, Idaho. This was an annual get-together of senior businesspeople, major investors, and other influential people from business and cultural life. The previous year I had given a presentation on Nokia. At this year's event the most interesting speaker was Apple's acting CEO, Steve Jobs.

Steve Jobs had been a wunderkind in the field of information technology. In the 1970s he and Steve Wozniak had set up Apple together. In the mid-1980s Jobs's team had launched the Macintosh, which was a major event. In 1985 Jobs was eased out of the company he had founded, and he made a fresh start as an entrepreneur, founding a new company called NeXT. He also started to finance and later lead Pixar, which made the first entirely computer-animated film, *Toy Story*. In 1996 Apple announced it was buying NeXT, and so Jobs returned to the company as an adviser. Apple was in deep difficulties at the time, and its CEO, Gil Amelio, was forced out in June 1997. Steve Jobs's appointment as CEO was intended as an interim measure, but the word *acting* was deleted from his job title in 2000.

Jobs was in Idaho not to talk about Apple products but about the movies Pixar made. Jobs walked from side to side on the wide stage, and described how the toys that gave *Toy Story* its name were summoned to life with the aid of computers. He was dressed in his signature jeans and black turtleneck shirt and was wearing round-lensed spectacles. He spoke about the technical basis for computer animation as intimately and attractively as a natural storyteller over a campfire.

Later we met several times at similar events and we had phone conversations to discuss possible joint ventures. Jobs came across as an exceptional and absolutist individual for whom everything was either/or; the middle way and compromises were unknown to him. Apple's products and services were "awesome, brilliant, overwhelming, the best." He believed almost fanatically in what he did.

Our explorations of possible cooperation were preliminary and it quickly became clear that it wasn't worth Nokia's while. Apple had the reputation for being difficult and for drafting agreements weighted in its favor.

We didn't work together, but Jobs had a big impact on me. His background had given him an excellent understanding of four things: the technical composition of a device (hardware), user experience (software), content (sound, image, and moving image), and external appearance (design). This combination was exceptionally powerful.

Nokia's rate of growth in the 1990s meant that everyone in the company had to concentrate on production, sales, and improving our processes. We set up new factories and took on new people all over the world. Our staff numbers breached the 40,000 barrier in 1998 and by 2000 Nokia employed over 58,000 people. I did my best to maintain connections with our employees and paid many visits to our offices and factories around the world. Nokia was now at least as multicultural as Atlantic College had been. Cultural differences made themselves felt in my meetings with employees. The Finns had no problem with using first names or giving direct feedback about the way things were organized. But in Asia the chief executive was a great personage, and my visits were all too often interpreted as meaning that somebody had done something wrong – which was not at all the message I wanted to send. Breaking the ice took its time.

Growth in the mobile phone market was so exceptional that even Nokia had its hands more than full in adapting to its demands. We needed every product development manager we could find in Finland and in other countries where we did product development. We needed more people who knew marketing, logistics, and sales. We needed ever more good managers for all our departments. All our energy was absorbed by growth, bringing growth under control, and lubricating our machinery. We couldn't afford to miss any opportunities that growth offered.

We looked at just the right issues in 1998, though we were probably not as decisive as we should have been. It's easy to say with the benefit of hindsight that we didn't invest enough of our profits from mobile phones in new areas, which might have led to new growth in the 2000s. In many areas we were too early. We followed events and wanted to be in at the beginning, but some-times it would have been better to wait and then taken bolder steps later.

Nokia placed a strong emphasis on research and product development. In 2000 we had 20,000 staff working on them, with around two-thirds in Fin-land. Our research centers generated many new discoveries and solutions to problems: our briefcase was bursting with patents. We had launched one wonderful model of phone after another, and our position in networks was also strong.

But in the future it would not be enough just to manufacture phones – phones had to have software that made them stand out from their com-petitors. We understood this and believed we could develop strong software expertise in our research centers. Later we had to accept that our efforts had been inadequate.

In the 1990s Nokia had found itself growing at a unique rate. Finnish pes-simism ensured that we didn't imagine an unrealistic future for Nokia. We began to think about the next phase. We understood that mobile phones alone weren't enough to take us into the next millennium.

PART IV

GROWTH AND
AN END TO GROWTH

CHAPTER 55

Profit Warning

O N 12 JUNE 2001 an era came to an end. Or rather, the era had ended the previous month, but it became news only in June. On 12 June Nokia gave a profit warning. We explained that sales were showing growth of less than 10 percent when at the end of April we had still expected 20 percent growth. That would have consequences for the bottom line: profits for the year's second quarter would be 15 to 20 percent less than we had predicted earlier.

The markets were less than delighted with Nokia's little summer surprise. In the first fifteen minutes after the announcement our share price spiraled down by 15 percent. Put another way, 20 billion dollars were wiped off the company's value. Our market worth thus shrank by 1.3 billion dollars a minute. The profit warning was Finland's main news story and the lead item in the world's financial media.

Summer in Finland was at its most radiant. The trees were festooned with pale green leaves and the sea shimmered outside Nokia's head office. People's thoughts were turning to their holidays. In a couple of weeks it would be midsummer, when the Finnish summer really began. In the center of Helsinki there was a brisk trade in ice cream, and the first new potatoes of the season would reach the open-air market down by the harbor at any moment. New potatoes and herrings are a special Finnish dish – imagine what it would be like if bacon and eggs or smoked salmon and cream cheese became available only with the arrival of summer.

But at Nokia we had other things to think about: with my team I was trying to work out what was going on. Had we come up against a brick wall? Could we get through it? If not, could we get around it? Or would Nokia have to turn itself into a different sort of company?

On the evening of the profit warning I had promised to speak at a global conference of communications specialists in Helsinki. Some were technical experts, some were senior executives. All would want to hear what I had to say about the profit warning. I tried to appear relaxed, confident, and calm. "I want to send out a clear message that we remain confident of our future and are ever more convinced that we're on the right track. Though as a company we're in good shape, the slowdown in economic growth is taking its toll," I said. I went on: "Companies have to make what people really need. Mobile services have to be individual."

I also tried to explain that we had moved into a new era and that my confidence in the future remained undimmed. But neither I nor anyone else at Nokia had a very clear picture of what that future held. What would life at Nokia be like without frenetic growth? Without constant new challenges? A life of cost savings, demands for strict efficiency, and battles for resources between different parts of the company?

I had learned that growth was as important for companies as oxygen was for people. Growth didn't just mean that sales figures increased or that shareholders could be certain of their dividends. Growth is important for other reasons. The whole of human life is a matter of physical and psychological growth. Individuals must search out what's best for themselves, to make more of themselves, to develop toward perfection. Growth in a company gives people opportunities to do that.

Without growth a company's employees turn into conservatives: they've lost the reason to exert themselves. If a company's leadership doesn't set sufficiently ambitious targets for growth, it's delusional if it believes that employees will stretch themselves. They won't. In the laboratories researchers won't bother to explore that one last possibility. Marketing people will be happy with the advertising company's initial proposal for a new campaign. Over in personnel they'll be satisfied with mediocre recruits when they should be taking on the best people possible. Products won't be fully tested, and mobile phones that don't work or are even downright dangerous will reach the market.

Without growth a company will shrivel. It will be forced to cut costs if it's to have any chance of making a respectable profit. These savings will hit product development, and the quality of the company's products will start to decline. When that happens the company's market position will collapse and its targets will again be in grave danger. The cycle will continue until the company is saved by new management or a new owner, or a merciful death ends its misery. The shareholders will have to make do with whatever is left over. Thus ends the tale of the company that's unable to grow.

Nokia had enjoyed exceptional growth for around ten years. Perhaps we should have done more to control the growth. Perhaps we should have thought harder about how fast our workforce was growing. Perhaps we should have thought about the organization in a different way. We could revisit many of our decisions, but everyone at Nokia knows in their hearts what growth feels like. In the 1990s it was exceptionally rapid. It made every heart beat faster. It created ambitious targets of its own accord, or so it seemed. Many of those targets were achieved.

We were an efficient machine that produced more money for its owners than any other company in our area. We had also become one of the world's most valuable brands, and promising young people all over the world were queuing up to work for us.

By the beginning of the 2000s people weren't buying mobile phones in such large numbers as earlier. Or, more precisely, people wanted to buy just the same number as before, but not more. In spring 2001 I estimated that about 405 million phones would be sold worldwide that year, roughly the same as the previous year. Sales of networks were no help in relieving Nokia's hangover from its years of growth. In July 2001 I said that better times would dawn again the following year, but in my heart I wasn't sure.

Nokia was a self-confident, efficient, and profitable company with a keen sense of its own worth and its own values. Its employees had earned this through hard work, sometimes at personal sacrifice. Many had also received a more concrete reward: options and bonuses had made many Nokia employees wealthy. A strong sense of one's own worth, however, may lead to self-satisfaction and slackness. When we were recruiting large numbers at the end of the 1990s, not all the applicants wanted to simply do their best or excel. And it wasn't a question of weakness within the company. Every expanding firm has to take on new people who are paid to solve ever more tightly defined problems, which isn't always good for efficiency.

Anssi Vanjoki came up with a telling example. "Now it really has happened. Nokia is now completely bureaucratized. A bloke came into my room, and I asked him what he did, and he told me he was a ringtone expert. Just imagine, now we have our own ringtone expert!"

Some of our new employees just wanted to grab a slice of the enchanted cake that Nokia had baked for itself. These people had seen only the years of exceptional growth, and they didn't experience the self-sacrifice that lay behind the company's initial phase of growth. When growth suddenly stopped, many of these people were lost. They slowed down the changes that Nokia had to make. Analysts wrote in the summer of 2001 that Nokia was no longer "immortal." Nokia had never been immortal, but many people in the company had experienced only those times when it had felt immortal. They didn't comprehend that companies are always mortal. Economic history is full of formerly well-known "immortal" companies, of which nothing is now remembered except the name, if that.

In 2001 the dotcom bubble burst and companies went back to square one. The mobile network operating companies had spent loads of cash on new mobile networks, but their ambitious plans evaporated as quickly as the money invested in them.

The dangers for Nokia were both internal and external. Internally we were following the same path that had brought such success at the end of the 1990s. We hadn't noticed that the world had changed. Our competitors had invested in product development, in the design of new phones, and in opening up new markets. The market share of the Korean company Samsung had started to grow. In China local firms were doing well. The average price of mobile phones had started to fall. Phones still sold well, as long as they were cheap, fun, and colorful – the sorts of items that teenage girls would want to be seen with and use on the streets of Beijing or Tokyo. The mobile phone seemed to be becoming so cheap that you could trade it in for a newer model on a whim. But phones also needed to become more complex. People, and especially companies, wanted phones that would enable you to work, read emails, and browse the Internet. Such phones required extra features and additional software. Nokia had made phones; now we had to become a software company as well.

Every firm that aspires to become a global software company will sooner or later run into Microsoft. Analysts and journalists started writing about a titanic battle that Microsoft and Nokia were waging against each other. We started to believe there really was such a battle when Bill Gates announced at ITU Telecom World in Geneva in 1999 that Microsoft intended to challenge Nokia. We started to prepare for victory in a struggle that seemed inescapable. Before that, though, we had to think about how we could get our company to start growing again.

In the early 2000s Nokia employed nearly 20,000 people who had completed a serious academic education. They were thinking people: they certainly took satisfaction from their salaries and other perks, but their real motivation came from elsewhere. It came from the company's ambitious goals, from growth, and from the fast-moving stream that carried them forward toward greater challenges. Now we had to find a way of creating those challenges or we would have trouble later on if our best people left us while we were still hoping for growth to turn up from somewhere.

CHAPTER 56

Timing Is Everything

THE CHIEF EXECUTIVE IS RESPONSIBLE for changes in senior management, whereas a change in chief executive is a matter for the board. But the chief executive should know when he has led the company long enough. In reality many chief executives want to hang on to power, even after they've lost their passion, their energy, and even their grip. The CEO's job isn't simple: there's more than enough to do twenty-four hours a day. You have to maintain your enthusiasm for new things, even if you've been in the job for many years. You have to recognize the limits of your own power if you're to keep your wits and your health.

By 2001 I had been Nokia's chief executive for ten years, and I had worked at Nokia for sixteen years. Nokia was a completely different company from the one I had joined. I had seen and experienced a great deal: ten years as chief executive of a leading technology company was an exceptional length of service. Our competitors had all changed their leaders rather often. One reason for that, of course, was that the companies' boards and shareholders hadn't been satisfied with their performance. I didn't have that problem.

I had told the board two things: I would carry on at least until 2003, and I thought Pekka Ala-Pietilä, who had been managing director since 1999, should be my successor. Olli-Pekka Kallasvuo was an excellent alternative; he was currently finance director. This was my "last will and testament," which I entrusted to the board in case something serious should befall me.

I had begun to discuss these issues with the board in the summer of 2001. I was the board chairman, but it wasn't for me to decide my own future. I spoke to the board members; the deputy chairman and chair of the personnel committee, Paul Collins, played a leading role. The board wasn't at all keen even to discuss a change of the CEO in 2003. Nor were they ready to nominate Pekka Ala-Pietilä as my successor.

"Fine. Then I propose that I stay on until 2006. I'll put that down on paper and we'll make it public," I said to Paul Collins. This seemed to have the support of the board, and that was how agreement was reached that I would stay at Nokia at least until 2006. The formal announcement was made at the end of October 2001. The press described this as "exceptional," perhaps because other companies seemed keener to change their CEOs than to keep them. For their part the Nokia board wanted to ensure that I would stay a few more years. The board felt comfortable having a familiar leader during such a turmoil in the industry.

The timing of a change determines everything. The wrong change, even when the time is ripe, may bring down a successful company once and for all. The right change, but at the wrong time, won't help the company but will cause opportunities to be lost. Perhaps the markets aren't ready for the change; or perhaps the consumers aren't ready for the new products.

Why can't chief executives time their decisions right, if everything depends on their ability to do so? Ultimately, the timing of a decision is based on intuition alone. There are no compelling, objective reasons, either general or specific, on which to base the change. To carry out a major change within a company is never a democratic decision. It's for the heads of the company to bear the responsibility for the changes. Very often their most important task is to sense when those changes should be made.

Complex changes are an everyday matter in the areas where Nokia is active. Technology changes. The consumption patterns of hundreds of millions of people change. Competitors change their way of operating. All this makes Nokia the world's most fascinating place to work. I have lived in the middle of it and made an impact. I couldn't hope for more.

I tried to sense those moments when the organization had to shake itself up and transform itself into something new. Change is in part an absolute value: people shouldn't be left to loll around in comfortable chairs in beautiful offices because human nature resists change. Without change we have no way of going forward: our development as human beings grinds to a halt. That's why I rotated, changed, and reorganized Nokia's leadership so many times. It's easy to push through changes if the company is in danger or if difficult times clearly lie ahead. Everyone then understands why change is necessary. The old road is no good. A better route to a brighter future has to be found. Crisis is the best catalyst of change.

The hardest thing is to sense the need for change, and then to put change into effect, just when everything seems to be going well. When the figures look good, revenue is growing, and profitability remains high, it's difficult even to talk about change. It's also very difficult to shift a manager whose life story is one of uninterrupted success. Even so, a transfer may be the only sensible thing to do if the old methods aren't working where it matters – in the market.

CHAPTER 57

Is Everyone Safe?

IN OCTOBER 2001 THE WORLD'S MEDIA had other things to think about than the timetable for the departure of Nokia's CEO. In September 2001 the world had changed in an instant into a different sort of place: even its most powerful people could no longer feel safe.

On 11 September Nokia made a preliminary announcement of its latest results at two in the afternoon, Finnish time. A little later I sat in my office on the seventh floor. The view out toward the sea was distinctly autumnal, though one or two sailing boats bobbed about in the distance. I was following on my computer how Nokia's shares were doing following our announcement. We were satisfied with the figures. We had said that our profits would be very much in line with what we had forecast.

Investors could trust Nokia. We expected a favorable reception, which is indeed what we got immediately; the share price rose by ten percent. We said we would organize a conference call for analysts, investors, and editors – anyone who wanted it – at 4 o'clock – 9 o'clock in the morning in New York.

Olli-Pekka Kallasvuo was responsible for the conference call. I continued to follow Nokia's share price on my computer screen. I felt rather carefree for once. Suddenly, at about two minutes past four, the share price plunged. I looked at the screen, perturbed. "What on earth have they told the investors?" I thought aloud as I sat in my office, which had neither a television nor a Reuters screen. I had always tried to keep these out of my room so that headline news couldn't deflect me from the fundamentals. And now headline news was fundamental.

I managed to find a news item circulated by the Finnish news service, Startel. This said that an aircraft had hit the World Trade Center in New

York, after which stock exchanges had started to slide the world over. About five minutes later came a report that a second plane had crashed into the World Trade Center. Then I dashed to the television in the adjoining conference room and turned on one of the Finnish channels. The finance minister was giving parliament an appraisal of the strengths and weaknesses of the Finnish economy. Then the opposition leader spoke at length, and then the finance minister defended his budget. The politicians were carrying on as if nothing had happened; for a moment they seemed to be part of a news blackout on global events. I couldn't afford not to know what had happened in New York. Next I invaded the sixth floor where our head of communications, Lauri Kivinen, and his team were tuned to international channels, which were broadcasting ever more shocking pictures of the terrorist attack.

At five o'clock Finnish television was still showing the budget, though a band of text informed viewers that a catastrophe had happened. It still only referred to an "aircraft collision," however.

I quickly called a little crisis meeting in my office. Veli Sundbäck, our director responsible for trade policy and an experienced diplomat, and Olli-Pekka Kallasvuo took part. We rang everyone on the executive board and tried to establish where our staff had been at the critical moment. Nokia had twenty employees at its Manhattan office. By about nine o'clock we knew that twelve of our employees had been in the office that Tuesday morning, and all were safe. We contacted the other eight and learned that they too were unharmed. Only the following day did we ascertain that none of our employees had been on the fatal flights.

We had survived the terrorist strikes in which thousands lost their lives or their health or loved ones. We had been lucky at Nokia, and we were profoundly grateful. Some of our employees might well have been visiting the World Trade Center that very morning, for many of our business customers had their offices in the Twin Towers.

At Nokia we had to tell people that all our own staff were safe. Our employees around the world were starting to send us their comments, questions, and views of where all this was likely to lead. I was shocked when I saw the pictures showing how the familiar landscape of lower Manhattan had been transformed into a smoking ruin filled with people fleeing for their lives. Most of my family was travelling abroad, and I had to make sure that they were safe. Liisa, my wife, was on a visit to Madrid with other officials from her department. I caught her on the phone in Spain, where the atmosphere was nervous and gloomy.

I'd promised a while back to have dinner with my daughter Anna that evening. On the one hand, I felt that I should stay at Nokia with my team on this particular evening; on the other, Liisa was away, there was no food at home, and I had to eat something. Perhaps, too, Anna would like to see her father on this evening in particular. She had spent the day coaching young gymnasts, and at around six one of the other coaches had told her that "something weird" had happened in New York.

"This is the most important thing to happen to our generation, because it really is going to change the world. Sadly it's both the most important thing but it's also really negative," I thought as my car took me to the center of Helsinki, which seemed empty. People had gone home. Everyone was watching the news on television. Everyone who could was sitting next to the people they loved. Many people were taking refuge in the familiar and the secure. Travel – and indeed globalization – came to a standstill that day. The belief in trade, in progress, in a civilized dialogue between cultures seemed to have died at the same time, overwhelmed by the clouds of smoke and dust the terrible explosions in New York had released.

My driver took me from our headquarters over the bridges to Helsinki. As we drove, the sun was setting on the Baltic horizon. There were still leaves on the trees on Helsinki's boulevards as the last rays of the evening sun reflected off the walls of the austere white Swedish theatre. I was a few minutes late at the cool new Italian restaurant, Via. Anna and I sat in a window seat; with my back to the window I surveyed the restaurant. There weren't many people there, and those who were didn't take much notice of me, which was unusual in a Finnish restaurant. Perhaps people had other things to think about. We ordered a stir-fry, which came promptly but represented no sort of culinary landmark. We talked about what would happen if the United States curled up into its shell or withdrew from the rest of the world.

My son was on a business trip to San Francisco, where his conference was carrying on as normal. On the West Coast they knew only that there had been a "plane accident" in New York. At dinner we still hadn't had word from him, and we were both a little worried though we tried not to be.

I made a few calls to Manhattan and got through to some of my friends surprisingly easily. Pentti Kouri was in good shape and ready to analyze what the terrorist attack meant for the world's future. Most of the mobile phone networks were working superbly. Only one network stopped operating, because its key antennae and other equipment had been mounted on the World Trade Center. I said goodnight to Anna and returned to Nokia at about nine-thirty. I checked the bulletins we were sending out and sent an email to the entire workforce. After an hour I left for my empty home, where I watched the news on CNN.

Well before midnight I got hold of my son and his wife. Now I knew that the whole of my international family was safe and well.

The following morning the world had changed. Companies had started to look at their own security arrangements. Travel was restricted. I was all too conscious that the arrangements for my own security had been beefed up: it meant I could no longer move around freely just anywhere as a private individual. Somebody somewhere knew all my movements, all the trips I made, everything I did. It wasn't a particularly inspiring thought.

But that following morning many other things carried on as before. I had promised to speak at a seminar at the labor ministry at 9 o'clock. At half past eight I rang the chief of staff at the ministry to ask whether the seminar would go ahead now that circumstances seemed to have changed. The official listened to me as if I were an idiot. "Of course it will," he said, so I went to the seminar and gave my presentation. We observed a moment of silence in memory of the victims of the terrorist attacks in New York.

I wanted at once to say something that wouldn't sound completely sorrowful. I said that the event was indeed tragic. It could well change the way in which we related to the world, to work, and to each other. It was, however, too early to say what its ultimate effects would be. In the midst of tragedy it was important to maintain a positive attitude. Although a knowledge-based society was extremely vulnerable in some ways, it had new strengths that would help it to function in a crisis.

"I managed to reach my friends in Manhattan from here in Finland without any trouble all yesterday evening. We should try to ensure that such things work in the future, whatever the circumstances," I said to the television cameras. The quote was then extracted and broadcast for the delectation of Finnish viewers on the main news bulletin that evening. A few days later I really got it in the neck for that. Some journalist or other complained that I had made a marketing speech when the world was trying to come to terms with its grief. He can scarcely have known what I said or meant. But I was labelled a greedy capitalist who tried to sell his phones even when more sensitive souls were mourning the tragic deaths of thousands. That wasn't how I saw it, but I didn't enjoy a right of reply to the media's condemnation.

I think the whole seminar should have been postponed. The morning after the attack Finland still seemed to be taking the whole event very much in its stride, though it would have a real impact on Finns, Americans, Muslims, and Christians. I didn't have any idea what would come next, but I could see that it wouldn't be anything terribly good. I knew that much already that first morning.

When I had given my speech at the seminar I returned to Nokia to see how things were. The world's future now looked different, and that meant that Nokia's future was also different from what it had been on Tuesday. Now we had to make a quick assessment of what had changed and how much.

We had arranged for a board meeting to take place in Bangkok and Singapore the following week. A first round of phone calls showed that life went on and our customers would value the visit. This was a good sign: Nokia would be there for its customers in bad times as well as good. That Wednesday I decided that the meeting would go ahead as planned. On Thursday I thought things through again and talked to my fellow directors. On Friday I changed my decision: the strategy and board meetings would be held in Finland. That was the surest and safest thing to do. Suddenly Finland seemed a rather wonderful location for the headquarters of a major company.

The terrorist attacks in themselves hadn't made any difference to Nokia's plans. The meetings didn't lead to changes in our objectives or our view of market fundamentals. But we did look more closely at the figures, and we reduced some of our forecasts. The global economy had been slowing since April, but now there was a separate discussion under way: what impact would the terrorist attacks have on the outlook for growth? How much would the U.S. recession deepen? What would it mean for growth elsewhere in the world? How long would the impact of the attacks be felt? My view was clear – the attacks would have a deep and long-term effect on the global economy. They were no small thing. The board didn't want to take firm positions or make hasty decisions; there would be time for that later.

Before the board meeting we considered many everyday matters. We decided that we should do something to help those who had suffered in the terrorist attacks. We would support the International Youth Foundation and set up a million-dollar fund for the education of children who had lost one or both parents. In addition we would at least match the money donated by our employees.

The terrorist attacks also affected Nokia's travel arrangements. We had 8,000 employees in the United States who now had to get used to tight security controls and new travel rules. We also needed to ensure that our supply chains would hold up. What would happen to our production in the United States? We lost a little production, but things were back to normal after a couple of days.

Almost the first thing we did was to look again at our marketing campaign. We were selling the Communicator on the basis of a lively television and newspaper campaign that showed a company chair brandishing a phone and jumping through a glass door so that the splinters flew in all directions. I decided we would drop this campaign as soon as we could. There were enough splinters in the world without Nokia adding to the debris.

Nokia's internal discussion on the impact of the attacks went on for some time. Our employees wondered in emails why the world had become the place it had. People were worried and panicky. They were also depressed: for about ten days Nokia didn't function at its usual energy levels because the horror of the recent events had demoralized people. Suddenly the future didn't seem quite as appealing as we had always believed it would be. Suddenly it seemed frightening, threatening, and unpredictable. People didn't try to put these thoughts into words, but I only had to look around me to see that the organization was running in a low gear. Our usual energy and enthusiasm had evaporated. People began to ponder ethical issues more than they had before.

At the beginning of the decade I had seen criticism of globalization grow ever louder as it became a stronger force for change. In Genoa 150,000 young people had protested against those they saw as responsible for globalization. These included leading politicians, the leaders of the biggest companies, and the international organizations that assisted them. I was certainly among them, although Nokia never appeared on the list of the five worst companies, perhaps because Nokia's products helped the demonstrators organize their own events. I suppose our market share among them was around 70 percent. The oil companies, Shell among them, tended to top the list, just ahead of clothing companies and pharmaceutical giants. The Finnish forestry industry came in for its share of vitriol too. In the summer of 2001 I asked two of Finland's most senior politicians what the anti-globalization movement meant. What would happen next? The politicians couldn't answer. They just said everything looked dreadful.

Jeffrey Sachs wrote in the *New York Times* that defenders of globalization shouldn't head for their bunkers when the demonstrators attacked. When the G8 leaders did that, and increased their security measures, the demonstrators started to go for companies and their leaders.

There hasn't been enough discussion with the critics of globalization. No one tries to understand the arguments against globalization before trying to defend it. I didn't then and I don't now believe that the world would be such a thriving place without a strong global economy. But we should listen to what the critics of globalization have to say. Our customers' understanding toward business will soon disappear if companies screw things up, though from the point of view of morale it's even worse if employees lose their pride in the firms they work for. Democracy and economic well-being always go hand in hand. If markets open on a global scale it's more likely that democracy will prevail.

Nokia is a business, and it can do good things only if it's both profitable and growing. Nokia can't save the world at the cost of its own profits, but we can try to make those profits responsibly.

Some people think that a company's only job is to turn a profit regardless of the costs or consequences. At the opposite extreme there are those who believe that companies should forget about profits and concentrate on good works. In my view both are wrong. A company's job is to produce a profit while recognizing its wider responsibilities. Otherwise the profits may turn out to be short-lived and the company will do badly.

The world rightly expects much from companies and their leaders. But it shouldn't demand that they do what they can't do. Senior executives are paid to think of where the interests of the company lie and how to develop it. Politicians are chosen, often through a democratic process, to balance wider interests. They carry their own responsibility and are answerable to their electorates. Company executives cannot replace politicians; that would wreck both political and business life.

Sometimes even talking about things can be difficult. In 2001 I was invited to a World Bank event where about ten leaders of global companies took part. The World Bank president, James Wolfensohn, wanted to talk about the global future. One of my American colleagues adopted a resentful tone when it was his turn to speak. "What is this international community you talk about so much?" he sneered. If you come from the Nordic countries the international community is a clear concept, but Americans think differently. My colleague was given the World Bank's official definition of the international community, but the answer didn't seem to satisfy him at all.

CHAPTER 58

Nokia Needs Renewal

GROWTH HAD COME TO A HALT AT NOKIA, sending us back to first principles in search of a future for ourselves and our company. At the end of 2001 I had kicked off discussions aimed at making Nokia readier to face the challenges of the future. The Five – our core group of the five most senior executives – held intensive meetings over several weeks. We asked ourselves all the fundamental questions: What should Nokia do? How should it be structured? Where will future growth come from? How can ideas and people circulate within the company to best effect? How can we ensure that our products are the ones the world's consumers want to buy?

I had decided it was time to reorganize Nokia, and this time I wanted to change the basic structure of the company. For years Nokia had been divided into two parts: mobile phones and mobile phone networks. For too long now we had served all the world's mobile phone customers through a single organization, without considering what customers really wanted. I also believed that Nokia needed to become stronger in software. We had to gear up for a possible battle against Microsoft.

We didn't fight in those meetings. No one shouted at anyone. We were used to talking things through with each other. We were sensitive to when someone was getting irritated, or when someone ought to give in. We had worked together for over ten years. We knew every mood, every glance, every frown; we knew who would start the ball rolling and who would have the last word. Sari Baldauf compared the relationship between the five of us to an enduring marriage where there wasn't any need to say much but everything was understood. It was our strength, but also our weakness.

This major reorganization of Nokia was the last thing the five of us would do together. We had had many adventures, we had created a great company, but now we had to prepare it for a new era.

I battered the group with endless questions. "What if we put mobile phones and networks together? Would we achieve greater growth and would we offer a better service to the operators?" Or: "What if we had four business units rather than two?" Or: "What if Nokia was organized along geographical lines rather than by business units? Perhaps then we would be better at taking local cultures into account?" I carried on with my questioning and I made the directors present counter-arguments, which enabled us to rule out unworkable ideas. After many meetings, after many sketch pads had been filled up with diagrams and ideas, we made our decision. The new organization was ready.

We hadn't used consultants because I don't believe they add much value to a company's deliberations on its basic strategy. I'm well known to be a bad customer for the services they offer. One of them once told me that when he was selling his ideas to the head of a company he wouldn't take a single piece of paper along with him, because top executives either couldn't or wouldn't read a word. He said that about half of chief executives never open a book, either for business or pleasure. So consultants needed the ability to sell The Next Big Idea to their clients as if they were Stone Age people sitting around their campfire. That technique wouldn't work with me: I need arguments and justifications, preferably set out on paper. If you need to read a couple of books, bring them on, let's do it!

Nokia has employed consultants, but their work has started only when we've completed our groundwork. My experience is that consultants have the most to offer when it comes to implementing a strategy. Creating the strategy is a task for the company's leadership, who must present it to the firm's owners and the board that represents them. After a dialogue the board accepts the agreed-upon strategy. The board is generally not the place where strategy or important organizational changes should be planned, except perhaps in small companies or those active in very mature areas. Otherwise the chief responsibility for pushing the strategy through must lie with the operational leadership.

"For the last ten years this company has made all its own decisions without outside help. There's no reason to assume that consultants can resolve our current challenges better than we can. Let's keep things in our own hands," is what I said to my colleagues.

Some consultants and management gurus did influence our thinking. I've already mentioned Gary Hamel and the ideas he gave us for searching out new openings. I've always urged people to read all the new books that come out and to learn something from them and apply what they've learned. But you have to have your own ideas and reach your own decisions, good and bad.

Nokia had long been one of the companies that management gurus followed closely. They told us what they thought, but often they asked us what we thought. This created a synthesis between how Nokia and other companies operate. The gurus summarize their ideas in books or in articles in the *Harvard Business Review*. I often saw Nokia's working methods described there and compared to those of other firms. But company cultures and circumstances will ultimately determine how ideas will be used and adapted.

Nokia's new organization was put in place at the beginning of May 2001. In Finland people go off on their summer holidays at the end of June, and I wanted to achieve something before that. The change was great, and analysts, investors, and journalists all picked up on it. And of course so did all Nokia's employees, who did their best to adapt to the new thinking.

We had split up our enormous mobile phone division into nine smaller units. About $28 billion-worth of revenue was divided between these units, some of which looked more like start-up companies than parts of the world's biggest mobile phone company. The names of these units showed the direction we were taking: Time-Division Multiple Access Unit, Code-Division Multiple Access Unit, Mobile Phones Unit, Mobile Entry Products Unit, Imaging Unit, Entertainment and Media Unit, Business Application Unit, Mobile Enhancements Unit, and Mobile Services Unit. The first two focused on two standards: TDMA-phones and CDMA-phones. The first of these was on its way out, though it was still important to Nokia in the United States and Latin America. Nokia's share of the market for CDMA phones was really too small, and the importance of this standard was growing, especially in Asian countries. We needed to get better at this technology.

The Mobile Phones Unit was the heart of our entire business. Its role was to concentrate on high-quality GSM phones and new models developed from them. This unit had to produce over half the company's profits in the next few years. The Mobile Entry Products Unit focused on developing markets and looked for opportunities for growth in countries such as China, Russia, and India. The phones it made had to be cheap. The unit was also expected to develop low-cost services in conjunction with local operators.

The Imaging Unit was just on the point of releasing the long-awaited camera phone, model number 7650. This unit's task was to design additional camera phone models, which Nokia had been too slow to develop. The Entertainment and Media Unit would develop new phones that would also play music, provide a platform for games and other media content. Nokia had just launched its model 5510, which had a music player and other media applications, but the phone didn't sell as well as we had hoped.

The Business Applications Unit was dedicated to phones and applications for professional use. Our main product was the Communicator. It hadn't made much impact yet in terms of sales, but it was very important in developing our brand.

Two other units, the Mobile Enhancements Unit and Mobile Services Unit, focused on accessories for mobile phones, such as earphones, covers, and loudspeakers, and on Club Nokia, which was intended to create a community of core customers. They would be offered special services, applications, and ringtones. This would also enhance loyalty toward Nokia as a brand.

Our new structure said all there was to say about what was happening in our business. We had different sorts of customers. There was no longer one mass of people to whom we could sell identical or even similar phones. For a while we had been like Ford in the 1920s, which had sold all customers its Model T in "any color as long as it's black." Ford's dominance ended when General Motors started to offer customers a range of cars with names such as Chevrolet, Oldsmobile, and Cadillac. The auto market was now divided into segments. If customers wanted to buy a different kind of car they didn't have to transfer their loyalties from General Motors to another manufacturer; they could simply switch to another of General Motors' brands. We thought the market for mobile phones would evolve along similar lines, as indeed had happened for many products since the 1920s. The world was no longer one gray mass but was differentiated into a rainbow palette according to tastes and desires, and this offered many new opportunities. Our reorganization put seizing those opportunities at the forefront.

CHAPTER 59

Bill Gates Picks Up
the Phone

IN 2002 WE REALIZED THAT WE DEFINITELY HAD A NEW COMPETITOR in the mobile business. It was based in Redmond in the United States and its name was Microsoft.

Microsoft had emerged from the shadows in 2000. The company announced then that it intended to move into two new areas of business. The first was games consoles, so that it could dominate home entertainment and electronics. Otherwise Sony would continue to reign supreme in home electronics. Microsoft's second target was mobile phones, where it didn't want Nokia to dominate the software and hence the consumers' souls. Microsoft didn't use those exact words, but that was how we interpreted their actions at Nokia. Microsoft had announced that it was coming to our patch, and we knew they played a hard game.

Microsoft had become an icon of the 1990s and 2000s and a monument to American enterprise. It had also grown into a colossus of the markets and went on the attack and defended itself from attack with varying degrees of success. The company concentrated on protecting its source codes and defending its rights in every part of the globe. Microsoft's culture didn't have much in common with Nokia's. It was a pure software company whose cash flow came from licensing payments. In the value chain Microsoft dominated one horizontal element, namely software. Nokia, on the other hand, grew through its products: mobile phones, for which it developed ever more sophisticated software as phones became more complex. By 2000 our mobile phones had capabilities similar to those of small computers. Our Communicator in particular was interoperable with computers and with Microsoft software, since it was only useful to an executive if information could readily be transferred between it and a computer.

We had actively sought out areas of cooperation. Pekka Ala-Pietilä and his team held discussions at Microsoft; from these had come the idea of a wireless phone with an Internet connection for office use. This project began in 1998 but it was quickly dropped as it became clear that there wouldn't be much demand for the product. After that we agreed that Nokia's smartphones would also work in the Microsoft Outlook environment. This didn't call for particularly dramatic steps since both sides had much to gain from the deal, and we quickly reached an agreement. It was an ordinary business decision.

In 1999 the founder and chairman of Microsoft, Bill Gates, introduced the Stinger phone and promised that it would be available by the end of 2001. Microsoft was trying to win over Nokia's competitors. They held discussions with at least Motorola and Sony Ericsson. They didn't succeed, but they did collaborate with Samsung to some degree, and they made arrangements for the production of the Stinger. The phone was never launched, however, but was buried in the graveyard where stillborn technology projects are laid to rest.

Microsoft had wanted to supply software for mobile phones, but we wanted to develop the software ourselves. The major mobile phone manufacturers had set up a software company called Symbian for that purpose. When we realized what Microsoft was trying to do we focused our software development ever more on Symbian. Its first achievement was the camera phone 7650, launched in 2002. Other companies, such as Sony Ericsson, Siemens, and Samsung, also invested more money in Symbian.

When Microsoft noticed that it was difficult to fight against Symbian, it changed its strategy once more. This time it focused on operating systems. Nokia's countermove was to bring together the Open Mobile Architecture Forum, which attracted two hundred practitioners from the mobile phone markets and elsewhere. This was such a high-profile move that Microsoft saw that it had to give up its dream of single-handedly dominating the market for mobile phone software.

Competing with Microsoft is never easy. We had the resources needed to do it, but once again we came up against cultural differences. The biggest problem was the software development community – Microsoft could mobilize a million software developers, where we could call on fifty or a hundred thousand at best. Symbian seriously lagged behind Microsoft in this.

I met Bill Gates for the first time in Sun Valley, Idaho, at one of the annual conferences that bring IT and media industry executives together. I don't have any particular mental image of Gates. He may well have seemed just as I had expected: he was more focused on technology than on leading people. I invited Gates to Finland, and he did indeed come to Nokia's new head office, which he immediately called PowerPoint Palace after one of his own success stories. We were certainly Microsoft's biggest customer in Finland, and PowerPoint perhaps loomed a little too large in what we did. Sometimes I banned its use when we were working on strategy, because it too readily became a substitute for independent thought.

We sat in our conference room for an hour and a half. Gates was on a post-Davos tour of Europe; he had just come from Brussels, where a Belgian anarchist had thrust a cream pie into his face. He was still slightly shaken up, at least to the extent that he had difficulty in firing himself up that morning.

Shortly after his visit I received a letter thanking me for the meeting and saying he looked forward to cooperation with Nokia.

In June 1999 I was with Liisa on a brief visit to our summer place in Orivesi. We were driving through the Finnish countryside. The fields where black and white cows grazed contemplatively were broken up by little huddles of trees, the sun was shining, and Finland's summer was at its zenith. It was all very restful. The phone rang, and at the other end was Bill Gates, straight from Redmond.

"Nokia has been anti-Microsoft," he yelled into the phone. He continued without a break for a quarter of an hour. I had to stop the car at the side of the road to avoid crashing. Liisa was astonished. Usually I manage to get a word in, but this time all I could do was listen. Bill Gates was accusing Nokia of unfair practices in some aspect of standards, which of course I knew nothing about. At last the call ended, I started the car again, and we continued on our way.

A month later I met Bill Gates again at another Sun Valley meeting. He apologized for the call. He explained that he had gotten the wrong company: the miscreant was Ericsson, not Nokia.

I went to Sun Valley again in 2002. After midsummer I had sent a message to Bill Gates telling him I hoped to meet him at the conference. At half past two in the afternoon of 12 July we met in a little meeting room, called the Sage Room, at our hotel. Bill Gates was armed with one of his own weapons, a laptop computer. I had brought Nokia's new model, the 7650, along with me. This was a camera phone, for which Symbian had developed some wonderful software. You could take photos with this camera, but you couldn't send them to anyone yet.

I put my brand new phone on the table. Gates had in front of him his laptop, which naturally had Microsoft's latest software. On the table there was also mineral water for us. We looked at one another, through our respective pairs of metal-framed glasses. "The markets aren't looking too good right now," Gates began. I couldn't have agreed more. The world had yet to recover from the shock of 2001, and technology seemed to have lost its appeal. No one could say what The Next Big Idea would be, or if there was to be one. "Things will get worse before they get better. We have three bad years ahead of us," Gates predicted. The chairman of Intel, Andy Grove, put it even more succinctly the following day: "The world is a shitty place."

The chairmen of the world's biggest technology companies were certainly not bubbling with optimism in the summer of 2002. Even so, I was satisfied with my conversation with Bill Gates. If we had started to discuss cooperation with Microsoft two years earlier they would have eaten us for breakfast. We wanted to be in a position where we would be playing with a reasonably strong hand.

Our strategy of defending open-source software and cooperating with many manufacturers had paid off. We had also managed to keep control of our own software development. Microsoft had perhaps begun to understand that mobile phones weren't as simple as laptop computers.

In a mobile phone the software and the device itself were almost indistinguishable: you couldn't tell where the software started and the hardware ended. The mobile phone had already started to become a personal product in which the design, features, software, and user interface were packaged into the smallest possible product, which was also a brand in itself. Nokia was on top of all this, while for Microsoft it was unknown territory. Microsoft was a software company, which had developed products that the whole world depended on. Nokia did its best to create attractive products that would appeal to individual consumers in an extremely competitive market.

We agreed with Bill Gates that almost everything possible in our world was going badly. The phone operators were in a bad way. Nokia's competitors had become weaker and we had our own problems, though I wouldn't have used quite those words to Bill Gates. "It would be a pity if our actions or arguments splintered the market so that there would no longer be just one single market for mobile phones," I said. Gates suggested we discuss what it was that Microsoft did that annoyed Nokia, and vice versa.

"What annoys me about Microsoft is that you believe you can use the same value chain for mobile phones as you use to create personal computers. But they're two very different things. Our model of vertical integration is designed to produce phones that appeal to consumers," I said. I didn't say that the way Microsoft was acting was hostile to Nokia, though in reality it was.

"In many decisions on standards you've opted for something other than the Microsoft model. You've chosen Java technology and RealPlayer for your phones," Gates said in his turn. "That's true," I replied in a conciliatory tone, "but now I'm sitting at this table in order to look again at these issues. That's what compatibility is about." I said. We spent twenty minutes or so on these painful questions. Then we sketched out a direction for future discussions on a notepad. We also agreed that Pekka Ala-Pietilä and Pertti Korhonen would soon get in touch to discuss strategy with their counterparts at Microsoft.

Two years earlier Microsoft had intended to capture the market for mobile phone software, come what may, and push Nokia into the sea. The only question had been which sea Bill Gates would choose for that purpose. Now his approach had changed, and all the arrogance had gone from the thinking of the world's biggest technology company.

There were two moments in our discussion when Gates got jittery. The first was of no significance. The second was when he shouted as he told me that three months earlier Nokia had supported a court indictment against Microsoft. We had to decide whether to intervene to give Microsoft a chance to offer an expert opinion in a court case. I had concluded that Nokia shouldn't get mixed up in courtroom disputes between Microsoft and the U.S. federal government, that we shouldn't intervene. It wasn't our business. But perhaps our representatives had said something incautious in the corridors that had found its way up to Bill Gates.

Finally I asked why Microsoft had ended its cooperation with Sony Ericsson. Cooperation had started a couple of years earlier but had come to a sudden end after a short time. "It wasn't going anywhere. It's impossible to work with a company that's falling to pieces the whole time," Gates said in his straightforward way. Directness was the Gates trademark, by which I had learned to know him. I knew it was better to be with him than against him. I also knew that if our efforts at cooperation didn't work, Microsoft would acquire fifty or so tanks from somewhere and try to crush Nokia beneath their tracks. Bill Gates was a typical exemplar of Andy Grove's famous dictum that "only the paranoid survive." Microsoft's methods had been extremely brutal, but its software had created entirely new ways of working and processing information. I had respected Bill Gates's clear intelligence and willpower when I first met him in 1998, but four years later I knew that Microsoft wasn't invincible.

"We realized that we would never make money in the wireless world," Gates said now. I drew a deep breath. I knew that Nokia had reached a critical point.

We shook hands after a long discussion. I picked up my mobile phone, Bill Gates his laptop, and the mineral water bottles remained on the table. Peace descended on the Sage Room as I returned with Gates to the dinner table in Sun Valley.

CHAPTER 60

Back to Reality

WE HAD RECONFIGURED NOKIA so the company could seize opportunities for new growth. We believed that the nine new business units were focused on the areas where growth would be found.

We were looking for growth over five years since we didn't know how long our current crisis would last. Our key aim was to build up our software capability so we could develop more complex products. We thought that mobile phone users should be able to read email, take pictures, and even regulate their heartbeats.

We were gearing up for a battle with Microsoft for supremacy of the wireless world. If we hadn't played our cards right I would have been in no position to take on Bill Gates when I met him in the summer of 2002. We had won our battle with Microsoft, even though we didn't yet know the final result. At the end of 2002 Microsoft's British partner, Sendo, switched sides; the company accused Microsoft of stealing its business secrets. Work on the smartphone that the two companies had developed together came to an end just before the phone was due to be launched.

We seemed safe from attack. About this time the *Economist* wrote about a new type of information technology: its cover featured not a laptop computer with Microsoft software, but Nokia's new phone. We were doing well in this battle, but for some reason we didn't notice that the real war was taking place somewhere else.

Companies usually make mistakes because they focus too much on the short-term future. Our mistake was the opposite: we were thinking too hard about what the world would look like in five years. We were losing our grip on what might happen next year. We believed our customers would move to more sophisticated and smarter phones and, at least in developed markets, leave the simpler models behind. We expected cheap phones to be dominant in developing markets. We had set up a unit to focus on just those markets – which is where all the growth in the world's mobile phone markets would come from.

In February 2003 we launched an entirely new line of Nokia products: phones on which you could play games. We called it N-Gage. It had been Nokia's dream to extend its range from phones to games consoles. You could load games on to the new phone by inserting a diskette. It looked more like a games console than a phone, and it was aimed at people aged sixteen to thirty-five. As well as games and a phone it contained a radio, a music player, and a web browser. For technical reasons, using it to make calls was a little awkward since you had to point its narrow edge toward your ear.

N-Gage had a big marketing budget. The phone had been designed by Anssi Vanjoki's unit, and Anssi was a marketing professional if anyone was. It was a rare individual at Nokia who wished to or would have dared disagree with Anssi on a marketing matter. The N-Gage was launched to a great fanfare at the London Eye, the giant Ferris wheel on the south bank of the River Thames.

N-Gage received a crushing reception from the very people who should have fallen in love with it. Young people thought it looked like a "taco gone wrong." As a phone it was rather clumsy because it was too big, and the way you had to hold it to make a call seemed ridiculous. The selection of games was too narrow and unsatisfactory in other respects. I even heard of one thirteen-year-old boy who, after he had seen our splendid new games phone, recommended to his father that he sell his Nokia shares.

We tried to put on a brave face. We put more money into marketing, and of course we received some positive or at least neutral publicity. We also started to think about what we might do with the N-Gage and why things had gone as they had. Perhaps we hadn't fully understood our new customers, or perhaps it wasn't as easy for Nokia to move from phones to games consoles as we had imagined. We believed we had created something new that would rewrite the rules of the game. We were sure we had succeeded in that, but our customers took a different view.

The sales figures for N-Gage fell far short of our targets, of course. We learned many new things, though some of that knowledge was quite expensive. N-Gage cost us around $352 million, which may sound like a great deal of money, but it's worth remembering that at that time Nokia's cash flow was around $587 million a month. N-Gage was our biggest single individual investment of those years. It wasn't a success but, partly through Nokia's support, Finland gained significant expertise in games design. In recent years Finnish companies such as Rovio and Supercell have again shown how Finland can compete at the top levels.

Our mistake was not that we took too big a risk, but that we made a loss. Our mistake was that we didn't take big enough risks when it would have been cheap to take them. Nokia's great profitability meant that our cash reserves had grown so big that stock exchange analysts kept demanding to know how the money might be returned to the shareholders to whom it really belonged.

Our focus on the N-Gage and other multimedia products cost us dearly in 2003. That spring we also launched a new media phone, which was a fine product, but it also failed to achieve much success. We were perhaps a little too early once again. It was only a little later that games and media content became common in phones.

In 2003 I took a two-week summer holiday, which was a record. I hadn't had such a peaceful break since 1980. In 2000 we had acquired a new holiday home, a manor house on a lake about seventy miles northeast of Helsinki. I looked out over the lake and realized how much I needed a holiday. We had acquired a puppy, Teri, and training her seemed much more demanding than running a global company. She was still bursting with puppyish life and energy and disobedience; these qualities were less in evidence at Nokia.

I had set major organizational changes in motion at Nokia. I assumed that splitting the mobile phone division into nine smaller units would be enough and would soon lead to fresh growth. Now I had to admit that I had been wrong. I should have overhauled the whole of Nokia, not just the way mobile phones were organized. Besides, the new division of responsibilities was pointing us in the wrong direction. We had focused on complicated smartphones and on cheap models for markets in the developing world. But between the two there remained a key market for mid-range phones, and we hadn't paid enough attention to that.

On top of that, in early 2003 our relationships with the mobile network operators had deteriorated. They wanted us to deliver tailored phones, as other manufacturers had, but that wasn't our preferred approach. The operators wanted specialized software for mid-range phones, such as high-resolution color screens and other high-quality features. We were gearing up to deliver large numbers of new phones, but we couldn't meet the requirements until 2004. Also, many operating companies thought Nokia had become too strong a company. They had difficulties of their own since the new 3G networks had yet to make a return on investment.

Nokia had smaller competitors who were ready to comply with the operating companies' tiniest wish. We had grown so big that every one of our competitors had just one aim: to attack Nokia's market share and push us off our pedestal. We had given many of our competitors the tools to do just that – every new product that failed or was late, every customer complaint, and every critical review gave them something to smile about in the boardrooms of Samsung and Motorola.

As well as the reorganization, I had made another decision. I would leave Nokia in 2006, whatever happened. My contract would have made it possible for me to stay on if the board and I both wanted that, but I had decided to do something else. Back in 2003 I didn't have any idea at all what that might be. For now I wanted to put Nokia back in shape and on the path to growth one more time; only then could I leave the company to my successor. It also seemed to me that I could no longer summon up as much enthusiasm as I needed to. And The Five had worked together long enough.

Nokia needed to enter a new phase; something had to be done. This wasn't the first time I'd found myself in this position: I had turned the company around twice already; I had made surprising organizational changes; and I had made all the necessary moves at the necessary times, to my own satisfaction. Of course, I hadn't achieved all this just by myself: Pekka, Matti, Sari, Olli-Pekka, as well as Anssi Vanjoki and Pertti Korhonen and others had all certainly done their bit to ensure that Nokia ascended back into the stratosphere just when the trees below had begun to seem too close for comfort.

At the moment of crisis there was more at stake than there had been earlier. Nokia was bigger than ever. It had become our life's work. It was a tale that we knew would go down in economic history. I didn't want to go down in history as the chief executive who raised Nokia to a commanding position and then let things fall apart and allowed its competitors to overtake it. No, I certainly didn't want that.

CHAPTER 61

Reorganization Once More

NOKIA NEEDED A COMPLETE MAKEOVER ONCE MORE. I had to give every one of our employees a clear message about the direction the company should take. You mustn't send an organization too many messages at one time. A company always has to seize the day and the opportunities it's offered. When in 2003 Nokia started to focus on work that wouldn't reach maturity until 2006, it started to fall behind. In every company the structures and the support functions should be designed with the front-line business in mind. If we had started to put our reporting systems or logistics straight in 1992, we would never have achieved our market position at the end of the decade. But neither would we have encountered the problems we did in 1995–96.

A company can't motivate its employees by sending a message saying: "get the structures into shape, and then we can expect growth." Employees can't strike a balance between objectives of different kinds, such as promoting growth on one hand and putting the right systems in place on the other. A company can't instruct its workers to step on the brakes and the accelerator at the same time. It is the job of senior management to see further. They should change the company's direction when it seems to be heading for a wall – not after it's already crashed into it.

At the end of the 1990s Nokia's revenue grew rapidly. Perhaps we should have been satisfied with a little less growth and left some energy for improving our systems. But that's a hard message to get across when people are relishing new victories, making the most of exciting new products, and experiencing new triumphs in China. An organization will never value the people who develop systems as much as it values those who innovate or sell things – someone who develops a new internal accounting system will rarely receive the same respect and recognition as someone who has just sold a million phones. It's the job of a company's board to strike a balance between these different factors. As the chief executive, responsibility for that ultimately rested with me.

In March 2003 I began to sketch out a new organizational structure. My core group gathered each morning in my meeting room. The days were lengthening; the sun had risen sometime around seven and would set again an hour or two after most people got home from work. The Finnish spring is a good time for everything new because the light increases so rapidly from day to day. We sketched possible models on notepads but didn't worry about who would go where. Our discussion concerned only what would be the best structure for Nokia regardless of who would do what. The time to consider individual roles would come later. I wanted to have that discussion with everyone separately. I already had some ideas of my own on where people should go, which would become clear later on.

The discussions went well and took the reorganization forward rapidly. The model was a simple but ambitious matrix: many people would now find themselves working with their colleagues, rather than competing against them, for the good of Nokia. That would demand a new maturity.

By 11 August I knew which individuals would change their jobs. In a way I also had to take a stance on who my successor would be, because the new arrangements would have an impact on who held power within Nokia. Some people would find themselves in a stronger position, while others would find their positions unchanged or apparently weakened. But I didn't want to have the press placing bets on who my successor would be. Indeed, my successor could in principle come from outside the matrix. Two of The Five would not be part of the group from which my successor would come. They were Matti Alahuhta and Sari Baldauf. Sari and I agreed, at her request, that she would leave Nokia in 2004. Matti would move to become the director responsible for strategy; later he would become chief executive of the elevator manufacturer Kone.

In itself the new organization was simple. There were four business groups: Mobile Phones, Multimedia, Networks, and Enterprise Solutions (which provided services for business customers). The matrix also included cross-cutting support functions. Olli-Pekka Kallasvuo would lead the Mobile Phones Unit, while Anssi Vanjoki would be in charge of Multimedia, where he would focus all his energies on smartphones and services linked to entertainment, music, and pictures. Sari Baldauf would continue to manage Networks.

Pekka Ala-Pietilä would move to run the global organization responsible for marketing, sales, logistics, and procurement. Pertti Korhonen would become Nokia's new chief technology officer, responsible for all technological development. We would find someone new to promote our services to business customers; Mary McDowell of Hewlett-Packard later took on that role. A second American, Rick Simonson, took over from Olli-Pekka as finance director later in September.

Our new structure was unveiled at the end of September and was in place by the beginning of January 2004. From September to December thousands and thousands of Nokia employees pondered their future, looked for new jobs in the new organization, and moved to work for new bosses. Those in charge of the new units fought the usual turf wars. Not all of them had enough good people to start with: there was certainly no long queue of gifted people outside the door of Olli-Pekka Kallasvuo's "ordinary" Mobile Phones Unit, for example, while Anssi Vanjoki's "unusual" group seemed to interest a disproportionate number of ambitious people. Despite that, the center of gravity of Nokia's business still lay with the Mobile Phones Unit. But the hard times weren't over.

CHAPTER 62

The Customers Strike Back

SUCCESS IS THE GRAVEST DANGER OF ALL. Success potentially makes major companies complacent and arrogant. Once a successful company has managed to change the rules of the market, it believes it can do so again and again. A successful company imagines that it understands its customers perfectly. It believes it knows what people want in Europe, in Asia, and in North America. Its board members watch well-crafted PowerPoint presentations showing how the customer base is evolving and what the new trends are. A successful company slips into talking about controlling its customers, when it should be talking about how the customers really control the company.

Many journalists and analysts thought that Nokia would be unable to sustain its profitability at such a high level. Mobile phone prices were falling, so they assumed Nokia would have to drop its prices too.

But we thought we could teach customers to use more expensive products and thus safeguard our future.

In 2003 we had launched the mobile games phone, the N-Gage, and also camera phones, but we weren't focusing on mid-range phones. We thought the future lay in expensive models for developed markets on the one hand, and very cheap, mass-market models for developing countries on the other. We believed we knew the customers, the markets, and the future, which we tried to control as best we could. Because of our success we were used to making our products the way we believed was right. We had become a proud company and didn't want to imitate others. For us it was a matter of honor that every insight and innovation was our own. It was important that we believed strongly in our own expertise and capability, but we might have done better if we had been humble enough to follow the moves our competitors made and the trends our customers followed.

Customers bring even the largest companies back to their senses. The mobile phone market moves so fast that no established position lasts more than a few seconds. Somewhere someone is coming up with a new way of making a phone. Somewhere a new fashion is catching on that dictates that phones have to be a certain shape and color. Somewhere in the world your customers are inventing a new way of using the camera in a phone. Somewhere one of your competitors is adopting a new kind of distribution system. The possibilities are limitless.

The telecom operating companies were important customers for Nokia. Our Networks Unit sold them mobile phone networks. Through them we sold vast numbers of phones, and they increasingly wanted us to tailor those phones to their own requirements. Phone manufacturers complied with the operating companies' wishes according to the degree that they wanted to or could.

The mobile network operators and the manufacturers carried on an interminable debate over who owned the customers. Inside Nokia's Mobile Phones Unit there were conflicting views on this: the more fundamentalist types thought that the operators were in much the same position as companies that make railway sleepers. Their view was that the operating companies didn't add any value for the customers, whose experiences depended on having good phones with lots of interesting features. The operators didn't provide significant services, because services and content were already combined in the manufacture of the phone. Nokia was involved in many projects where new content was installed directly into the phone. That was how mobile television got under way in 2005.

But many people did understand the role the mobile network operators played in business. Close to 50 percent of phones were sold by the operators. The operators saw and knew what was happening in the market, so it was worth listening closely to what they had to tell us.

In the summer of 2003 the operators' concerns reached our ears. Their trade association was adopting a more critical tone: Nokia was rapidly becoming their Public Enemy Number One. One of their representatives called on us to say that they wanted to buy clamshell phones, but all Nokia had to offer were the familiar "candy bar" models.

Nokia had already started to design a clamshell phone, but it was running late. Once again we had decided to do everything ourselves even though we hadn't previously made clamshell or hinged models for the mid-range market. We encountered many technical difficulties that we tried to explain to our friends, but we didn't take their concerns seriously enough in 2003.

In September the anti-Nokia front gained strength. Many operating companies feared that Nokia would tread on their toes as it developed its Nokia Club concept. Customers would find themselves directed to Nokia's web pages rather than to the operating companies' pages. Our initiative had never been directed against the operators, but to some it looked as if it had.

The board of the association of mobile network operators, the GSM Association, met every third month. At the end of 2003 the meeting took place in Milan, where several major operators declared open war on Nokia. Their war cry was "Kill Nokia!" The phrase undoubtedly contained more rhetoric than reality, but it reflected the thinking among the operators.

Our friend in the world of the mobile network operators got back in touch. He was worried about what the future would hold for Nokia if its relationships with the operating companies didn't improve. He had taken it upon himself to tell us what was bothering the operating companies. From Milan he rang Matti Alahuhta and said that death threats were raining down on Nokia from every direction. Matti took his concerns seriously, which led to an immediate reappraisal in the Mobile Phones Unit. The operators' concerns had registered with Nokia, but our reaction speed left much to be desired.

One of the world's largest operating companies, Vodafone, was in the vanguard of the anti-Nokia movement and found it easy to bring smaller companies along with it. The operators' secret operation culminated in Cannes in February 2004, when over a hundred operators gathered for their annual meeting. They simply agreed to reduce their purchases from Nokia by a certain proportion.

They wanted to teach Nokia a clear lesson. Someone had asked at Cannes if what the operators were doing was even legal. The lawyers were clear on that point, however. This wasn't a matter of a cartel, but a recommendation for a common action. Nokia had to go back to school, to a hard school where rapid results were expected.

CHAPTER 63

Clams Are Predators

IF I KNOW THINGS AREN'T GOING WELL, I feel it physically, as a horrible sensation in my stomach. I feel it when I have to give a profit warning, even when everyone has done their best. I feel it when I've been subjected to unfair criticism. And I feel it when someone I've trusted can no longer be relied upon.

From time to time I also have an unpleasant feeling when intuition tells me that things aren't going in the right direction. I get annoyed when things don't seem to be fully under my control. I always try to look as far into the future as possible, to head off any little problems that might cause uncertainty.

In 2003 we had decided to change direction. Nokia's leadership had been reorganized. The whole company had taken on a new form and thousands of people brigaded in line with the new structures. We made vast numbers of decisions, large and small. *Business Week* was really talking of past glories when it placed Nokia sixth in its annual survey of the world's most valuable brands. It was the most valuable in Europe and the most valuable mobile phone company. Our profitability and market share remained high. However, it felt as if we were losing the battle on several fronts.

In November 2003 I gave an interview to the *Wall Street Journal*. They asked what kept me awake at night. I replied that I always slept well, even on airplanes. I said I was pondering what would happen in the next three or four years. In 1999 and 2000 everyone had believed in the triumph of technology, until 11 September 2001 changed everything. Thus my worry was whether Nokia was structured to absorb every unexpected change the following years would undoubtedly bring. I couldn't know what those changes might be. But I reckoned that any surprises were likely to come either from technology or from Nokia's competitors.

It was a good guess. I still didn't have the faintest idea of what awaited us as we entered 2004. Everything looked good at the beginning of January. The last quarter of 2003 had been a good period – our results were better than they had been for a long time. When I returned to Nokia after my Christmas break, morale was high. Our order books were still full in the first week of January.

In the second week there was a turn for the worse: we didn't get any orders. Our phones weren't selling as we had expected. Things didn't get better the following week, either. This wasn't a good start to the year. I quickly realized something was wrong.

These situations have their own charm. I feel energized when I can roll up my sleeves and solve problems, and I expect a great deal from the people around me. They have to carry heavy responsibilities and make almost superhuman efforts. But innovation and failure are both permitted. If people give everything in a crisis you can't punish them if they make mistakes. At Nokia I've always tried to strike a balance between the demands I make and the excitement that work can bring. We won't achieve anything if we don't expect enough from people. But we would quickly lose good people if they didn't enjoy their work. This balance is absolutely essential.

In a crisis the chief executive's job is to show by their own behavior and actions what's important. They have to go where changes have to be made. They also have to admit where the company has made mistakes, and where they have made mistakes; but they must also look ahead to the future. They must demand systematic results when the crisis begins to be resolved. Their decisions have to be right and proportionate. Everyone has to do their bit, but not more. In a crisis no one wants leaders who are weak or have lost their nerve.

It soon became clear that the mobile network operators were acting on their threat. Their share of Nokia sales in Europe was usually around 50 percent; they had decided to bring that down to 30 percent. The major companies were reducing their purchases, but the smaller ones were buying as many phones as before. When we calculated the impact of the partial boycott, we found that our market share in Europe had fallen by 12 percentage points in six months. The meeting at Cannes in February had sent a message to Nokia, which we had most certainly received. Nokia fell off its pedestal in a matter of weeks. The operating companies' smart weapon had hit its target, with destructive force. Our market share had fallen from 38 percent in 2003 to 32 percent in 2004.

Nokia started to do its homework. Our discussions with the operating companies began on a new basis. If we had shown arrogance in the past, we certainly couldn't afford it now. I divided responsibility for dealing with individual operating companies between the members of our management team. I wanted my most experienced colleagues to report directly to me on their dealings with specific operators. I jumped on planes to meet the most important companies myself. I talked through our problems with Vodafone at their head office. I wanted to show them that we were serious and were offering a concrete response to their concerns.

The world would have been a simpler place if we could have blamed our difficulties entirely on our relationships with the operating companies. Unfortunately, we had to look in the mirror. There we could see an inadequate range of products, defective processes, carelessness, and arrogance.

On top of that, we had concentrated so hard on maintaining our profitability that we were shutting ourselves out of expanding markets.

Suddenly we found ourselves competing in the market for mid-range phones. Really it was only now that mid-range phones had appeared; they were a new phenomenon for us all. They didn't compete on the basis of their new applications; they competed on the basis of their design and physical properties. They were called flip-phones or clamshell phones because they opened with the aid of a hinge.

Our competitors had tried in various ways to destroy Nokia by changing the rules of the game. Now the clamshell phones brought them success. The phones weren't a step forward in technical terms, but they offered a different experience to customers using old technology. The fault for Nokia's problems also lay in our organization, for which I was responsible. In 2003 Matti Alahuhta was in overall charge of Mobile Phones, but Anssi Vanjoki was responsible for the product development and reported to Matti. With hindsight this arrangement turns out to have been our Achilles' heel.

Matti and Anssi were, and are, very different in their approach to leadership. Matti is a strategist who likes to work things through to their conclusion, while Anssi moves fast like a cruise missile. He works on the basis of intuition, paying close attention to market signals. Anssi was a strong believer in smartphones and didn't believe at all in clamshell phones. He thought we ought to make a handful of them because the operators seemed to want them, but basically he believed that clamshell phones were a passing fad. He turned out to be right. But that didn't help Nokia when our competitors' clamshells were nibbling away at our market share and profitability. We didn't have the phones on the market we should have had.

Matti Alahuhta was committed to producing Nokia's own clamshell phone. But Matti and Anssi couldn't find enough common ground for the investment that was needed, for positioning the new product in the market, and for allocating the necessary resources. The upshot was a failure to create phones that were good enough. We were out of the game in this particular competition.

Asian manufacturers, especially Samsung, made money from clamshell phones, which went down very well with young people in Asia and beyond. This wasn't Nokia's only problem. Our arch-rival Motorola rose again thanks to a phone called the Motorola Razr. The Americans ingeniously combined three things: a large screen, a slender body, and a clamshell casing. All this was wrapped up in a marketing campaign that had touches of genius. The Razr started out as a phone aimed at rich and tech-savvy customers at the upper end of the market. Then Motorola lowered the product's price and the results spoke for themselves. The phone was designed in 2003, launched in 2004, and by 2006 there were 50 million of them in use. Eventually 130 million Razr phones would be sold, a record for a clamshell.

For the second time in Nokia's recent history we had to examine the anatomy of the clamshell, because Motorola had surprised us. The previous time had been when Pertti Korhonen took a Motorola phone to bits in Nokia's Oulu laboratory back in 1989. Now there was no need to disassemble a phone because we could already see what had happened.

In 2004 Nokia finally succeeded in producing a clamshell phone for the European market, six months late. Some people predicted that in a few years half the world's mobile phones would be clamshell models. The clamshell had become a dangerous beast of prey, which Nokia attempted to domesticate much too late. Our first clamshell phone couldn't compete.

Samsung had achieved not just lift-off, it had practically gone into orbit on the fuel provided by its clamshell phones. They were now in their third or even fourth generation. Samsung knew how to stuff its mid-range phones full of features that would appeal to consumers: cameras, big screens, and designs that were easy to use and worked well. Suddenly Nokia's phones were no longer enticing.

We had thought once more that we could change the rules of the game and everyone else would fall into line. When we decided to make our clamshell phone we wanted it to be different from everyone else's. So we developed a new type of hinge. We tried to go through two stages in one leap. The new phone too was notably late, and we had come up with such expensive solutions that the customers weren't satisfied. They wouldn't pay extra for our education in the fine art of clamshell phones.

We should have thought longer and harder about what customers really wanted. Looking back, it appears that customers didn't want clamshell phones as such; what they wanted were phones that looked and felt different and new. If a customer had bought a phone costing $130 a year or two back, we should have come up with a much better phone that would cost $260. Now all we had to offer was a supermodel costing $650. We were victims of our own elementary mistakes.

My agonies intensified. Responsibility for the Mobile Phones Unit had moved to Olli-Pekka Kallasvuo, and I knew he would get things right. There was a profit warning ahead, which would knock billions off our market value. The press was saying that I was in exactly the same position that I had been in a couple of years earlier. We had to make some major corrections.

The CEO of a company can never escape responsibility for his or her own mistakes. On 6 April I made a conference call explaining to shareholders where we stood. I had travelled the previous day to Atlanta to meet one of our important customers, Cingular. From there I flew to New York in the evening. I woke at five in the morning to read my papers, had breakfast at the Peninsula Hotel at seven, and knew then that I had a long and arduous day ahead. There was a shortage of financial news: only the results for Rupert Murdoch's NewsCorp and for Nokia were due. I could see that we would attract a great deal of attention, all of it negative. The worst of it was that I couldn't really make promises to anyone. All I could do was repeat the same message to the investors: things are under control. We're doing the right things. This is a much smaller crisis than the one we faced in 1995. But I didn't know when our profits would improve, or to what extent. All I could do – and it was what I wanted to do – was trust our new organization. It had to succeed. Otherwise everything would go badly for us. My stomach was burning for three or four days. At least my body understood what was up.

The first thing we did was something straight out of textbooks. If your goods don't sell, you should drop the price. Our phones were well packaged and commanded premium prices. We could afford to sell them more cheaply, though that might go against our traditional principles. A price cut would stop our market share crumbling, though of course the markets wouldn't like the move. Our profitability would also be in danger.

The crucial thing was to crank our machinery into action. At its heart sat a group of product directors responsible for designing new phones that would

The Nokia 6101

sell in our various markets. A product director's job was to ensure that the customer's voice was heard at an early stage in our design process. If, for example, we wanted to create a phone for developed markets costing $200, it would be up to the product director to say which compromises could be made in the design and which weren't possible. A product director's job was made up of countless small decisions that were the basis for a new product that would stand or fall in the market for which it had been designed.

In the mid-1990s we launched perhaps three new models of phone a year. By the mid-2000s this figure had grown to at least forty. Ten years earlier a product director had a great deal of power and responsibility – every new model was a major event that could determine Nokia's fate for the coming years. Now a product director's job had become more mundane.

Our announcement that Nokia intended to develop new and complex multimedia phones had brought a new creative glow. There had certainly been a glow when we developed N-Gage. The company devoted its most valuable resources to these products, which were not yet ready to be launched. We had also skimped on design. The ease of use and features of our mid-range phones were not on a level that would win back our market share.

Now the product directors had to focus on new tasks with a fresh attitude. Olli-Pekka Kallasvuo queried almost every aspect of the Mobile Phones Unit's conventional wisdom. He was enough of an outsider to do that; but he also knew practically everything and brought a great deal of authority to bear. He didn't want to hear old explanations of why Nokia hadn't made clamshell phones. He asked basic questions until the people he spoke to had to admit there was really no rational basis for how things had been done. The product directors had to be transferred to different roles and new people brought in, and we also had to find new experts.

In spring 2004 I gathered all our mobile phone product directors together. I opened the meeting and put my neck on the line as far as I could. I tried to acknowledge both my own and Nokia's mistakes. I emphasized how important this issue was to the entire company. Once again I saw serious faces in front of me. Everyone knew, once again, that Nokia's future was at stake.

Matters gradually started to move in the right direction. In spring 2004 the decision to produce a new clamshell model was made, and it was launched a year later. This model – the 6101 – worked well, sold well, and showed that Nokia was an organization that could learn. Before this Olli-Pekka Kallasvuo had started to turn the whole organization's thinking in a new direction. Copying good ideas wasn't forbidden.

Design, colors, features, and marketing were all ways of creating added value for individual customers. If customers wanted cameras in their mid-range phones, Nokia's job was to find a way of making them. If Americans were only interested in buying clamshell models, Nokia had to make them. We at Nokia wanted to be reasonable, but our customers around the world didn't necessarily want to be as reasonable as we were in Finland. At the last moment we had admitted that it was the customers' money that kept us going, and that they might well be right.

CHAPTER 64

Three Crises

IN GREEK CULTURE the word *crisis* originally meant a turning-point. As a medical term a crisis means simply a fork in the road: the patient either recovers or dies. The same holds true for business life, though the diagnosis isn't always as exact as in the medical world. In business it's only with hindsight that you can work out where things went wrong, why the forecasts turned out to be inaccurate, or how a major company came to lose not just its place in the market but its credibility and its brand as well. And, by the same token, how the company came to lose its senior management; or to put it a better way, how the senior management came to lose the company and their jobs. Then a new age dawns, and no one wants to remember the bad old days or undertake detailed investigations into what went wrong.

Nokia went through at least three crises in the 1990s and 2000s. In 1992 its cash flow dried up and it was on the point of sinking. That crisis was all too visible. Confirmation of its existence came from the Swiss bankers, who were unwilling to extend finance to Nokia, and from Ericsson, who decided not to buy us in 1991 because we were in such bad shape.

In 1995 we encountered a new crisis. We had been growing fast – we had taken off like an airplane built in a back yard. Just as soon as we were properly airborne and had started to congratulate ourselves that the plane could indeed fly, we began to hear some alarming noises. The engine was starting to cut out and the steering didn't seem to work. We had to make an emergency landing and rebuild our craft. Our system couldn't stand up to vigorous growth. Within eight months we got things back into shape, and we were soon aloft once more. If we hadn't succeeded Nokia would be no more, and you wouldn't be reading this book.

We came up against the real world again in 2001, though *crisis* might be a little too strong a word to describe the situation. Growth was now much weaker. Instead, there was ever more aggressive competition, ever more ambitious products, and ever more demanding customers, both individual consumers and operating companies. The market for mobile phones was growing, but Nokia seemed to be getting a smaller share of that growth. Nokia was also suffering because it wasn't strong enough in the Japanese or American markets. Nokia hadn't focused enough on the technological requirements of those markets, which worked to the CDMA standard.

From March to June 2004 Nokia was again on the critical list. We had made some very serious mistakes. We had aimed at the wrong target, and we had lost touch with our customers, both the operating companies and individual consumers. These were the worst mistakes a company could make. I bore my own responsibility for them.

The crisis in 2004 showed that we had to stick coolly and deliberately to our own line, regardless of what anyone else might say. That did not, however, mean withdrawal from reality, from customers, from markets, from the right technology. Building a major company means humility, practicality, flexibility, alertness, and responsiveness. Although Nokia made mistakes, getting back on the right track was possible. We found in spring 2004 that the company could be guided; we could still dispense with the automatic pilot if we needed to.

By June our figures still hadn't improved. In July we issued our results for the first six months, and our share price slumped further. But July was also the turning point. This wasn't visible in the first week of the month, but by the second week, when practically every Finn is on holiday, Nokia's figures seemed to be turning the corner. The battle had perhaps been won, after all.

In that year we didn't manage to address the reasons for our failure. We altered our course, but it took time to implement lasting changes. By 2005 we were back on track for growth. At the beginning of 2006 we succeeded in improving our market share and our profitability, and Nokia was once again a growing company. It had taken a year and a half.

We had, however, learned something from our earlier crises – even though one of the most important things we'd learned was that crises don't resemble each other. In 1992 there hadn't been time to weigh alternatives because Nokia was running out of money. Olli-Pekka Kallasvuo, then our finance director, and I had had to go to the banks, cap in hand. We had to create confidence in the company's future, even though our own confidence almost ran dry at times. The company was small and in bad shape. If money and confidence had run out, the Nokia story would have ended there and then. When finally we got our hands on some money, we started to worry that someone would buy the company, because it had become far too cheap.

In 1995 we had bumped up against the limits of our own growth. We had not stocked up in advance. We lost control of the company. Over the course of eight months Pekka Ala-Pietilä and Pertti Korhonen in particular managed to put the company back on the rails. If we had failed, the Nokia story would have ended abruptly. It was only on account of the crisis that we learned how to configure a global company for sustainable growth.

In 2004 we were the biggest company in our own field. We had reached a position where the main dangers were arrogance, indifference, and remoteness. We had become such a big player that our customers and our business partners began to see us as a threat. We hadn't listened closely enough to the telecom operators. After the crisis we were sharper and more sensitive and travelling on the right track toward the next round of change.

CHAPTER 65

The Right Ideas,
Some Wrong Assumptions,
and Prisoners of Success

NOKIA HAS BEEN ACCUSED, in retrospect, of failing to understand how the world was changing in 2004 and thereafter. I simply don't agree. We knew what was happening: where we failed was in applying our knowledge effectively. We made poor decisions, we didn't think things through clearly enough, and we didn't get where we wanted to go. We were also prisoners of our own success. Nokia's results were good, even exceptional, once we were clear of the crisis of 2004. In 2007 we had our best results ever. None of us would have imagined that just a year or two later the company would produce one of the worst results in its history.

It all began in 2004, however. The previous year we had planned a radical reorganization, intended to reflect what had happened in the market for mobile phones. Markets evolved, and every company tried to predict the direction, speed, and intensity of change. We believed that smartphones were on their way. We believed it so strongly that we established a new business unit to focus on them, and we poured lots of money into product development and marketing. The purpose of the reorganization was to ensure that we would make the right phones for new markets. Nokia's Mobile Phones Unit – NMP – had grown too big within Nokia. It made vast numbers of mobile phones, and quantity had become a substitute for quality.

Logistics, procurement, and sales all worked well: NMP was an efficient machine.

But the efficient machine was unable to make the new products that Nokia sorely needed. If production is directed solely at satisfying the demand that already exists, there's no room for new ideas. Furthermore, Nokia's structures had stayed pretty much the same since 1998. As one by one the other business units ceased to operate, only two were left: Nokia Mobile Phones and Nokia Networks, which built and sold networks to operating companies. These two giants were like companies within the company, and their managing directors ran them in the style of CEOs.

We needed a new organization where NMP would be divided into three: the Mobile Phones Unit, the Multimedia Unit, and Enterprise Solutions. Nokia had tacitly admitted that smartphones and mid-range phones now formed distinct market segments. Also, in the new matrix structure marketing wouldn't be treated as a single function; it would be integrated vertically with the new business units. The same was true of technology, which was perhaps the single most important driver of activity: we reconfigured Nokia's engineering department as well. It suited some of the engineers, but others found the new structure uncomfortable.

In fact the new organization was unremarkable. This is how major companies were and are organized everywhere and in all areas of business. Matrix organizations compel people from different units to make decisions together and to take notice of other people's views. They demand the maturity to understand the interests of the whole firm, which is not the same as the profit or success of one's own unit. They also compel senior management to be where the action is, because there are always issues that only the chief executive can rule on. Lastly, matrix organizations develop friction and heat, which are essential for creativity.

Some have assumed that Nokia's later difficulties resulted from the matrix organization introduced in 2004. I don't agree with them, though not all of Nokia's senior managers functioned effectively within the new structures. Perhaps we didn't train people enough, or maybe power struggles caused problems. Perhaps I too was unable to work in the best possible way in the new organization. And maybe people were jostling for my position and this had started to affect their behavior.

I think now that the reorganization of Nokia put in place in 2004 was correct and an improvement on what had gone before. Even so, we weren't hugely successful. The problem is perhaps that organizations are made of people.

In 2004 one strand of Nokia's history was coming to an end. Perceptive people sensed this. From the early 1990s the company had developed a particular culture, which its closely-knit leaders sustained for many years. I was of course one of those leaders. When I announced that I was stepping down the situation changed, though of course the question was not only about me. After that the position of many other senior managers and divisional chiefs changed: people were concerned about their future, there were more discussions in the corridors, and the large-scale reorganization took many people out of their comfort zones.

All of Nokia's most important people had put a great deal of energy into the company over decades. By 2004 Pekka Ala-Pietilä had been with the company twenty years, Matti Alahuhta twenty-seven, Sari Baldauf twenty-one, Olli-Pekka Kallasvuo twenty-four, Pertti Korhonen eighteen, and Anssi Vanjoki thirteen years. These wonderful people had shaped the company with their own energies and after their own characters. Within the company they were living legends. Of course media exposure, success, and their financial rewards all had something to do with this. The Five and some other senior managers were more than just salaried staff: they embodied the company's values.

When I restructured the senior leadership at Nokia for the last time in 2003–04, I may not have given enough thought to the significance of these people. They helped plan the new organization. I didn't foresee a future in which they wouldn't be around. But that soon became the reality: by 2006 Pekka Ala-Pietilä, Matti Alahuhta, Pertti Korhonen, and Sari Baldauf had all left Nokia. My role changed too when I moved to be chairman of the board of directors and Olli-Pekka Kallasvuo took over as chief executive.

The change in senior leadership was great. Perhaps we lost too much tacit (and indeed vocal) knowledge at the time of the restructuring. Some of the departures were agreed upon well in advance, but some were more surprising. Either way, the result was that only Olli-Pekka Kallasvuo, Anssi Vanjoki, and I remained of the core team that had led Nokia from the mid-1990s on. I don't want to disparage the new generation of leaders who had grown up at Nokia, who tried to step into their shoes in the restructured company. But the break with the past was perhaps too abrupt. Many employees were perhaps too ready to believe that the good times would continue to roll, and that both they and the company would continue merrily on their way.

We wanted to create structures that weren't built around individual managers. Our goal was the world's best organization in the service of the world's best manufacturer of mobile devices. It didn't occur to any of us that the key managers would depart, taking with them their expertise, energy, ideas, experience, and leadership ability. Perhaps we should have done more to hang on to at least some of them.

I certainly made other mistakes. The new structure forced the chief executive to be more intimately involved in the management of the company. Ever smaller issues started to cross my desk. In the new model I should have been

The Nokia N95

closer to the machinery, but psychologically I was already moving to my new position as chairman of the board. I recognized this problem and did everything I could, but as so often happens it was a state of affairs that I needed a twenty-fifth hour in the day to resolve.

Companies often do things either too early or too late. Nokia restructured itself both too late and too early. Only later did it become clear that we had invested in the right ideas, but too soon. We believed that the market wanted expensive, high-performance phones, but we were wrong. It was only later that the operating companies could offer the services that made smartphones appealing. The Apple iPhone came on the market only in 2007.

The new structure didn't mean just new leadership; our working methods had to change as well. We were addressing the right issues, but even so our results remained weak. We were trying to do the things that Apple, Google, and Microsoft would all implement later.

The old Nokia had made many basic products and modified them when necessary, whereas we wanted to focus on a handful of software platforms and the products based on them. Now this change seems self-evident, but in Nokia's thinking at the time it was revolutionary. It was a change in Nokia's behavior that has continued to this day. I understood also that the world of software was changing. Previously, every phone model or group of models had its own software, but now we had to move to wide software platforms. Phones had to be designed to fit the software, not the software to fit the phone. This was a crucial change, and we wanted our restructuring to enable us to move forward with it.

I put Pertti Korhonen in charge of this. At the beginning the changes in organization produced a brilliant result. In 2006 Nokia announced it was launching a smartphone named the N95. It had a cover that slid back to reveal a keyboard. It also contained our first 5-megapixel camera.

The new phone was launched in 2007, immediately after Apple announced its own alternative smartphone, which was called the iPhone. Steve Jobs talked about this phone at a trade fair in the United States in January 2007, and it came on the market at the end of June.

Thus began a duel between Nokia as reigning champion and Apple as its challenger. The prize was the global smartphone market. Many put their bets on Nokia. We knew how to design, manufacture, and market our phones. Our infrastructure was far superior. You could use our phones with confidence in every country, on every network, in all conditions. Nokia's engineers were the world's best. We had conquered all the world's markets; even if our market share had dropped a little in the United States we were trying our hardest there as well. If anyone who followed mobile phones had been asked in 2007 who would win this duel, the answer would have been clear – Nokia was overwhelmingly the best bet.

CHAPTER 66

Could Nokia Have Been a Software Company?

W HEN A COMPANY RUNS INTO DIFFICULTIES they always seem new and unpredictable. In fact they will have been around for a while, in the form of unanswered questions, careless thinking, or half-baked decisions. Every company tries to evade difficult issues, and it's the leader's job to spot them in time and try to find the right solutions before they become too big. Solving them on paper isn't enough: you have to find a way of putting your decisions and solutions into effect.

Companies have to change, and sometimes extremely fast. As with a sailing boat tacking to windward, the turn has to be extremely smooth, fast, controlled, and decisive, otherwise the craft will capsize. You can only turn rapidly if you're sure of your direction. Uncertainty and differences of opinion will slow down the decisions. The boat may already have washed up on the rocks because the turn should have been made much earlier.

We tried to change at Nokia between 2004 and 2007. We wanted to change direction but didn't know what, in practice, that meant. At the same time we were all – and I mean everyone at Nokia – prisoners of our own past.

We had long seen that Nokia was shifting from manufacturing to service provision, which demanded greater expertise in software design. We knew that Nokia had to become a software company. We talked about this internally and to the media. We also announced, long before our competitors, that the Internet would soon fit in people's pockets. And so it did, though much later than we had forecast.

Nokia never had its own operating system or a unit within the company that might produce one. Nokia had established itself as a developer of telephone equipment. We had acquired the template for an operating system by taking over a small company that had by chance come up for sale in 1998. The company was based in England and its name was Symbian. It was bought jointly by Nokia, Ericsson, and Motorola.

Symbian had begun as a company called Psion, which had made little palmtop computers. One of its most successful products was the Psion Organizer, which had a database and a diary. Psion continued to operate after it had sold its software expertise along with Symbian to the mobile phone companies. Motorola took over what was left of the original company in 2012.

Phones were no longer just phones by the beginning of the 2000s. They were smart, high-performance devices with numerous applications – they had become computers. The phone that offered the best experience to its users would be the victor, and the operating system was the very heart of the battle.

Anssi Vanjoki and Pertti Korhonen disagreed about many things, but about this they were of one mind. They both believed that Symbian software would give us a competitive edge, if we could use it as a base to which we could add applications. If we could create a smartphone in this way, it would be a roaring sales success. Central to our thinking was a conviction that our more expensive smartphones would eventually use a Linux-based operating system, which at some point would replace Symbian. This line of thought eventually gave rise to the MeeGo operating system.

Naturally there was one question that made us pause: was Symbian still a competitive option in the new world? We had a brisk internal debate on this issue from 2005 to 2007.

At Nokia it was our long-standing practice for each model of phone to have its own version of the operating system. Now we tried to change things so that a single software platform would support a common operating system for many different models. The basic idea was clear and simple, but it demanded a major cultural shift inside the company. This was anything but easy. The mobile phone mentality had to move to the smartphone era.

I really wasn't an expert on software, so I had to rely on my key advisers, Pertti Korhonen and Anssi Vanjoki. Pertti knew more than anyone at Nokia what our products were made of and how they worked. But Pertti wasn't a child of the new software age: his experience came chiefly from the 1990s and the beginning of the 2000s. Still, he was the one who knew most about software in our senior management team. Anssi had a comprehensive understanding of our products and the demands that users made of them.

Once again, looking back, it's easy to be wise after the event. None of us – Anssi Vanjoki, Pertti Korhonen, or me – were software experts. Nor were Matti Alahuhta or Olli-Pekka Kallasvuo. We could ask penetrating questions, but to answer them we depended on the expertise of the next level down in the organization. What would happen in the software world in the next five to ten years? How could Nokia best turn itself into a software company? And if it could, what would be the consequences? What should we do? We feverishly sought good, evidence-based answers to these questions in 2004–07.

Nokia really needed its own home-grown software experts, with a deep knowledge of the field, to tackle these burning issues. But we didn't have them. Indeed, there didn't seem to be such people anywhere in Europe. As far back as 2001 we had talked of strengthening our software expertise, and we had begun to get a grip on the problem.

First we applied the lessons of some positive experiences from the 1990s. We had boosted product development, in both mobile phones and networks, by bringing in Finland's leading experts in radio technology. We had worked closely with the universities on that. The best example was Yrjö Neuvo, who joined us in 1993 and became the chief technology officer. As the world's leading researcher on digital signal processing his fingerprints were all over Nokia's technological lead. The results were exceptional, truly world class.

We tried to repeat this in software. Nokia took on a large group of professors and key researchers from the universities and polytechnics. They spent a year or two either at Nokia's Research Centre or in individual business units. But the second time around the results were modest, downright feeble.

When around 2005 we really started to understand what we were up against, we tried to recruit more experienced software experts. We also strengthened the Research Centre and our product development work in the United States, both in Boston and in Silicon Valley. Again the results turned out to be very weak. Using these methods it simply wasn't possible to develop a strong team of software experts in a short time.

Symbian was Nokia's smartphone operating system until 2011, when the company announced it was moving to the Microsoft operating system.

PART V

WHAT'S A CHIEF EXECUTIVE FOR?

CHAPTER 67

The January Decision

I HAVE MADE MANY MAJOR DECISIONS JUST AFTER CHRISTMAS. I usually take a break then until the second week of January. When I returned to my office on the seventh floor of Nokia's headquarters in January 2005, I knew I wouldn't continue as the company's chief executive much longer. Actually, I had known that for some time, but I hadn't let anyone know. Now it was time to leave and to choose a successor. I was relieved, but I knew the process wouldn't be easy.

I had wanted to relinquish the CEO responsibilities earlier as well. I had thought of leaving in 2003, but it would have looked as if I were fleeing from the difficulties that were then just starting. The company's board of directors appealed to me to stay on. I had an agreement whereby I could leave the company in 2006, if I wished, though I was committed to staying at least until then.

Not everyone had taken the agreement seriously, but for me it was important. It seemed to me that I had done everything I could do as the CEO of Nokia, and from now on I really didn't have anything more to add. Also, I felt that Nokia needed some clear changes. There should be opportunities for new people, the executive committee needed to be more international, and I wanted to do something different. In January 2005 I still didn't have any idea what that something might be.

When I was chosen to become Nokia's chief executive, the company's owners at the time, Finnish banks and insurance companies, invited me to a dimly-lit conference room and asked me to take on the role. That was how Finnish companies still did things in the early 1990s. They didn't interview other candidates, or even consider them. Nor did anyone ask whether the new CEO should come from inside or outside the company. Some Finns wanted Nokia's CEO to be selected the same way even now. I couldn't have disagreed more. I wanted the alternatives to be examined closely. I wanted the candidates interviewed. I wanted to explore the option of an external candidate, even though I thought there were many brilliant candidates for the job within Nokia.

When Nokia's new leadership structure began to operate at the beginning of 2004, many people saw it as the first stage in the competition for the new CEO. But the organization hadn't been transformed in order for potential candidates to compete, although the new organization certainly gave them a chance to demonstrate their competence, motivation, and ability to work with others.

Pekka Ala-Pietilä, Olli-Pekka Kallasvuo, and Pertti Korhonen were the key candidates. Matti Alahuhta, after becoming strategy director, left the company in the autumn of 2004, and Sari Baldauf had also decided to leave at the end of 2004, so they were no longer in the running.

I discussed the selection of the new CEO with Deputy Chairman Paul Collins, since he was preparing personnel matters for consideration by the board. He was fully abreast of modern governance procedures and told me bluntly at the outset that "you're not to participate in the selection process at all."

He did however have one request to make. He asked if I would compile a list of between five and ten possible internal candidates to succeed me. I spent half a day thinking the names through. My list consisted of Pekka Ala-Pietilä, Olli-Pekka Kallasvuo, Anssi Vanjoki, Pertti Korhonen, Timo Ihamuotila, and Mary McDowell. I wanted to give the board of directors the opportunity to weigh the merits of both familiar figures and candidates from a new generation. Pekka, Olli-Pekka, and Anssi were in the former group, Pertti had risen to his current position a little later than them, and Mary and Timo belonged to Nokia's new generation. It was a good list and gave the board enough to proceed with.

It was then the board's job to interview these candidates. At some stage a consultant was brought in to tell us whether our internal candidates would satisfy international requirements. If they weren't good enough we would have to consider external candidates.

A working group set up by the board bore the main responsibility for the selection process. It consisted of Paul Collins, Marjorie Scardino, and Per Karlsson, with Bengt Homström as an additional member. I wasn't there when the candidates were interviewed, and I don't know how well each of them did. The working group did, however, ask me to write for them a page on each candidate, describing their strengths and the areas where they needed development.

The only genuine surprise in the whole process came on Saturday, 19 March. Pekka Ala-Pietilä told me that he didn't want to be the CEO. He had thought about it and talked it through with his family and decided that he didn't have the necessary fire for the job. He would leave Nokia later that year.

Pekka's announcement made the selection process more difficult. He had been appointed deputy chief executive in 1998, and a year later he had become president when I was appointed chairman, after which he had been a clear candidate to be my successor.

I had told the board back in 2001 that I wanted to step down as CEO in 2003, and that I saw Pekka as my successor. When the board didn't go along with my proposal I agreed to extend my term until 2006. Pekka was visibly younger than me. We had worked together for many years. I valued his brilliant grasp of strategy and his ability to lead people within an organization. I was disappointed and sad at his decision, and I couldn't help thinking that Pekka should have seen it as his duty to pursue the CEO role. On the other hand I respected his decision and his decisiveness. He didn't want to be in the public eye, as a media target; but as CEO of Nokia you can't avoid that. It's one of the less agreeable features of the job.

After Pekka withdrew, the process needed speeding up. If Pekka had in principle decided to leave Nokia, we had to move up a gear to appoint a new CEO at the board meeting in July. If we did that we wouldn't lose time or cause uncertainty within the organization. The board met in London on 26–27 July. The most important item on the agenda was the appointment. Having deliberated the matter, the working group had whittled the list down to two candidates, and Olli-Pekka Kallasvuo was the stronger. The board wanted a chance to explore whether Nokia should be led by a younger man. I too had said this option should be examined closely.

As the meeting went on I debated with Paul Collins whether Nokia should go for experience or for youthful promise. The board clearly tended toward experience, and I really had no objections to raise. Olli-Pekka Kallasvuo would be my successor as the CEO of Nokia. He was on hand if the board wanted to talk to him, but no further interview was needed – the board knew him well enough and the working group had given him a thorough grilling already.

Nokia had appointed a new CEO, who would assume his duties in June 2006. Responsibility for this decision was in part mine, though I had not participated at all in the official selection process. We also discussed my own role. I'd announced that I wanted to do something new in a distinctly different field. Paul Collins told me that the board wanted me to continue as their chairman, even though it was extremely important to give Olli-Pekka the space he needed to build his own management team organization and to develop his own plans and strategy.

I wasn't keen on staying on as chairman. After some persuasion I agreed to it, but only after my role had been clearly defined for the benefit of the media, investors, and Nokia itself. We agreed that my role as chairman would be the same as Casimir Ehrnrooth's in the Nokia of the 1990s. I would spend one or two days a week on Nokia business, and I would focus on being a supportive but challenging interlocutor to the chief executive. Marjorie Scardino, who headed the appointments committee, informed the company's general meeting of this arrangement in spring 2006.

All the candidates to succeed me were excellent, and some were outstanding. I was proud of my company, which had nurtured people who could continue my work. I felt we had reached the right decision, even if there had been some surprises along the way. I was also satisfied that everything had been done thoroughly and by the book. As well as the interviews, we had commissioned comprehensive external analyses of the candidates' strengths and weaknesses. We had gotten to know them inside out: no one had a right to just walk into one of the most difficult but fascinating jobs the business world could offer.

At the beginning of August the world's media were told who would take over from me. At the same time we announced Olli-Pekka's appointment as a member of the board with operational responsibility starting 1 October 2005. Although I would be responsible for the company as CEO until 1 June 2006, I wanted to give Olli-Pekka full responsibility for the planning process for 2006.

On 3 August Pekka, Olli-Pekka, and I sat at the front of the auditorium at our head office to give a press conference. There was a slight air of sadness in the room, a sense that an era was drawing to a close and a new one was beginning. Pekka spoke honestly about the reasons for his own decision. He wanted to do something new after all the years he had spent at Nokia. He explained that he didn't really have the fire in his belly to take over the role of CEO. Olli-Pekka, for his part, was certain that he did have what it would take to lead Nokia into its next phase.

With these men, these two men who were so close to me, I had fought for Nokia fifteen years before. They both belonged to the elite of the world's business leaders, and it was good to sit between them. For me it was time to do something else.

Our press conference was open and honest. I suppose the foreign journalists suspected that some complex plot was going on behind the scenes. No one could have spoken more openly of their motives than Pekka and Olli-Pekka. The journalists seemed to believe them since neither of them had any other agenda. All three of us said what we thought and how we had reached our decisions.

Two weeks later there was more news. The *Financial Times* wrote on its front page "Shell snatches Ollila." Shell had decided to appoint me as chairman of the board. A firm of headhunters had rung me back in March and I had given my preliminary agreement. I confirmed this in the summer when I saw that Nokia would reach a quick decision on my successor. I was overjoyed. At Shell I would have a chance to apply my long-standing interest in the global economy and in energy. It had been a long journey from the world of high school nature clubs, and later my economic awakening during the 1970s oil crisis, to my new role as chairman of the board of one of the world's largest energy companies.

CHAPTER 68

Twenty-One Years and a Few Months More

PEOPLE TALK OF THE LAME DUCK PHENOMENON, when a leader has announced his departure and then finds his powers ebbing away. But with so much happening at Nokia there was no danger that I'd run out of steam during the transition.

In 2005 and 2006 we had made major decisions on the future of our network business. The changes were significant. Mobile network operators had begun outsourcing their network operations and maintenance, so our service business was growing at a remarkable rate. Nokia no longer merely supplied base stations and other network equipment – now we also looked after its care and maintenance. Networks required constant research and development. We did fewer deals, but those we did were significant. Competition to sell services, equipment, and software to operators was intensifying. We had beaten off our competitors, especially Ericsson and, above all, the new companies emerging from China. We had to show some muscle.

There had also been changes within Nokia. Simon Beresford-Wylie, an Australian who had joined Nokia at the end of the 1990s, had taken over from Sari Baldauf, who had been responsible for the success of mobile phone networks. Sari had run the unit like her own start-up, with strong support from a small, dedicated team. Simon Beresford-Wylie's role as Sari's replacement was truly a challenge for him.

The market had given us clear indications that the American company Lucent might be for sale. We took a closer look, and when our hunch was confirmed we approached the company. Lucent had been split off from AT&T as an independent enterprise. As a listed company it had become a favorite with investors in the 1990s. It had a voracious appetite and grew through acquisition into a global enterprise. But at the beginning of the 2000s Lucent found itself in difficulties and was forced to divest some of its non-core businesses.

Negotiations began in the early spring of 2005. I met Lucent's chairwoman, Patricia Russo, whom I already knew slightly. Russo had long experience in the IT field and had led Lucent since 2002. She was regarded as one of America's most influential women executives. Later the negotiations were conducted between the business leaders and finance staff, and we got a good idea of where Lucent was coming from and what sort of company it was.

I didn't make any major acquisitions when I was the Nokia CEO. We had grown organically for the most part, and I was cautious about acquisitions. Their success rate isn't very high. Too often they're pursued for the wrong reasons – to expand egos and empires. Too often executives underestimate the energy needed to acquire and absorb a company and successfully merge two company cultures. Economic history is full of sad tales of unsuccessful acquisitions, which on occasion have sunk the company making the purchase. Perhaps my subconscious caution was due also to Nokia's little banquet of acquisitions in the 1980s. I had spent a long time cleaning up the consequences.

Our position now was perhaps a little more complicated than that. Lucent's shareholders had concluded that the company couldn't survive on its own. If Nokia didn't buy it, one of our competitors would. We knew Lucent was also in negotiations with two other companies. One was the French company Alcatel. The other was probably Motorola or Ericsson, but we weren't sure.

While I was pondering whether to buy Lucent, I was also considering the future of Nokia's network business. The Americans, who were commendably clear cut in everything, always thought that if they couldn't buy, they could at least sell – and at a good price. Business there was a constant round of deals and trades, where the shop was always open. In Europe things were a little different. Siemens, for example, had rarely sold any of its businesses.

Should Nokia have sold its network business? Absolutely, if you asked a stock exchange analyst in the spring of 2005. It would have freed up some cash and made the area more dynamic. And of course it would have left Nokia as a mobile phone company, pure and simple. In practice, the only possible buyer would have been Siemens, and I for one would have been emotionally allergic to that.

Lucent wanted a quick answer, however. Our first impressions were that the company's fixed costs were far too high and that it was too well staffed:

it had 30,000 employees and its revenue was \$8 billion. The more closely we looked at the company, the more strongly our impressions were confirmed. On the plus side, the company's market share in the United States was growing. But the negative factors became clearer, too. Lucent needed a complete restructuring, with its unprofitable units in various parts of the world shut down. There were questions about many liabilities on the company's balance sheet, which was not uncommon.

After painstaking deliberation we decided that buying Lucent wouldn't be a smart move for Nokia or for its shareholders. The board made this decision before Easter, and we knew we were setting in motion a series of changes in the market for networks. We had made the opening move, and other moves would necessarily follow. Lucent announced at the start of April 2006 that it would merge with Alcatel, which was one and a half times bigger.

Time showed clearly that Alcatel didn't get the benefits from the deal that it had expected. The hoped-for opportunities for cooperation didn't materialize, as is so often the case. Alcatel had to write down much of the value of Lucent, which showed that the deal had wasted the shareholders' money, which was now available for the sellers – Lucent's shareholders – to enjoy. Another common story.

After all this we had no reason to mourn our decision on Lucent. We knew that it was time for us to plan our next move. Thus in the spring and summer of 2005 we began to negotiate with Siemens, which for Nokia was a familiar story. Back in the 1980s Nokia's prowess in selling to the Soviet Union had aroused the interest of Siemens in West Germany. In 1986 its CEO, Anton Hasholzner, proposed that we undertake joint projects in telephone technology, but the talks didn't reach a conclusion. Early in the 1990s Siemens approached Nokia again, wanting to buy our network business. At that time we decided to turn down the offer. Now we were discussing new forms of cooperation – in other words, a joint enterprise. Siemens had other joint ventures, such as the computer company Fujitsu Siemens, or Bosch and Siemens Hausgerate, which made white goods. But such cooperation was a departure from our normal way of doing business.

Negotiations went ahead on two levels. I discussed the concept and broad direction with the Siemens CEO, Klaus Kleinfeld. The director of Nokia's network unit, Simon Beresford-Wylie, discussed the operational side with his German counterparts. During the spring and summer we developed an excellent mutual understanding on most issues. But we couldn't agree on one key principle: how was the company to be led? Siemens drew on its previous experience in cooperative ventures and stressed that the firm should be run so that both parent companies had equivalent powers and responsibility. We didn't agree. We warned that this model would lead to two head offices, uncertainty over who was in charge, and duplication. There would be no economies of scale.

Between Christmas and the New Year I was skiing in Switzerland. I gazed at the stunning Alpine scenery and for a moment thought of something other than Nokia. Until my mobile phone rang. At the other end was Olli-Pekka Kallasvuo, Nokia's CEO-in-waiting, who had taken on additional operational responsibility in October. During the call we decided that we couldn't accept the model Siemens proposed. There would be no agreement unless Nokia took charge of the nascent joint enterprise. In the spring we discussed practical issues, and Siemens finally came around to our way of thinking. On 19 June 2006 we announced a joint venture with the name of Nokia Siemens Networks (NSN). At the press conference Nokia was represented by Olli-Pekka Kallasvuo. I was in Canada on Shell business, learning about the oil shale project and the gas fields there.

The new company would bring together the bulk of Nokia's and Siemens' network operations. Nokia and Siemens each owned half the company, which officially began its work on 1 April 2007. The launch was delayed because Siemens was caught up in a bribery scandal. Nokia's Simon Beresford-Wylie was the CEO – Nokia was in the driver's seat, as we had demanded. Siemens saw its investment as a purely financial decision, which it would relinquish if the occasion arose. Nokia did eventually buy Siemens' half of the company, taking the whole firm into ownership in the spring of 2013.

Preparation of the NSN deal was the last major event of my time as CEO. On the afternoon of 31 May 2006 Olli-Pekka Kallasvuo took over the CEO's office and the meeting space that went with it. I was given another room at Nokia HQ, a long way from Olli-Pekka's. Now that I think about it, I recall that I never visited the CEO office after that day, though Olli-Pekka did come to mine.

Removal crates had been stacked up in my room for weeks, full of books, papers, and photographs. I also took one important painting that had long travelled with me to the room of the chair of the board. I had gazed at it in good times and bad. The painting was by Akseli Gallen-Kallela, a key figure in Finnish culture. As often happens when one is moving, the picture spent a long time leaning against the wall and was put up only after several months.

I had received many email messages from colleagues at Nokia, and these were collected into a little book. Every message was truly heartwarming. In my last days as chairman there was, however, a sad undertone, because our colleague on the board, Édouard Michelin, had died tragically and unexpectedly five days earlier. It was a shock for all of us.

How at Nokia did we celebrate an employee whose career with the company had lasted twenty-one years and a few months and was now approaching its conclusion? Modestly, that's how. I've already explained that Nokia's culture had no room for elaborate ceremonies, and at my own wish we made no exception for me. At 4 o'clock Olli-Pekka, my secretary, and I raised our glasses of champagne.

The event lasted barely fifteen minutes. The removal crates were transferred that evening out of the CEO's room and into the room of the chair of the board, in another part of the building. The celebrations were over and work would continue with Olli-Pekka at the helm.

The following morning I was at Helsinki airport. The flight to Amsterdam left at 8:15 a.m. and I was in The Hague at 10:35 a.m. local time. I had taken an apartment in the city and agreed to spend two to three days a week on Shell business.

My concluding months as the CEO were as hectic as the preceding fourteen years. The business correspondent Anna-Liisa Lilius of the Finnish magazine *Talouselämä* (*Business Life*) reported on my last hundred days. When she began she was particularly struck by the fact that the longest time slot she'd be allocated in my diary was just two minutes. Perhaps I would have a little more time in the future.

CHAPTER 69

What Did I Learn at School?
Fourteen Years as Nokia's Chief Executive

NOKIA IS A STORY OF GROWTH ON MANY LEVELS: of how the company took shape, developed, and grew, and of how Nokia's young leaders took on the greatest responsibilities in Finland's economic history.

Nokia was a place of growth in many senses. I worked as chief executive for over fourteen years, which in this field is a truly exceptional length of time.

"Those are my principles and if you don't like them ... well, I have others," said Groucho Marx. He was scarcely serious, but talk of values and company culture is sometimes regarded as pointless waffle. So the most senior people must show by their own example that creating and following clear principles is both important and appropriate. Every enterprise competes for good employees, and the company's identity, values, and leadership culture are crucial to attracting them.

"Maailma alkaa Arlandan lentokentän takaa," was the slogan at Nokia in the early 1990s, when Finnish was still our working language: "The world begins at Stockholm airport." Later, political changes and better connections brought unfamiliar cultures closer together. The change was captured in the phrase "the world is flat." That meant that Finland should treat the whole world as its domestic market. Top management must live and breathe internationally and ensure that the company knows in every fiber what it must do to succeed globally. Because it is possible.

A company is healthy when it grows, and the emotional bonus that growth provides for its workers is remarkable. Ambitious growth objectives are an important motivator, though one must guard against growing pains. An internationally listed company can't work in the same way as a start-up. The need to balance ambitious growth objectives and disciplined behavior was one of the most important lessons from the Nokia story.

A company's most valuable assets lie between its employees' ears. As chief executive I was ultimately responsible for Nokia's staff. I tried to get to know the most senior three hundred to four hundred executives well while also keeping in touch with all our areas of activity. Factories, research laboratories, and canteens are better places to learn than the boardroom. Until they're given the opportunity, gifted individuals can't show what they're capable of. That's why I promoted some talented young people into some surprising positions. We also respected education and expertise and supported continuous learning. Intuition and creativity are important, but you also need careful research and good analysis if you're to make the right decisions.

Leadership is about discussion. As chief executive I tried to take both internal and external communication seriously. It's all too easy to be seduced by PR because you have to work with the media. A company's position is never as strong as the most positive stories suggest, or in such a deep crisis as the most negative accounts would have you believe.

The chief executive's work is very lonely. It's important to have people with whom you can discuss things openly, say what's on your mind, and be understood. I often spoke to Lew Platt at Hewlett-Packard, Michael Dell at Dell, Andy Grove at Intel, and Scott McNealy at Sun Microsystems. But discussion with the external world isn't enough on its own – you have to have people inside the company who will be honest with you. That's why a company needs an open, supportive culture with the right processes underpinning it, such as a comprehensive appraisal system. No one can make decisions on the chief executive's behalf. Consultants and investment bankers are important advisers, but one must take rigorous care that the desire and ability to make decisions are kept strictly within one's own organization. Consultants all too easily become too cozy with a company's top management as it grows and matures. I tried to stay sensitive to areas where the organization seemed at risk of getting stale.

Consultants aren't the only people worth talking to. But some senior executives' understanding of wider society seemed to have a bewilderingly rickety base. They didn't understand how politicians set about solving problems, and they couldn't talk to the trade unions or shop stewards. I tried to set up a continuing conversation with the political elite both in Finland and abroad. My years as president of the National Union of University Students in Finland helped in understanding wider society. When I say "talking to politicians" I don't mean that business people should try to make their decisions for them, or that they should start to operate like politicians. I had observed how Kari Kairamo and Simo Vuorilehto operated as chief executives, and I had seen their successes, defeats, and the pressures they'd been under. But I understood what such work was about only when I experienced it for myself.

CHAPTER 70

China is Different

WHEN I STEPPED DOWN AS CEO OF NOKIA, China was our biggest market. We had a market share of 31 percent in mobile phones and had left our arch-rival Motorola far behind. Our achievement was no mere matter of luck, for Nokia had a long history of involvement in China. Nokia had exported cables there as far back as the 1950s. By the 1980s cable machines and computer networks had taken their place, and a decade later Nokia was exporting mobile phone networks and handsets. Nokia set up its first office in the country in 1985.

At the beginning of the 1990s we learned that the Chinese were thinking hard about which digital mobile phone standard to opt for. Nokia and Ericsson naturally encouraged them to go for GSM. The Chinese ultimately made the right decision, and Nokia sold its first GSM phone in China in 1994.

The Chinese presumably decided early on that their inadequate and poorly maintained fixed landline network wasn't worth bringing up to scratch. If they had, the impact on the global economy would have been dramatic: the Club of Rome forecast back in the 1970s that a comprehensive, fixed-link phone network in China would have used up the world's entire reserves of copper. The Chinese decided early on that the future lay in a wireless network, and the country leapfrogged into a new era, but the resulting network was a mixture of fixed and wireless. In the mid-1990s China also acquired a CDMA network at the behest of our American competitors, after intense lobbying.

In the mid-1990s we saw that the Chinese market would also be the decisive battleground for mobile phones. The country was forging ahead economically, and a new, prosperous, middle class was emerging. Young Chi-

Nokia opened a factory in China in 2003, accompanied by fireworks. Finland is represented by Veli Sundbäck , Minister of Finance Sauli Niinistö and me.

nese people wanted fashionable phones. We had arrived in China at a good time and we tried to do our groundwork. I had learned the most important lesson on my first visit to China in 1988: you had to get to know the country inside out. If a company wanted to know what was happening in the markets there, the chief executive had to meet politicians, officials, and the managers of Chinese companies – that was the only way to make the contacts every company needed. Only by talking to Chinese people could you get solid information about the country's politics and economics. For me China was always a vivid experience. I saw firsthand how the world's new economic locomotive was gathering power, and how Chinese decision-makers saw the world and put their own ideas into action.

The traffic was not one way – the Chinese were very interested in Nokia in the 1990s. I remember very well how they paid their first "state visit" to Nokia. On 10 April 1997 Deputy Prime Minister Wu Bangguo landed at Helsinki airport after having wangled himself an invitation to Finland. His team wished to spend two days with Nokia: in Espoo near Helsinki and at Oulu in the north. The Chinese wanted to find out whether the company would be a partner with adequate resources for China in its expanding GSM project. I remember the meeting especially well because my mother had died the day before. The Chinese guest of honor gave the matter due atten-tion in his elegant comments, since mothers are greatly respected in Chinese culture. We became good friends of the deputy prime minister later on.

On my trips to China I also tried to meet people outside of business and look around a lot. Visits to regional cities often give a clearer picture of what the future holds than dry reports or PowerPoint presentations.

At Nokia I shared my interest in China with Sari Baldauf. She built up our network operations, and became a world-class expert on doing business with China. We often held long discussions of how Nokia could best succeed there. I travelled to China three or four times a year, Sari even more often. Together we established a unique network of decision-makers, entrepreneurs, and other people, and through our Chinese managers and employees we learned about the country's political and social climate.

On a visit to China in 2001 I listened to a young and gifted Chinese woman who had just started work at Nokia. She could have gotten a job at any international company on the basis of her top-class education. But she had chosen Nokia on the grounds that there "she could one day become chief executive." When I heard that I smiled to myself. Her remark rang true: Nokia appealed to talented Chinese because it was so much less concerned with bureaucracy or the pecking order than even American firms. Promotion could be much quicker at Nokia, and the company felt informal.

As a country China was not in the least informal. On my own visits I often received a reception tantamount to what a head of state might expect on a state visit. A police escort would conduct the procession of cars along the streets of Beijing. My active connections with China were recognized when I was formally awarded the Freedom of the City of Beijing.

Nokia's hike around the Chinese markets was not always as glorious as in 2006, however. In 2003 we received a timely reminder of our mortality. Nokia had three offices in China. We found ourselves off balance when Chinese manufacturers began opening up the distribution network for mobile phones. We rapidly found a new way of selling phones. In a few years we had seventy distributors and soon we had a presence in every one of China's most important regional cities. We also started making phones that were better adapted to the Chinese market and allowed the use of Chinese characters.

The Chinese leadership quickly understood that industrial production alone wouldn't guarantee a durable basis for the economy. They were pleased when industrial jobs were created, but joint ventures in product development between international companies and Chinese counterparts were seen as better still. Companies that provided both jobs and opportunities for product development could expect to increase their share of a market that was getting tougher.

Chinese phone manufacturers were starting to compete strongly against international companies, and the Chinese government wanted to support them for its own nationalistic reasons. We had to change our strategy rapidly. We beefed up our sales network in the Chinese countryside, removed some layers, and ensured that our sales commissions went to the people who actually sold the phones. Motorola wasn't really in the game, and our market share rose.

In 2004 Nokia's total sales in China were around $3.9 billion. Nokia had become the market leader in mobile phones, and we had also maintained our lead as supplier of mobile phone networks to China. In 2005 our sales rose to $4.6 billion. We employed nearly 5,000 people there. We had succeeded in the fastest-growing market area in the world. Nokia's success lasted several years, but the tide turned in 2008 when Apple's iPhone conquered the Chinese market and the Android operating system was adopted for use in Chinese mobile phones.

What else did I learn from China? That the Chinese, and other Asians, value long-term relationships with and commitment from their customers. China also demands a tremendously competitive spirit if a company is to thrive among ambitious local firms. You need outstanding products that the emerging middle class is keen to buy. But the most important thing to remember is that China is different from other markets – it's not an extension of either Europe or the United States. Nokia, like other firms, must bear this in mind if it's to succeed in China in the future.

CHAPTER 71

Agonies of a Chief Executive

SENIOR APPOINTMENTS CAN GO WRONG. One leadership guru reckons that 30 percent do. For chief executives the failure rate may be even higher. Many failures, perhaps most, are quietly buried. Changes of CEO may not look like sackings, but sackings do happen in major global businesses. CEOs leave to spend more time with their families, move on to new jobs, take up new board positions, or even become chief executives of other companies.

The time chief executives spend in their jobs has become ever shorter. Organizations grow tired of their leaders after five or six years. Leaders need renewal, fresh ideas, and new approaches. Rapid communication has made their lives more difficult. A chief executive must continually fight in a hostile environment. The head of a global company may have to travel to three continents in the course of a single week. They may be richly remunerated for this, but we each have only one life.

I've been through all this. I've experienced stratospheric success, but I also know what it's like when a company plumbs the depths, letting down its shareholders, its workers, and everyone else who believed the wonderful fairy tale could go on forever. A few times I wanted to throw in the towel, but those feelings never lasted long.

There's no way of knowing in advance who will make a good chief executive. There are many reasons for that. You don't know what the job entails until you start to do it. Many a board member has watched the CEO at work and thought they could do the job as well, if not better. A good CEO makes the job look easy, even effortless, just as a successful athlete does. In reality it's never easy, but some learn that awkward truth better and faster than others; many never learn it at all.

An incoming CEO will be surprised by the issues that cross his or her desk. About 70 percent is the sort of stuff they would never expect to see. These aren't big issues – on the contrary, they're mostly small but horrid. Ultimately they may evolve into major threats that put the company's brand and reputation at risk. Or the organization may seize up while it awaits decisions that aren't made soon enough.

In highly competitive global markets delays in decision-making can be disastrous. Key executives will draw their own conclusions about the chief executive's ability or lack thereof. A company's leadership team can disintegrate very quickly, and no one can lead alone, at least not in a global company. And this is just one way to fail as CEO – there are at least dozens if not hundreds of others.

When Nokia overhauled its product development structures after the failures of 2004, I made it our goal to have the company on the way up again by 2006. I expected the following year to be good as well. So the new chief executive, my successor, would start from a strong position. They wouldn't spend time bemoaning the mistakes of the recent past or trying to put them right. I created the best beginning I possibly could, passing on the baton with honor.

Everything went even better than I imagined it would. The N95, launched in autumn 2006, would carry the company through 2007 and into 2008, perhaps beyond. The N95 showed clearly that Nokia had the smartphone market at its feet, until the iPhone changed everything by making the Internet fit the pocket or palm. We'd been talking about that for many years.

Nokia's results in 2007 were its best ever, and by November its share price had reached nearly $44. These exceptional results were due to the company's strength both in China and elsewhere. Only in the United States was our market share declining. Overall, Nokia's share of the mobile phone market hovered around 40 percent. In retrospect it turns out that Nokia peaked around this time.

Perhaps this made the life of Olli-Pekka Kallasvuo, the new chief executive, a little too easy. He finished the 2006 budget and took over the hot seat the following spring. Growth was strong in 2007, but the company's fixed costs also grew rapidly. It was too easy for the new CEO to assume Nokia would remain in a strong position because the figures were all good and still trending upwards. This was deceptive, though, because the foundations for the glowing results of 2007 had been laid well in advance.

CHAPTER 72

The Game Changes

MEANWHILE, IN ANOTHER PART OF THE FOREST, our competitive position shifted radically when Steve Jobs launched the iPhone in the United States in June 2007. By the end of the following year the iPhone was available worldwide. Looking back it's easy to accuse Nokia of complacency. We knew how to make mobile phones, and some people at Nokia undoubtedly believed that Apple could never overtake our market share or even make a mobile that worked properly. Teething troubles with the iPhone, such as its malfunctioning antenna, tended to confirm that view. Nokia's long experience in manufacturing mobile phones enabled it to minimize such problems.

Back in 2007 I wanted to be confident that the new executive committee wouldn't be blinded by its own excellence. And I wanted to learn things for myself. There was so much going on: technical advances, new trends in design, and a rapid evolution in the way customers used their phones. They were all happening at an exhausting rate, and all had an impact in the contest for dominance in the global mobile phone market. I have no idea how many models I must have tried out during my time as chief executive. Now I wanted to come to grips with the turmoil the advent of the iPhone was causing Nokia.

As autumn approached I decided to undertake a little survey of Nokia's senior people. I chatted with a dozen of them, asking if they saw the iPhone as a dangerous competitor. Of the dozen, two thought the iPhone posed no danger, because our Symbian operating system was better than Apple's iOS. The other ten thought the iPhone would prove a serious competitor that we shouldn't underestimate. Some of them expressed their views in terms not fit for publication. The message was clear: most of Nokia's key people were alert enough to grasp that Apple really had thrown down the gauntlet in the contest for the smartphone market.

Books have already been written about the success of the iPhone and doubtless there are more to come. Its touchscreen is a triumph and its overall design is unique, functional, and simple. The iPhone showed once and for all that the most important thing isn't the engineering, the materials, or even a phone's batteries, which iPhone users can't change for themselves. No, the most important things are the apps, the programs and services that iPhone users can buy for their phones. These comprise the user experience that makes one phone special and another ordinary. An entire ecosystem had come into being, of a sort that Nokia had been unable to create itself. Club Nokia had perhaps been a gesture in the right direction, but that was as far as we had gone.

If you bought an iPhone you were buying not just a phone but a passport to an ever-growing and rapidly evolving world – the phone gave you entry to a digital community. And the phone worked beautifully with other Apple products. The iPhone offered something Nokia couldn't. Even so, in retrospect it's good to recall that the iPhone was far from an instant success; it sold slowly when it was first released in 2007. By the spring of 2008, though, every smart person knew it was going to be really something.

We at Nokia saw what was happening. Then why didn't we do something about it? There are many answers to that question. At Nokia we used to say that a new manager was stuck with their predecessor for the first eighteen months. What this really meant was that the new manager was stuck with the products their predecessor had launched. On the other hand, Nokia's success never depended on a single product, but always on a range of products.

My own influence on Nokia's product range continued into 2007, though I had stepped down as chief executive the previous June. Things were still going well back then because we made the best possible Symbian phone, the N95. Everything seemed to be under control at Nokia, and we weren't aware of any threats.

Nokia had chosen Symbian as the operating system for its smartphone much earlier. Symbian too was in the throes of change. Nokia owned just 48 percent of Symbian shares, and the other owners hadn't so far allowed us to acquire a majority, so Nokia was to a certain degree a prisoner of Symbian's other shareholders. But their interest had dwindled, so Nokia finally succeeded in taking over the business in its entirety. Nokia decided to make Symbian a free provider of source code; thus the Symbian Foundation came into being. Nokia and the other owners moved their operating systems to the new Symbian so that open source code would stimulate innovation in software and services.

The open Symbian began its work in spring 2009. It didn't publish all its software because various agreements prevented that. Even so, the release of code in 2010 was the largest yet undertaken.

In 2007 the board accepted the biggest deal in Finland's economic history. Nokia bought the NAVTEQ Corporation, which was one of the world's largest cartographic companies. The deal was worth $7.7 billion in total, for which we paid cash. The deal was announced in October. The sale price may seem rather high, but it reflected a clear vision and Nokia's strategic interests. Digital maps and their applications were bound to grow in importance and would offer a new dimension in web services. Consumers wanted to find facts, services, and each other with the help of their phones. Above all, they wanted to reach their destinations. Nokia's maps would make the lives of its phone users easier.

CHAPTER 73

Difficulties in Germany

SYMBIAN WASN'T NOKIA'S ONLY PROBLEM, though even on its own it would have given us enough to worry about. We had other issues too. Once again Nokia needed to close a factory at Bochum in Germany.

Bochum in 2007 awoke old memories. A good ten years earlier Nokia had closed a television factory there. Now a German mobile phone factory no longer contributed much to our global production. The board agreed that the factory was no longer competitive. It was in the wrong place and needed a level of investment we weren't ready to provide, because we had just made a major investment in Romania, in Transylvania to be exact. But we could all see far enough ahead to know that the announcement was likely to play badly in Germany. It would be easy to play politics with the idea that Romanians were stealing German jobs, thanks to decisions made in Finland.

Nokia's board was of one mind about all this in the autumn of 2007. We knew on the basis of our previous experiences that the closure of a factory in Germany would provoke a sharp reaction. We knew Germany's powerful trade union movement would want to flex its muscles. Everything had to be planned very well and very thoroughly. We had to take good care of our political relationships so that the closure wouldn't damage Nokia. One can't afford a single mistake if one intends to close a plant in Germany.

We went through the plans for Bochum at the December board meeting. We emphasized the need to manage relationships with the trade unions and politicians very carefully. It would make sense to brief Chancellor Merkel and the prime minister of Rhineland-Westphalia well in advance. A week later I reminded Olli-Pekka of this, and told him I was ready to help. "That's good," he replied. The board also discussed how the news should be made public in the New Year. And that's where matters rested.

In January I asked Olli-Pekka what was happening. He told me the factory would close on the fifteenth of the month. When I asked how briefing the senior Germans was going, he told me it had been decided to do things differently.

The board found this incomprehensible. We had decided at our previous meeting how things should be done. After that meeting Olli-Pekka and our director of corporate relations, Veli Sundbäck, had discussed how to take matters forward. The company's German legal advisers had told them there was no point in preliminary discussions with the trade unions since they would only try to string things out as long as possible. The lawyers' view was that a short sharp shock might be more painful, but it would be faster. An isolated explosion was preferable to protracted negotiations, even if it did produce a lot of hot air.

Nokia had to make 2,300 employees redundant in Bochum. The closure of the factory and the redundancies went according to plan, but the communications strategy failed utterly. The news took Chancellor Merkel completely by surprise. On 18 January she criticized Nokia severely for its decision to close "a viable factory." Four days later 13,000 Germans mounted a demonstration against Nokia.

Nokia made the redundancy payments in April. It also had to set up a training institution for those workers who had failed to find new jobs. All this cost around $280 million: significantly less, however, than the slower and more traditional route of negotiation would have cost. A couple of weeks later Olli-Pekka conceded that Nokia's market share had fallen "temporarily" from 40 percent to 35 percent. Reputation had its price.

For example, the *Financial Times* noted in May that Nokia's strategy for communicating the decision to close the plant had succeeded in angering the whole of Germany. Little mistakes led to bigger mistakes. Olli-Pekka tried to apologize for them, but without much success. From the board's point of view it was disconcerting that the closure at Bochum had been handled almost entirely contrary to Nokia's culture and practice, so carefully nurtured over fifteen years. This left its mark. When Nokia reduced its workforce in 2011–12, the board kept an exceptionally close watch.

The local negotiations in Bochum concluded in July, while operations at the factory ceased at the end of June. Nokia had seen things through, but the affair left a lasting dent in its reputation, in its market share, and on Olli-Pekka Kallasvuo's reputation as chief executive.

At the end of May we had a difficult strategy meeting, where the board was dissatisfied with the strategy presented by the leadership team. The board's view was that Nokia had no real answer to Apple, whose breakthrough in the market for mobiles was now absolutely clear. A couple of months later even Finns – whom we might have expected to stay loyal to Nokia – queued through the night to buy iPhones.

There seemed to be too many gaps and uncertainties in Nokia's strategy. It had far too few clear goals or suggestions for concrete activity, which the board found unsettling. It was agreed that the draft strategy would be the basis for further discussions over the summer and into the autumn.

We had strengthened the board. Henning Kagermann, the former CEO of the German software company SAP, joined us in spring 2007 and Risto Siilasmaa, the founder of F-Security, a year later. They brought with them the best understanding of software that Europe could offer. The board was also keen for me to do a little more. We had agreed earlier that I would devote one or two days a week to Nokia, but now the board wanted me to give "a bit more time," in the words of Marjorie Scardino, who was one of its members. What I was not, though, was an "executive chairman."

Everything went well in Olli-Pekka's first eighteen months. The board often quizzed the CEO on whether I was breathing down his neck or an obstacle to making the right decisions. Olli-Pekka's answer was clear: I knew the company inside and out and our dialogue was always to the point. He also said that things were going well.

In autumn 2008 the global economy took a dramatic turn for the worse. In September the investment bank Lehman Bros. went bankrupt and shares sank on the world's stock exchanges. The roots of the crisis lay in the U.S. housing market. Subprime mortgages scattered like confetti and the loans were then packaged as complex derivative products. In 2007–08 everything turned sour and the financial sector suffered its worst crisis in recent history.

Nokia's vital statistics were still good in the autumn of 2008, though the share price dipped like all the others.

In December 2008 the crisis hit Nokia directly. At the turn of the year the mobile phone group received a flood of order cancellations. Sales were extremely weak. The mobile phone market stalled but more or less recovered by the end of the year. Nokia's senior management focused on survival. The company felt the pressure on costs and started looking for savings, by trimming travel costs, for example. At the critical moment attention shifted from the most important objectives, which were to knock Symbian into shape and to bring successful products to market.

CHAPTER 74

A Tough Decision

My original plan of spending between two and four years on the board before stepping down had to be put on ice when the board asked me to stay longer. I agreed to my terms with Olli-Pekka. Our secretaries fixed a time, and we ran through the issues. Olli-Pekka ran the company; my job was to ensure that it followed the right path in accordance with the board's decisions. And I would always be ready to help.

We wanted to give the board some breathing space until spring 2009. The N97 was announced at the end of 2008 and launched in the United States the following June and in other countries soon after. It had a touchscreen and also a sliding keyboard. It used Symbian software and was Skype-enabled so it could be used to make calls via the Internet. It was released three years after the N95.

The N97 didn't trouble the iPhone. Its software capacity was inadequate, and it suffered from other basic technical problems. Anssi Vanjoki later described it as a let-down as a customer experience. This was a polite way of saying the N97 was an utter failure just when Nokia most needed to succeed.

Sadly the board's impression in 2008 had been correct. The picture then had not been clear, however, since the results were still good. The N95 – a great success story – sold well, and this gave us a strong cash flow. We saw, though, that the strategy wasn't clear, and the results were dismal. In spring 2009 messages started to emerge from Nokia that the company was drifting. Things had started to clog up, decision-making had slowed down, and discussion was increasingly referred to committees. These messages came from various directions and weren't very loud, but they should have received closer attention.

Olli-Pekka Kallasvuo had carried out a restructuring in 2007 and its results were now clear. Every chief executive creates an organization in their own image. Olli-Pekka's functional organization allowed for enough delegation and set up numerous working groups, but ultimately decisions returned to the chief executive's desk. At least, that was the hope. In practice matters tended to stay with the working groups, giving rise to internally insoluble disputes. These issues were identified when the board discussed the restructuring plans in 2007. After a long discussion the board decided to support the chief executive and accepted his proposed changes.

A change in chief executive is always a risk for a company. At Nokia the bar for changing chief executive has always been set high. The board has always focused on strategy, not on operational questions. Careless or hurried decisions have never been part of Nokia culture. So Olli-Pekka was given the opportunity to show what he was capable of. He was an experienced corporate manager but inexperienced as the top person at a great global concern. In that sense his appointment was a gamble. You can never predict a chief executive's capacity to develop. Olli-Pekka was a perfect fit for the job. He brought to the game expertise gained over 25 years at Nokia and elsewhere. No one could have questioned his genuine desire to do his job in the best possible way.

The company Olli-Pekka led faced not just internal challenges but a bloody contest with Apple, iPhone, and Steve Jobs. Nokia's chief executive didn't spend his days peacefully. Competitors often emerge from where they're least expected. So it was for Olli-Pekka.

Olli-Pekka was the first to admit he wasn't a software expert. That was true, but then neither was I. Steve Jobs wasn't just a software expert; he also understood customers, design, and marketing. Bill Gates was a software expert, though even he was reputed to have pinched software designed by others at the outset of his career.

The chief executive doesn't have to be an expert in software or any other technical area. What they do need is a burning interest in understanding the basic principles and the ability to find the right people for the right jobs. Nokia was unable to find the people who could have transformed it into a software company. It was stagnant and feeble on account of its reliance on Symbian. The board believed that the company had enough software expertise, and senior management assured them there were no problems with basic competences and that the problems with Symbian would be solved.

The warning signals became serious in the summer and autumn of 2009. I had experienced a number of summers when worries had started to mount up. It felt bad – the body senses that trouble is in store before the mind or the brain. So it was in 2009. I felt a sense of powerlessness and physical pain. For at least a year ahead it would be a difficult time, perhaps the most difficult Nokia had gone through.

A crayfish party in August was the first occasion where a Nokia board member asked if all was well with the company. He said out loud what I had been thinking, that things didn't seem to be going the way the board wanted them to go. Toward the end of the year the board held its annual review of its own operations and the role of the chair. Deputy Chair Marjorie Scardino led the discussions, which focused on the way the company's operations were managed. Almost every board member asked whether the chief executive had gotten things right. These discussions set events in motion.

At the January 2010 board meeting we held long discussions about the company's competitiveness. I was tasked with discussing the company's leadership in a broad sense with the members of the executive committee. The committee was nearly unanimous on this, though one member – a Finn – found the decision hasty and surprising.

I held my discussions between February and April with Olli-Pekka's knowledge and consent. Each conversation lasted between half an hour and ninety minutes. I spread the discussions over a long period because I didn't wish to give the impression that we were in a crisis demanding rapid resolution. I tried to find out where the pressure points lay and how they affected the company's effectiveness. I concluded each conversation with a question: was Olli-Pekka Kallasvuo the right person to lead Nokia?

These conversations weren't easy. However, I knew everyone I was talking to. They all chose their words carefully, and they all wanted to give serious answers to the chairman's questions. There were a dozen interviews in all: most took place in meeting rooms at the head office and one during a visit to London.

About half of those I consulted supported Olli-Pekka without reservation, but a similar proportion were so skeptical of his prospects as to stretch the limits of polite speech. Olli-Pekka is a sympathetic individual and doesn't arouse antipathy, but the doubts about him were clear and strong enough to act upon. These discussions with board members didn't seal the chief executive's fate on their own, but they provided important supporting material. At the beginning of May the board was ready for its next decisive move. Nokia would appoint a new chief executive as soon as possible. We set up a working group – a search committee – to handle the matter. It consisted of Marjorie Scardino, Per Karlsson, and me.

CHAPTER 75

A New Leader

I N MID-JUNE MARJORIE SCARDINO, PER KARLSSON, AND I met in London. The location was the Berkeley Hotel, where I usually stayed. We quickly agreed on the next steps. Marjorie Scardino would get in touch with Spencer Stuart, a firm specializing in the recruitment of senior executives for IT and communications technology companies.

The consultants quickly got to work and prepared a list that the three of us went through together. This took less than a week, after which we chose five candidates from the United States. There were also two internal candidates: Anssi Vanjoki, who now headed the Mobile Solutions Unit, and Niklas Savander, who was in charge of the Services and Devices Unit. Both were executive board members and had been with the company for a long time. We decided to interview them at the same time as the external candidates.

Finding Nokia's new chief executive was my task, once the headhunter had put together his own list. I had to start travelling straight away – there was no time to waste. I left Helsinki on a private flight to San Francisco at the end of June. I'd arranged to meet the five candidates over three days. Three of my meetings were at the Four Seasons Hotel, over breakfast, lunch, and in a private meeting room. After this I continued to Redmond and the heart of the Microsoft empire. There aren't many hotels in Redmond, so I had to meet one candidate over breakfast in my suite so that no secrets would be spilled. In the evening I once again boarded my plane and flew from the West Coast to the East Coast. With the final candidate I shared supper in Southampton on Long Island, an area made famous in F. Scott Fitzgerald's novel *The Great Gatsby*. After this last meeting on the East Coast my task was almost complete. I met the headhunter in the car on the way to the airport and then boarded the plane and took off for Helsinki.

I was happy with my three-day trip and the candidates I had met. Even so, as I turned things over in my mind during the flight, I wasn't sure we'd find the right person for Nokia from that group. We had to be confident of our choice. And the candidate we chose had to want to lead Nokia. These were my thoughts before I nodded off to the sound of the aircraft's peaceful hum.

There were still two candidates to go, in short order. Both had the right background, and both could have led Nokia, though in slightly different directions. It was easy for me to put all these candidates in order in my mind. My first choice was an American, the second-in-command of a well-known technology company. He was about fifty and had spent a long time with the same firm, rising through the ranks to his present powerful position.

I met my favored candidate a second time and spoke to him a third. He would certainly have been the right choice for Nokia and Nokia the right choice for him. My candidate knew the world's technology companies inside out, and I liked his leadership style. His values seemed to fit Nokia well, too. But after an extended period of reflection my candidate decided to withdraw. The reasons were personal and had nothing to do with Nokia.

One external candidate remained for the final round. This was the Canadian Stephen Elop. He was head of Microsoft Office and a member of the company's executive team. Before that he had had a long career in American companies. He had worked at Adobe and Juniper. He seemed to be a good salesperson and a decisive manager. He also had experience and expertise in software technology. These were the qualities Nokia needed. He also loved ice hockey, which is important to Finns, but this played no part in his selection.

I liked Stephen Elop's Finnish-style directness when he spoke of his experiences, of Microsoft, and of Nokia. There was nothing unnecessarily slick about him. He was both enthusiastic and capable. He had also done his homework exceptionally well. He knew the company he wanted to lead. He had gotten to know the company well a year earlier when Nokia and Microsoft announced their joint venture, in which he'd had a significant role.

Nevertheless I put lots of questions to myself. Stephen Elop seemed a good communicator, bursting with ideas, but could he delegate effectively? Was he sufficiently "product-minded," by which I meant someone capable of achievements similar to those of Steve Jobs? Beneath his Canadian exterior, was Stephen Elop really an American-style leader, with all the implications, both positive and negative, that that entailed? Would he understand Nokia?

Stephen Elop and me in 2010.

Both the search committee and Nokia's full board considered these questions. The answers were satisfactory and so we continued our discussions.

The external candidate had thus been identified. There were still the two internal candidates, whom I'd hurriedly interviewed in spring 2010. Niklas Savander was ruled out following an interview, so that just two candidates remained in play: Stephen Elop and Anssi Vanjoki.

Anssi Vanjoki had had a long and distinguished career at Nokia. He had believed in the Nokia brand when no one else had trusted it. Anssi aroused strong feelings, for and against, on account of his self-assurance, irritability, and slightly American style. If he had been chosen as Olli-Pekka Kallasvuo's successor some senior executives would have left the firm. At least, that's what they said. Even so, no one questioned Anssi's achievements in sales and marketing. He returned from his travels with sales concluded, even if the customers weren't always his most enthusiastic fans.

Over the years Anssi Vanjoki had matured, as do we all. His hard edges had softened, but we didn't base our choice on personal qualities this time. The business Anssi brought in didn't seem a strong enough qualification to give him the job. Within Nokia he had been in charge of the unit that should have produced a rival to the iPhone. He had been responsible for the MeeGo project, which had employed two thousand people. Google's Android had needed just four hundred to five hundred people. And the MeeGo project hadn't produced the desired results. (Nowadays the smartphone company Jolla uses the same platform in its phones, but more efficiently so that it gets results.) We asked Anssi where he hoped to take Nokia when he was at the helm. His answer didn't put him ahead.

I explained our decision to Anssi, who was naturally surprised and disappointed. In August I also told Olli-Pekka that we were about to appoint a new chief executive. He was surprised that the process had been so rapid. But it shouldn't have come as a complete surprise to anyone, since my journey to the United States had been leaked to the *Wall Street Journal*, which helpfully told its readers that Nokia was seeking a new, foreign CEO. This story appeared on 22 July and its details were pretty accurate, so whoever leaked it must have been one of the candidates. It was a damaging leak, but even though it caused us to accelerate the process, it didn't affect the result.

When Nokia's board approved the new chief executive in August, one board member marveled at how quickly we'd done it. He thought we should have given Olli-Pekka more time. Everyone else thought differently, that there wasn't time to fritter away. The decision was made at the last minute.

At 8:30 a.m. Helsinki time on 10 September 2010 journalists and analysts read the news that Stephen Elop had been selected to be Nokia's chief executive. Later in the day we held a crowded press conference in the auditorium where I had held so many similar events. I had announced my departure as chief executive there five years earlier. Cameras snapped and I sat under the hot spotlights as I thanked Olli-Pekka for his long career at Nokia. The company was once again setting off in a new direction. Now it was Stephen Elop's turn. I didn't know how things would go. I would, however, play my own part as well as I could.

EPILOGUE

NOKIA'S SUCCESS IN THE 1990S was no foregone conclusion. It was based on the courageous decision that the company's future lay in mobile phones and networks. Nokia was a company with its back to the wall: it was hemorrhaging money, and its core business had crumbled. The world didn't owe Nokia a living, and if the company was to survive it had to make clear decisions rapidly. The opportunity wouldn't come again. If Nokia had been in a better place, the company's youthful leadership – The Five – couldn't have made such radical decisions. The company's very existence was in question, as well as its leadership's credibility.

We saw where our future lay, but it seemed to us that no one shared our vision. Within Nokia there was a great deal of uncertainty. People were suspicious of our change of direction. Things weren't helped by a consultants' report that poured cold water on the prospects for both mobile phones and markets. Indeed, the report took a gloomy view of the future in every area where Nokia was active.

Our choice turned out to have been the right one, and indeed the only possible one. Our focus on phones and networks was the prime mover of our success. But on its own it wouldn't have been enough. We could succeed only on the terms set by customers and users. Nokia was known for its engineers and its engineering ability, and we applied that experience to the development of mobile phones. A phone had to look and feel good and fit into an envelope. You should be able to buy one in any color you wanted. Today these points are self-evident, but back then they were revolutionary insights. In this our youth and lack of preconceptions helped. We were truly, and at times passionately, fascinated with and enthusiastic about our products. Without that passion we wouldn't have dared take such bold steps.

Our vision was global. We decided not to restrict ourselves to the Nordic region, as Finnish firms had traditionally done, but to make the whole of Europe our market. In time we extended into Asia, especially China, because growth in developing markets would change the whole world.

Our products derived from our vision. Nokia had something for every consumer on the planet, wherever they lived or however much money they had. We didn't stubbornly try to push the same model on everyone; we tried to adapt to local tastes and customers' evolving wishes. And we often succeeded. We understood that the birth of international mass-marketing would help us. We were tightly bound to those technical protocols that we believed to be the best, such as GSM technology. The same couldn't be said for our competitors, Motorola and Ericsson, let alone the Japanese or European conglomerates.

We also succeeded in winning over the operating companies. Our product range was broad and enticing. We had succeeded in making our products economically and also in adapting our production to the operating companies' wishes and changes in the market.

When, at the start of the nineties, we realised that our vision would save Nokia, we had to make a lot of decisions in a hurry. We had to knock our plans, our logistics, and our production into shape so we could grow into a globally effective company. We were nimble, happy to improvise, and nifty in adapting our strategy, so we were able to pull the company back from oblivion. Now we had to focus on our management systems, strategic planning, and building up the company's resources. Tension between our "fast" implementation and our "slow" processes was always at the heart of Nokia.

In 1995–96 we received warning that our management structures were unfit for their purpose, when the whole company became impossible to steer. After that Nokia designed the world's most efficient machinery for logistics, production, and employing sub-contractors. These weren't areas where we made mistakes in the 2000s; our structures never let us down again after 1996. We had learned our lessons.

We at Nokia were an efficient, capable bunch. The hierarchy was fairly flat and information flowed rapidly within the company, both officially and informally. The five of us who led the company set examples to everyone in it. We worked as if we were establishing a start-up – communication was easy, we didn't go in for politicking, the company always came first. This way of working spread throughout the organization: to the governing board, the executive board, and the 200 most senior managers, and through them to the company's entire expanding workforce. We lived the Nokia story, which was the story of a company that challenged old ways of thinking and doing and grew to dominate a whole new market. It was a story of unexpected triumph. Our work certainly didn't lack meaning.

Everyone at Nokia pushed themselves to the limit for the company. We faced unfamiliar and difficult issues – we had to overcome the problems of dealing with multiple time zones, for example, and we had to come to grips with the cultures of our new markets. A lot of this was pioneering work. People at Nokia were responsible for much more than they could ever have imagined, even in their wildest dreams. Their achievements were staggering, as much in terms of their personal growth as in the company's expansion.

Nokia's furious growth in the 1990s greatly expanded the opportunities open to its employees. This suited my own approach to leadership since I liked to stir things up by regularly promoting people to new positions and moving them to unknown corners of the earth. It made Nokia a workplace where good employees didn't get stuck in silos or their own cubicles, defending their little patch of territory. The collision between traditional and new ways of thinking drew the company forward.

That a small Finnish company in poor shape could succeed in a demanding global market would have seemed impossible at the beginning of the 1990s. It seemed equally improbable that the overwhelmingly dominant market leader could lose its position in just a few years. Why did Nokia get into such terrible trouble from 2008 on?

It would be simple and simplistic to say that Nokia was the prisoner of its own success. Nevertheless, many background factors came together to make Nokia's pre-2007 success possible. The N95 smartphone, developed between 2004 and 2006, was a beauty that sold extremely well. The impressive cash flow it produced created a deceptive sense of security, when we should have been focusing on the future. Nokia became bloated in 2007–08 and its costs mushroomed. The company should have examined its working practices ruthlessly; instead we wrongly thought that Nokia's old recipes would continue to do their job. But the world had moved on.

Nokia had been forced into a contest that would be decided by the competitiveness of the operating system, the users' experience (which was based on our software expertise), and the apps. Nokia's software capability was inadequate, as we had recognised and tried to remedy – which made the position all the more bitter. Our efforts hadn't succeeded, however. We saw for ourselves how even the best strategy is useless unless one can implement it.

We knew that in the future most mobile phones would be smartphones, but our software and apps left us in an uncompetitive position.

We understood the problem, but at some deep level we couldn't accept what was happening. Many big projects just carried on. We examined the sales projections for the following quarter, when our eyes should have been focused much further ahead. Earlier we had sometimes looked too far ahead too soon. Now we were looking down the wrong end of the telescope.

Symbian was on the right track. However, at least until spring 2008 it was too remote from Nokia and especially from our internal debates on operating systems. This wasn't by design; it was because Symbian's other shareholders weren't ready for Nokia to become the majority shareholder. When Symbian finally became part of the Nokia organization, it didn't integrate properly and there were overlaps.

At the beginning of the 2000s I overhauled Nokia's organization, working on the matrix principle. This compelled the company to operate in a more unified way. The direction was right, but it didn't really fit with Nokia's traditional culture. Direct reporting based on profit centers had been a good model in the 1990s, well suited to the smaller Nokia of the time, so the matrix organization met with resistance. Some of the managers didn't understand how to work within a matrix.

The matrix also placed new requirements on the chief executive. Thousands of employees switched units, line managers, and job descriptions. As several members of The Five left around the time reorganization took place, too many people wondered where the next Five would come from. But The Five's contribution had been unique, and nothing like them could emerge again. They weren't an organizational structure, but a team of five distinct individuals. The group's dispersal left a huge hole in the organization that wasn't possible to fill.

In 2007 Nokia took a step back, toward organizing on functional lines. As a consequence the company was unable to grasp the software problem creatively and decisively. The company spent its time on firefighting, a purely reactive activity, when it should have been looking for new worlds to conquer. Decision-making got bogged down in working groups and committees. Nokia slowed down like an old, worn-out car. And the leadership team didn't show the same unity, determination, and agility as before. The matrix organisation needed more time to put down roots if it was to be the basis for lasting change.

Now Nokia faced three challenges. It had to adapt to a new competitive situation, carry on with its restructuring, and deal with the impact of a global recession – all at the same time. The absence of The Five certainly caused problems. Previously it had made decisions without delay, but now the functional organization with its endless and over-populated review meetings made decision-making cumbersome. When sales volume grows globally, making profits demands both innovation and discipline. At the same time Apple showed how an effective matrix organisation could make a company extremely competitive.

The media offered a critical assessment of the governing board's role in Nokia's difficulties. Some outsiders thought the board should have taken a more hands-on approach. But in a company employing more than 100,000 people such a confusing mix of roles could hardly have made matters better.

As a former chief executive I too must answer similar accusations. Many people suspect that as chairman I was still pulling the strings from behind the scenes. But it wasn't like that. The governing board and the executive board maintained a constant dialogue, but they were both clear on their own roles and responsibilities.

Against the din of the disconcerting and highly personalized public discussion in Finland I naturally examined my own role in the way Nokia had developed. I'm sure that while I was chief executive I could have tried more aggressively to boost the company's software expertise. We recognised the need, and did a lot, but if we had bought a company specializing in operating systems software it could have had a powerful practical and symbolic impact. It might have made people at Nokia understand what modern software is all about.

During my time as chairman, from 2006 to 2012, my role was clear. The board looked on as Olli-Pekka Kallasvuo, with his 25 years of experience in the company, took over as chief executive. The board, which now had fresh, high-level software expertise, collectively monitored and actively appraised Kallasvuo's work. It would certainly have been possible to change the chief executive sooner, though it would have been painful at any time. The timetable we followed had been thoroughly discussed and agreed upon.

Nokia's main competitors in the United States and Asia had long been hunting for material for a counterattack that would knock the company off its pedestal. Between 2007 and 2010 they succeeded at last. They identified top-of-the-range mobile phones as our weak point. Central to the success of both Apple and Google was the unique experience in computers and operating systems to be found in Silicon Valley. This enabled computers to be incorporated into smartphones, rather than phones into computers. They ambushed us in the same way we had ambushed Motorola in the 1990s.

The story of Nokia in the U.S. market went back much earlier, however. We began to sell mobile phones in the United States at the beginning of the 1980s, and they started to take off after 1984 when we set up a joint venture with the American firm Tandy. Together we set up a factory to manufacture phones in Korea. They were sold through Nokia's own distribution network and also through Radio Shack, a chain of electronics shops owned by Tandy, which many Americans will fondly remember. Our collaboration with Tandy increased both our production capability and our understanding of the U.S. market.

The U.S. mobile phone market had traditionally been difficult for every non-American company, so we savored Motorola's defeat to the full. Motorola had dominated the U.S. market, and Nokia's share remained modest up to 1998. During that time our market share was between 5 and 20 percent. In the United States phones were chiefly sold through the nationwide operators, and they took a close interest in the features the phones had to offer. So Nokia had to adapt to local conditions. In 1996 we began to collaborate with AT&T Wireless, with rapid results: by 1998 we were the market leader, and later our U.S. market share went over 40 percent. It was still more than 20 percent in 2006.

We had long believed that the power of the U.S. operating companies to dictate the market would last forever. This belief was proved wrong between 2007 and 2010.

The operating companies had long tried to tell us that in the United States there was no demand for smartphones costing more than about $300. Nokia had tried hard to make what the customer wanted. Then Apple came along and launched the iPhone with a price tag of more than $600. But Apple had created something really new: a wonderful experience for the phone user where the phone was the key to an entire ecosystem of services and applications.

We also learned a lot about how the wider U.S. market worked. The sheer size of the market demanded a degree of humility since it always required us to adapt our thinking. This was true for technology, distribution, consumers' preferences, and other things as well.

Americans are patriotic when it comes to technology. They hold it to be self-evident that their own products are the world's best. They're proud of them, but they're also ready to put up protectionist barriers based on technical differences from other countries' products.

Non-American companies have only rarely been successful in the United States. U.S. products usually dominate the market, though they may be manufactured in Chinese factories. SAP, which fought effectively against Oracle, is a rare exception. Siemens often comes in only third in its categories. Sony Playstation is probably the best non-American consumer product.

In this environment Nokia had to work hard against strong headwinds. Although we did pretty well, there was usually an atmosphere of uncertainty during our discussions with the operating companies. While Nokia seemed to be highly regarded, it felt as if our customers were just waiting for the day when U.S. substitutes for our products would be available.

All in all the United States is an extremely competitive market where success requires better marketing and distribution than anywhere else. It's the ultimate test for any global company. It's a tough job, but if you don't rise to it the deepest essence of global markets will elude you.

After I stepped down as chairman of Nokia in the spring of 2012 I began to put the finishing touches to this book. It was nearly ready at the beginning of September 2013, when it was announced that ownership of Nokia's mobile phone division would be transferred to our historic arch-enemy Microsoft. The main reaction in Finland was one of shock and disbelief. Strong feelings came to the surface. But against the background of history the decision doesn't seem so exceptional. Nokia had made significant disposals in the past. The spinning off of the paper division in the 1980s, which I myself had pushed forward, had been a personally painful decision. After all, Nokia had had its origins in the forest industry, back in the 1800s.

The mobile phone had a greater symbolic significance. Finns had formed a strong emotional bond with their Nokia mobiles, although in the historical context the brand had been built up in rather a short time, less than 25 years. This shows the power of the Nokia story. To many outsiders mobiles and Nokia are one and the same; it's an issue of the company's and even Finland's identity. Nokia's board's decision to sell was dramatic and courageous. Even so, for me and for everyone else who had a long association with Nokia it was sad to see more than 40 years worth of Finnish engineering expertise sold abroad. But we should look ahead: can the company rebuild itself to benefit from the expertise it retains?

Other questions come to mind, since Nokia isn't known for quitting. Many feel disappointed and wonder why Nokia should throw in the towel when there's still so much to play for. Is this really a mature area? Nokia had rejected takeover bids, even when the company was in a dire situation. For example, when Siemens approached the board in 1992 with the intention of buying our Cellular Systems Unit, we barely gave them the time of day. We had a clear vision of the future and it was on that basis that we solved our problems one at a time. Selling wasn't on our agenda. The Cellular Systems Unit had a place in our strategy for the next five years, and that worked out as it should. It was the same story in the logistics crisis. Nokia had already been condemned as a loser, but we put our structures straight, doubled our investments and our work hours, and returned as victors.

Soon after the deal Microsoft's real plans became clear, and there was nothing good for Finland about them. Microsoft wound down its Finnish operations, leaving only a product development center, because it had decided not to invest in phone production. The change in the company's chief executive had an impact on this.

Though Nokia had been sidelined it still took on new business. The most important move was the decision at the beginning of 2015 to buy Alcatel-Lucent; the deal was completed in December 2015. This was the biggest acquisition in Finland's history: it enabled Nokia to reach the same level as Ericsson and Huawei, which had previously dominated the global network business between them.

The profitability of Nokia's network business also strengthened, overtaking Ericsson's in 2015.

I believe that amalgamating Alcatel-Lucent and Nokia will consume a lot of leadership time and organizational energy over the next couple of years. But it offers the chance to become first in the field both by size and capability. The opportunities for growth are modest, but the sector will be absolutely central in building a networked infrastructure. Once more it will demand brilliant technical ability, such as in developing the Internet of things.

From humble origins in the forests of Finland, Nokia developed into a great technology company that conquered global markets, changing the world as it did so. This was a big thing for a small country. At its peak Nokia's share of Finland's GDP reached nearly 4 percent, accounting for 10 percent of exports and almost 30 percent of the value of shares traded on the Helsinki Stock Exchange. Nokia employed 23,000 people in Finland, most of whom were highly educated.

Nokia's greatest significance for Finland was not, however, economic, but psychological. Nokia showed that a small country, and a small country's businesses, could conquer the world and capture its customers' hearts. Nokia helped create networks and connections within Finnish industry that could never have existed before. Nokia created a model for Finnish enterprises that embodied best practices, attracted the attention of the international media, and promoted expertise in leadership. Its employees spread these strengths to many other companies.

The new Finnish video games industry sprang from Nokia's need to include games on its mobile phones. These new start-ups weren't built on the ruins of Nokia, as has been suggested, but took Nokia as their inspiration.

Many ordinary Finns benefited as employees or subcontractors of Nokia, or as its shareholders. The ensuing prosperity spread throughout Finland.

Nokia may have sometimes been "too big" for Finland, in that it may have taken too large a share of available resources. But a small country doesn't always have the means to develop a fully diversified economy.

What next for Nokia? I'm an optimist. History gives a hint that after a metamorphosis Nokia will probably find a new area into which it can grow. This won't happen on the basis of the ideas of one or two leaders, but through a broad group of motivated Nokia engineers for whom good leadership will act as a stimulus. I've had the chance to observe several such situations, and every one of them has been fascinating. The key word is trust. Trust in people and in letting them do what they want. In today's increasingly individualistic atmosphere a team spirit, expertise, and a humble approach still have a crucial role to play. More easily said than done, perhaps, but I believe I will yet see many such miracles at Nokia.

APPENDIX

Nokia's Financial Performance Indicators: 1992–2010

NET SALES
(MILLION EUROS)

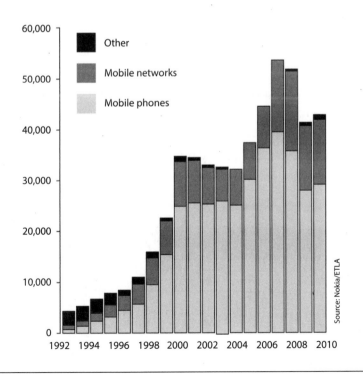

Source: Nokia/ETLA

SHARE OF FINLAND'S GDP
(PERCENTAGE)

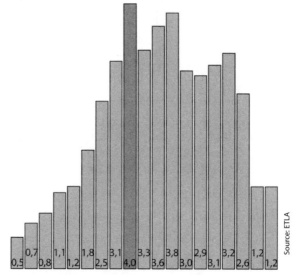

0,5 0,7 0,8 1,1 1,2 1,8 2,5 3,1 4,0 3,3 3,6 3,8 3,0 2,9 3,1 3,2 2,6 1,2 1,2

1992 1994 1996 1998 2000 2002 2004 2006 2008 2010

Source: ETLA

MARKET SHARE
(PERCENTAGE)

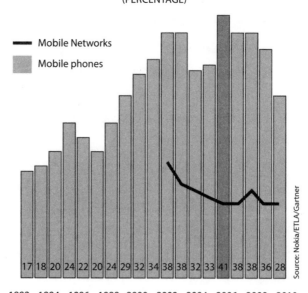

— Mobile Networks

▮ Mobile phones

17 18 20 24 22 20 24 29 32 34 38 38 32 33 41 38 38 36 28

1992 1994 1996 1998 2000 2002 2004 2006 2008 2010

Source: Nokia/ETLA/Gartner

MARKET PRICE
(EUROS)

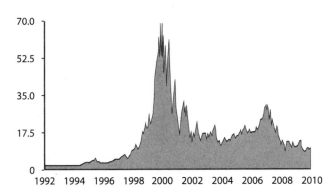

NUMBER OF EMPLOYEES
(THOUSANDS)

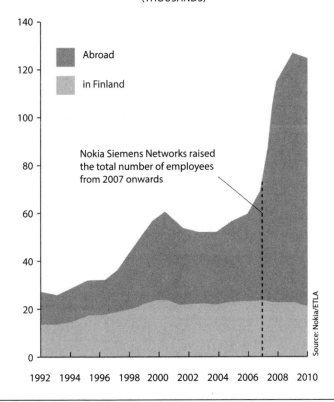

MOBILE PHONE SALES
(MILLIONS)

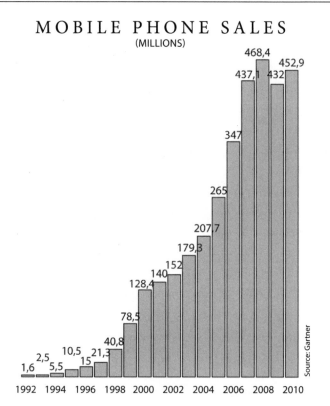

Source: Gartner

PEOPLE INDEX

SUBJECT INDEX

ABOUT THE AUTHORS

JORMA OLLILA became the pre-eminent European businessman of his generation during his time as Nokia's CEO from 1992 to 2006 and Chairman from 1999 to 2012. He served as Chairman of the Board of Royal Dutch Shell from 2006 to 2015 and Chairman of the European Round Table of Industrialists from 2005 to 2009. Currently an Advisory Partner at investment bank Perella Weinberg Partners, Ollila is Chairman of Outokumpu Oyj and Miltton Oy. He is also Vice Chairman of Otava Books and Magazines, a board member of Tetra Laval Group and the University of Helsinki, and Chairman of The Research Institute of the Finnish Economy ETLA and Finnish Business and Policy Forum. He holds master's degrees in economics from the London School of Economics, in engineering from the Helsinki University of Technology, and in political science from the University of Helsinki. He is an Honorary Fellow of the London School of Economics and holds honorary doctorates from the University of Helsinki, the Helsinki University of Technology, and the University of Vaasa.

HARRI SAUKKOMAA, Chairman and founder of the public relations firm Tekir, is a distinguished journalist, entrepreneur, executive, and author of several nonfiction books.